T5-AGS-129

A UNIVERSAL APPEAL

ASPECTS OF THE REVIVAL OF MONASTICISM IN THE WEST IN THE 19TH AND EARLY 20TH CENTURIES

RENE KOLLAR

A UNIVERSAL APPEAL

ASPECTS OF THE REVIVAL OF MONASTICISM IN THE WEST IN THE 19TH AND EARLY 20TH CENTURIES

RENE KOLLAR

International Scholars Publications

A CATHOLIC SCHOLARS PRESS BOOK

SAN FRANCISCO • LONDON • BETHESDA

BX
2475
. K65
1996

Library of Congress Cataloging-in-Publication Data

Kollar, Rene.
    A universal appeal: aspects of the revival of monasticism in the
West in the 19th and early 20th centuries / Rene Kollar.
    p. cm.
Includes bibliographical references and index.
ISBN 1-57309-003-4. -- ISBN 1-57309-002-6
1. Monasticism and religious orders--History--19th century.
2. Monasticism and religious orders, Anglican--History--19th
century. 3. Monasticism and religious orders--History--20th
century. 4. Monasticism and religious orders, Anglican-
-History--20th century. I. Title.
BX2475.K65 1996
271'.009'034--dc20
                                       96-14664
                                       CIP

Copyright 1996 by Rene Kollar

All rights reserved. Printed in the United States of America. No part of this
book may be used or reproduced in any manner whatsoever without written
permission except in the case of brief quotations embodied in critical articles
and reviews.

Editorial Inquiries:
International Scholars Publications
7831 Woodmont Avenue, #345
Bethesda, MD 20814

To the Students of Saint Vincent: Past, Present and Future

ARCHABBOT BONIFACE WIMMER (1809–1887)
FOUNDER OF SAINT VINCENT ARCHABBEY (1846)

꽃

CONTENTS

❧

FOREWORD

Rene Kollar's contribution to the history of monasticism through this volume centers on an area less well-known to historians of that phenomenon, namely, the revival of monasticism, especially in the Church of England, in the 19th century. The major portion of the essays printed here describes those origins in minute and fascinating detail, with ample descriptions of the creative, forceful, and tenacious people involved. To this history he has added some of his critical essays about English Roman Catholic monasteries of that same period. He describes at length the confused and, at times, bewildering negotiations with Herbert Cardinal Vaughan concerning possible pastoral ministry and administration at Westminster Cathedral, at first proposed to the French Benedictines and then to the English. Nationalism and national pride played a role in this confusion.

The history of monastic revival on the Continent during the same period is better known, beginning with the renewal in France of the Abbaye Saint-Pierre at Solesmes under Dom Guéranger in the 1830's and its important role in the revival of Gregorian chant and an appreciation for Roman liturgy. In addition, historians of German culture during the same period have studied thoroughly the re-establishment of monasticism in Bavaria under Ludwig I, again in the 1830's, with the restoration of the abbeys of St. Michael in Metten, St. Stephen in Augsburg, St. Bonifaz in Munich, and a host of others. The history of the founding of the Beuronese Congregation a few decades later by the Wolter brothers, Maurus and Placidus, the influence of such historically important monasteries of that Congregation as the abbeys of Beuron and Maria Laach, and its rapid growth throughout Germany and Austria is also well documented.

The Beuronese Congregation extended itself into Belgium through the founding of Maredsous Abbey in 1872. New houses in America, first St. Vincent in Latrobe, Pennsylvania, and St. John in Collegeville, Minnesota, were founded from the Bavarian Congregation. Soon after, the

Swiss Congregation came to the new world with the foundation of St. Meinrad in Indiana and Conception Abbey in Missouri. It is important to remember that these monasteries were begun very soon after the revival of their founding houses in Europe. The Romantic period, thus, could boast of a flowering of the monastic movement throughout the whole of the older and more traditional Catholic countries in Europe, as well as in the new areas of missionary endeavor. The revival of monasticism became a part of the missionary thrust of the same period. The missionary spirit of Abbot Boniface Wimmer captured the intensity of that revival in the United States in the middle of the 19th century, a spirit that coincided so well with the frontier mentality of the new world.

The interest in the Middle Ages as an inspiration for the revival of monasticism in Catholicism of the Romantic period and the new missionary thrust of the Church were natural allies for an awakening of renewed interest in monasticism in the other churches of Christianity that had their origins in the period of the Reformation. For the Church of England and for the Reformation churches in general the revival of monasticism posed a special problem that naturally surfaced at once. Much of the ethos of the Reformation period had been centered around a bias against monasticism. Luther, it will be remembered, had harsh words to say against the monastic tradition and a similar negative spirit abounded in the Church of England. Overcoming that bias, swimming against that current, was one of the challenges to be faced by anyone who wished to restore monastic traditions in those churches with a Reformation tradition. Rene Kollar, O.S.B., in these essays traces that conflict, describing the history of the strong-willed and colorful characters involved in it. It took people of exceptional stamina and courage to accomplish the renewal.

It was inevitable that, eventually, as centuries passed after the Reformation, this question of monasticism in the churches of the Reformation would arise. The roots of monasticism find themselves solidly embedded in the first centuries of Church life; they are not just a remnant of a late or dubious medieval tradition. Any revival of interest in the Patristic period—as Professor Kollar points out with regard to Cardinal Newman and his influence in the monastic revival—must bring about a renewed interest in the monastic phenomenon, so important in the early history of the Church and in the subsequent centuries. Last century Anglicans naturally spawned groups with such an interest and thus had to confront the monastic phenomenon in Church life, why it had been suppressed during the Reformation period, what importance it had in the early Church and in the Middle Ages, and what was lacking in a Church tradition that did not have this phenomenon. In addition, the Romantic period, as mentioned, saw a rebirth of interest in the high Middle Ages and could not ignore the strength and power of the evolved monastic tradition in that period both on the Continent and especially in England itself. In fact, that monastic tradition was so much a part of the history of the English nation and its culture that the question of a monastic revival within the Church of England had to be posed again to do justice to its history and older tradition.

The struggle of that interest to find concrete realization forms the story of these illuminating essays. As one reads them, one poses even the larger question of whether the monastic witness is not a part of every more developed religious culture, springing from some inner urge of human nature itself, a need to make one's belief in a loving and providential God the center of one's whole existence. In the Christian witness it includes the belief in the end-times as determinative of how these in-between-times should be lived to make sense out of them. In any case, these essays will also stimulate historians of the monastic phenomenon in general to examine those churches that had abandoned the monastic tradition only to seek to re-establish it centuries later. In our own day that includes not only this phenomenon within the Anglican tradition but also the interesting more recent monastic movement of Taizé in the Reformed tradition.

We are happy that Rene Kollar has gathered together in one place all these informative essays that contribute so much to understanding the monastic revival of the last century and especially within the Church of England.

—Rembert G. Weakland, O.S.B.
Archbishop of Milwaukee, Wisconsin

INTRODUCTION

The year 1846 opened an important chapter in the long and significant history of Benedictine monasticism. In that year Boniface
Wimmer, a monk of Metten Abbey in Bavaria, crossed the Atlantic
"with the expressed intent of transplanting the Benedictine Order from
Europe to North America."[1] After a brief stay in Carrolltown, Pennsylvania, Wimmer and his followers eventually moved to Saint Vincent Parish
in Westmoreland County at the request of Bishop Michael O'Connor, the
Bishop of Pittsburgh.[2] Wimmer arrived at the future site of Saint Vincent
Archabbey, the first monastery founded in America, on 18 October 1846,
and six days later he clothed sixteen candidates for his new monastery in
the Benedictine habit. Wimmer wanted to establish communities of monks
who would foster learning, educate the American youth, and minister to
the spiritual needs of American Roman Catholics, especially the German
immigrants. By all standards, Wimmer did succeed: Saint Vincent
Archabbey currently has over 200 monks; it was the founding abbey of
monasteries in Alabama, Colorado, Florida, Illinois, Minnesota, New
Jersey, North Carolina, and Kansas; and Saint Vincent at present operates
a liberal arts college, a seminary which trains men for the Roman Catholic
priesthood, numerous parishes throughout Pennsylvania, a preparatory
school in Savannah, Georgia, and missions in Brazil and Taiwan.

Boniface Wimmer's arrival and the foundation of Saint Vincent
have not been forgotten. Beginning in the spring of 1995 and continuing
into the autumn of 1996, Saint Vincent Archabbey, College, Seminary,
and Parish have scheduled a series of events and special projects to
commemorate the 150th anniversary of Wimmer's arrival in Western
Pennsylvania. This sesquicentennial celebration is appropriate and worth-
while, but there might be a temptation to see the foundation of Saint
Vincent outside of a broader revival of Benedictine monasticism which
began during the nineteenth century. This would be unfortunate. The
establishment of a monastery in America by Boniface Wimmer, however

1

important and significant, represents part of a larger mosaic of a Benedictine renaissance which took place during the last century. This collection of essays attempts to place the foundation of Saint Vincent Archabbey within that context.[3]

The Reformation, the Enlightenment, and finally the policies of the French Revolution had all dealt serious blows to the monastic ideal in Europe. According to Dom David Knowles, "At the end of the domination of Napoleon I the monastic order, and in particular the traditional Benedictine family, was in worse case than at any time since the days of Benedict himself."[4] It appeared that monasticism had passed into history. Knowles argues that the revival of monasticism which took place after Napoleon's defeat was influenced by the keen interest in Romanticism, which recognized the value of the Middle Ages, and also by the belief that "an imitation of medieval achievements and institutions was the best way of combating the ills of the past century." This rebirth of monasticism originated in France, Italy, and Germany, and from these three countries Benedictinism eventually took root throughout Europe, England, and North America. Boniface Wimmer's monastic dreams for North America developed in this environment.

Benedictine monasticism survived the revolutionary and secular movements of the past centuries, and has also recently found expression in certain Anglican circles. Consequently, several articles (Chapters I-IX) discuss the revival of monasticism within the Anglican Church. Abbot Aelred Carlyle's vision of Anglican monasticism, Anglican sisterhoods, and the relationship of the Established Church and Roman Catholicism to Anglican religious life will be examined. Some material on Abbot Carlyle appears in my recent study of Carlyle published by Peter Lang Publishing, Inc.[5] Sections from my book, *Westminster Cathedral: From Dream to Reality* (Chapter X) make reference to the growth of Benedictine monasticism in England during the nineteenth century as well as aspects of modern French monasticism. Chapters XI-XIII deal specifically with the English Benedictine Congregation during the nineteenth and twentieth centuries and the successful foundation of a monastery in London. Chapter XIV discusses an early eighteenth century plan to establish Benedictinism in Western Pennsylvania, and Chapter XV explores the plans of Bishop Charles Grafton to establish the conventual life in the American Episcopal Church. The photographs have been eliminated from *Westminster Cathedral: From Dream to Reality*. For the most part, I have used the same spelling and punctuation which appeared in the original publications.

My interest in modern Benedictine history grew out of my 1981 doctoral dissertation written for the University of Maryland. Since that time, I have received encouragement from numerous friends and scholars on both sides of the Atlantic. I would like to acknowledge the following journals for permission to print material from copyright works: *The Downside Review, Studia Monastica, Cistercian Studies Quarterly* (Printed with Permission of *Cistercian Studies Quarterly), Harvard Theological Review* (Copyright 1983 by the President and Fellows of Harvard College. Reprinted by permission), *Tjurunga, Church History* (Reprinted with Permission from *Church History* 53 (June 1984): 218–230), *The Heythrop Journal, Recusant History, Journal of Ecclesiastical History,* and *Word and Spirit.* Numerous people have played an important part in the publication of this book of essays. The monks of Saint Vincent Archabbey have always been my chief source of inspiration. I especially thank Archabbot Douglas R. Nowicki, O.S.B., for his kind and fraternal support, and I am indebted to Archbishop Rembert G. Weakland, O.S.B., Archbishop of Milwaukee, for finding time in his busy schedule to write the Foreword for the book. In London, the monks of Ealing Abbey have always shown me the true meaning of monastic hospitality. Throughout the years, numerous research grants from Saint Vincent College and Saint Vincent Seminary have made my trips to English archives and libraries possible. The Rev. John F. Murtha, O.S.B., a church historian by training and President of Saint Vincent College from 1985-1995, has always shown enthusiasm for my endeavors. His support is largely responsible for the publication of this book. My greatest inspiration, however, still remains those special students whom I have taught.

Notes

[1] O. Kline, *The Sportsman's Hall Parish Later Named Saint Vincent 1790-1846* (Latrobe: Saint Vincent Archabbey Press, 1990), 84.

[2] For a biography of Boniface Wimmer and the establishment of Saint Vincent Archabbey see, J. Oetgen, *An American Abbot. Boniface Wimmer, O.S.B.,* (Latrobe: The Archabbey Press, 1976).

[3] The following is the order in which the articles appear: "The Oxford Movement and the Heritage of Benedictine Monasticism." *The Downside Review* 345 (October 1938): 281-91;"Dr. Pusey and Ft. Ignatius of Llanthony." *The Journal of Welsh Ecclesiastical History* 2 (1985): 27-40; "A Question of Authority: The Anglican Nuns of West Malling." *Studia Monastica* 27 (1985): 135-56; "The 1897 Lambeth Conference and the Question of Religious Life in the Anglican Communion." *Cistercian Studies Quarterly'* 26 (December 1991): 319-30; "Anglo-Catholicism in the Church of England, 1895-1913: Abbot Aelred Carlyle and the Monks of Caldey Island." *Harvard Theological Review* 76 (April 1983): 205-24; "Ritualism in a Gloucestershire Village: Anglican Monks, Clergymen, and the Parishioners of Lower Guiting." *Tjurunga* 43 (1992): 54-81; "Lord Halifax and Monasticism in the Church of England." *Church History,* 53 (June 1984): 218-30; *"Pax:* An Early Ecumenical Journal." *The Heythrop Journal* 26 (July 1985): 294-309; "The Caldey Monks and the Catholic Press: 1905-1913." *Recusant History* 17 (April 1985): 287-98; *Westminster Cathedral: From Dream to Reality* (Edinburgh: F & L Publications, 1987); "The Return of the Benedictines to London." *Tjurunga* (September 1987): 36-52; "Bishops and Benedictines: The Case of Father Richard O'Halloran." *Journal of Ecclesiastical History* 38 (July 1987): 362-85; "The Reluctant Prior: Bishop Wulstan Pearson of Lancaster." *Recusant History* 20 (May 1991): 402-13; "Plans for an Eighteenth Century Benedictine Settlement in Western Pennsylvania: Bishop Carroll and the English Benedictine Congregation." In *Word and Spirit: Aspects of Monasticism in America,* 3-11. Petersham, Massachusetts: St. Bede's Publications, 1992; and "Bishop Charles Grafton's Dream for Religious Life in the American Episcopal Church: The Influence of the Monastic Revival in the Church of England." *Studia Monastica* 33 (1991): 133-43.

[4] David Knowles, *Christian Monasticism* (New York: McGraw-Hill Book Company, 1969), 170.

[5] R. Kollar, *Abbot Aelred Carlyle, Caldey Island, and the Anglo-Catholic Revival in England* (New York: Peter Lang Publishing, Inc., 1995).

CHAPTER I

THE OXFORD MOVEMENT AND THE HERITAGE OF BENEDICTINE MONASTICISM

After the destruction of the Benedictine houses by the Henrican Reformation, the monastic system in England seemed dead. But examples of men and women could be found who continued to promote aspects of the monastic ideal. Little Gidding and the numerous voluntary prayer groups of the Restoration were popular, but short-lived. By the turn of the nineteenth century, however, the historical climate made the Anglican soil of England hospitable to Benedictine monasticism. The piety and suffering of the refugee French priests who fled to England to escape the horrors of the Revolution, for example, helped to change the anti-Roman prejudices of some Britons. But it was the Oxford Movement and its claim to the inheritance of monasticism which helped to give renewed strength to the monastic spirit.

The goal of the Oxford Movement was a renewal of pastoral duties and a refurbishing of the Anglican moral fibre. The Tractarians emphasized the importance of the pre-Reformation or Catholic tradition in the Church of England, and consequently, the theologians began to discover the value of many monastic practices.[1] One can detect three major themes in the Oxford Movement: a reaction against the secularism of the age, a desire to elevate the importance of the pre-Reformation tradition, and consequently a dedication to the principles of the ancient pristine Church. These characteristics, consequently, nurtured the growth of monastic ideals in nineteenth-century England.

It was the Catholic tradition, and not the spirit of the Reformation, which inspired the Tractarians. Three specific historical epochs influenced the Oxford writers: monasticism in the patristic era, the achievements of mediaeval Benedictinism, and the stability of seventeenth-century French monastic life.[2] Each period was an expression of monastic greatness. Through their study of history, therefore, it became apparent that certain monastic traditions were meaningful. Certain investigations showed that it was only custom and not official regulations that had led to the abandonment of many of the historic agents of worship.'[3] When the Oxford theologians studied the Church of the Fathers, they discovered such values as elaborate liturgies, communal recitation of the psalter, community living and celibacy. In respect to the liturgy, one historian of the period stated that 'it was a distinction to the Oxford Movement to help the Church of England to regain the Benedictine sense of worship in itself, the *Opus Dei*.'[4] The Patristic writers, therefore, became a source of authority for scriptural exegesis and ecclesiastical problems. John Keble, for example, urged that their tradition should be consulted in three areas: in the formulation of essential articles of faith, as a guide to the interpretation of Sacred Scripture, and as a guideline for the discipline and liturgical practices of the Church.[5] 'With the dawn of the Oxford Movement and the publication of the first of the *Tracts for the Times* in 1833, the dry bones of Anglicanism began to stir.'[6]

When one thinks of the Oxford Movement, the names of Pusey and Newman lead the list of seminal thinkers. These theologians were the most prolific writers on the value of monastic life, but it would be a mistake to assume that these were the only ones who appreciated the importance of monasticism. John Keble saw the importance of such a lifestyle and went to great lengths to defend the concept of celibacy as a way of life. In one writing, he stated:

> ...your letters imply two things: first that Scripture gives no encouragement to persons to devote themselves to a single life...on the first of these points, I feel quite sure that you are under a mistake. Our Lord's words which your letters do not notice are so very expressive....[7]

Hurrell Froude popularized the virtues of unmarried clerics living together in colleges.

> It has lately come into my head that the present state of things in England makes an opening for reviving the monastic system...[and] certain colleges of unmarried priests would be the cheapest possible way of providing for the spiritual want of a large population....[8]

Frederick William Faber, one of Newman's students, also championed the celibate life for Anglican priests[9] and founded a small community at his vicarage in Elton.[10]

Edward Bouverie Pusey was fascinated with Froude's intention to establish a brotherhood of single priests. Pusey understood and urged the importance of monastic life for the well-being of the Anglican Church, and the way to achieve this goal would be the re-establishment of groups of unmarried clerics living a community life. Their apostolate would be social work. In 1838, Pusey proposed the following to Newman: 'what I should like then would be a place for twelve fellows, but beginning with not less than two...with an endowment of one thousand pounds...and so enable one to make a rule for them.'[11] As the brotherhood expanded, men would leave and begin new foundations. In addition to social work, these colleges might even become bases for the training of missionary priests. According to Pusey, 'the more I think of Froude's plan, the more it seems to me the only one, if anything is to be done for our large towns. I have the same conclusion for missionaries.'[12] Pusey, therefore, dreamed of foundations which would not be only centres of prayer and meditation, but would also involve themselves in work among the urban poor. He also saw the need for similar communities of single women, and these sisterhoods were modelled on the principles of the French Sisters of Charity. Both groups, however, would admit only celibates.

Pusey argued that it was erroneous to equate celibacy with Romanism or Popery, On the contrary, one should regard it as a special gift from God. The theological basis for celibacy, moreover, can be discovered in the practices of the primitive Christian communities. 'But what has this, my Lord [Bishop Richard Bagot of Oxford], in common with Rome and Romanism? The preference of celibacy as a higher state is Scriptural, and, as being such, is primitive.'[13] Celibacy, however, must remain optional. To use Pusey's words, 'I am not advocating celibacy my Lord, as the general rule of the Church, nor imposing upon others "a yoke, which I touch not with one of my fingers"... but surely there is room for all.'[14] This style of life was an essential part of his plan for brotherhoods, and it was also the cornerstone of his views on conventual life for women.

The importance he attached to sisterhoods was mirrored in a letter to Keble: 'Newman and I have separately come to think it necessary to have some *Soeurs de Charité* in the Anglo-Catholic Church.'[15] In 1841, Pusey visited Ireland to observe at first hand the workings of Roman Catholic nunneries, and in the same year Miss Marion Hughes committed herself to vows in his presence. From this date on, there were constant references to a μονή that is, a monastery, in his correspondence with Keble and Newman. The goal of these sisterhoods would be a chance for certain people to flee from the secular lures of the world and its distractions. These institutions would not be eremitical, but would engage in pastoral activities among the poor of England. In 1844, Pusey wrote to the Reverend H. Ellacombe: 'I cannot doubt this drawing of people's minds toward a more devoted life, giving themselves to His service, and the ministering to His poor, is, in the main, of God.'[16] In his correspondence with Reverend Doctor Hook, Pusey enumerated other factors which would justify the establishment of societies for single women. They would be exemplars of Christian ideals and outlets for those who felt called to community life. The convents could also absorb those individuals who might convert to Rome. This fear of secession to Rome was a real fear. Pusey theorized that if one found the Church of England narrow and sterile, he might switch allegiance to Rome. Newman appreciated Pusey's anxiety and also believed that the conventual life might stem a mass conversion to Rome. 'Pusey is at the moment eager about setting up Sisters of Mercy. I feel sure that such institutions are the only means of saving some of our best members from turning Catholics.'[17]

John Henry Newman became the chief spokesman for the establishment of monasticism in the Anglican Church. Newman argued that monasticism was the means for the preservation of the truths and essentials of Christianity. Also, monastic life could protect the Church of England from the dangers of indifference and rationalism.

> I would request of them to compare it with the sort of religion into which the unhappy enthusiast of the present day is precipitated by the high and dry system of the Establishment, and he will see how much was gained to Christianity in purity, as well as unity, by that monastic system....[18]

He recognized a growing schism in the Church of England and believed that he could heal this split by providing for some spiritual outlet. Monasticism was the cure. Newman maintained that monasteries should become havens for piety and holiness, and he believed that 'such provisions in one shape or another will always be attempted by the more serious and anxious part of the community wherever Christianity is generally professed.'[19] Newman's desire for monastic life achieved fruition on 25th April 1842, when he and a group of friends retired to Littlemore to live a quasi-monastic life centred around praying the breviary. Newman defended his decision by pleading that 'monastic houses became...nothing else than a peculiar development of Christian ministry — a ministry not of sacraments or clerical, but especially of the word or doctrine.'[20] Prior to Littlemore, however, Newman had developed his theology of monastic life in the Church of England.

All commentaries on the Benedictine Rule maintain that monastic life was one of withdrawal or, to use another description, a *fuga mundi*. One fled from the world and its evils. Although he did not preclude work such as hospital service or pastoral duties, Newman appreciated the importance of this withdrawal. Moreover, he argued that the future of religious life in the Church of England would have little success until the thoughts of the clergy turn from the preoccupations of this world to the next.[21]

Newman's theory of monastic life may appear negative or reactionary since he believed that 'monasticism was one and the same everywhere because it was a reaction from the secular life which has everywhere the same structure and characteristic.'[22] But on the other hand, there was a positive dimension. According to Newman, 'one great purpose answered by monasticism in the early ages was the maintenance of the truth in times and places in which the great masses of Catholics had let it slip from them.'[23] This appeal to the spirit of the ancient Church was the main argument in Newman's writings, and from this period he developed his justification for the monastic system. Newman criticized his contemporaries who condemned monasticism as an evil associated with a pre-Reformation papacy. He retorted that a monastic style of life existed in Christian history not only from the fourth century, 'but from the time of St. Philip's daughters in the *Acts, viz.,* the private and domestic observance of an ascetic life for religion's sake and to the honour of Christ.'[24] In a letter to Froude in 1833, he defended monasticism by an appeal to antiquity.

> Now someone has told me that, in defending monasticism, I have become peculiar. I can but throw myself in answer upon the general Church and avow (as I do) that if any one will show me any opinion of mine which the Primitive Church condemned, I will renounce it.[25]

Newman also valued the cultural inheritance derived from the monastic movement.

In *Historical Sketches* (London, 1873), Newman traced the decline of western civilization in the Middle Ages and posited that monasticism filled the void which followed. According to Newman, the scholarship of the monasteries, the copying of manuscripts and the strengthening of learning through the establishment of palace schools were the gifts which monasticism bequeathed to Europe. 'The old order of things died, sure enough, but then a new order took its place and they themselves by no will or expectation of their own were in no small measure its very life.'[26] Consequently, Newman valued monasticism because it personified the patristic system of values and contributed to the development of order and education in Europe. A celibate brotherhood whose life revolved around the monastic breviary, Newman maintained, would serve as a spiritual stimulus for the Anglican Church. Newman's belief in the efficacy of celibacy and his devotion to the breviary, therefore, help to flesh out his approach to monasticism.

In *Tract 90,* one can see the culmination of Newman's ideas concerning the celibate life. He stated that 'our Church leaves the discretion with the clergy; and most people will allow that, under our circumstances, she acts wisely in doing so.'[27] One should embrace celibacy freely, and ecclesiastical canons must not legislate for the celibate life. Although the majority of the Anglicans believed that celibacy was Romish or unnatural, Newman remained unmarried. He did not belittle the married clergy, but he maintained that the celibate was the superior of the two. Early in his life he concluded that the single state could sanctify and enrich the Church of England, and personally, he thought that celibacy was the means to attain his salvation. In *Apologia Pro Vita Sua,* Newman explained why he renounced the married life.

> I am obliged to mention, although 1 do it with great
> reluctance, another deep imagination, which at the time,
> the autumn of 1816, took possession of me — there can
> be no mistake about the fact that it would be the will of
> God that I should lead a single life.[28]

He believed that 'vows (e.g. celibacy) are evident of want of faith.'[29] The Church, therefore, cannot legislate for celibacy; one must freely accept this state of life. One must stress the importance of celibacy in Newman's spiritual and intellectual thought since it was one of the main reasons which led him to abandon Anglicanism for the Roman Church. According to Newman, '...her zealous maintenance of the doctrine and rule of celibacy, which I recognize as Apostolic, and her faithful agreement with Antiquity in so many points...was an argument as well as a plea in favour of the great Church of Rome.'[30]

The monastic breviary also found a place of honour in Newman's writings. At Littlemore, he established a horarium which emulated the Roman schema of Matins, Lauds, Vespers and Compline. He abandoned the Book of Common Prayer in favour of the more primitive, that is, Catholic rite. Newman defended the reason behind his devotion to the Benedictine breviary in *Tract 75*.

> And there is a further benefit which, it is hoped, will result from an acquaintance with the Breviary Services, *viz.*, that the adoption and arrangement of the Psalms therein made will impress many people with a true sense of excellence and profitableness of those inspired compositions than it is the fashion of this age to entertain.[31]

Along with celibacy, therefore, devotion to the breviary were essential elements of Newman's attempt at common life at Littlemore.

In 1840, Newman tried to explain the nature of Littlemore to the Reverend Thomas Mozley: 'We have bought nine acres and want to build a μονή...the cells to be required, being (say) nine or ten feet high...the oratory or chapel, a matter altogether for future construction.'[32] Newman had no wish to establish Roman Catholic monasticism, but on the other hand, his devotion to a universal monastic ideal led him to this experiment. At Littlemore, there were no permanent vows, no distinctive uniform or habit, and no enforced stability. With the exception of the daily schedule, Newman refused to legislate for the life at Littlemore.

> I suppose a religious house ought frankly to receive anyone who shows himself in earnest, without respect of persons...The principle of obedience does not exist in our Church — i.e. (as regards a religious house) the principle of assimilation, or a digestive power. We have no head to whom obedience is due. We have no ecclesiastical authority, no episcopal blessing. We have no vows, obliging people to be resigned, when the spirit or flesh rebels. We have no sacramental services, compensating for hardships, relieving the dreariness or monotony (as some would find it) of a retreat.[33]

Nevertheless, Newman established a community which can be termed monastic. In 1840, Newman informed Pusey that 'since I have been up here an idea has revived in my mind, of which we have before now talked,

11

viz., of building a monastic house in the place, and coming up to live in it myself.'[34] Writing years later, he stated: 'I had in view a monastic house there.'[35] Although he recognized the value of solitude, Newman viewed Littlemore as a service institution with the membership involved in a preaching apostolate or in pastoral work. He also wanted Littlemore to become a source of inspiration for those who were drawn to an Anglo-Catholic theology. The community, therefore, would foster those ideals and traditions which were lost during the Reformation, especially monasticism. At Littlemore, '...it will be attempted to wrest a weapon out of our adversaries' hands...a treasure which was ours as much as theirs, and then, on our attempting to recover it, they accuse us of borrowing what we have lost through inadvertence.'[36]

In *Parochial and Plain Sermons,* Newman explained the principles behind Littlemore. He canonized those individuals who had put all aside, renounced the world and devoted all to the service of God.

> The life here advocated is one of which Prayer, Praise, Intercession and other devotional services are made the object and business, in the same sense in which a certain profession or trade is the object and business of life to the mass of men: one to which everything else gives way. This explanation will answer the question, how much of each day it supposes to set aside for devotion. Callings of this world do not necessarily occupy the whole, or half or a third of our time, but they rule and dispose of the whole of it.[37]

He also believed that monasticism could meet an emotional or spiritual need for certain people.

> I am almost in despair of keeping men together. The only possible way is a monastery. Men want an outlet for their devotional and penitential feelings, and if we do not grant it, to a dead certainty they will go where they can find it.[38]

There were some spurious indictments against Littlemore. A number of hostile Anglicans caricatured the community as a popish monastery. Consequently, the Bishop of Oxford demanded an explanation of the 'so-called Anglo-Catholic Monastery that is in the process of erection at Littlemore.'[39] The Bishop also inquired about the dormitory, the chapel and the refectory, and he ended his query by complimenting Newman. The Bishop stated that he had the greatest trust in Newman, and also believed that he would be the last person to advocate a revolutionary or unorthodox experiment. Newman responded immediately with a lengthy description of the brotherhood. He emphasized the personal nature of the venture and assured the Bishop of his loyalty to the Church of England. Newman reported that he was not departing from Anglican traditions, but was merely performing the ordinary duties of a curate. 'I propose to live there myself a good deal...In doing this I believe I am consulting for the good of my parish, as my population in Littlemore is at least equal to that of St. Mary's in Oxford...I am doing a very great benefit to my people.'[40] Littlemore, according to Newman, was a response to the needs of the local parish. He concluded his reply to the Bishop by stressing the orthodox nature of Littlemore. 'Of course I can repeat your Lordship's words that I am not attempting a revival of the monastic orders in anything approaching to the Romanist sense of the term.'[41] In 1845, Newman disbanded the brotherhood and Littlemore ended. The importance of Newman's experiment was its influence on others; individuals began to ponder the feasibility of monasticism in the Church of England.

The best summary of Newman's thoughts on religious life are contained in a philippic written against a critic who claimed that monasticism was inconsistent with the Gospel message. Newman argued that the early monks personified the poverty and humility of Christ. Moreover, the monastic communities mirrored the spirit of the Gospels because the monastic ideal was the 'nearest approach to the perfection of the Christian spirit.'[42] Moreover, it 'is the greatest fulfillment of both the first and second commandment of the law.'[43] When Newman left the Anglican Church and converted to Roman Catholicism in 1845, the Oxford Movement and the Anglo-Catholics lost their chief spokesman for religious life.

By mid-century, therefore, there was a strong movement to establish monasticism in the Anglican Church. The arguments were many. Some maintained that the monks could do valuable social work, while others espoused an enclosed or ascetic brotherhood. But it was the prestige and theological arguments of the Tractarians which made the conventual life appealing to Anglicans. Monasticism, they believed, was the common heritage of all Christians, not only of Rome, and its introduction would enrich the Established Church.

Notes

[1] O. Chadwick, ed., *The Mind of the Oxford Movement* (Stanford University Press, Stanford, 1960), p. 12.

[2] A.M. Allchin, *The Silent Rebellion: Anglican Religious Communities: 1845-1900* (SCM Press, London, 1958), p. 37.

[3] W.J.C. Wand, *Anglicanism in History and Today* (Weidenfeld and Nicolson, London, 1950), p. 102.

[4] C.C. Martindale, *The Life of Monsignor Robert Hugh Benson* (Longmans Green Co., London, 1916), p. 268.

[5] O. Chadwick, ed., *The Mind of the Oxford Movement*, p. 38.

[6] P. Anson, *The Benedictines of Caldey* (The Catholic Book Club, London, 1940), p. xvi.

[7] B.W. Randolph, ed., *Letters of Spiritual Guidance by John Keble* (A. R. Mowbray Co., London, 1909), p. 156.

[8] L. Guiney, *Hurrell Froude* (Methuen Co., London, 1904), p. 122.

[9] J. Bowden, *Life and Letters of Frederick Faber* (John Murphy, Baltimore, 1869), pp. 93-94.

[10] R. Chapman, *Father Faber* (Burns, Oates, Washbourn, London, 1961), pp. 93-116.

[11] H. Liddon, *Life of Edward Bouverie Pusey*, vol. 2 (Longmans Green Co., London, 1893), p. 38.

[12] Ibid.

[13] E.B. Pusey, *A Letter to the Right Reverend Father in God Richard, Lord Bishop of Oxford, on the Tendency to Romanism Imputed to Doctrines Held of Old, as Now, in the English Church* (Charles Henry, New York, 1839), p. 142.

[14] Ibid., p. 144.

[15] H. Liddon, *Life of Edward Bouverie Pusey*, Vol. 3, p. 5.

[16] Ibid., p. 14.

[17] Ibid., p. 6.

[18] J.H. Newman, *Historical Sketches*, vol. 2 (Longmans Green Co., New York, 1906), p. 102.

[19] Ibid., p. 165.

[20] J.H. Newman, *The Church of the Fathers* (John Lane, New York, 1900), p. 258.

[21] J.H. Newman, *Discussions and Arguments on Various Subjects* (Longmans Green Co., New York, 1907), p. 41.

[22] J.H. Newman, *Historical Sketches*, vol. 2, p. 373.

[23] A. Mozley, ed., *Letters and Correspondence of John Henry Newman* (Longmans Green Co., London, 1890), p. 100.

[24] J.H. Newman, *Historical Sketches*, vol. 2, p. 166.

[25] A. Mozley, ed., *Letters and Correspondence of John Henry Newman*, p. 100.

[26] J.H. Newman, *Historical Sketches*, vol. 2, p. 442.

[27] J.H. Newman, *Tracts for the Times: Remarks on Certain Passages in the Thirty-Nine Articles* (AMS Press, New York, 1969), p. 64.

[28] J.H. Newman, *Apologia Pro Vita Sua* (Longmans Green Co., New York, 1947), p. 6.

[29] A. Mozley, ed., *Letters and Correspondence of John Henry Newman*, p. 194.

[30] J.H. Newman, *Apologia Pro Vita Sua*, p. 49.

[31] J.H. Newman, *Tracts for the Times, Number 75* (AMS Press, New York, 1969), p. 2.

[32] A. Mozley, ed., *Letters and Correspondence of John Henry Newman*, p. 272.

[33] The Birmingham Oratory, ed., *Correspondence of J.H. Newman with John Keble and Others,* 1839-1845 (Longmans Green Co., London, 1917), p. 311.

[34] H. Liddon, *Life of Edward Bouverie Pusey*, p. 135.

[35] J.H. Newman, *Apologia Pro Vita Sua*, p. 119.

[36] J.H. Newman, *Tracts for the Times, Number 75*, p.1.

[37] J.H. Newman, *Parochial and Plain Sermons* (Longmans Green Co., New York, 1891), p. 334.

[38] The Birmingham Oratory, ed., *Correspondence of J.H. Newman with John Keble and Others*, p. 172.

[39] A. Mozley, ed., *Letters and Correspondence of John Henry Newman*, p. 350.

[40] Ibid., p. 352.

[41] A. Mozley, ed., *Letters and Correspondence of John Henry Newman*, p. 352.

[42] J.H. Newman, *Essays: Critical and Historical*, vol. 2, (Longmans Green Co., New York, 1907), p. 418.

[43] Ibid., p. 415.

CHAPTER II

DR. PUSEY AND FR. IGNATIUS
OF LLANTHONY

D r. Pusey, the scholar, and Fr. Ignatius, the eccentric champion of the revival of Benedictine life in the Church of England, conjure up pictures which represent opposite extremes in the world of Victorian religion. Pusey's biographers portray him as a scholar, teacher, erudite theologian, and the leader of the so-called 'Puseyites.' More importantly, he did not follow the urges of his Oxford contemporaries and bolt to the Roman Catholic Church. In spite of his acknowledged influence and importance, he still remains the 'most neglected of the Tractarian leaders.'[1] Pusey's life and accomplishments have failed to attract the attention of church historians. Because he wrote as 'a warm admirer and a rigid adherent of his master,' even Liddon's standard biography has obvious shortcomings.[2] Fr. Ignatius, on the other hand, has captured the imagination of several biographers.[3] Studies dealing with the monk of Llanthony range from Baroness De Bertouch's fantastic study, complete with its theophanies, apparitions, and miracles, to the more sober works by Attwater and Calder-Marshall. Consequently, Pusey has emerged as the mainstay of the Tractarians, Ignatius as the impulsive, eccentric, and strong-willed pioneer. Pusey is remembered as a saintly academician, but the career of Ignatius is tainted by scandals, financial disasters, and frequent bouts with ecclesiastical authorities. One recent study even accuses Fr. Ignatius of sexual impropriety of a homosexual nature.[4] The different personalities and interests of the two are apparent, but a relationship did develop between Pusey the realist and Ignatius the idealist. The extent of the influence of Dr. Pusey on Ignatius's career, however, is debated.

Pusey's biographers labour to avoid any association between their revered subject and Fr. Ignatius. Liddon does not mention or discuss Ignatius in his four volume work, but he does devote a great amount of space to Pusey's support of sisterhoods.[5] Leonard Prestige simply notes that 'Pusey had, through Miss Sellon, some dealings with the brilliant and erratic Father Ignatius...' and encouraged him in his monastic vocation.[6] The series of essays edited by Butler entirely avoid any discussion of the relationship between Pusey and Fr. Ignatius. But the sympathetic studies of Ignatius never fail to emphasise the association between the two churchmen.

The name of Pusey, therefore, tends to lend a sense of respectability to the checkered career of Ignatius. Calder-Marshall, for example, gives Pusey a central part in his biography of Ignatius, and maintains that the Oxford theologian functioned as 'his spiritual father.'[7] Attwater records that Pusey's early association with Ignatius at Plymouth represented 'the really important happening of the period.'[8] Peter Anson describes the close relationship which existed between the scholar and the monk as 'a friendship which, considering the differences in their character, was remarkable.'[9] Not surprisingly, De Bertouch canonizes the influence of Pusey, 'the saintly spiritual warrior,'[10] on her subject: 'it is no exaggeration to state that these two distinguished souls (Pusey and Sellon) were the ghostly foster parents of the Monk's vocation.' 'Well-nigh up to the very year of his death,' she writes, 'Dr. Pusey was the chosen administrator of the Sacrament of Penance to the monk, his friend, his confident in all things, his arbitrator in all situations difficult or tense.'[11] Even Dr. Pusey realised that his name and reputation would be used to give authority to Ignatius. Writing to Archbishop Charles Thomas Longley in 1866, Pusey noted that 'he (Ignatius) is not unlikely to maker much use of my name.'[12]

If one totally disregards the influence of Dr. Pusey on the development of Fr. Ignatius, one also ignores historical fact and evidence. But to link the career of Ignatius to Pusey, to picture the Oxford professor as the monk's mentor, or to argue that Fr. Ignatius enjoyed the wholehearted and uncritical support of Dr. Pusey also misses the mark. Their paths did cross and Pusey did extend some encouragement to the young idealist, but the relationship was not as intimate as the monk's supporters argue or as barren as Pusey's biographers would have us believe.

In 1860, Joseph Leycester Lyne, an ordained Anglican deacon, was assigned to assist George Rundle Prynne at St. Mary's Plymouth. Here, Lyne established a small religious community for men and eventually came into contact with Dr. Pusey and Priscilla Lydia Sellon. Consequently, Pusey began to encourage young Lyne in his plan.[13] According to Lyne's recollection, 'nothing daunted, and by Dr. Pusey's emphatic advice...(I) decided to start...(my) community on a modest basis.'[14] Both Pusey and Sellon supported this brotherhood, the Society for the Love of Jesus, and suggested that the membership inhabit a residence owned by

Sellon so that they could easily assess and evaluate the deacon's qualities.[15] According to Lyne, Pusey became his trusted confidant. Dr. Pusey's testimony confirms this friendship: '...up to the time of his leaving Plymouth I was his advisor.'[16] When he allegedly cured a fourteen year-old girl, Lyne relates that Pusey told him that 'you are too young...for the notoriety, whether favourable or the reverse, to be anything but a spiritual temptation and hindrance.'[17] But Dr. Pusey did not remain uncritical: 'Pusey encouraged his monastic purpose, while maintaining a wholesome distrust of his judgment.'[18] Attwater also believes that Pusey and Sellon were not blind to the monk's faults, 'but in many ways he was a most promising young man, sincerely attracted to the religious life, and one who might be most valuable to the cause of Catholicism in the Church of England.' Consequently, they 'sympathized with him, they encouraged him, they helped to form the monastic idea definitely in his mind.'[19] Pusey's memories of Lyne at Plymouth are positive: 'he was very successful... among the daughters and effective...'[20]

However, this experimental brotherhood failed, Lyne became ill, and his family decided to take him to Belgium to recover. Before he departed, an incident occurred which drew Pusey into a controversy with Lyne's father which would span two decades. Determined that Lyne should not become discouraged in his vocation, Lydia Sellon had an ersatz habit made for the young monk, and Pusey sent the garment to Lyne, who immediately donned it.'... I transmitted it under a wrong impression of the way in which your son would use it,' Dr. Pusey wrote to Mr. Francis Lyne twenty years later: 'My own conviction is, that it is better not to make marked outward changes in things done for God. I had not in my mind that He would wear the dress in any marked way.'[21] In another letter to Mr. Lyne, Pusey again recognised the folly in giving the impressionable deacon the monastic garb.[22] This habit, consequently, became both a sign of defiance and a seal of Pusey's approval which would haunt and embarrass Pusey throughout his life.

From the continent, Lyne 'wrote frequently to Dr. Pusey and Miss Sellon, trying to obliterate the bad impression which his first failure must have made on them.'[23] Moreover, this Belgium experience had a marked influence on the neophyte Anglican monk. Bedecked with Pusey's habit, Lyne was drawn quickly and inevitably into the romantic world of monks and monasteries. Pusey later diagnosed the ill effect Belgium had on young Lyne. 'His father spoiled him...by sending him to Belgium,' Pusey explained to the Archbishop of Canterbury, Charles Thomas Longley, where 'he had nothing to do, visited all the Benedictine monasteries, and henceforth nothing would satisfy, but to adopt the whole Benedictine

Rule.'[24] According to Pusey, Lyne learned his Benedictinism in Belgium: 'I understand afterwards that having nothing else to do, he spent his time visiting the Belgium convents, and he came back, believing himself to have a vocation to unite with others in restoring the Benedictine order in the English Church.'[25] Pusey later chided Mr. Lyne for taking his son to the continent and told him that, 'if you had not done this, you would not have had the anxiety which you...had.'[26]

Inspired by the desire to become the first Anglican Benedictine, Lyne returned to England, and the habit became his trademark. His stay at St. George's-in-the-East was cut short when Charles Lowder demanded that Lyne abandon his treasured monastic habit. Ignatius refused and resigned. Shortly afterwards he adopted the title 'Fr. Ignatius' and began to publish and preach in favour of the necessity to introduce Benedictine monasticism into the Anglican Church. According to Anson and Calder-Marshall, Fr. Ignatius professed his solemn vows in the presence of Dr. Pusey in 1864.[27] That year also marked a change in the friendship between Pusey and Ignatius. The Anglican monk began to enjoy his notoriety and independence, and his antics also began to embarrass Dr. Pusey. In April 1864 Pusey informed Ignatius's father that 'it is long since your son acted upon the advice of mine...' 'I am in no way responsible for anything he does...' and he stands 'in no relation to me.'[28] The reason for this distance was Ignatius's desire to live as a Benedictine monk, something Pusey thought inappropriate and impractical. Consequently, Dr. Pusey later informed Archbishop Longley that 'his relation to me and my influence began to cool.' [29] Even when Ignatius struggled in vain to found another brotherhood near Ipswich in 1862, 'Dr. Pusey and Miss Sellon, while not dissuading him from his monastic vocation, were a trifle less certain of his ability carry the project through...'[30]

When Ignatius moved this community to Norwich, he immediately came into conflict with the local bishop, John Thomas Pelham, and some loyal Anglicans who thought that he was introducing popery into the Church of England under the cover of monasticism. Internal dissension within Ignatius's community and damaging publicity in the press also weakened its fragile existence. Eventually in 1866 Ignatius was dispossessed of his property in Norwich due to a technicality in the title deed. During this time, Dr. Pusey had recognised that his influence over the Anglican monk had diminished, but Ignatius still clung to the belief that Pusey was his spiritual godfather. Commenting on a visit to Norwich by Pusey and Sellon, Ignatius later. reminisced: '...(both) had kept anxious watch over every deed and word which recorded a progressive footprint in the career that they had done so much to launch upon its deep waters.[31] Dr.

Pusey did, however, admit that be had received favourable reports from laymen about Ignatius's preaching in Norwich.'[32] While Ignatius was struggling in Norwich, Pusey began to formulate and clarify his ideas on what direction Ignatius's career should take.

Ignatius's activities, especially his alleged Romish practices, had scandalised and shocked his parents. Both tried to urge their son to abandon his monkish pretenses and to return to the order and discipline of the Anglican Church. In the eyes of Mr. Francis Lyne, Dr. Pusey appeared to be the culprit who encouraged his son to pursue a Benedictine vocation. While Ignatius was still at Norwich, Mr. Lyne wrote and complained to the Archbishop of Canterbury, Charles Thomas Longley. Lyne objected to Ignatius's liturgical practices, but he singled out the Pusey habit for special scorn.[33] After an exchange of letters between Pusey, Ignatius and Mr. Lyne, Dr. Pusey proposed that Ignatius modify his monastic dress and wear a cassock. But Lyne protested to Longley: 'the Cassock Dr. Pusey approves...' because 'it is a protection to the clergy against themselves." Moreover, Lyne thought that his prerogative as a father had been usurped by Dr. Pusey, and he complained that 'I feel I have no right to a voice in such a matter.'[34]

During the summer of 1866, Mr. Lyne wrote to Pusey and sought his help, as an arbiter to force his son to moderate his views. However he would not permit an interview or meeting between Ignatius and Pusey. In June Pusey replied to this request to act as a mediator. But Pusey believed that a meeting with Fr. Ignatius was essential: 'intercourse with myself is calming to him, not exciting.' 'How can I give an opinion if I am not allowed to see your son,' Pusey queried. 'I have no object,' he continued, 'except that your son should live to the glory of God...'[35] Pusey also accused the father of exerting unnecessary pressure on his son, and ended his letter begging Mr. Lyne to allow Ignatius to travel to Oxford to meet with him.

Mr. Lyne responded to Pusey's letter and reminded Dr. Pusey that earlier in 1864 he had appealed to the professor's conscience for assistance to 'oppose...those of the clergy who were misleading him.' According to Lyne, Pusey replied that he no longer exerted any influence over Ignatius. Lyne failed to accept this argument and maintained that Pusey's influence still remained strong. 'I have other letters from you,' he informed Pusey, 'that left an impression on my mind, that, at the first you took my son under your wing from a desire to rescue a valuable child from an ungodly parent.' Mr. Lyne castigated Pusey for meddling in a matter which was a family affair. He acknowledged Pusey's wish that Ignatius visit him at Oxford, and pointed out to Pusey that 'my wish was to prevent the meeting.' 'I desire to keep my son in his natural...state.'[36] Lyne sent a copy of this letter to Lambeth Palace and threatened to publish an expose of Pusey's alleged evil influences on his son in the *Church Times*.[37]

Sensing a possible scandal or damaging publicity, Pusey sent a long letter to Archbishop Longley. This letter contained his estimation of Ignatius and discussed the extent of his influence on the Anglican monk. 'I wish to mention to you,' Pusey began, 'what I think of the young man, and what I have had to do with him.' Dr. Pusey quickly pointed out some positive and noteworthy characteristics. 'He has (as his actions show) a great deal of natural energy, a strong will, a very affectionate and loving heart, a real love for our Lord...(and) I was told that he was an eloquent Preacher.' Moreover, Ignatius always exhibited a great devotion to the Church of England. Pusey also noted that he advised Ignatius during the monk's stay at Plymouth, but his influence had since waned. Dr. Pusey told Longley that Ignatius's trip to Belgium damaged him; he returned to England with romantic notions to establish Benedictinism along the lines of the Roman Catholic monasteries which he visited on the continent. Pusey also explained that Mr. Lyne's words and actions might harm his son: 'My fear now is that his father (who has very strong religious prejudices) will avail himself of his son's present weakness and commit him in some opposite direction, to induce him to give up that devotional life to which he feels himself to have been called.' This might result in a disastrous conversion to Roman Catholicism because Anglicans like Ignatius 'have no vent for their aspirations in the Church of England, or think they have not.'

What path, then, did Dr. Pusey want Fr. Ignatius to follow? Clearly he would not encourage Ignatius to pursue a vocation as a Benedictine monk; his flirtation with European monasticism contributed to his current problems. Because of Ignatius's gusto and preaching skills, Pusey believed that he could easily develop into an effective urban missionary. 'What I wish for him,' Dr. Pusey told the primate, 'was that...living under a simple religious rule of life he should work as a missionary in one of our heathen populations.' Sounding similar to the Settlement House Movement, Pusey argued that 'our heathen population can be reached only by bodies of clergy dedicated to this work of conversion and living for that end alone.' Consequently, 'I wished him to live quietly and let people see the fruits of his mode of life.' But Ignatius should not be made a curate. If he were ordained a priest, Pusey doubted if Ignatius would persevere. Although 'he would sacrifice a great deal for the present to obtain them (orders),' Pusey believed that Ignatius lacked stability. Dr. Pusey ended his lengthy letter by defending his earlier suggestion that Ignatius abandon his controversial monastic dress and adopt a cassock. 'Other clergy had worn it with the permission of the Bishop,' Pusey reminded the Archbishop, and he stated that 'my young friend also wishes it as an outward token that he is leading a life apart from the world.'[38] Soon after this the disaster struck at Norwich, and Pusey offered Ignatius assistance.

Dr. Pusey immediately invited Fr. Ignatius to stay with him at the Isle of Wight, and it appears that Pusey's magic began to work on the evicted Anglican monk. On 30 June 1866 Ignatius contacted Archbishop Longley, informed him that he was staying with Pusey, and indicated that he was anxious to visit the Archbishop.[39] Pusey's moderating influence continued to surface. A month later, while still lodged at the Isle of Wight, Ignatius again expressed a desire to regularise his status as an Anglican clergyman. Ignatius told Longley that he intended 'to submit myself to you.' 'I am very anxious to see you again, and hear from you what you wish me to do and how to continue my work for Jesus and the lives of my fellow sinners in a quiet and unobtrusive way if that is possible.'[40] Pusey, therefore, forced Ignatius to re-think his vocation, and Ignatius remembered his stay on the Isle of Wight with affection and devotion.

> Dr. Pusey's invitation was conveyed in terms which admitted of no refusal, and in due course of time the Reverend Father (Ignatius) found himself comfortably installed with his devoted old friends...[41] He also complained of 'being a burden on the loving hospitality of my faithful friends, Dr. Pusey and Miss Sellon.'[42]

Dr. Pusey's evaluation of his guest and his future in the Anglican Church remained unchanged. 'I invited him here,' Pusey told Archbishop Longley, 'because I felt sure that he would get no better.' 'He wanted rest for his mind and he had none.' Pusey again drew the primate's attention to Mr. Lyne's 'religious harshness.' Pusey described Ignatius as 'simple as a child, enthusiastic, impulsive,' and emphasised his past successes in Plymouth and even in troublesome Norwich. For Pusey the conclusion was obvious: 'This points to his being employed in some way as a missionary in some of our heathen towns.' Pusey also portrayed Ignatius in the language similar to the famous ritualist slum priests such as Lowder and Mackonochie: 'He has a great sense of beauty and this leads to a great value...' Although Dr. Pusey maintained that Ignatius was 'no judge of character,' he argued that a brotherhood under the direction of Ignatius could positively influence large numbers of 'lay persons, who besides saying more prayers than usual,' might carry out 'works of love as laymen can do, leading a strict life in common.' If Dr.

Pusey recognized the potential for an urban settlement, he also pointed out problems.

> At present, I do not think that he has health for more. And it would be good for him to be put on a probation himself for which has not been tried yet in his persever-ance. His impulsive nature would be carrying him off to something else.[43]

Although Pusey's realism clashed with Fr. Ignatius's romantic and idealistic Benedictine lifestyle, the latter continued to seek Pusey's advice during the summer of 1866. It also appears that Ignatius began to modify his views in accordance with Pusey's plan for an urban mission. During an unpublicised trip back to Norwich in August, Ignatius wrote to Archbishop Longley that he was 'more anxious than ever to do what is our dear Lord's will for me, and I do not care what I give up of my own tastes to prove this to you...' He also drew attention to Pusey's moderating influence: 'I continue to ask Dr. Pusey's advice in...things that I do.'[44] Ignatius later informed the primate that Dr. Pusey 'has been very pleased with me as regards my duty towards my father,' but he also revealed a sign of anxiety when he hinted that conversion to Roman Catholicism was a real possibil-ity.[45] By the end of September Ignatius's rebellious and contentious spirit again surfaced. Acknowledging that Pusey still inspected some of his publications and public statements, Ignatius lashed out against Arch-bishop Longley: 'You have mistrusted me once and I have publicly said so and should never feel again that rest and comfort in your Grace when I was trusted.' Yet Ignatius continued to appeal to the reputation of Pusey. 'I am...to see Dr. Pusey soon,' he informed the Archbishop, and will continue 'consulting him in spiritual matters as I have for years been accustomed to do so.'[46]

The reason which prompted this sour attack against Longley might be attributed to the Archbishop's hesitancy to sanction Ignatius's monastic dream or to give in to the monk's insistent demand for priestly orders. As Ignatius began to attack and question the motives of the primate, his friendship with Dr. Pusey also began to cool. The year 1867, therefore, marked the end of Ignatius's attachment to Pusey. Dr. Pusey continued to refuse to give his approbation to a monastic settlement; in his mind Ignatius could only succeed as a missionary to the urban outcasts of Victorian England. Moreover, Pusey had urged Longley to approach the question of ordination with caution and diplomacy. Pusey had even called for a period of probation and waiting before orders; Ignatius'a lack of stability troubled him. Pusey's refusal to sign a petition calling for Ignatius's ordination widened the gulf between the former advisor and the impetuous monk. On 5 December 1867 Pusey replied to Mrs. Lyne's plea to support the ordination of her son. 'I am very sorry that I cannot sign the enclosed,' he replied, 'I appreciate...your son's gifts and good qualities, but with the disposition which I have seen and *watched* for several years I should dread the priesthood for him.' Pusey's position was firm and uncompromising: 'I *dare not* take part in trying to obtain it for him.'[47] Pusey's view did not change with time. Writing to Lord Halifax in 1870 he informed the viscount that 'Father Ignatius is a most impractical man.' 'He is a good revivalist preacher wasted; very amiable, vain and ignorant of human nature in the concrete.'[48]

If Dr. Pusey divorced himself from Ignatius because of the latter's romantic nature and erratic personality, Ignatius also separated himself from Pusey. In 1870 Fr. Ignatius started another monastic community at Llanthony Abbey in the Black Mountains, and the correspondence between the monk and his former advisor ceased. Ignatius quickly initiated a monastic horarium and planned for the creation of a grand congregation of Anglican monks centred at his Welsh abbey. Preaching and writing became the chief occupations of Ignatius, who still dreamed of priestly orders. But without Pusey's help or recommendation Ignatius realised that no Anglican bishop would ordain him. Consequently, Ignatius confirmed Pusey's fears and approached an Old Catholic bishop, Joseph René Vilatte, also known as Mar Timotheus, and petitioned him for ordination. In July 1898 Vilatte ordained Ignatius of Llanthony, an event which Pusey had earlier discouraged.

Realising that Dr. Pusey had formed definite plans about his future in the Anglican Church which conflicted with his dreams, Ignatius distanced himself from Pusey's influence, guidance and wisdom. Negotiation, caution and counsel gave way to that romantic, eccentric and flamboyant personality of Victorian religious history. For a time, Pusey did exert a moderating influence on Fr. Ignatius, but the latter's vision exceeded the boundaries of the mature Oxford scholar. On the other hand, those who see Pusey as the unquestioning and uncritical champion of Ignatius's Benedictine dream are shortsighted. To believe, as Ignatius did, that 'either directly or indirectly, it would seem that Dr. Pusey was never very far away from the momentous hours of his monk-pupil's life'[49] distorts the facts of their friendship.

Notes

[1] P. Bulter, ed., *Pusey Rediscovered*, (London, 1983), p ix.

[2] Ibid.

[3] D. Attwater, *Fr. Ignatius of Llanthony*, (London, 1931); A Calder-Marshall, *The Enthusiast*, (London, 1962); The Baroness De Bertouch, *The Life of Father Ignatius*, O.S.B., (London, 1904). See also P. Anson, *The Call of the Cloister*, (London, 1964).

[4] D. Hilliard, 'Unenglish and Unmanly: Anglo-Catholicism and Homosexuality,' *Victorian Studies*, 25 (Winter 1982) pp. 181-210.

[5] H. Liddon, *Life of Edward Bouverie Pusey*, (London, 1893), 4 vols.

[6] L. Prestige, *Pusey*, (Oxford, 1982), p 122.

[7] Calder-Marshall, *The Enthusiast*, p 61.

[8] Attwater, *Fr. Ignatius of Llanthony*, p 8.

[9] Anson, *The Call of the Cloister*, p 58.

[10] De Bertouch, *The Life of Fr. Ignatius*, p 82

[11] Ibid., p 83.

[12] London, Lambeth Palace Library, Longley Papers, LV4, Pusey to Longley, 15 June 1866.

[13] Prestige, *Pusey*, p 122.

[14] De Bertouch, *The Life of Fr. Ignatius*, p 94.

[15] Calder-Marshall, *The Enthusiast*, p 65.

[16] Longley Papers, Pusey to F. Lyne (Ignatius's father), 15 June 1866.

[17] De Bertouch, *The Life of Fr. Ignatius*, p 87.

[18] Prestige, *Pusey*, p 122.

[19] Attwater, *Fr. Ignatius of Llanthony*, p 8.

[20] Longley Papers, Pusey to Longley, 2 August 1865.

[21] Pusey to F. Lyne, September 1881, printed in *Dr. Pusey's Defence of 'Father Ignatius,'* (London, 1882).

[22] Pusey to F. Lyne, 27 September 1881, printed in *Dr. Pusey's Defence*.

[23] Calder-Marshall, *The Enthusiast*, p 68.

[24] Longley Papers, Pusey to Longley, 5 June 1866.

[25] Pusey to F. Lyne, September 1881, printed 1n *Dr. Pusey's Defence*.

[26] Longley Papers, Pusey to F. Lyne, 10 June 1866.

[27] Anson, *Call of the Cloister*, p 58; Calder-Marshall, *The Enthusiast*, p 103.

[28] Quoted in Longley Papers, F. Lyne to Pusey, 13 June 1866.

[29] Longley Papers, Pusey to Longley, 15 June 1866.

[30] Calder-Marshall, *The Enthusiast*, p 96.

[31] De Bertouch, *The Life of Fr. Ignatius*, p 238.

[32] Longley Papers, Pusey to Longley, 2 August 1866.

[33] Longley Papers, Lyne to Longley, 28 May 1866.

[34] Ibid.

[35] Longley Papers, Pusey to Lyne, 10 June 1866.

[36] Longley Papers, Lyne to Pusey, 13 June 1866.

[37] Longley Papers, Lyne to Longley, 13 June 1866.

[38] Longley Papers, Pusey to Longley, 15 June 1866.

[39] Longley Papers, Ignatius to Longley, 30 June 1866.

[40] Longley Papers, Ignatius to Longley, 27 July 1866.

[41] De Bertouch, *The Life of Fr. Ignatius*, p 238.

[42] De Bertouch, *The Life of Fr. Ignatius*, p 353.

[43] Longley Papers, Pusey to Longley, 2 August 1866.

[44] Longley Papers, Ignatius to Longley, 3 August 1866.

[45] Longley Papers, Ignatius to Longley, 6 September 1866.

[46] Longley Papers, Ignatius to Longley, 22 September 1866.

[47] Pusey to Mrs. Lyne. 5 December 1867, printed in *Dr. Pusey's Defence*.

[48] Pusey to Halifax. 1870, quoted in Calder-Marshall, *The Enthusiast,* p 104.

[49] De Bertouch, *The Life of Fr. Ignatius*, p 552.

CHAPTER III

A QUESTION OF AUTHORITY: THE ANGLICAN NUNS OF WEST MALLING

Authority in the Anglican Church has always presented a problem. Beginning with the Reformation settlement, divines have debated the nature and extent of ecclesiastical authority. The conscience of individual believers, the local congregation, and the episcopacy have at times been designated as the *fons et origo* of church power. After the Restoration, the hierarchy reclaimed this prerogative, which the minister and parish had usurped during the Commonwealth. The nineteenth century proclaimed the theory that true authority rested with the episcopal hierarchy, but in reality bishops enjoyed little real power. The growth of ritualism with its attendant "surplice riots," the new scientific and critical spirit associated with Darwin, Christian Socialism, and the publication of *Essays and Reviews* and *Lux Mundi* demonstrated not only the scope of comprehensiveness and freedom within the Anglican Church, but also the inability or reluctance of individual bishops to demand conformity. In 1874, Disraeli attempted to bring some order and supervision into what he believed was the chaotic condition of the Established Church. By the provisions of the Public Worship Regulation Act, individual parishioners could bring charges against priests who deviated from the rubrics of the Book of Common Prayer. After the scandalous imprisonment of several saintly vicars for alleged ritual abuses, however, the bishops used a safeguard written into the Act, the "Bishop's Veto," to halt future prosecutions and thus effectively stripping the statute of all power.

By the end of the century, therefore, the lines of church authority were confused. Comprehensiveness, Anglo-Catholicism, and liturgical experiments were popular. Consequently, the theory and practice of Anglican authority stretched from a position which demanded rigorous discipline to a *laissez-faire*. The case of the Anglican nuns at West Malling is an example of the dilemma which plagued the Church of England. Viewed as a microcosm of the Church, this sisterhood and its dealings with two

Archbishops of Canterbury illustrate different approaches toward ecclesiastical authority. Archbishop Frederick Temple gave blanket permission to a number of practices and devotions which, according to some, were contrary to the Church of England. Archbishop Randall Davidson, on the other hand, demanded that the convent abandon these usages and conform to the accepted practices of the Church. Davidson maintained that a bishop might be compromised by the actions of his predecessors, and he must be careful not to jeopardize the freedom of his successor. For the individual Anglican, the situation was confusing.

The West Malling community was originally part of a Benedictine sisterhood founded and supervised by Fr. Ignatius Lyne in 1868.[1] After consultation with Mother Lydia Sellon, superior of the Davenport convent, Ignatius appointed Sister Ella, who took the name of Mother Hilda, O.S.B., as the first superior of his new foundation. The community settled first at Feltham, Middlesex, but in 1881, a schism occurred and a group led by Mother Hilda revolted against Ignatius's arbitrary leadership. To quell any future show of independence, he excommunicated the discontents.[2] Eight years later, Mother Hilda led her rebel group to Twickenham and established a foundation still loyal to the Benedictine Rule. Forced to move again, West Malling in Kent became the home of the Anglican nuns in 1893.

By the end of the century, sisterhoods were infamous as havens for ritualism. According to Horton Davies "the most striking advances in ritual as well as ceremonial were to be sought out only by the initiated and the trusted in the sequestered chapels of religious communities that were such a remarkable manifestation of Anglo-Catholic spirituality in the second half of the nineteenth century."[3] West Malling was no exception. The most unyielding opponent of "popish abuses," Walter Walsh, mentioned this sisterhood as a sinister threat to the integrity of the church of England.[4] The convent at West Malling achieved a degree of stability under Mother Hilda, and in 1903, she wrote what appeared to be an innocent letter which sought the permission of the Archbishop of Canterbury to have one of her nuns professed.

On September 22, 1903, Mother Hilda informed Archbishop Randall Davidson that "one of the community is desirous of 'Profession.'"[5] Moreover, she stated that Frederick Temple, Davidson's predecessor at Lambeth Palace, was routinely notified of any profession in the community, and "...permission he always kindly gave." "In accordance with this custom," she concluded, "I now write to ask your Grace's permission which we trust you will graciously accord."[6] Archbishop Davidson's reply was unexpected. "Before I can express an opinion as to what I ought to do in this matter about which you enquire, I should like to be in possession of more particulars... [for example] the constitution and work of the community."[7] Davidson confessed his ignorance of the West Malling nuns, but expressed the hope "that we shall be able to arrange matters satisfactory both in the present instance and for the future..." The existence of sisterhoods in the Church of England was problematic, and he mentioned the ambiguity surrounding the 1897 Report of the Lambeth Conference on religious communities as an example.[8] In order that he might "have all the facts before... coming to a decision as to what ought to be our ordinary course of action in these cases," the Archbishop directed Mother Hilda to send him a copy of the convent's constitution.[9]

The Mother Superior's response revealed a sense of bewilderment and confusion: Why this sudden scrutiny and investigation? Her reply pointed out that Archbishop Temple had already seen the constitution, "asked one question on a point I was able to satisfy him, and [he] gave permission for a sister's profession."[10] She maintained that the sisterhood was " a small *insignificant* community" which avoided publicity. Moreover, its inclusion in The *Official Year Book of the Church of England* was ample proof of the convent's loyalty and orthodoxy.[11] Mother Hilda continued to appeal to the earlier approval of Archbishop Temple, "...whom we knew when Bishop of London and who then gave his permission as well as later when at Canterbury."[12] She also claimed that the sisters were Benedictine. In conclusion, the superior promised that the constitution would soon follow. Archbishop Davidson, therefore, faced two dilemmas. Did Frederick Temple give his sanction to the existence and practices of this sisterhood, and if so, were his successors constrained by his actions? Secondly, did the West Malling constitution embody and express the spirit of the Established Church?

When Frederick Temple became Archbishop of Canterbury in 1896, he was seventy-five years old and nearly blind. As Bishop of London (1885-1896), he distinguished himself as a social and educational reformer.[13] Temple recognized the plight of the poor in London's slums and supported the foundation of parochial brotherhoods to work among the urban outcasts. Religious communities might alleviate the poverty and suffering of his flock. In 1891, for example, he addressed the Upper House of Convocation and argued "that the clergy want very large assistance, and they want the assistance of men who will be willing to give such assistance... We want a number of men who would do a great deal of voluntary work... to meet the enormous amount of practical heathenism that is to be found in the poorer parts of great towns."[14] These urban foundations must "... work in strict subordination to the authority of the bishop of each diocese... and only on the invitation and under the sanction of the Incumbent or Curate in charge."[15] He also recognized the value of vows and encouraged members "to undertake lifelong engagements to the life and work of the community." But at the discretion of the bishop, one could be released from this religious commitment.[16] For Temple, therefore, religious communities were not alien to the character of the Church of England. Moreover, sisterhoods, such as West Malling, could strengthen the Church's dedication to the welfare of the poor and needy.

Frederick Temple was certainly acquainted with the West Malling women, but it appears he was not clear on the extent of his authority over the sisterhood. In 1897, for example, a former chaplain sent Temple a list of complaints drawn up by some of the members which dealt with some aspects of the convent's life. The Archbishop's reply was succinct: "What right have I to interfere."[17] The priest, therefore, pointed out that Temple did have the authority "to interfere with the Malling community."[18] "I can only say," he continued, "that the last two Chaplains held a license from Your Grace's predecessors... [and] the community wishes to maintain this connection in the future." Temple's response revealed a sense of bewilderment and confusion. "...If I am a Visitor, I can interfere and if I am asked to license a Chaplain, I can enquire, but I do not understand how I can... do anything in the case as it stands."[19] Other interested Anglicans also queried the Archbishop about the ecclesiastical status of West Malling. One suggested that the sisterhood existed "...for the purpose of seclusion from the external world as much as the strictest Roman Catholic convent."[20] Another simply asked "whether the Sisterhood at Malling Abbey is recognized by the Archbishop and under his authority."[21] A third, who was corresponding with Mother Hilda, desired to know if West Malling enjoyed episcopal sanction.[22] The Primate's response to this was characteristically noncommittal: "Do you know anything of the community?"[23]

Although the sisterhood boasted that they possessed the approval of the Archbishop of Canterbury, Temple was ignorant of the convent's lifestyle. Because of the number of questions about West Malling, Temple asked the Suffragan Bishop of Dover, William Walsh, to report to him on the sisterhood. "They are a very strict Order, and are practically enclosed," he informed the Archbishop, and "I have seen the Mother Superior two or three times and I think she is a sensible and certainly very humble minded..." The Bishop also stated that he believed that the former Primate, Edward White Benson, had licensed a priest to minister to the women.[24] Two days later, Bishop Walsh commented on the apostolates of the Anglican sisters. "The work of the community is done within the walls. They receive sick cases and nurse them, but what else besides prayer, I know not..." Consequently, he recommended that the Archbishop approach Mother Hilda for more information.[25] In spite of Temple's lack of knowledge and the confusion surrounding the nature of his authority over the convent, in 1898 he licensed a clergyman, M.J. Richards, to attend to the spiritual needs of the sisters.[26] When Richards later reminded Temple that he had been given "permission to officiate here," the Archbishop was still unclear about conditions at West Malling. If "there are any other papers about the community," he told the chaplain, "let me have them."[27] Nonetheless, the nuns contended that they were a legitimate foundation living under the approval of the Archbishop of Canterbury. The Primate's subsequent dealings with the convent's chaplain and his approbation of vows strengthened this interpretation.

After the resignation of Richards, Rev. C.H. Berry[28] asked Temple to allow him to accept the chaplaincy at West Malling along with permission to officiate there until he could formally petition for a licence.[29] Berry told the Archbishop that "the post of Chaplain to Malling Abbey was offered to me by the Superior of the Sisters there."[30] Temple replied that application must be made by a legitimate representative of the sisterhood.[31] Mother Hilda, therefore, formally petitioned the Primate to license Berry as their chaplain.[32] Temple's reply was ambiguous: "What is Constitution and who is your visitor?"[33] The Mother Superior, sensing danger, reminded the Archbishop that he had previously licensed a priest for the convent. She also promised to forward the document. Temple studied the document, and after an exchange of letters concerning the wording of the Constitution and the nature of the sister's vows, he assured Mother Hilda that "you may employ Mr. Berry in the way you propose."[34] West Malling could now boast a chaplain approved by the Archbishop of Canterbury. According to this interpretation, Temple's silence signaled episcopal sanction; the nuns were a legitimate foundation with the blessing of the Primate of the Anglican Church.

Archbishop Temple's position on vows, likewise flexible, also conveyed what the sisterhood believed was sanction and approval for their way of life. As Bishop of London, Temple had recognized that vows *per se* were not contrary to the teaching of the Established Church. He also maintained that one could receive a dispensation from this obligation by approaching the local bishop.[35] Vows, for Temple, need not be indissoluble. In response to a woman asking his opinion about her daughter who planned to pronounce life vows in another Anglican convent, Temple responded that "all vows are dispensible."[36] He told the worried mother that the bishop can release the sisters from their responsibilities.[37] Although not permanent, vows were serious and should not be entered into lightly. When a nun, for example, requested a release from her vows and argued that they were invalid, Temple demanded strong evidence. "I have no sufficient information to satisfy me of the invalidity of these vows," he informed the petitioner.[38]

Whether they were binding or not, Temple's approval of vows at West Malling strengthened the credibility of the sisterhood in the Anglican Church. Early in the 1901 correspondence with Mother Hilda about Berry's chaplain's license, the Archbishop requested some information on the nature of the nuns' vows. Moreover, he wanted to know the process for dispensation.[39] The Mother Superior informed Temple that "the Sisters take the usual three vows [poverty, chastity, obedience] after first a postulancy for a year."[40] Following this, there was a further probationary period. Finally, "provided they [the sisters] have not wavered in the desire for the life and are of a sufficient age," about 30, "one can petition to make life vows." Dispensation was definitely possible. "If a sister finds she had made a mistake, the Chapter [of the convent] can release her from obedience... and she is free to request dispensation altogether from Your Grace or Bishop of [the] Diocese in which [the] convent is..." situated. The Superior reminded Temple, that when Bishop of London, he had demanded that the convent seek his permission before any profession. She also stated that he had given special leave for a young woman who was twenty-one to make final vows. But more important, "no one has been professed without Your predecessors' or Your Grace's permission since my interview with you when Bishop of London..."[41] In the following year, Mother Hilda sought approval for one of her nuns to make final vows, and Temple replied: "Let the profession proceed."[42] On April 8, 1902, the ceremony took place, and Mother Hilda thanked the Archbishop for his valuable help.[43]

In addition to the appointment of a chaplain and the sanctioning of final vows, Archbishop Temple's flippant and casual approval of the sisterhood's constitution strengthened the nuns' belief that their community was loyal to the teaching of the Anglican Church. The constitution which Temple condoned, however, clashed with some accepted Anglican guidelines for religious communities. Numerous Church Congresses and Convocations had examined the arguments for the existence of brotherhoods and sisterhoods in the Church, but it was not until the 1897 Lambeth Conference that the hierarchy expressed their views on conventual life in the Church of England. In general, the Conference wanted to prevent the formation of any brotherhood or sisterhood which was free from episcopal supervision. It was suggested, therefore, that the local bishop become the *ex officio* visitor, and moreover, the religious community "...must not be allowed to work in any diocese without the consent of the bishop."[44] An episcopal visitor was an unnegotiable prerequisite.

In devotional and liturgical matters, all religious bodies must use the Book of Common Prayer, and to ensure this, a "constitution... should be submitted to the Bishop's approval."[45] Moreover, "all liberty... must be regulated as to ensure the maintenance of the faith, and the order and discipline of the Anglican Church."[46] The bishops also recognized the dangers surrounding the ownership of property. Consequently, "provision for due rules as to the possession and disposition of property" should be stipulated in the community's by-laws. Ownership of the property must not escape the supervision and control of the Anglican Church.[47]

In spite of the Lambeth Conference proposals, it was not until August 23, 1901, that Archbishop Temple asked Mother Hilda about the constitution. Within a week, she sent the Archbishop the document. In the cover letter, she emphasized that the constitution was" ... nearly all in spirit though not actually in Words taken from the Holy Rule of St. Benedict..."[48] She also explained why the sisterhood did not have an episcopal visitor. "We have never had a visitor, and nothing about one [is] in the Holy Rule, but if desirable, a beneficed priest, and old friend, would very likely act as such." However, she concluded, the constitution contained a provision for appeal to the bishop of the diocese where the convent was located.[49] With the exception of some queries about vows,[50] Temple remained mute about this curious document. This silence, in the minds of the nuns, supported Mother Hilda's boast that the Archbishop of Canterbury had sanctioned and approved their statutes.

On examination of his attitude towards the West Malling constitution, Temple's negligence becomes clear.[51] Visibly absent from the constitution was any reference to the Book of Common Prayer. Instead, the public prayers of the convent were "to be said or sung as they are found in the Monastic Breviary..." Moreover, the constitution described the Anglican nuns as "a Community of Women living under the Rule of St. Benedict in accordance with the traditional interpretation of the above Institute." Also obvious by its absence was the office of visitor. Some episcopal supervision was mentioned, but only in the case of unsettled or unresolved disputes within the community. The bishop, "if he is willing to act," would be approached only as a final arbiter. The Mother Superior was omnipotent; she even appointed the chaplain. Finally, no clause safeguarded the property of the sisterhood, as recommended by the Lambeth Conference, for the Church of England.[52]

Archbishop Temple's actions or lack of direction gave some measure of episcopal blessing to the West Malling sisterhood. Consequently, in the 1903 correspondence between the nuns and his successor, Randall Davidson, Temple's behavior was the argument used to force Davidson to acquiesce or approve some questionable practices. But was the new Archbishop bound to honor the commitments of his predecessor? An able administrator, Archbishop Davidson despised Temple's haphazard manner of dealing with ecclesiastical questions. According to Davidson, Archbishop Temple refused to delegate power and seldom consulted with his advisors. "His habit of doing everything for himself extended from the petty trifle... to the biggest things in the Church. His chaplains had no knowledge of his correspondence... He told them very little or nothing, and they had to pick up the facts as best they could."[53] Consequently, "it would be very easy to give abundant instances of mischief which ensued."[54] The claims of West Malling might be one example.

On his appointment to Canterbury, Randall Davidson could boast of more than a decade of experience on the episcopal bench.[55] He brought to Lambeth Palace a dedication to efficiency and professionalism which Temple lacked. As Archbishop, he promoted a vision of a peaceful, harmonious, and unified Church of England; public discord and scandal must give way to compromise.[56] Moreover, religious orthodoxy could destroy itself by a policy of episcopal oppression.[57] Decisions were made only after lengthy consultations and meetings with ecclesiastical experts and advisors. However, Davidson refused to make concessions on accepted Anglican doctrines, especially the use of the Book of Common Prayer for worship. Freedom of expression, he maintained, must conform to "a general loyalty to principles and usages which have come down from the past..."[58] Firm and determined, Davidson confronted what he believed to be more than a decade of episcopal negligence. Consultation, correspondence, and discussion, but ultimately the goal was loyalty to the teaching of the Established Church. Consequently, Archbishop Davidson would not be compromised by Temple's dealings with the West Malling convent.

After he received the 1903 petition from Mother Hilda, concerning one of her sister's final vows, Archbishop Davidson's first request was to demand a copy of the constitution. He received the document, the exact one Temple had earlier approved,[59] and immediately began to probe. At once, Davidson asked for the following information: the number of sisters, the work of the community and its relation to any parishes, and the names of the current chaplain and the official visitor. He also raised some questions about the role of the bishop as arbiter.[60] Before the above letter arrived, Mother Hilda wrote and continued to push for the profession of the sister, which was the object of the initial contact with Davidson. The candidate was over thirty, an orphan, and had received the approval of the community. "She is naturally anxious," the Superior continued, since she wanted the ceremony to take place "in [the] middle of the month... [and] there are arrangements to be made."[61]

After the Archbishop's searching letter, the tone of Mother Hilda's response was less urgent and demanding. The membership consisted of fourteen sisters, who were engaged in care for the old, sick, and children. Some embroidery was done, but the women "... do not undertake parochial work."[62] Moreover, she continued, "we have no visitor." "Appeal to the Bishops means the Bishop of the Diocese where [the] Community lives." The Rev. C.H. Berry held the position of Chaplain for the past two years. He had been licensed by Archbishop Temple.[63] The question of episcopal authority and jurisdiction over the convent was to become the subject of the emotional correspondence between Berry and the Archbishop of Canterbury. For Archbishop Davidson, the issue was whether the Anglican Church could recognize certain practices of Malling Abbey as orthodox.

Fr. Berry and Archbishop Davidson met in early March, 1903, and discussed the religious practices and the lifestyle of the sisters.[64] Based on this interview, the constitution, and the exchange of letters with Mother Hilda, the Archbishop sketched for Berry what he believed to be a just description of the observances of the convent and his relation to the sisterhood. Davidson acknowledged Berry's license.[65] He assumed that the chaplain followed the guidelines of the Anglican Prayer Book in the "outer" or public chapel, but in the convent's private, the "inner chapel," Davidson noticed that there was "perpetual Reservation of the Holy Sacrament, a Reservation which it cannot be contended is required for urgent ministrations of the sick." Archbishop Davidson stressed that he had "no desire in matters of this kind to be over-scrupulous or fussy," but certain practices could not be condoned. "If on the strength of my formal license," he explained, "you take part in maintaining usages or a usage which I believe to be contrary to the spirit and rule of the Church of England, I am distinctly responsible for the sanction thus given."[66] He also pointed out that the absence of an episcopal visitor ran counter to the wishes of the Lambeth Report. This office was the responsibility of Edward Talbot, the Bishop of Rochester. Moreover, Archbishop Davidson did not view the petition for the sister's profession as a simple and easy matter. "I am bound to consider such questions in the light of the precedent which will be set by my actions," he concluded, and "it is possible that the Mother Superior, or even yourself, might not have fully weighed the position in all its gravity."[67]

The discussion then shifted from the profession of a West Malling nun to an investigation of the soundness and orthodoxy of the convent's liturgical practices. Fr. Berry claimed that he was writing to the Primate without Mother Hilda's knowledge, but this does not seem plausible because of the lack of independence enjoyed by the West Malling chaplain.[68] Berry, therefore, expressed the mind and wishes of the sisterhood. He maintained that the Blessed Sacrament was reserved for the benefit of those nuns over eighty years old and several others whose condition might suddenly turn critical. In addition to keeping the Sacrament for the spiritual needs of the sick, Berry argued for Reservation on the basis of custom and past approval. The chaplain asked Davidson for "tacit permission if not actual sanction 'because' it has been the privilege of the Rev. Mother Superior and elder Sisters for some 30 years... and round it their devotional life circles." Again he appealed to Temple's past actions. Reservation, Berry suggested, "was allowed by the late Archbishop Temple, when Bishop of London."

Berry admitted the absence of a visitor, but argued that the Lambeth Report did not intend "that the Bishop of the Diocese has... jurisdiction, as Bishop, in the Community Houses within his Diocese." He ended his letter by stating that he had no desire to act without the Archbishop's consent. Instead of approaching the Bishop of Rochester, which was the appropriate procedure, Rev. C.H. Berry offered the office to the Archbishop of Canterbury. This would greatly increase the prestige of the convent. The question of an episcopal visitor, therefore, could easily be solved: "May I ask Your Grace... if ...Your Grace would consent to become the Visitor of the Community here, or on what terms Your Grace would sanction the nomination of another priest as Visitor?"[69] In reply, Davidson did not comment on the invitation to become the convent's visitor, but instead singled out the liturgical abuses. He expressed his sorrow that the women insisted "upon a usage [Reservation] for which I am bound to say no exceptional need seems to be shown such as would justify a Bishop in treating it as lying outside ordinary rules wither for Communities or for Parishes."[70] The Archbishop promised to continue to study the matter.

Berry's lengthy response to this letter was a classic example of Anglican comprehensiveness. It also illustrated the absence of effective episcopal supervision in some sections of the Church of England, which could be perceived or interpreted as ecclesiastical approval. Berry quickly appealed to the memory of Archbishop Temple. "We obtained the sanction of the then Bishop of London, (Dr. Temple) and when we removed to West Malling, we did it under his express sanction; and were established by his authority as Archbishop."[71] "It is by his authority," Berry continued, "that the Community exists, and follows the Benedictine Rule of life." The convent did nothing without his knowledge. Consequently, "we always recognized this, and it is our earnest desire to recognize that Your Grace is our Ecclesiastical Superior, not only as individual Christians domiciled in Your Grace's diocese, but as a Community, we recognize in a most loyal sense that Your Grace *is* our Visitor." According to this logic, Archbishop Davidson was limited and hampered by Temple's actions. Because Archbishop Temple sanctioned the sisterhood, the nuns insisted that successive Primates must accept this approval and act accordingly.

Berry argued that an important element of Davidson's inheritance was his role as the official visitor of the convent. He had earlier queried the *ex-officio* position of the diocesan bishop as visitor, and had invited Davidson to apply or nominate someone for the post. Now the chaplain informed the Archbishop that "we submit that the Diocesan is *ipso facto* Visitor of any Religious House established by his sanction in the Diocese." But because of Temple's extraordinary patronage, Berry contended that the post belonged to the Archbishop of Canterbury, not the local bishop, Edward Talbot of Rochester. The provincial took precedence over the local bishop in this instance. Fr. Berry quoted from an ancient constitution in *Lyndwood's Provinciale* to bolster his point.[72] Berry's line of argumentation led to one conclusion.

> We claim... by virtue of the late Archbishop's actions in sanctioning and establishing us, a recognized Canonical position in the Church, and to be as much an Ecclesiastical institution of the diocese, and as such subject to Your Grace in all things lawful and honest, including the observance of the Rule and all the ancient customs of those who follow it, as the Cathedral Body is.

If this limited the freedom of Archbishop Davidson, the justification for Reservation of the Blessed Sacrament severely curtailed episcopal control of the convent's liturgy and doctrine.

Berry claimed that if the Archbishop forbade Reservation, the convent would naturally comply. However, "we recognize that in regard to Reservation the Church or Chapel of a Religious House is in an entirely different position from a Parish Church; inasmuch as the permission of the Bishop is required for Reservation in the former case." But Berry's logic was inconsistent. While arguing that Temple's sanction extended archiepiscopal approval to West Malling, he ignored Temple's decree which forbade Reservation in the Church of England.[73] This position was based, Berry contended, on the Act of Uniformity and "had that statute not existed, it is highly probable that the opinion would have been different."

The chaplain's argument continued: "But we as a Religious House have nothing to do with any Act of Uniformity." The services of the nuns were private and "by the very terms of the Act we are outside its scope." Berry pleaded that this "was the view of Archbishop Temple." Moreover, Temple "was fully informed of all our proceedings [and] never... raised any objection to our reserving the Blessed Sacrament." The chaplain's main argument, therefore, was the precedent set by Temple: "We humbly submit... [and] plead that a privilege that has been allowed us for so long a time should (if possible) be continued to us." Reservation was also "of great significance as hallowing, spiritualizing," and was entirely in harmony with the traditions of the apostolic church.

Temple's questionable approval and Berry's references to the early church were not the only justifications for Reservation. The Rule of St. Benedict also sanctioned it. Berry maintained that the Rule granted a certain freedom from Anglican control. Again, it was Temple who had given his blessing to the nuns who lived under Benedict's precepts. Berry stated that "while the Rule does not prescribe Reservation, yet the surroundings of the life cannot be like that of the Benedictines of the earlier and purer days, if the hallowing influence of the Blessed Sacrament be not perpetually with us." Because of Temple's approbation, therefore, "that sanction to live under his [Benedict's] Rule carries with it —by implication— the permission to reserve." Berry maintained that if Davidson prohibited Reservation, the nuns would endure "intense spiritual strain and consternation... [and] there would be grave spiritual danger to their souls in any such prohibition..." The chaplain promised, however, that the sisters would make certain changes, for example, move the Blessed Sacrament from the chapel to a private room or eliminate any prayers said openly in the presence of the Sacrament, if only the Archbishop would continue to allow the practice. Moreover, Berry reiterated that "we submit ourselves, as in duty bound, wholly to Your Grace's spiritual authority."[74]

Archbishop Davidson's response was not reassuring. In respect to Reservation, the Primate stated that he was "ready to treat in an exceptional way exceptional needs," for example, he would permit Reservation in hospitals or during epidemics, but did not "honestly feel that such evidence is forthcoming... with regard to the necessities of the community."[75] The Archbishop also assaulted the contention that the sisterhood was shielded from any future episcopal authority or supervision because of Temple's past support and sanction. "The very reference which you make to some action of Archbishop Temple's shows the danger in a very clear way." Davidson stated the problem succinctly: "...my action in such matters extends far beyond the moment or place." He also questioned the validity of what might have been some implicit approval or encouragement granted by his predecessor. "Nothing, as I understand, exists in writing or in any formal shape to show that your belief is correct or that Archbishop Temple knowingly or deliberately sanctioned a usage which he has in such explicit terms condemned." Finally, his action must be considered as a precedent which might "gravely embarrass my successor and other Bishops who desire to adhere to the rules and formularies of the Church of England."[76] Consequently, Archbishop Davidson would not compromise his disapproval of Reservation at West Malling, even if Temple had permitted it.

In the opinion of Archbishop Davidson, the West Malling situation was not trivial or unimportant. In the first place, here was a community which claimed official ecclesiastical approbation for some practices which the Anglican Church had clearly and forcefully condemned. Secondly, should these objectionable "usages" be allowed to continue because of his predecessor's implicit or questionable authorization? Other religious communities might use the same argument. The problem facing Davidson was whether authority in the Church of England depended on the whim or personal interpretation of an individual bishop, or whether there was some objective and constant guideline for doctrine and liturgy. If Davidson refused to act now, some Anglicans might claim his inaction, like Temple's, signified the approval of the Archbishop of Canterbury. Consequently, the Archbishop penned another letter to the West Malling chaplain.

Davidson pointed out that it was nonsense to designate a bishop *ipso facto* visitor, and then emasculate him of any real power. As for Berry's contention that Archbishop Temple permitted the nuns to use the Benedictine Missal in place of the Book of Common Prayer, Davidson expressed astonishment. "You will realize that this is a somewhat startling statement, and I cannot accept it without detailed documentary proof."[77] Temple's *laissez-faire* attitude was not sufficient; formal condemnation was not the only requirement for a practice to be judged unlawful. As for Reservation, Davidson stated that he did not share the chaplain's view that it was not a superstitious custom. He pointed out the illogical notion suggested by Berry that the Archbishop of Canterbury could sanction Reservation of the Blessed Sacrament at West Malling, and then limit or prescribe the manner of its observance. Reservation for the sick might be an exception, but it was "not the mind of the Church of England" that it become an object of prayer and devotion. Davidson remained firm and stated that he would not be moved by appeals to Temple or primitive Christian customs to sanction practices he believed to be objectionable. The Archbishop stated how careful he must be "in dealing with the kind of request thus made to me." His final word was resolute.

But when the line which you have taken in the matter is adopted it is obvious that a Bishop who desires to keep the promises made at his Consecration with regard to maintaining the doctrine and discipline of the Church in which he is appointed to rule, must leave no opening for future misunderstanding or create precedents which may hereafter be used to the detriment of the true teachings of our Church.[78]

Archbishop Davidson's position was clear. All objectionable practices, even those not specifically forbidden by bishops, must be abandoned if they were contrary to the teaching of the Established Church. Reservation of the Blessed Sacrament was an example, and he would not tolerate its continuance. Moreover, there was no hint of compromise or negotiation on Davidson's part. Berry also recognized the Archbishop's intransigence, and merely acknowledged reception of the Primate's letter of February 22.[79] Davidson now addressed himself to the subject which precipitated the correspondence, namely, a sister's desire to make final vows.

After a gap of two months, Fr. Berry again petitioned Archbishop Davidson on behalf of the sister who desired to make final vows as a member of West Malling.[80] The chaplain stated that he believed "her to be well prepared and... [was] fully satisfied as to her devotion and purpose."[81] He emphasized that she had been waiting six months and was eager to make her profession. "May I hope that Your Grace will allow me to proceed in this matter," he urged Davidson, "even though Your Grace still suspends judgment of the other points which have been raised."[82] If Berry believed that this request would be approved quickly and easily, he received an unexpected shock. Archbishop Davidson scrutinized the entire question of vows and the ceremony of profession as ruthlessly as he studied Reservation.

Because he had not seen any indication of West Malling's conformity to the liturgical reforms he demanded, Archbishop Davidson challenged Berry's request. "I have felt unable," Davidson told the chaplain, "to give any sanction, direct or indirect to a community which avowedly declines to be satisfied with the Service of the Book of Common Prayer for the celebration of Holy Communion, and which regards as vital the maintenance of usages which I deem contrary both to the spirit and letter of the Church's rule."[83] The Primate could not approve the proposed vow ceremony because he believed that he could not "rightly exercise jurisdiction within a community which has decided to set my rulings at naught..."[84] Fr. Berry replied and contended that he believed that the Archbishop had never demanded any change or alteration in the community's service. If this were the case, he claimed he would "certainly feel bound in conscience to obey any definite direction..."[85] The chaplain pleaded that he was not ignoring the wishes of the Archbishop. He also hoped that Davidson's opinions, "strongly expressed though they were... left some hope for compromise..."[86] For the Archbishop, the sensitive point remained West Malling's refusal to modify its custom of Reservation of the Blessed Sacrament.

Davidson admitted that it was "most painful to give any decision which is calculated to cause distress to devout minds."[87] He also recognized how certain practices, "even if these usages be out of harmony with the spirit and teaching of our church," have become sacrosanct because of the lack of supervision from proper authority. The Archbishop confessed that "the usages in question have received a quasi-sanction of Archbishop Temple's supposed approval or acquiescence in their continuance." But if he did not interfere, this might "... easily obtain as a precedent a wider importance than those who are locally concerned can realize." "It is absolutely incumbent upon me," he argued, "to deal with local problems upon the lines of general principle, even if this occasionally involves what seems like hardship to individuals whom one shrinks from paining." Before the discussion on vows could proceed, therefore, Davidson required that the Book of Common Prayer be used as the sole source of all ceremonies at West Malling. Reservation must be discontinued, and he reiterated his belief that it was "contrary both to the spirit and letter of the Church's directions..." But he softened the harshness of this demand with the following promise: "if the directions I have given are complied with, I am quite willing to authorize you to profess the novice about whom the Mother Superior has written to me..." A bishop must not act otherwise. According to Davidson, if one read the promises made at an episcopal consecration, one would realize the solemn responsibility and burden which belonged to the office of bishop.[88]

After some provision was made for the spiritual needs of the convent's sick,[89] Berry finally gave in to Archbishop Davidson's demands about curtailing Reservation. However, the question of the sister's profession still needed to be resolved. On June 3, Berry asked the Archbishop for permission to profess the candidate at the end of the month.[90] In his petition, the chaplain asked Davidson for his authorization, "as brief and formal as possible," which would be read to the congregation during the ceremony.[91] Archbishop Davidson, however, still refused to be hurried into granting his personal sanction. Without proper investigation and study, this might embarrass the Church or compromise the authority of his successor. Consequently, the Primate's response was consistent with the history of his dealings with West Malling. He asked Berry to post him a copy of the ceremony, including the text of the vows. "I cannot doubt that all is right," he tried to reassure the chaplain, "but before sending such a letter... I should wish to have everything before me."[92] Berry agreed to the Archbishop's demand.[93]

Archbishop Davidson again seriously questioned the propriety and orthodoxy of the material sent from West Malling. He thanked Berry for the copy of the ceremonial, but immediately challenged it: "at first sight it seems to me that there are passages... to which I could not appropriately give my imprimatur."[94] Davidson wanted to know the origin of the vow service, and asked "whether it is really the Roman use in its entirety." With reference to the wording of the formula, the Archbishop questioned the meaning of the phrase "according to the Rule of St. Benedict." Did not his earlier stipulations prohibit any compromise with this specifically Roman Catholic document? Consequently, Davidson stated that "...no promise must be made that would be inconsistent with the directions which I have already given."[95]

Berry's response revealed that he finally realized that appeals to past episcopal sanction or justification by custom and tradition meant little to Davidson's commitment to uniformity. The chaplain's answer was not apologetic or argumentative, but a straightforward reply to the Archbishop's queries. He claimed that the ceremony differed "a great deal" from the Roman Pontifical.[96] Berry confessed he did not know its exact origin, but the service was similar to one found in the *Priest's Prayer Book*.[97] In respect to vows "according to the Rule of St. Benedict, he explained that this did not weaken one's allegiance to the Established Church since the candidate promised fidelity to the Rule as interpreted by a faithful Anglican sisterhood. The chaplain renewed his pledge of loyalty to the Archbishop and restated his request that Davidson approve the vow ceremony. But Berry also claimed, however, that he was justified in officiating at the service even without Archbishop Davidson's sanction. "Therefore I wrote asking explicit permission," he boasted, "rather than act on implicit permission already given."[98]

As in the case of Reservation, the Archbishop was unmoved by the chaplain's arguments. West Malling must in this instance also conform to the conscience of the Anglican Church. "...I am quite willing that the Sister in question should be professed, provided of course that the Form of Profession is one that I can approve,"[99] Davidson informed Berry. The Archbishop then explicated his idea of authentic episcopal authority. "Either I am responsible for what is done within the walls of the community, or I am not." If not, then the request for sanction and approval for the profession was meaningless. But, he continued, "if I am responsible, I must know, not only what is to be done, but in what manner it is to be done." Authority, therefore, was not permissive. Davidson complained that the West Malling profession formula raised serious questions concerning some accepted Anglican teachings. He admitted that the wording of the text "...jars myself personally," but also promised to seek the advice of others who were more familiar with religious communities in the Church of England.[100]

The Suffragan Bishop of Reading, J.L. Randall, was such an expert. Davidson told him that he was "greatly worried about a little community" of Anglican nuns.[101] The Archbishop outlined some practices, "little short of outrageous," which took place within the sisters' chapel. Archbishop Temple, he admitted, probably gave leave to these "without himself inquiring into the details." Use of the Roman Missal in lieu of the Book of Common Prayer and insistence upon Reservation of the Blessed Sacrament had until recently been the custom of the convent. These issues had just been settled. But a proposed ceremony for a sister's final profession, Davidson explained, appeared to his "...perhaps too Protestant mind... almost alien." The Archbishop, therefore, asked Bishop Randall to examine the document and report to him on its acceptability. Davidson also sketched three possible courses of action: sanction the form for regular use; prohibit it and demand that a new one be composed; or allow the present text for the profession in question. If he adopted the last option, he would make it clear, however, that the ceremony "must never be used again under my sanction and that another form must be prepared."[102]

The Bishop of Reading replied and pointed out that the West Malling document did not correspond to anything he had ever seen or experienced in his dealings with other recognized Anglican sisterhoods. This ceremony, he contended, was essentially Roman Catholic. "The Malling Service is a very servile and jejune Translation of the Roman 'Benedicto Virginum' in the Pontificale, and the Variations from that are all in the wrong Directions."[103] As for the right course of action, Bishop Randall maintained that the first was impossible, the second problematic, yet reasonable, but "in the present distress" the last might be the most prudent. But it must be made clear that the sisters could use the proposed form only in this specific case. Randall could not avoid reference to Frederick Temple. In his opinion, Temple's actions were not responsible. "It seems to me unfortunate," he concluded, "that any Direction or Permission by Bps. in such matters should rest only on word of mouth, surely they sh[ould] be given in writing."[104] This advice strengthened the Primate's wish to reform West Malling and eradicate any questionable customs or liturgies. Any lingering doubt that he was acting out of ignorance or dislike of High Church practices also vanished. The Bishop of Reading's condemnation of Temple's past behavior and the unfavorable comparison of West Malling with other established Anglican sisterhoods made Archbishop Davidson more resolute and determined to end the convent's unsupervised life.

Davidson immediately informed Fr. Berry of the result of his deliberations and what action he would take. Realizing that an uncompromising approach might force some of the women to convert to Rome,[105] the Archbishop nevertheless condemned the ceremonial to be used at the convent's vow ceremony.

> I feel that my own view as to its inapplicableness to the Church of England system and spirit is born out by those whom I have consulted, and I have purposely taken counsel with men of experience on these particular matters and in sympathy (speaking generally) with the School of Churchmen to which your Community belongs.[106]

He quoted verbatim the Bishop of Reading's remarks about the "servile and rather jejune" translation of the vow ceremony which he maintained was based on the Roman Catholic Pontificale. Davidson was extremely harsh in his stinging condemnation. "Superstition and... an unwholesome forcefulness" were the marks of the West Malling ceremonial. "The variations may be ancient," he conceded, "...but they are characterized by the weaker features of medieval usage and phraseology." Although the Bishop of Reading urged some latitude, Davidson ignored this suggestion. Under the present circumstances, he would permit no vow ceremony to take place at the convent. The decision was final, and he would tolerate no compromise: "I do not feel that I can rightly sanction... a service entirely foreign to the spirit and teaching of the Church of England..."[107]

Archbishop Davidson had no idea how Berry and the nuns would react to this drastic ultimatum. Beginning with the revolt against its founder, Fr. Ignatius, the sisterhood had enjoyed a long tradition of independence and isolation from the mainstream of Anglican life. Since some customs and practices had been enshrined and unquestioned for such a long time, an attack against their orthodoxy might be resisted. Moreover, the legacy of Archbishop Temple had created a myth of legitimacy. Consequently, Archbishop Davidson was aware that a rebellion or secession to Rome was possible. If the conflict became public, West Malling might attract the support of sympathetic High Churchmen. One anonymous letter, for example, pleaded with Davidson to allow the nuns the freedom to enjoy their traditional religious practices. "Surely the *service* of the Church of England could include a few for religious," she begged, and "*Sodom* might have been saved by such."[108]

But the threat of resistance on the part of the nuns or a public outcry from friendly Anglicans failed to materialize. Fr. Berry surrendered quietly. He informed Archbishop Davidson that he had labored to be faithful to the Primate's wishes, and on the other hand, wanted to comply with the desires of the sisters. These two positions, he believed, were irreconcilable. "I am obliged—by my own personal affairs—to ask Your Grace to release me," he asked Davidson, and "I trust Your Grace will grant my petition."[109] This resignation ended the impasse. Archbishop Davidson's desire to bring West Malling within the bounds of uniformity and his duty to impose legitimate episcopal authority and supervision on a convent of Anglican nuns triumphed. For the time being, a direct confrontation between the women and the Archbishop of Canterbury was avoided.

Little information exists on the internal life of West Malling after Rev. C.H. Berry's resignation. Mother Hilda died in December, 1906, and in the spring the community invited Sister Mary Pauline Ewart of the All Saints Convent, London, to become their superior. Mother Scholastica, as she became known, was installed and blessed as Abbess by the Anglican Abbot of Caldey Island, Aelred Carlyle. The permission of the Bishop of Rochester gave this ceremony some legitimacy. Peter Anson described the liturgical life of the convent during Mother Scholastica's tenure as Roman and the "teaching being based entirely on the standard works found in any Roman Catholic Benedictine novitiate."[110] By 1910, there were rumors that Mother Scholastica was on the verge of conversion to Rome. In the same year, the nuns recognized Abbot Carlyle as their visitor and became affiliated to his Anglican Congregation of the Primitive Observance.[111] The sisterhood continued to flourish, and in April, 1911, the nuns moved to St. Bride's Abbey, Milford Haven. Mother Scholastica's attraction to Rome grew stronger, and following the example of Abbot Carlyle's secession, she led her sisters to Rome in February, 1913. Mother Scholastica told the members of her community that "submission to Rome... would bring no outward change, for they had never had a single service of the Church of England since they had been in the house."[112] In 1904, the Anglican nuns accepted the authority of the Established Church, but in 1913, they publicly renounced the Church of their baptism and embraced Roman Catholicism.

Notes

[1] For the origins and early history of the West Malling sisterhood, see: P. Anson, *The Call of the Cloister: Religious Communities and Kindred Bodies in the Anglican Communion* (London: SPCK, 1964); De Bertouch, *The Life of Father Ignatius* (London: Methuen, 1904); and *The Benedictines of Talacre Abbey* (Exeter: The Catholic Records Press, 1927).

[2] P. Anson, *The Call of the Cloister*, p. 420.

[3] H. Davies, *Worship and Theology in England: From Newman to Martineau* (Princeton: Princeton University Press, 1965), p. 130.

[4] W. Walsh, *The Secret History of the Oxford Movement* (London: Swan Sonnenschein, 1898), p. 184.

[5] Mary Hilda to Davidson, 22 September 1903, Davidson Papers, vol. 84, Lambeth Palace Library, London.

[6] Ibid.

[7] Davidson to Mary Hilda, 30 September 1903, Davidson Papers, vol. 84.

[8] See p. 34.

[9] Davidson to Mary Hilda, 30 September 1903, Davidson Papers, vol. 84.

[10] Mary Hilda to Davidson, 20 October 1903, Davidson Papers, vol. 84.

[11] *The Official Year Book of the Church of England* contained the following: "St. Mary and St. Scholastica, St. Mary's Abbey, West Malling Kent. A community of Sisters who devote themselves to the devotional life. They also undertake Church embroidery, plain needlework, and the care of a few aged and infirm persons. A Home of Rest, especially meant for aged or disabled domestic servants, being attached to the Convent, and a few children also being received. Priests and lay people are admitted as associates of the Convent, and keep a slight rule; also oblate ladies who desire to lead a stricter life and more in accordance with the rule followed by the Sisters, but who are unable to live always in Community. Lady Boarders received." *The Official Year Book of the Church of England* (London: SPCK, 1903), p. 161.

[12] Mary Hilda to Davidson, 20 October 1903, Davidson Papers, vol. 84.

[13] For biographies of Temple see DNB; E. Carpenter, *Cantuar: The Archbishops in Their Office* (London: Cassell, 1971); D. Edwards, *Leaders of the Church of England 1828–1978* (London: Hodder and Staughton, 1978); and E.G. Sandford, *Frederick Temple* (London: Macmillan Co., 1907).

[14] *The Chronicle of Convocation, Upper House, 1891* (London: National Society's Depository, 1891), p. 47.

[15] Ibid., p. 53.

[16] Ibid., p. 55. See also pp. 8-9.

[17] Browley to Temple, 14 July 1897, Temple Papers, vol. 25, F. Temple Papers, Lambeth Palace Library, London.

[18] Browley to Temple, 16 July 1897, Temple Papers, vol. 25.

[19] Temple to Browley, 19 July 1897, Temple Papers, vol. 25.

[20] Smith to Temple, 21 August 1897, Temple Papers, vol. 25.

[21] Turner to Temple, 17 December 1897, Temple Papers, vol. 25.

[22] Butt to Temple, 13 August 1897, Temple Papers, vol. 25.

[23] Ibid.

[24] Walsh to Temple, 17 August 1897, Temple Papers, vol. 25.

[25] Walsh to Temple, 19 August 1897, Temple Papers, vol. 25.

[26] *Crockford's,* 1899.

[27] Richards to Temple, 4 January 1898, Temple Papers, vol. 25.

[28] *Crockford's,* 1904.

[29] Berry to Temple, 17 August 1901, Temple Papers, vol. 47.

[30] Berry to Temple, 20 August 1901, Temple Papers, vol. 47.

[31] Mary Hilda to Temple, 23 August 1901, Temple Papers, vol. 47.

[32] Ibid.

[33] Mary Hilda to Temple, 26 August 1901, Temple Papers, vol. 47.

[34] Mary Hilda to Temple, 4 September 1901, Temple Papers, vol. 47.

[35] See pp. 30–31.

[36] Daniel to Temple, 24 May 1898, Temple Papers, vol. 11.

[37] Daniel to Temple, 18 June 1898, Temple Papers vol. 11.

[38] Sister to Temple, 14 December 1898, Temple Papers, vol. 47.

[39] Mary Hilda to Temple, 26 August 1901, Temple Papers, vol. 47.

[40] Mary Hilda to Temple, 4 September 1901, Temple Papers, vol. 47.

[41] Ibid.

[42] Mary Hilda to Temple, 5 April 1902, Temple Papers, vol. 54.

[43] Mary Hilda to Temple, 8 April 1902, Temple Papers, vol. 54.

[44] "Proceedings on the Religious Communities," Lambeth Conference, 1897, LC. 38, Lambeth Palace Library. The most recent history of the Lambeth Conference is A. Stephenson, *Anglicanism and the Lambeth Conference* (London: SPCK, 1978). A good early history is S. Dark, *The Lambeth Conferences* (London: Eyre, Spottiswoode, 1930). Archbishop Davidson's *The Five Lambeth Conferences* (London: SPCK, 1920) contains selections from the official reports and resolutions.

[45] Ibid.

[46] Ibid.

[47] "Report of the Committee Appointed in 1897 to Consider the Relation of Religious Communities Within The Church to the Episcopate," Lambeth Conference 1908, LC 100/28, p. 5, Lambeth Palace Library.

[48] Mary Hilda to Temple, 28 August 1901, Temple Papers, vol. 47.

[49] Ibid.

[50] See p. 34.

[51] "Constitutions of the Congregation of S. Mary and S. Scholastica," 1901, Temple Papers, vol. 84.

[52] Ibid.

[53] Quoted in G.K.A. Bell, *Randall Davidson* (London: Oxford University Press, 1952), p. 291.

[54] Ibid.

[55] The best biography of Randall Davidson is G.K.A. Bell, *Randall Davidson* (London: Oxford University Press, 1952). See also E. Carpenter, *Cantuar: The Archbishops in Their Office;* DNB; S. Dark, *Archbishop Davidson and The English Church* (London: Philip Allen Co., 1929); D. Edwards, *Leaders of the Church of England;* C. Herbert, *Twenty-five Years as Archbishop of Canterbury* (London: Wells, Gardiner, 1927).

[56] S. Dark, *Archbishop Davidson and the English Church,* p. vi.

[57] A.M. Ramsey, *From Gore to Temple* (London: Longmans, Green Co., 1962), p. 82.

[58] R. Davidson, "The Character and Call of the Church of England," 1905, Lambeth Palace Library, p. 47.

[59] See p. 34.

[60] Davidson to Mary Hilda, 12 October 1903, Davidson Papers. vol. 84.

[61] Mary Hilda to Davidson, 10 October 1903, Davidson Papers, vol. 84.

[62] Mary Hilda to Davidson, 13 October 1903, Davidson Papers, vol. 84.

[63] Ibid.

[64] Davidson to Berry, 10 November 1903, Davidson Papers, vol. 84. This letter contains a reference to the March meeting. No record of the meeting survives.

[65] Ibid.

[66] On May 1, 1900, Archbishop Frederick Temple issued the following statement condemning Reservation of the Blessed Sacrament: "...after weighing carefully all that has been put before us, I am obliged to decide that the Church of England does not at present allow Reservation in any form, and that those who think it ought to be allowed, though perfectly justified in endeavouring to get the proper authorities to alter the law, are not justified in practicing Reservation until the law has been altered." *The Archbishop of Canterbury On Reservation* (London: Macmillan Co., 1900), p. 12.

[67] Davidson to Berry, 10 November 1903, Davidson Papers, vol. 84.

[68] Berry to Davidson, 7 January 1904, Davidson Papers, vol. 84.

[69] Ibid.

[70] Davidson to Berry, 12 January 1904, Davidson Papers, vol. 84.

[71] Berry to Davidson, 16 January 1904, Davidson Papers, vol. 84.

[72] Berry referred to a canon of Archbishop Edmund Rich (1234-45), *Quoniam religionum:* "in as much as great diversity of religious engendereth great confusion in the Church of God we command that they which found a new hospital or monastery receive of the ordinary of the place the ordinance and rules after which they may live religiously in order, moreover we strictly command that neither men, neither women, be shut up in any place without special license of the Diocesan, the place, the manners, the quality of the persons being diligently considered: and also wherewith... no secular persons shall sojourn in their house without an honest cause and a manifest." H.C. Bell and J.V. Vullard, eds., *Lyndwood's Provinciale* (London: The Faith Press, 1929), p. 87.

[73] Berry to Davidson, 16 January 1904, Davidson Papers, vol. 84.

[74] Ibid.

[75] Davidson to Berry, 22 February 1904, Davidson Papers, vol. 84.

[76] Ibid.

[77] Ibid.

[78] Ibid.

[79] Berry to Davidson, 23 February 1904, Davidson Papers, vol. 84.

[80] See pp. 30-31 for the beginning of the correspondence between Mary Hilda and the Archbishop concerning the final profession of one of the West Malling nuns.

[81] Berry to Davidson, 16 April 1904, Davidson Papers, vol. 84.

[82] Ibid.

[83] Davidson to Berry, 28 April 1904, Davidson Papers, vol. 84.

[84] Ibid.

[85] Berry to Davidson, 29 April 1904, Davidson Papers, vol. 84.

[86] Ibid.

[87] Davidson to Berry, 10 May 1904, Davidson Papers, vol. 84.

[88] Ibid.

[89] Berry proposed that he be allowed to carry the Sacrament to the eighty-year old housekeeper and to a blind and paralyzed young woman after the Communion service ended. Berry to Davidson, 23 May 1904, Davidson Papers, vol. 84. Provided that this ceremony take place "immediately after the Service and not at another time in the day," Davidson agreed to Berry's suggestion. Davidson to Berry, 23 May 1904, Davidson Papers, vol. 84.

[90] Berry to Davidson, 3 June 1904, Davidson Papers, vol. 84.

[91] Ibid.

[92] Davidson to Berry, 4 June 1904, Davidson Papers, vol. 84.

[93] Berry to Davidson, 5 June 1904, Davidson Papers, vol. 84.

[94] Davidson to Berry, 7 June 1904, Davidson Papers, vol. 84.

[95] Ibid.

[96] Berry to Davidson, 10 June 1904, Davidson Papers, vol. 84.

[97] According to its preface, *The Priest's Prayer Book* was an attempt to provide parochial clergy with prayers for certain occasions not included in the Book of Common Prayer, "not to suspend the use of the Book of Common Prayer, but to be merely ancillary and subordinate to it..." R. Litterdale and J. Vaux, eds., *The Priest's Prayer Book* (London: J. Masters Co., 1876), p.v. Berry's comment to Archbishop Davidson referred to "Form for the Profession of a Sister" (pp. 292-97).

[98] Berry to Davidson, 10 June 1904, Davidson Papers, vol. 84.

[99] Davidson to Berry, 11 June 1904, Davidson Papers, vol. 84.

[100] Ibid.

[101] Davidson to Randall, 11 June 1904, Davidson Papers, vol. 84.

[102] Ibid.

[103] Randall to Davidson, 14 June 1904, Davidson Papers, vol. 84.

[104] Ibid.

[105] Davidson to Randall, 11 June 1904, Davidson Papers, vol. 84.

[106] Davidson to Berry, 1 August 1904, Davidson Papers, vol. 84.

[107] Ibid.

108 A letter to Davidson, 22 May 1904, Davidson Papers, vol. 84.

109 Berry to Davidson, 5 August 1904, Davidson Papers, vol. 84.

110 P. Anson, *The Call of the Cloister,* p. 426.

111 Ibid., p. 427.

112 *The Benedictines of Talacre Abbey, p. 10.*

CHAPTER IV

THE 1897 LAMBETH CONFERENCE AND THE QUESTION OF RELIGIOUS LIFE IN THE ANGLICAN COMMUNION

Monastic life had always played a significant role in the political, social, and economic life of England. By the time of the Reformation in the sixteenth century, however, the monastic system had become wealthy, complacent, and desperately in need of renewal; many Britons saw monks and nuns as drones and parasites. King Henry VIII seized upon this animosity and engineered the dissolution of the English monasteries by acts of Parliament. But old traditions could not easily be legislated out of existence by statute law, and the monastic ideal continued to survive both in memory and in voluntary prayer groups of the new national church. The nineteenth century proved to be a watershed. The English romantic writers glorified the country's medieval past and the important contributions made by religious orders. The "Catholic" spirit of the Oxford Movement also helped to re-awaken Anglican interests in monastic life. The Oxford theologians "did more than help to repolish her forgotten teachings."[1] But "it also introduced into the Church practices and devotions which had in fact lapsed entirely since the divisions of the sixteenth century, particularly by the revival of the Religious Life..." Edward Bouverie Pusey, John Henry Newman, and Frederick Faber all praised England's monastic heritage and longed to see the introduction and growth of religious life in the Church of England.

Some heard and assented to the arguments of the Oxford Movement. Consequently, conventual life again began to appear in the Church. The interest in sisterhoods started this trend. In 1841, Marion Rebecca Hughes took vows and placed herself under the tutelage of Doctor Pusey. The first Anglican sisterhood was established in 1845 at Park Village West in London; others soon followed: the Community of Saint Mary the Virgin at Wantage (1848), the Society of the Most Holy Trinity at Devonport

(1848), the Community of Saint John Baptist at Clewer near Windsor (1851), and the Society of Saint Margaret at East Grinstead in Sussex (1855). By the turn of the century, approximately sixty sisterhoods had been founded, although many were short-lived.[2] Brotherhoods, following monastic models, appeared next: the Society of Saint John the Evangelist (also known as the "Cowley Fathers") in Oxford (1866), the Order of Saint Paul (1889), the Community of the Resurrection at Mirfield in Yorkshire (1892), and the Society of the Sacred Mission, Kelham, Nottinghamshire (1894). Others, for example, the brotherhood founded by Father Ignatius of Llanthony, were not to survive.[3]

To the Victorian eye, therefore, it seemed that the monastic system and religious life had gained ground within the Church of England. The growing spirit of religious toleration[4] and the work undertaken by these Anglican communities, which was missionary and pastoral as opposed to a life of contemplation and withdrawal from the world usually associated with Roman Catholicism, contributed to their growth and success in nineteenth-century England. In 1871, a Select Committee of the House of Commons vindicated Anglican conventual life.[5] The support of the Convocation of Canterbury,[6] which in 1852 again began to function, along with the resolutions of Church Congresses did much to dispel any taint of disloyalty or "popery ." A small but vociferous Anglo-Catholic party also championed the merits of religious life and argued for its right to exist within the Church of England. On the other hand, an equally determined evangelical party tried to discredit brotherhoods and sisterhoods.

Monastic life still maintained an ambiguous position within the structure of the Church of England. What exactly was the relationship between a religious community and ecclesiastical or episcopal authority concerning supervision? Who would monitor the worship or liturgy? Could a community substitute a Roman Catholic rite, more suitable to monastic practices, for the rites of the Book of Common Prayer? The question of vows, roundly condemned by the reformers, still needed to be resolved. Were there certain guidelines a community must follow to remain within the wide comprehensiveness of Anglicanism? More importantly, could the Church of England embrace monks and nuns as loyal members? These unanswered questions and the uncertainties concerning the nature of religious communities forced the Anglican Communion to consider the issue of religious life at its 1897 Lambeth Conference.

"It was not until the Lambeth Conference of 1897 that the Anglican episcopate as a body first discussed religious communities, or suggested lines of closer relationship between them and ecclesiastical authorities."[7] Meeting for the first time in 1867, the early Lambeth Conferences reflected the changing nature of Anglicanism. "In the 19th century the universality of the Church had an increasing place in the minds of many Anglicans in different parts of the world, and their relationship to one another, and to one another's problems and prospects, indicated that clarification might be best achieved by some kind of conferring together."[8] The impetus came from outside of Great Britain. Disturbed by the publication of *Essays and Reviews* and the confusion associated with the Colenso affair,[9] the Anglican Church in Canada pressed for the establishment of a general council or assembly to guide the Anglican Communion. This proposal initially met fierce opposition, but the Archbishop of Canterbury, Charles Thomas Longley, who later presided over the first Lambeth Conference in 1867, modified the Canadian proposal:

> It should be distinctly understood that at this meeting no declaration of faith shall be made, and no decision come to which shall affect generally the interests of the Church, but that we shall meet together for brotherly counsel and encouragement...I shall refuse to convene any assembly which pretended to enact any Canons or affected to make any decisions binding on the Church.[10]

Longley's intervention and support for a consultative assembly, therefore, ensured its acceptance by his fellow bishops.

Since 1867, Lambeth Conferences, which met every ten years, have discussed problems or issues which touched the Anglican Church throughout the world: ritualism, prayer-book revision, the Colenso affair in Natal, the role of the laity (1867); unity between Anglican churches, boards of arbitration, Anglican chaplains in Europe, the needs of various churches (1878); and social involvement in respect to intemperance, purity, emigrants, socialism, better relationships with other Churches, especially the Eastern Orthodox, Scandinavian and Old Catholic churches, divorce, and acceptable standards of doctrine and worship (1888). By the end of the century, the Lambeth Conferences had become a recognized and trusted platform for episcopal discussion and consultation. As with the past conferences, events tended to determine the agenda. Ritualism and the Lincoln judgment, discussions between Anglicans and Roman Catholics which eventually produced *Apostolicae curae,* confusion over the Book of Common Prayer, problems associated with industrialism and the colonies all needed attention in 1897.[11] The bishops had addressed many of these issues previously, but in the opinion of some, a new item—the rapid growth of religious communities within the Church of England—needed serious attention. The episcopate could not ignore the numerous sister-hoods and brotherhoods any longer. "Here was one of the definite fruits of the Oxford Movement upon which the bishops needed to pronounce."[12]

The fourth Lambeth Conference met in London during July, 1897. The membership had grown to 194 bishops; Frederick Temple, the Archbishop of Canterbury, presided and introduced the topic dealing with the relationship of religious communities to the episcopate. Bishop William Stubbs of Oxford spoke first and told the meeting that his "diocese contains...[some] most influential brotherhoods and sisterhoods."[13] More-over, he continued: "These communities never caused any serious trouble," but Stubbs did confess that he had "certain anxieties on the subject." And he listed these areas: matters of law, the subject of vows, and the rights and jurisdiction of bishops over these communities.

Many communities had acquired property either by their own efforts or through gifts of friendly patrons, and Bishop Stubbs suggested that it "should be certified that the corporate property of brotherhoods and sisterhoods is held in a proper and legal form."[14] The diocesan bishop should shoulder this responsibility. The question of vows, long associated with suspicious Roman Catholic practices, took up more of his time. Stubbs admitted that he had no problem with vows *per se,* but to "what extent is it wise for us to recognize those vows as binding in any dealings..." with the religious communities?[15] Dispensation or release from vows presented serious and sensitive problems. Stubbs declared: "I refuse to grant dispensations." But the Bishop of Oxford did recognize the need for some guidelines or procedure to deal with possible dispensations. He believed that a release from one's vows "should be in the hands of some episcopal authority...[either] the bishop of the diocese, whom I think ought to be the visitor...or if not...their own chosen visitor..." However, this should not minimize the seriousness of a vow, "which I think is indispensable."

Religious communities of women and men, moreover, should not live a life independently of the local bishop who, as the episcopal visitor, should exercise control and jurisdiction over the brotherhoods and sisterhoods. "In most cases, one would hope that the [local] bishop would be the visitor of the community," Bishop Stubbs told the bishops.[16] "Brotherhoods...must not be allowed to work in any diocese without the consent of the Bishop, [and] without the license of the Bishop." He warned that if the church allowed "priests to exercise their office without any relation to the Bishop of the diocese, I think you will find that difficulties will arise and difficulties extremely difficult to solve." Stubbs then related how he treated members of the Cowley Fathers who resided in his diocese:

"I give the license after examination and testimonial as I should do in the case of a licensed curate..."[17]

The granting of a license, however, does not excuse the local diocesan from his responsibilities. A bishop, he stated, "can withdraw the license in case of misconduct." Religious communities must "be incorporated in the work of the church in the diocese...[and] if the Bishop thinks that things which are contrary to the law...are carried out, he should interfere by remonstrance..." But Stubbs wanted to avoid any accusations of despotic and tyrannical episcopal behavior. Bishops Stubbs believed that it was not "necessary to lay down hard and fast laws beforehand..." Bishops should not employ "inquisitorial powers." The Bishop of Oxford argued for nothing more than adherence to the laws and formularies of the Church of England on the part of those living the conventual life. His closing remarks addressed the problem "which must be at the root of the decision of the committee...[namely] how they can reconcile obedience to the bishop with obedience to a superior."[18]

After Bishop Stubbs finished, other members of the Lambeth Conference offered their views on Anglican religious life. The Bishop of Wakefield, William Walsham How, began by bemoaning the lack of support shown for communities of men, whereas greater encouragement had been extended to sisterhoods. He then quickly pointed out some problems associated with conventual life. The bishop believed that the "sanction of the incumbent of the parish"—that is, the parish priest—was necessary before members of a religious community enter the parish boundaries. But his chief concern dealt with the authority and jurisdiction of the diocesan bishop. He asked, "How far has the visitor a right of objecting and interfering, what power has he?"[19] "What power will these communities allow him to have," especially where practices "inconsistent with the Church of England...create immense difficulty?"[20] Moreover, Bishop How queried what measures a bishop could take to correct a community. The bishop finally told the assembly that it must face the issue of vows and dispensations at once, and he revealed his own position: "...there must be some power somewhere of removal of unworthy or disloyal members of communities."[21]

The Bishop of Bloemfontein, J.W. Hicks, followed and spoke on the subject of vows. Hicks supported the idea of promises, which could be dispensed, but argued against release from solemn vows. Agreeing with Bishop Stubbs, he believed that all priests living in community must possess an episcopal license. Hicks did not "see that they need be licensed by the Bishop to a particular parish and diocese."[22] He suggested an alternative. "They may have a general license and at the same time may be able to exercise their function with the consent or at the desire of the local authority in each particular case..." A founding member of the Cowley Fathers, the American Bishop of Fond du Lac (Wisconsin), Charles C. Grafton, always smiled on the establishment and growth of religious life within Anglicanism. Grafton told the Lambeth Conference that the "development of religious life apart from the true ministry and the sacraments is absolutely impossible..."[23] He then argued for the freedom of religious communities. The early church "never legislated for them but left communities quite free."[24] Historically, episcopal legislation injured the spirit of community life. But his plea for more freedom and less centralized control did not mean a *laissez-faire* atmosphere; bishops should maintain a scrutiny over the financial affairs of the communities and also have the power to dispense from vows.

Taking a different approach from Grafton, A. B. Webb, the Bishop of Grahamstown, South Africa, pleaded for the acceptance of religious life, but also emphasized the need for episcopal supervision. "If a body of Bishops recognizes this life ," he stated, "then they certainly have a right to require submission to order and submission to order depends upon its relation to the Bishop's...visitation."[25] This episcopal visitor, therefore, would keep ecclesiastical law and order. He should even oversee and supervise the liturgical life of the community. "Undisciplined devotion," the bishop noted, "...is too often a source of practical pervading heresy in the Church..."[26] Also, a constitution detailing the life and activities of a community "should be submitted to the Bishop's approval...and no alteration whatever allowed without his consent..." Subject to the consent of the bishop, dispensation from vows "should be a possibility...under certain conditions."[27] Likewise reacting to Bishop Grafton's plea for freedom, the Bishop of Ely, Alwyne Frederick Compton, took a hard-line approach and pointed out that episcopal "...legislation arose because difficulties had already been found with regard to brotherhoods and sisterhoods."[28] This bishop wanted some procedure for the possible dissolution of a community, for example, upon the decision of both archbishops, with the advice of the Lambeth Conference, and after an official investigation.

The flow of the discussions continued to emphasize the desire for a close and intimate working relationship between the religious communities and properly constituted church authority, namely, the bishops. Consequently, the Bishop of Saint Andrews in Scotland, G. H. Wilkinson, wanted some communication or dialogue between representatives of the religious communities and the bishops. This would ensure cooperation. Moreover, "... it is of vital importance to the Church that she should know, and know in some detail, what are the kinds of prayer and the kind of devotion that is being offered in that [the community's] Chapel."[29] Randall Davidson, the Bishop of Winchester and the next Archbishop of Canterbury (1903), also sounded an alarm: "...Community life [is] growing by leaps and bounds...[and an] element of danger which accompanies it is also growing...in a very decided and definite way..."[30] This serious matter, he continued, "...urgently needs the guidance and direction of the episcopate." He ended his address with a sense of urgency. "There is undoubtedly a peril at least, in the growing independence or lawlessness on the part of some Religious Communities." And in response to these words of Bishop Davidson "the assembled bishops signaled their approval with shouts of 'Hear, hear.'"

Bishop Mandell Creighton of London attempted to blunt the criticism and harsh language of the previous speakers. He spoke of the desire on the part of communities living in London to obtain episcopal recognition: the brotherhoods and sisterhoods in his diocese had always opened their ears to his counsel and advice. Moreover, Creighton argued, to impose strict liturgical guidelines on their devotional services would create difficulties. "It is obvious that a body living in a community must have more offices than are contained in the Book of Common Prayer," he reasoned, "and must have a greater variety of services than any Anglican formularies have hitherto contemplated..."[31]

The president of the Lambeth Conference, Frederick Temple, spoke last. The Archbishop of Canterbury moved that "a Committee be appointed to consider the subject 'the relation of the religious communities within the Church of England to the episcopate' and to report in the concluding session of the conference..."[32] This committee could, however, ask to postpone the report for a year. After the membership had been agreed upon,[33] the next question concerned the name of the chairman. "The committee dealing with the religious communities was chaired by the Bishop of Oxford, William Stubbs, who was Bishop of a diocese where several communities were established."[34] His personal knowledge and experience would prove invaluable. But the perplexity of the issue necessarily meant that the committee could not finish its work and present a final report during the summer of 1897. The committee's preliminary findings, however, addressed the problems and questions raised by the bishops, but it did not offer any concrete proposals. "We desire to secure to Communities all reasonable freedom of organization and development," this report stated, and "such freedom is essential to the due exercise of special gifts."[35] But on the other hand, "a liberty...must be so regulated as to ensure the maintenance of the Faith, and the order and discipline of the

Church, together with a due recognition of family claims and the rights of individual members of a Community." The report cautiously abstained from making any specific recommendations concerning vows and dispensations; the superiors of the various brotherhoods and sisterhoods had to be interviewed first. Equally vague was the subject of visitation: "right relations to the Episcopate involved some well-defined powers of Visitation; the consideration of what these powers should be, we reserve for our final report." The committee made no mention of a community's liturgical devotions.

On two points, however, Bishop Stubbs' committee offered some direction. All priests "ministering to a religious community should be licensed for that purpose by the Diocesan Bishop." The report stressed that priests owed their canonical obedience to the bishop of the diocese where they ministered, and that a priest's membership in a religious community should not jeopardize or compromise this obedience. Questions dealing with property rights and ownership did not receive much attention during the Lambeth Conference debates. The committee did recognize, however, the importance of this question and urged the adoption of two principles: first, before a community receives episcopal recognition, the trust deeds should be examined by legal counsel to guarantee that the property could not be diverted or alienated from the Church of England; second, provision should "be made for the disposal of property in the event of the dissolution of the Community or the withdrawal of an individual member."

The 1897 Lambeth Conference did, however, pass two resolutions which drew attention to the important work of the committee, and granted the committee additional time to compile a thorough and satisfactory report. The first recognized "with thankfulness the revival alike of brotherhoods and sisterhoods...and commends to the attention of the Church the Report of the Committee appointed to consider the Relation of Religious Communities to the Episcopate."[36] The second resolution acknowledged the "importance of the further development of such Communities, [and] the Conference requests the Committee to continue its labours ." The final report, it suggested, should be in the hands of the Archbishop of Canterbury by July 1898.

An encyclical letter issued by the bishops attending the 1897 Lambeth Conference commented and enlarged upon the resolutions dealing with Anglican religious communities. Moreover, it captured in compact and condensed form the opinions voiced during the discussions. This letter began by noting that more time had to be devoted to this important topic, and it clearly acknowledged "that such communities are capable of rendering great services to the Church, and have indeed already done so."[37] It did not avoid or minimize the serious reservations raised by some bishops. "But we think more regulation is needed if they are to be worked in thorough harmony with the general work of the Church as a whole ." In the mind of the Lambeth Conference it was not clear what form this supervision should take, and consequently the committee had to define the extent and force of episcopal supervision. The encyclical letter ended with words of encouragement and caution to those individuals who wanted to embrace the religious life and urged future candidates to understand the seriousness of their choice. With these resolutions and directives from the 1897 Lambeth Conference, the committee began its task.

After several meetings, the committee finished its task and sent to Archbishop Frederick Temple the final report on 28 November 1898. The archbishop thought that it was incomplete; he wanted a section dealing with deaconesses to be included before publication. Three years later, however, Bishop Randall Davidson of Winchester, a member of the committee, wrote to Temple and urged him to take action on the report even though it did not meet the archbishop's expectations. According to Bishop Davidson, "it has seemed to your Committee to be desirable to present again to your Grace the original Report, notwithstanding the fact that the second branch of the subject [the deaconesses] has not yet been dealt with."[38] "And a prolonged delay might," Davidson suggested, "in the opinion of your Committee, lead to misapprehension as to the cause." He apologized for the delay and promised to finish the section on the deaconesses as soon as possible. Archbishop Temple agreed with Davidson's position and, consequently, he circulated the unfinished report in 1902.

Before the 1908 Lambeth Conference assembled, the committee had thus completed its task, but still had to postpone its report on deaconesses. Some familiar faces, however, had disappeared. Of the original 1897 committee, eight bishops had died. And a new archbishop occupied Lambeth Palace; Randall Davidson succeeded Frederick Temple after his death in 1902. Davidson had also replaced Bishop Stubbs, who died in 1901, as chairman of the committee on religious life. In this capacity, the archbishop wrote the introduction to the committee report. He recounted the background and history of the deliberations and noted that the members had met frequently and had sought the advice of the superiors of numerous religious communities. Davidson, with reference to the world-wide nature of Anglicanism, stated that "the development of the Community system in different parts of the world is necessarily subject to very different conditions, and it is important that all features of these variations, in different parts of the Anglican communion, should be well and duly considered..."[39] Moreover, "every opportunity should be given for the expression of local opinion on the basis of well-weighed experience before the final adoption of any line of definite recommendation as to the policy of the Church at large." The present committee, according to Archbishop Davidson, also suggested that a copy of the report should be sent to every diocesan bishop of the Anglican Communion, who would then have the opportunity to respond. From this data, the Consultative Committee of the Lambeth Conference, or any other body, could draw up a series of recommendations.

The committee's report to the 1908 Lambeth Conference faithfully reflected the spirit of the 1897 conference, especially the need to strengthen episcopal authority over brotherhoods and sisterhoods. Conventual life within Anglicanism must not be allowed to develop independently of proper Church supervision and control. To achieve the appropriate and satisfactory relationship, the committee thought it essential "that there should be on the part of the Episcopate a recognition of Religious Communities within the Church of England and of Religious Life as expressed in the Rule of such communities." But on the other hand, "...there should be on the part of the Communities a distinct recognition of the authority of the Episcopate." The office of visitor, with specific duties and responsibilities, and an officially approved constitution would safeguard the rights and prerogatives of the bishops and protect Anglican interests.

The visitor, who "should be, *ex officio,* Visitor of the Mother-House of any community established in his diocese ," would guarantee that the community would not stray beyond the wide boundaries of Anglican comprehensiveness. If the diocesan bishop refused to accept the office, the community would elect its own candidate, subject to the approval of the archbishop or metropolitan of the province. The report clearly spelled out the duties of the episcopal visitor: to ensure that the original constitution of the community had received "authoritative sanction," either from the visitor or from the archbishop or metropolitan of the province; to see that the community observes the letter and spirit of its constitution; to license the clergy; and to monitor the religious services, making sure that the community uses the Book of Common Prayer.

Along with the office of visitor, an acceptable constitution would limit the freedom of a religious community to operate independently of episcopal supervision. The committee believed that a proper constitution should touch the following aspects of community life: "the distinct recognition of the Doctrine and Discipline of the Church of England"; conditions for the formation of a governing board; provisions "as to additional Offices, books of Devotions and ornaments and appliances of House and Chapel"; and the procedures for the establishment of "rules as to possession and disposition of property." The constitution must also address the issue of vows, a sensitive issue to all segments of Anglicanism. According to the report, the regulations of a religious community should contain "provision for rules for imposition of and release from vows, solemn promises, or engagements with the Community..." To ensure propriety, members of a community should make their "Formal Profession" in the presence of "the Bishop of the Diocese or some deputy appointed by him for that purpose." Finally, the committee suggested that recently formed brotherhoods and sisterhoods be given time "to deliberate over their Statutes under provisional sanction."

But the report did not give *carte blanche* authority to those bishops who wanted to control every phase of a community's life. It allowed some freedom and latitude of action. The committee's report noted that the members had studied "several points relating to the life and works of Religious Communities ," and decided not to address or comment on these topics since "they do not fall within the terms of our Reference." Moreover, "we have made no special reference to the means by which the inner life of their members can be directed, their mental powers strengthened, their capacities for usefulness in the Kingdom of our Blessed Lord developed." The last act of the committee on religious communities dealt with the successful passage of a resolution, which directed the Archbishop of Canterbury to submit a copy of the report to all diocesan bishops and invite a response.

The committee appointed in 1897, therefore, played a fundamental role in drawing the attention of the Anglican Communion to the existence of brotherhoods and sisterhoods within its churches. The report also helped to dismiss the stereotypes of conventual life as unnatural or popish. By trying to bring the religious orders close to the episcopate, the committee's report tended to regularize community life and thus ensure it a proper place within the fabric of Anglicanism. Moreover, the 1897 committee represented the first of many attempts to tackle questions associated with brotherhoods and sisterhoods. The American Episcopal Church, for example, formally recognized religious orders of women and men in 1913. The topic of sisterhoods appeared on the agenda of the 1920 Lambeth Conference, and discussions at the 1930 conference eventually resulted in the establishment of the Advisory Council on Religious Communities in 1935. This organization successfully served as a bridge between bishops and the Anglican religious communities. Within the Church of England herself, Anglican brotherhoods and sisterhoods currently occupy an important place and participate in a confederation called the Communities' Consultative Council.

Notes

[1] Bernard and Margaret Pawley, *Rome and Canterbury Through Four Centuries* (London: Mowbray, 1981). P. 133.

[2] Peter Anson, *The Call of the Cloister: Religious Communities and Kindred Bodies in the Anglican Communion* [Hereafter Cloister] (London: SPCK, 1964). Pp. 595-97.

[3] *Cloister*, p. 594.

[4] See Edward Norman, *Anti-Catholicism in Victorian England* (London: Allen and Unwin, 1967).

[5] See Walter Arnstein, *Protestant versus Catholic in Mid-Victorian England. Mr. Newdegate and the Nuns* (Columbia, MO: University of Missouri Press, 1982).

[6] Rene Kollar, "Anglican Brotherhoods and Urban Social Work," *Churchman* 101 (1987), Pp. 140-145.

[7] *Cloister*, p. 482. The Lambeth Conference is an assembly of bishops of the Anglican Communion held every ten years under the presidency of the Archbishop of Canterbury. Consultative in nature, the Lambeth Conference passes non-binding resolutions dealing with questions or problems confronting the church. The first Lambeth Conference was held in 1867. For a short history of the Lambeth Conferences, see Alan M.G. Stephenson, *Anglicanism and the Lambeth Conferences* [Hereafter ALC] (London: SPCK, 1978).

[8] John Howe, *Highways and Hedges: Anglicanism and the Universal Church* (London: CIO Publishing, 1985). P. 59.

[9] The publication of *Essays and Reviews* (1860) and the writings of Bishop John Colenso of Natal (1814-1883) stirred controversy within the Anglican Communion. Both contributed to the religious crisis which resulted in the convening of the first Lambeth Conference in 1867. *Essays and Reviews*, a collection of seven essays, challenged accepted thought on numerous issues related to biblical scholarship. Colenso also disturbed many Anglicans by questioning the traditional authorship and historical accuracy of several books of the Old Testament.

[10] Quoted in Stephen Neill, *Anglicanism* (London: Mowbray, 1977). Pp. 360-61.

[11] For a discussion of the 1897 Lambeth Conference, as well as the previous meetings, see ALC.

[12] ALC, p. 100. The 1897 Lambeth Conference also discussed the growth of deaconesses. The German Lutheran pastor, T. Fliedner, founded the first order of deaconesses at Kaiserwerth in 1836. This revival spread quickly to England. In 1861, the Bishop of London, Archibald Tait, ordained Miss Elizabeth Ferard a deaconess. Diocesan Deaconess Institutions grew in number and they embraced pastoral work as their chief apostolates. Based broadly on monastic principles, "from the earliest years members shared a common life and a common rule of prayer..." *Cloister*, p. 393.

[13] Proceedings on Religious Communities [Hereafter PRC], Lambeth Conference 1897, Min. I, July 5-7, LC 38, Lambeth Palace Library, Lambeth Palace, London.

[14] PRC, p. 131.

[15] PRC, pp. 131-132.

[16] PRC, p. 134.

[17] PRC, p. 135.

[18] PRC, p. 138.

[19] PRC, p. 139.

[20] PRC, p.141.

[21] PRC, p. 143.

[22] PRC, p. 148.

[23] PRC, p. 150.

[24] PRC, p. 154.

[25] PRC, p. 160.

[26] PRC, p. 161.

[27] PRC, p. 162.

[28] PRC, p. 163.

[29] PRC, pp. 168-169.

[30] PRC, p. 170.

[31] PRC, p. 179.

[32] PRC, p. 185

[33] The bishops of the following dioceses made up the membership of the committee: Albany, Bloemfontein, Calcutta, Christchurch, Corfe, Fond du Lac, Grahamstown, Goulburn, Lincoln, London, Marlborough, Oxford (chairman), Pennsylvania, Quebec, Reading (secretary), Rockhampton, Saint Andrews, Vermont, Wakefield, Washington, and Winchester.

[34] ALC, p. 105.

[35] Report of the Conference Committee 1897, LC 62/5, Lambeth Palace Library, London.

[36] "Resolution of Lambeth Conference, 1897," printed in Randall Davidson (comp.), *The Six Lambeth Conferences 1867-1920* (London: SPCK, 1929). P. 201. The resolution also directed the committee to study and to report on the revival of the office of deaconesses.

[37] "Encyclical Letter Issued by the Bishops Attending the Fourth Lambeth Conference," July 1897, printed in Randall Davidson (comp.), *The Six Lambeth Conferences 1867-1920*, p. 188.

[38] Davidson to Temple, 11 November, 1901, printed in the Report of the Committee Appointed in 1897 to Consider the Religious Communities within the Church to the Episcopate, 1908, LC 100/28, LPL.

[39] Report of the Committee Appointed in 1897 to Consider the Relation of Religious Communities within the Church to the Episcopate, 1908.

CHAPTER V

ANGLO-CATHOLICISM IN THE CHURCH OF ENGLAND, 1895-1913: ABBOT AELRED CARLYLE AND THE MONKS OF CALDEY ISLAND

From 1906-13, Abbot Aelred Carlyle (1874-1955) enjoyed immense popularity as an Anglo-Catholic, and, according to some, could have easily become the spokesman for this section of the Anglican Church. Through perseverance and diplomacy, he single-handedly founded the first Benedictine monastery in the Church of England since the Reformation. Unlike others who sought and failed to bring Roman Catholic practices into the Established Church, Abbot Carlyle enjoyed the explicit ecclesiastical sanction of an Archbishop of Canterbury for his work, and with this seal of approval he could dismiss critics and disbelievers. By 1910, Abbot Carlyle and his community on Caldey Island, South Wales, had become a paradise for High Churchmen. The Abbot's charismatic and hypnotic personality attracted many who nostalgically longed for the glories of a medieval and united Christendom. Armed with a High Church theory of Benedictinism, Caldey became an enclave of ritualism, the "naughty underworld" of the Edwardian Anglican Church. Caldey was, at its peak, an exemplar of pre-Reformation Roman Catholic monasticism. In 1913, the experiment was in ruins. Carlyle refused to yield to the reforming zeal of the Bishop of Oxford and his attempts to force Caldey to conform to the comprehensiveness of the Anglican Church. The result was sensational: a group of monks renounced the church of their baptism and sought admission to the Church of Rome.

1. Anglo-Catholicism and the Revival of Religious Brotherhoods

After the nationalization of the church under Henry VIII and the suppression of the monasteries, which were already vulnerable to such attack, the monastic system seemed dead.[1] But a small underground stream of the monastic life continued to flow through some channels of English religious life. Little Gidding and the voluntary prayer groups of the Restoration were short-lived and transient.[2] The French Revolution with its attendant movement of French priests to Britain as refugees,[3] the emotionalism of the Wesleyan awakening[4] and then the Oxford Movement all helped to give renewed strength to the monastic ideal. In 1838, Edward Bouverie Pusey, for example, outlined a plan for a religious brotherhood to John Newman: "What I should like then would be a place for twelve fellows, but beginning with not less than two...with an endowment of one thousand pounds...and so enable one to make a rule for them."[5] Newman also appreciated the value of the monastic system for the Anglican Church.

> I would then request them to compare it with...[the] religion into which the unhappy enthusiast of the present day is precipitated by the high and dry system of the Establishment, and he will see how much was gained to Christianity in purity, as well as unity by that monastic system.[6]

In addition to a favorable religious climate, other factors encouraged the foundations of religious communities in the Established Church: the praiseworthy work done by convents of nuns,[7] the support of Convocation and Church Congresses,[8] and the vindication of religious life by a Select Committee of the House of Commons.[9] The orthodoxy and valuable pastoral work of three brotherhoods, the Cowley Fathers, the Society of the Resurrection, and the Society of the Sacred Mission, helped to destroy the stereotype of religious life as evil and popish. The meritorious achievements of the Settlement House Movement in London's East End forced the Anglican hierarchy to recognize the value of religious brotherhoods working in urban slums. At the 1891 Convocation of Canterbury, Frederick Temple, the Bishop of London, captured the consensus of the membership. He claimed

> that the clergy want very large assistance, and they want the assistance of men who will be willing to give such

> assistance...We want a number of men who would do a
> great deal of voluntary work . .. to meet the enormous
> amount of practical heathenism that is to be found in the
> poorer parts of the great towns.[10]

The 1897 Lambeth Conference concurred, but argued for the absolute authority of the local bishop over any fraternity and demanded loyalty to the formularies of the Church of England. If the Anglican Church should recognize a brotherhood, then it certainly has "a right to require submission to order, and submission to order depends in its relation to the Bishops."[11]

A vigorous Anglo-Catholic movement also promoted a revival of monastic life in the Established Church. During the latter part of the nineteenth century, ritualism had reached epidemic proportions. It had evolved from the passive antiquarianism of the 1840s into a movement which flouted ecclesiastical law, the rulings of church courts, and official pronouncements of bishops. This second generation of Tractarians was also more concerned with liturgy and ceremony. The Anglo-Catholic priests, consequently, were determined to "adopt the liturgical practices of the pre-Reformation church in England and, in not a few cases the extra-liturgical devotions of the post-Tridentine Roman Catholic Church in Europe."[12]

In the 1890s, however, the emphasis of the Anglo-Catholics blossomed into a passion which sought to revive the ceremonial and sacramental theology of sixteenth-century Rome. The High Church clergy scorned the destructiveness of the Reformation and the shallowness of its liturgy. In his evidence before the 1904 Royal Commission on Ecclesiastical Discipline, the Archbishop of Canterbury, Randall Davidson, stated that "it became clear that during recent years a development of the use of special services outside the Book of Common Prayer, most of them profitable or harmless, but some of them open to grave exception as inconsistent with the doctrine and discipline of the Church of England or as definitely excluded from her services"[13] had become common in the Anglican Church. Moreover, an increasing number of Anglican clergy "had tended, almost inevitably to the disregard of authority and...to act in ritual matters on their own individual discretion or on the advice of irresponsible societies."[14]

Comprehensiveness and *laissez faire* in religious matters, therefore, appeared to have triumphed over the appeals for uniformity and clerical discipline. By the turn of the century, moreover, the Anglican bishops had become the supreme arbitrators in ritualist disputes. The use of the episcopal veto in the 1874 Public Worship Regulation Act,[15] the growing power of Convocation, and the courage of the Anglican hierarchy are examples of the increasing power of the church in determining its policies. Ecclesiastical law and discipline had passed from Parliament and the secular courts to the conscience of the diocesan bishops. According to Professor Owen Chadwick, "the important consequence...was the development in the authority of the bishop, as the guide of the clergy amid disagreements, as the maintainer of a reasonable measure of agreement in modes of worship, and as a safeguard for a reasonable liberty in liturgical experiment."[16] A wide measure of freedom, therefore, was obvious in the Anglican Church. In some dioceses, conformity to the established norms was demanded, but in others, benign neglect or encouragement to experiment in liturgy and Roman Catholic practices was the rule. When the Royal Commission on Ecclesiastical Discipline published its findings in 1906, the evidence overwhelmingly supported the allegations that comprehensiveness and freedom were the predominant tendencies in the Established Church.

The main conclusions of the Commission were that the law concerning public worship was too narrow, the machinery for discipline had broken down, and the law, when reformed, should be enforced.[17] "Despite mobs, episcopal inhibitions, parliamentary legislation...imprisonments and the condemnation of the Courts of Arches and the Judicial Committee of the Privy Council, the Anglo-Catholics had won freedom for most of their distinctive ritualistic claims and thus changed the character of the worship of the Church of England in many parishes."[18] Consequently, this spirit of toleration, along with the positive view of monastic life which developed in Victorian England, fostered an atmosphere conducive to the growth of conventual life in the Church of England. Aelred Carlyle, therefore, could rely on the support of interested clerics and laymen in his desire to establish an Anglican Benedictine monastery.

2. An Anglican Benedictine Monastery in the Church of England

During the early phase of Aelred Carlyle's life, 1874-94, he developed into an extreme ritualist.[19] By 1894, he was Roman Catholic in devotion and belief, but still professed loyalty to the Church of England. His early family life lacked stability, and the sudden death of his father in 1890 destroyed his future at Oxford. While Carlyle was a medical student at St. Bartholomew's, he became captivated by Anglo-Catholic thought. Attracted by the pomp of Catholic liturgy, he frequented ritualist churches and Roman Catholic monasteries,[20] and his studies suffered. After failure at medicine, he devoted his time and energy to dreams and fantasies about reviving religious life in the Church of England. Since 1891, Carlyle later confessed, "a very definite wish was formed in my mind to a life as far as possible according to the Rule of St. Benedict."[21] In 1892, he became an associate of a brotherhood based on Benedictine principles,[22] and by 1895 he had composed two rules for future monasteries.[23] Supported by a stipend from his mother, Carlyle and a few friends attempted to establish a number of monastic fraternities throughout Great Britain, but without much success. Friendly vicars and bishops tolerated these canonically irregular brotherhoods.[24] Even without any visible signs of success, the evangelical or Protestant wing of Anglicanism saw Carlyle as a threat to the integrity of the Established Church.

When a member of his brotherhood became involved in a theft of books in 1898, the evangelical press warned Anglicans of the dangers of Carlyle's revival. A writer for the *Church Review* told his readers that there was more at stake than a question of stolen books, and questioned the legality of Carlyle's brotherhood: "It is news to me that there are monks in the Church of England."[25] The *Church Intelligencer* published articles on "Secret Societies in the Church of England," "Revelation of Anglican Monkery," and "Monkery and Water."[26] *The Rock* reported that "there is a deliberate and persistent attempt...to make monasticism, with all its revolting self-torture, unscriptural and unnatural regulations...a recognized part of the English Church."[27] Religious brotherhoods like Carlyle's are "unEnglish, sneaking societies," who seek to "destroy the manly frankness of the British character."[28]

When Carlyle arrived at Lower Guiting, Gloucestershire, in the spring of 1898, the *Church Intelligencer* described his brotherhood as "a complete betrayal of the Church of England" and pointed out the "rottenness of the allegiance of the Anglican brotherhood" to the Church of England.[29] Carlyle's alleged ritualism, lighted candles, a Roman Catholic baptism service, the sacrificial character of the Mass, incense, and auricular confession,[30] enraged the parishioners of Lower Guiting. The arrival of a "Protestant Van" on 2 July became the catalyst for a confrontation between the villagers and the monks. Encouraged by the preachers, crowds attacked the monastery with "eggs, destined neither to be eaten nor to produce chickens, but simply to exhale a most disagreeable odour."[31] On 29 July, the parishioners drove Aelred Carlyle and his remaining monks out of Lower Guiting.[32] While the press and preachers vilified Carlyle, the Archbishop of Canterbury, Frederick Temple, sanctioned and gave approval to his dream to establish Benedictine monasticism in the Anglican Church.

In June 1897, Carlyle petitioned Archbishop Temple to authorize his solemn profession and "license him to erect a Congregation."[33] It was not until February 1898, however, that Carlyle met Temple. According to Carlyle, "His Grace has given me his sanction and Blessing and special authorization for my profession as a Benedictine."[34] On 20 February, Frater Aelred Carlyle pronounced solemn vows of stability, conversion, and obedience as an Anglican monk of the Order of St. Benedict.[35] Four years later, the small brotherhood sent "a petition to the Archbishop for his sanction for the Election and Blessing of our Abbot."[36] With the request, Carlyle enclosed a letter which urged the Primate "to consider the accompanying petition and to sign and seal it in a token of your sanction, and so establish our little community."[37] Because he misplaced the Charter, it was not until May 1902 that Temple signed and returned the document to Carlyle.[38] Carlyle's reaction was sheer joy. He thanked Temple, exclaiming, "We are most grateful to Your Grace for your kindness in signing our schedule and thus establishing our little community."[39] Regardless of his motive or the expediency of his actions, Archbishop Temple's Charter signified episcopal approval and the sanction of the Archbishop of Canterbury. The support or indifference of other members of the hierarchy, however, also helped to ensure the success of the Anglican Benedictines.

Even though the villagers of Lower Guiting demanded that their bishop, Charles John Ellicott, remove Carlyle and banish the brotherhood from the parish because of alleged Roman practices, he did not act.[40] During the sojourn of the monks in Yorkshire, 1902-6, Archbishop William Maclagan did not trouble the community. When they moved to Caldey, Maclagan recommended Carlyle to their new diocesan, John Owen: "They gave me no trouble, and have been engaged in various good works in their own neighbourhood."[41] A number of Maclagan's actions, moreover, strengthened Carlyle's official standing in the Anglican Church. With his permission Charles Grafton, the Bishop of Fond du Lac, Wisconsin, installed and blessed Carlyle as abbot and superior of the new brotherhood.[42] Again with Maclagan's permission,[43] Bishop Grafton ordained Carlyle a priest on 15 November 1904 in Wisconsin. On his return to England, Archbishop Maclagan issued Carlyle a provisional license authorizing him to minister to the needs of his monastery.[44]

When Abbot Carlyle and nineteen Anglican followers occupied Caldey Island in 1906, the continued absence of episcopal control gave him freedom to experiment with Roman liturgy and devotions. The relation between the Bishop of St. David's and Abbot Carlyle was admittedly passive.[45] Owen avoided "any official relations with the community as a community."[46] "I have always felt that the question of the community was very difficult," Owen later admitted, "and I have been specially anxious to be just to a movement with which I am afraid my sympathies are imperfect."[47] Upon the Abbot's arrival in his diocese, Bishop Owen informed Carlyle that any sign of favor from him should not be interpreted as official recognition of the community.[48] The English hierarchy, therefore, must accept some responsibility for the success and appeal of the Anglican brotherhood and the increasing prestige of Abbot Carlyle. A word of disapproval or censure would have branded Carlyle a maverick and the orthodoxy of the monastery questionable. Because of episcopal indifference, however, Caldey Island quickly developed into an Anglo-Catholic paradise.

Contemplative in spirit and catholic in liturgy, Abbot Carlyle adhered to the Rule of St. Benedict in its strict and literal interpretation. The membership of the brotherhood had also grown. When Carlyle went to Yorkshire in 1902, there were nine members, but by March 1912, the community numbered thirty-five monks.[49] Abbot Carlyle legislated for every aspect of the monks' daily life from how one should enter and leave church to the manner in which a monk should make the sign of the cross or genuflect during services.[50] He instituted an exacting ceremonial for the refectory: specially made aluminum tins were used for coffee, a detailed rubric ruled the use of napkins and eating utensils, and the frugal meals were eaten in silence. Novices were taught never to cross their knees. Since silence was strictly observed, "Silence Books" were kept in case one had to ask an important question. Carlyle also insisted on daily cold baths, nude swimming, and a daily conference with each of his monks.[51] He later acknowledged that one might think "Caldey was exotic in relation to normal Anglicanism, but that was accidental rather than concerted."[52] Carlyle also maintained that he "wanted the Real Catholic Benedictine life...with its spiritual strength and its traditional observance."[53] He did not believe that Caldey "was either quixotic or illogical," but that it represented "a real innocent and ardent desire to possess something in our own church that was lacking."[54]

The basis of Abbot Carlyle's monastic theology was a longing to found monasticism in the Anglican Church. "As it did not then exist," he said, "I set out to establish it."[55] "I saw a Revival of the Spiritual Life spreading through England with here and there men waiting and longing for the opportunity of withdrawing...to seek the peace and regulation of the cloister."[56] Regretfully, the observance of Benedict's Rule had been absent from Britain too long. "True, for many years the Church of England has been bereft of this life, but now the Holy Spirit is stirring in pious hearts for its revival."[57] But the essence of Carlyle's monasticism was catholicity. "Our position in the Church of England is that of Catholics separated from the rest of Western Christendom by the events of the Reformation."[58] Carlyle, like most Anglo-Catholics, deplored the destructiveness of the sixteenth century. He attacked the Reformation "in its origin and in its consequences." Moreover, he was convinced "that it was through no personal fault of our own that we are separated from the communion of the Latin Church."[59] Consequently, the customs, manners, and liturgical devotions of Caldey were copies of Roman Catholic practices, and the majority deviated from the Anglican norm.

The liturgy and devotions of Caldey were Roman Catholic in letter and spirit, and Carlyle openly boasted of practices condemned by the Royal Commission. Wilfred Upson, Carlyle's successor as Abbot, described the spirit of Caldey's liturgical life in terms of catholicity. When he joined the community in 1908, he found that "there was reservation of what we believed to be the Blessed Sacrament, and Exposition...a great devotion to our Lady[and] we acknowledged the Pope to be the Head of the Church, satisfying ourselves...if he could not acknowledge us, that was not our fault."[60] The neo-Roman practices were part of the Catholic heritage and reflected the spiritual needs of Caldey.[61] "The whole Liturgical Revival," *Pax* declared, "springs out of the revived sense of pageantry, together with the breakdown of isolation, and a realization of the fact that the Church of Christ is meant to be one universal or cosmopolitan society."[62]

The Ceremonial of Caldey stipulated that "the Holy Sacrifice of the Mass is celebrated in Latin according to the Monastic Rite *(Missale Monasticum, pro omnibus sub Regula Sancti Benedicti militantibus)* after the Use finally published in the year 1604." Furthermore, the rubrics of this Roman Catholic missal were "observed in their entirely, save only that Holy Communion is administered under both species."[63] Only monks, however, were permitted to offer the Tridentine Mass, and the ceremony was restricted to the Abbey Church. "Secular Priests who offer the Holy Sacrifice in the Caldey Village Church or at the side altars in the Monastic Church use the Prayer Book Rite without any audible interpolation or alteration."[64] *Pax* was equally vocal in this restriction. "While our more ornate Benedictine Rite is of course in use at the monastery chapel, the Prayer Book is equally of course in the village church."[65] All services were conducted in Latin, and as the only priest in the monastery, Abbot Carlyle celebrated Mass wearing the vestments of a medieval prelate.[66] No effort was spared to emulate Roman Catholic ceremonies. A monk, for example, was dispatched to the Roman Catholic monastery of Quarr, Isle of Wight, to observe their ceremonial and the singing of Latin plainchant.[67] The result was an elaborate Roman Mass, uncanonical for the Established Church and illicit for the Roman Catholic Church. An eye-witness commented on the beauty of the sung Latin Mass, the use of incense, and the beauty of the ceremony,[68] and *The Organist and Choirmaster* (13 September 1908) praised a pontifical Latin Mass celebrated by Carlyle. The author was impressed with the "beauty of the ritual" and the singing of the Tridentine Mass.[69] Roman Catholic devotions, however, were not limited to the Mass.

Candidates were admitted into the monastery in a ceremony copied from the Roman missal,[70] and pronounced solemn vows in the same manner and form as their Roman counterparts.[71] When the Abbot's Chapel was dedicated in 1912, the ceremony, complete with exorcism and intercessory prayers, was identical to the Roman Catholic ritual.[72] Certain feast days and devotions condemned by the Royal Commission were also celebrated on Caldey.[73] Eucharistic devotions such as Corpus Christi, Benediction, Reservation, and Exposition of the Blessed Sacrament posed challenges to the Anglican teaching concerning Transubstantiation and the Real Presence.[74] Abbot Carlyle's devotion to the Blessed Virgin was well known. The ceremonial legislated that during May "a special altar is erected in the church in honor of the Blessed Virgin Mary, and special hymns, litanies, etc., are used during this month."[75] The Assumption of the Blessed Virgin Mary and the Feast of the Immaculate Conception were designated as special holidays.[76] The monastic office was also performed according to Roman Catholic custom.

Instead of the Book of Common Prayer, Carlyle preferred the Roman Monastic Breviary for the public choral prayer of his monks. The eight times of prayer prescribed for Roman Catholic monks "are recited in Latin according to the disposition of the Psalter provided in the Holy Rule of St. Benedict."[77] According to High Church theology, the use of the Monastic Breviary by the Caldey monks was not exceptional or illegal. *Pax* told its readers that the Breviary was not peculiar to Rome. "Here we have an Office, many features of which, certainly, have been suggested by the Roman Office, but which, taken as a whole is distinctly the creation of the mind of St. Benedict."[78] The Caldey liturgy, therefore, was Roman Catholic and contained devotions and practices abhorrent to the Anglican Church, but there was no attempt to curtail or prohibit them. Abbot Carlyle was not forced to defend or justify his community until 1912.

The freedom from episcopal supervision, a credible Anglo-Catholic theology, and the Roman devotions and liturgy appealed to High Churchmen who rejoiced in the establishment on Caldey of a monastery in the

Church of England. The Abbey Guest House offered hospitality to those men who wanted to participate in the daily life and schedule of a monastery, and a large number of priests, laymen, and university students took advantage of this opportunity. *Pax* advertised that the guest house had been "built for the purpose of enabling the Community to receive its friends, or those who are introduced by friends."[79] The reception of guests was an important apostolate for Carlyle: "The Guest House means much to us, as to those who come to stay with us...Though the two houses are apart, and the guests come in touch with the Abbot and Guest-Master, yet the spiritual links are felt and the gain is mutual."[80] For a small donation, visitors were invited to participate in the life of the monastic community. Although they ate their meals separately, Carlyle invited the guests to attend the full schedule of the monks' devotions and to meet with him for conferences.[81] Silence was encouraged, but lively discussions on theology and the condition of the Anglican Church constituted an important part of the life at the Guest House. One guest recorded that "there will be frank and buoyant intercourse with other guests, at one with them in sympathy and interests and aims."[82] The Guest House was always crowded,[83] and the register reflected the diverse backgrounds of those who visited Caldey.

The majority of guests were prominent Anglo-Catholics, clergymen, and Oxbridge students. Of the High Church leaders, Lord Halifax continued to be Carlyle's most enthusiastic patron. His visit to Caldey in July 1908 strengthened his conviction to promote the revival. The Viscount described his sojourn on Caldey to his son Edward with great excitement. "I must tell you about Caldey: it was delightful—a paradise...very comfortable arrangements."[84] "The liturgy was very well sung and most moving...If Caldey did not belong to the monks I would give anything to have it myself."[85] In addition to friendly conversations with the Abbot and exploring the island, the High Church liturgy pleased him immensely. "At 6:30 Evensong in the old church and then Exposition of the Blessed Sacrament with intercessions and Compline in the Monastery Chapel. It really was the chief dream of my life realized."[86] In October 1908, he told Athelstan Riley, a Vice-President of the English Church Union, that "Caldey and the Abbot appeal to all things I care for very much."[87] On the Abbot's part, he was anxious to maintain this friendship. "Your loving interest has given fresh heart and filled me with thankfulness to our Lord for so good a friend," Carlyle wrote after the Viscount's visit, and he rejoiced at the opportunity "to show you the place where God has planted the seed which you preserved and cared for at Painsthorpe."[88]

Between 1906-10, the Caldey Guest House developed into an enclave of Anglo-Catholicism. Fr. Ronald Knox, a frequent visitor, related how "in the guest-house all the gossip of the Church was told and retold...A stranger listening to the conversation might have imagined 'bishops' to be the name applied to some secret band of criminals."[89] During his holidays on Caldey, he admitted he met priests who "said the Mass everyday,...assimilated the doctrine of the intercession of saints,...became enamoured by...the ever-varied monotonies of the Divine Office," and became convinced of "the value of devotions to the Blessed Sacrament [which] was now a clear attitude of my creed."[90] Although he did not personally approve of the doctrines of the Immaculate Conception and the Assumption, Knox later confessed that "it is to the Summer of 1909 that I trace my first real consciousness of the unique position of the Mother of God."[91] The Roman Catholic spirit of Caldey, therefore, impressed him greatly and consequently influenced his conversion to Rome.

3. The Conversion of the Caldey Monks to Roman Catholicism

By 1912, many Anglo-Catholics questioned the loyalty of Caldey to the Anglican Church and the ecclesiastical status of Abbot Carlyle. In 1910, Rev. H. F. B. Mackay of All Saints, Margaret St., London, informed Lord Halifax that the Abbot had openly boasted to a parishioner that the Caldey monks would seriously consider conversion in the autumn.[92] Rev. E. H. Day also told Halifax that Carlyle allegedly stated that if a secession did take place, it "would be the greatest blow to the Church since Newman."[93] At the end of 1911, Abbot Carlyle expressed doubts about his position in the Established Church and wrote Lord Halifax that he was "watching affairs in the Church with interest and some anxiety."[94] More important, however, was the mystery surrounding the Abbot's credentials as an Anglican priest. Some critics pointed out that the omission of his name in *Crockford's,* the official register of clergymen in the Church of England, meant that he did not possess the required license to function as an Anglican priest. Consequently, Carlyle informed Halifax that he wanted a meeting with the Archbishop of Canterbury, Randall Davidson, "chiefly in regard to granting the Archbishop's license in the province."[95] This decision was crucial. In the past, individual bishops tolerated the Abbot's Roman tendencies, but it was a different matter to ask the Primate of the Anglican Church to sanction doctrines and practices that were anathema to the Church's tradition and teaching.

Abbot Carlyle met Archbishop Davidson at Lambeth Palace on 6 March 1912. The Abbot immediately addressed himself to the "granting of a Provincial License...and the doubt that had risen in the communities about their position in the Anglican Church."[96] For the first time he acknowledged his unlicensed position: "Will you give me now a license under the Colonial Clergy Act for officiating in the province of Canterbury, although I neither hold nor ask for Diocesan accrediting or license, or office."[97] Moreover, Abbot Carlyle sought permission to have a number of his monks ordained, but they would not pledge allegiance to the Established Church in the normal manner.[98] If Davidson granted this request, the Caldey priests would be absolutely free from diocesan supervision and at liberty to deviate from ecclesiastical laws and Anglican practices.[99]

Davidson's sense of diplomacy, however, defused the urgency of Abbot Carlyle's demands and, for the time being, avoided a crisis. Carlyle maintained that the Archbishop "was careful all the way through to avoid expressing any personal opinion, but many times showed himself kindly and well disposed."[100] Davidson admitted that he "was much attracted by him," but did not see his "way clearly yet."[101] Trying to find a solution, the Archbishop contacted the Bishop of Oxford, Charles Gore, and asked how he should deal with Carlyle's petition. Gore replied that the Primate must restrain Abbot Carlyle and bring a halt to the episcopal neglect Caldey had always enjoyed. He told Archbishop Davidson that "the Abbot has been spoilt by his friends and that we must try and get the matters into order."[102] Consequently, Bishop Gore pleaded with the Archbishop to appoint him official Visitor to study and reform Caldey: "if I can be of any use as a visitor, with the ordinary power of an episcopal visitor...I would...act."[103]

On 20 May 1913, Archbishop Davidson informed Abbot Carlyle that he would take no action with respect to his license or the status of the monastery until the community elected an Episcopal Visitor. Davidson recommended Bishop Gore.[104] In August, Carlyle told Davidson that the community would "be glad to welcome the opportunity of electing a Visitor in the person of Bishop Gore," and by this action, Caldey could boast of "a distinct recognition of the authority of the Episcopate."[105] With the Abbot's consent Bishop Gore sent two Anglican priests, Rev. W.H.B. Trevelyan and Darwell Stone, the Principal of Pusey House, to visit Caldey and report back on the spiritual life and doctrine.[106]

Stone and Trevelyan arrived on Caldey Island on 3 January 1913. After talking with the Abbot, reviewing the rules and constitution of the community, and inquiring about the liturgy and devotions of the monastery, they drew up a report for Bishop Gore, which Abbot Carlyle endorsed.[107] The Stone-Trevelyan Report[108] was truthful and objective. It mentioned several points which might require modification, but it did not condemn or judge. The Report singled out the following questionable practices: the feasts of the Immaculate Conception and Assumption, Exposition of the Blessed Sacrament, veneration of relics, eucharistic processions, Benediction, and perpetual Reservation of the Blessed Sacrament. Nevertheless, Stone and Trevelyan gave a positive view of the Caldey community. "The whole conduct of the Services made a very favourable impression on us. We were also favourably impressed with the apparent healthy tone of the community, and the evident care taken in all arrangements." Moreover, they emphasized "that the Community as a whole is wishful to be in close relationship to the Episcopate, and that you [Bishop Gore] should become the Episcopal Visitor."[109]

With typical bluntness, Bishop Gore informed Abbot Carlyle that he could not become Caldey's Visitor unless the Abbot would accept four conditions. According to Gore, the "preliminaries...seem to me to be obvious and to lie outside all possibilities of bargaining and concession, and I do not think it is worth going on until these preliminary points are taken for granted."[110] Gore demanded the following: the property of Caldey to be legally secured to the Church of England;[111] the Book of Common Prayer must be used exclusively; the doctrines of the Immaculate Conception and Assumption must be abandoned; and Benediction, Reservation of the Blessed Sacrament, and the exposition of relics must be curtailed. But this was not all: "I cannot promise that this list is exclusive," Gore informed Abbot Carlyle, "I should have very carefully to attend to a number of details and bear in mind on the one hand the general principle of policy and on the other hand the exceptional position of your Community."[112]

The resolute and uncompromising nature of Bishop Gore's demands shocked Abbot Carlyle. "It seems to me hardly fair to the Community," the Abbot retorted, "to put before them at once what is merely a series of negotiations that 'lie outside all possibilities of bargaining and concession.'"[113] Carlyle tried to have him reconsider his position, but Gore refused. The monks of Caldey, therefore, were faced with a decision: to accept Bishop Gore's demands would mean a surrender of Anglo-Catholic practices which they treasured; to reject would mean Carlyle's status as a clergyman and the relationship of the monastery to the Anglican Church would remain unresolved. Consequently, the majority of monks voted to renounce the Church of England and to seek admission into the Roman Catholic Church.[114] As for Bishop Gore's position, the Abbot believed that "as an Anglican Bishop [he] is perfectly justified in his demands, but to submit would be a denial of catholic principles."[115] Speaking with the authority of the Established Church, Gore wanted to impose "drastic limitations upon our faith." Certain doctrinal beliefs were involved.[116] As members of the universal church, Carlyle argued that "we have no right to be bound by an individual Bishop to his own particular views on matters of doctrine."[117]

The reaction of the Anglican Church to the secession was mixed. Archbishop Davidson wholeheartedly supported Bishop Gore's actions. The Primate told Gore that he did not "demur to what you have done and written...[and] what I have seen strikes me as eminently reasonable and considerate on your part.[118] The Low Church party violently scorned the conversion and criticized the encouragement extended to the Caldey monks by the English episcopacy. A spokesman for the Protestant Alliance scolded Davidson and warned that "the Bishops would do well to clear the Church of such religious orders" whose primary object was to undermine the Church of England.[119] The *Churchman's Magazine* asked "Who'll be the next to follow Caldey," and described the monks as "born of inflated and misconceived ideas, nurtured by traitorous archiepiscopal patronage, and matured in medieval extravagancies."[120] With the exception of Lord Halifax, who was furious with Bishop Gore's rigid demands,[121] the response of the Anglo-Catholic party was mild. Most were sorry to see the monks depart, but also believed that the life on Caldey was irreconcilable with the comprehensiveness of the Established Church. *The Church Times,* for example, regretted the action of the Caldey monks "because it seems to have been taken with a haste which bodes ill for the future of those concerned."[122]

A sense of triumph and pride, on the other hand, characterized the reaction of the Roman Catholics. The *Catholic Times,* which had earlier described Abbot Carlyle as a fraud and hypocrite, called the conversion a "gallant attempt" which exhibited "real moral courage."[123] Influential churchmen such as Aidan Gasquet, the President of the English Benedictines, and Columba Marmion, the renowned Abbot of Maredsous Abbey, expedited Carlyle's entry into the Roman Church. On 29 June 1914 he made his solemn profession as a Benedictine monk at Maredsous Abbey, and on 5 July the Bishop of Namur ordained Carlyle a Roman Catholic priest. In August of the same year, Aelred Carlyle was blessed as Abbot of the convert community.

A different assessment of the conversion, however, appeared in the columns of *The Times*. The article inveighed against the "London clergy [who] were not unwilling that their parishes should become the scene of his [Carlyle's] experiments" and "aged Archbishops [who] gave permission for various purposes about which they would have been more doubtful in the days of their earlier vigour." It ended on a cautious note: "Must the Church be prepared for further losses resulting from this one? The trouble is that there is a large archipelago of Caldeys."[124]

Notes

[1] George Herbert Cook, *Letters to Cromwell and Others on the Suppression of the Monasteries* (London: Baker, 1965); David Knowles, *Christian Monasticism* (New York: McGraw Hill, 1961); *The Monastic Order in England* (Cambridge: Cambridge University, 1904); *The Religious Orders in England* (3 vols.; Cambridge: Cambridge University, 1950); Ernest K. Milliken, *English Monasticism: Yesterday and Today* (London: Harrap, 1967); Joyce Younings, *The Dissolution of the Monasteries* (New York: Barnes and Noble, 1971).

[2] Arthur M. Allchin, *The Silent Rebellion: Anglican Religious Communities, 1845-1900* (London: SCM, 1958); Desmond Bowen, *The Idea of the Victorian Church* (Montreal: McGill University, 1968); S. J. Cumings, *A History of Anglican Liturgy* (New York: St. Martin's, 1969); Alan Maycock, *Chronicles of Little Gidding* (London: SPCK, 1954); *Nicholas Ferrar of Little Gidding* (New York: Macmillan, 1938); A.M. Williams, *Conversations at Little Gidding* (Cambridge: Cambridge University, 1938).

[3] Peter Anson, *The Call of the Cloister: Religious Communities and Kindred Bodies in the Anglican Communion* (London: SPCK, 1964); John Bossy, *The English Catholic Community 1570-1850* (London: Darton, Longman and Todd, 1975); J. Derek Holmes, *More Roman than Rome: English Catholicism in the Nineteenth Century* (London: Burns and Oates, 1970); Ralph Sockman, *The Revival of the Conventual Life in the Church of England in the Nineteenth Century* (New York: W.D.Gray, 1917); Bernard Ward, *The Dawn of the Catholic Revival* (New York: Longmans Green, 1909).

[4] Stanley Ayling, *John Wesley* (London: Collins, 1979); Edward P. Thompson, *The Making of the English Working Class* (New York: Vintage, 1963).

[5] Quoted in H. Liddon, *Life of Edward Bouverie Pusey* (4 vols.; London: Longmans, Green, 1893) 2. 38.

[6] John Henry Newman, *Historical Sketches* (New York: Longmans, Green, 1906) 2. 102. On 25 April 1842, Newman and a group of friends retired to Littlemore, Oxfordshire, to live a quasi-monastic life centered on the Benedictine breviary.

[7] According to Peter Anson, seventy-three convents were established between 1847 and 1914. Twenty-seven died out quickly, but the remainder were still in existence at the outbreak of World War 1. See Anson, *Call of the Cloister*, 595-98. The patronage of influential people (for example, Pusey, Lord John Manners, Gladstone, and Bishop Samuel Wilberforce) all lent respectability to sisterhoods.

[8] See Allchin, *Silent Rebellion*, 139-55.

[9] Parliament (Great Britain), "Report from the Committee on Conventual and Monastic Institutes," *Parliament Papers* (Commons) (1871) vol. 7 *(Reports,* vol. 1). The *Report* concluded: "Members of the Church of England, of the Greek Church, or of any other Church other than the Church of Rome, are perfectly free to make monastic vows, to enroll themselves in communities of a conventual or monastic character..." (p. iii).

[10] *The Chronicle of Convocation, Upper House, 1891* (London: National Society's Depository, 1891) 46-49. The Convocation eventually passed a resolution endorsing brotherhoods bound by vows and working in parishes under the supervision of the vicar. Ibid., 208-9, 235.

[11] Lambeth Conference, "Proceedings on the Religious Communities" (London: Lambeth Palace Library, 1897) LC 38, 161.

[12] *Report of the Royal Commission on Ecclesiastical Discipline* (London: Wyman and Sons, 1906) 62. In 1904, there was a recrudescence of the ritual debate. The English episcopacy

recognized that some sort of action was required. Certain people wanted the appointment of a select committee of the House of Commons to investigate ecclesiastical disorders. But to many churchmen this was unthinkable. Under the leadership of Archbishop Davidson, a compromise was reached: a Royal Commission composed of members of both Houses.

[13] Ibid., 62.

[14] Ibid.

[15] Under the provisions of the Act, a bishop could block a prosecution in his diocese. Consequently, the Act never had the power and force its supporters envisioned. For the background and the working of the Public Worship Regulation Act, see James Bentley, *Ritualism and Politics in Victorian England* (London: Oxford University, 1978).

[16] *The Victorian Church* (London: Black, 1971) Part 2, 325.

[17] *Report of the Royal Commission,* 75-76. On the recommendation of the Commission, the Public Worship Regulation Act was repealed in 1906.

[18] Horton Davies, *Worship and Theology and England. From Newman to Martineau* (Princeton: Princeton University, 1962) 126.

[19] For the life of Abbot Carlyle and the Benedictine revival in the Church of England see Peter Anson, *Abbot Extraordinary* (New York: Sheed and Ward, 1958); *Benedictines of Caldey* (Gloucester: Prinknash Abbey, 1944).

[20] Among them, St. Alban's, Holborn, All Saints, Margaret St., and St. Matthew's, Earl's Court, which were famous London ritualist Anglican churches. Roman Catholic churches on the Continent, especially Namur and Chartres, and the Carmelite Church in Kensington, West London, also impressed him. Carlyle visited the Cistercian monastery of St. Bernard's, Leicester, and also spent a great amount of time at Buckfast Abbey, where he almost converted to Roman Catholicism in 1895.

[21] Aelred Carlyle to Frederick Temple, 24 January 1898 (Caldey: Davidson Papers, London: Lambeth Palace Library).

[22] This religious fraternity was not sanctioned by the parish authorities in Ealing, London. Nor was there any desire on the part of the brotherhood to seek official recognition. It was essentially a lay fellowship composed of idealistic young Anglo-Catholics. See "Notes on the History of the Community," *Pax* (September 1904) 8. *Pax* was the publication of the Caldey monks, and was published by the monks of Prinknash Abbey, where the Caldey community eventually moved in 1928.

[23] Aelred Carlyle, "Constitutions of the Oblate Brothers of the Holy Order of St. Benedict"; "The English Order of St. Benedict: A Sketch" (Carlyle Papers; Cranham, Gloucester: Prinknash Abbey Archives, 1894, 1893). Lacking originality, these rules were based on Roman Catholic monastic writings. Carlyle also acknowledged his indebtedness to S. Fox, *Monks and Monasteries: Being an Account of English Monasteries* (London: James Burns, 1845) and the nineteenth-century French monastic writer, Jean Baptiste Muard.

[24] With a few friends, Carlyle tried unsuccessfully to establish a monastic brotherhood at the following places before a period of stability, 1902-6, at Painsthorpe, Yorkshire: Ealing and the Isle of Dogs, London, Lower Guiting in Gloucestershire, Newton Abbot, and a short stay on Caldey Island in 1902.

[25] *Church Review* (London, 3 February 1898).

[26] *Church Intelligencer* (London, June 1898).

[27] *The Rock* (London, 25 February 1898).

[28] Ibid.

[29] *Church Intelligencer* (March 1898).

[30] *Cheltenham Free Press* (21 May 1898).

[31] *Cheltenham Chronicle* (6 July 1898).

[32] *Cheltenham Free Press* (6 August 1898).

[33] Rev. D. Cowan to F. Temple, 1 June 1897 (Caldey: Davidson Papers).

[34] Carlyle to Rev. J. Green, 15 February 1898 (Carlyle Papers; Slough: Nashdom Abbey Archives).

[35] "Vow Formula," 20 February 1898 (Carlyle Papers; Prinknash Abbey Archives).

[36] The original Charter is either misplaced or lost. Reproductions appeared in "Notes on the History of the Community," *Pax* (March 1905) 81.

[37] Carlyle to Temple, 24 February 1902 (Caldey: Davidson Papers).

[38] Idem, 28 May 1902 (Caldey: Davidson Papers).

[39] Ibid.

[40] Rene M. Kollar, "Abbot Aelred Carlyle and the Monks of Caldey Island: Anglo-Catholicism in the Church of England, 1895-1913" (Ph.D. diss., University of Maryland, 1981) 159-64.

[41] Maclagan to Owen, 6 December 1906 (Caldey: Davidson Papers).

[42] W.R. Shepherd, ed., *The Benedictines of Caldey Island* (Caldey Island: The Abbey, 1906) 32; Halifax to Hill, 31 October 1903 (Halifax Papers; York: The Borthwick Institute).

[43] "Letter Dismissory," Maclagan to Grafton, 26 September 1906 (Carlyle Papers; Prinknash Abbey Archives).

[44] Archbishop Maclagan told Grafton that he would receive Carlyle as a priest in Colonial Orders, but instead issued a provisional license to officiate in York under the provisions of the *1871 Private Chapel's Act,* 34 & 35 Victoria, chap. 66

[45] J. Owen to R. Davidson, 28 December 1911 (Caldey: Davidson Papers).

[46] Ibid.

[47] Owen to Davidson, 29 December 1911 (Caldey: Davidson Papers).

[48] Idem, 28 December 1911 (Caldey: Davidson Papers).

[49] Aelred Carlyle, *Our Purpose and Method* printed in *The Benedictines of Caldey Island,* 67-111.

[50] Aelred Carlyle, "Customary and Ceremonial of the Regular Observance of the Fathers of the English Congregation of the Strict Observance of the Rule of Our Most Holy Father Saint Benedict" (Carlyle Papers; Prinknash Abbey Archives, 1908).

[51] Peter Anson, *A Roving Recluse* (Cork: Mercier, 1946) and *Abbot Extraordinary.* Anson was a monk of Caldey during the Anglican period.

[52] Carlyle to P. Anson, 21 January 1938 (Carlyle Papers; Elgin: Pluscarden Abbey Archives).

[53] Ibid.

[54] Ibid.

[55] Ibid.

[56] Carlyle, *Purpose and Method,* 90.

[57] Aelred Carlyle, "The Monastic Life," *The Holy Cross Magazine* (August 1907) 178.

[58] Carlyle to D. Prideaux, 6 November 1912 (Carlyle Papers; Prinknash Abbey Archives).

[59] Quoted in Anson, *Benedictines of Caldey,* 139.

[60] W. Upson, "Fifty Years Ago," *Pax* (Spring 1963) 1.

[61] Carlyle to Gore, 17 October 1912 (Prinknash Abbey Archives).

[62] F. Claude Kempson, "The Church in England, 1833-1908," *Pax* (March 1908) 433.

[63] "The Ceremonial of Caldey" (Prinknash Abbey Archives). The "Customary and Ceremonial of the Regular Observance" explained in detail the rubrics for Mass at Caldey.

[64] Ibid.

[65] "Community Letter," *Pax* (September 1930) 30.

[66] *The Ceremonial of Caldey* stated: "The Reverend Father Abbot also uses the mitre, the gloves, the dalmatic and tunic, when singing Mass *in pontificalibus* as provided in the Rubrics of the Missal *Ritus servandus in celebratione Missae.*"

[67] Carlyle to Anson, 25 April 1910 (Prinknash Abbey Archives).

[68] *The Church Times,* 25 June 1909.

[69] The author was also impressed with the romantic effects of the liturgy. "As the office [Compline] proceeded the shades of evening became more and more intense; the two candles below the taller ones on the altar were extinguished, and the only light came from the red light suspended before the tabernacle."

[70] *Ordo ad recipiendum et induendum novitium* (Prinknash Abbey Archives).

[71] "The Form of Receiving Monks to Solemn Profession" (Prinknash Abbey Archives).

[72] "The Dedication of the Abbot's Chapel," 8 December 1912 (Prinknash Abbey Archives).

[73] Holy Week services, especially Mass of the Pre-Sanctified, Rogation Days, All Saints and All Souls Days, Veneration of Relics, Mass for the Departed, Festival of St. Peter's Chair and numerous patron feast days. See "Ceremonial of Caldey."

[74] Benediction was given according to the Roman rite on Sundays and Wednesdays. The Blessed Sacrament was in continued Reservation and Exposition took place on high holy days and the monthly day of recollection. See "Ceremonial of Caldey" and "Customary and Ceremonial."

[75] "Ceremonial of Caldey."

[76] Ibid. These were both condemned by the *Report of the Royal Commission,* 41-43.

[77] "Ceremonial of Caldey." The schedule of psalms was contained "in the *commune de tempore* of the Monastic Breviary." Carlyle favored the edition "issued by the House of Descles et Cie of Tournay, finally revised for the use of the Benedictines in the year 1912. All members of the Congregation...are bound to attend the recitation of the Divine Office in choir."

[78] A. Barlay, "The Monastic Breviary," *Pax* (March 1908) 393.

[79] "The Abbey Guest House," *Pax* (September 1910) 45.

[80] "The Guest House," *Pax* (Michaelmas, 1906) 36.

[81] "The Guest House," *Pax* (March 1907) 152.

[82] E. H. Day, "A Day at Caldey," *The Benedictines of Caldey Island,* 5.

[83] *Caldey Abbey Guest Book.* There were few days when there were no guests staying in the monastery's guest house. During the first year, over 225 visitors stayed on Caldey. By August 1908, 139 visitors had registered in the guestbook for the year.

[84] Halifax to Edward, 20 July 1908 (Halifax Papers). Halifax was part of a party consisting of the prominent Anglo-Catholics W.J. Birkbeck, Athelstan Riley, and Sir Samuel Hoare.

[85] Halifax to Agnes, 20 July 1908 (Halifax Papers).

[86] Ibid.

[87] Halifax to Riley, October 1908 (Halifax Papers).

[88] Carlyle to Halifax, 25 July 1908 (Halifax Papers).

[89] Ronald Knox, *Spiritual Aeneid,* (London: Longmans Green, 1918) 80.

[90] Ibid., 80-81.

[91] Ibid., 82. Knox remained in close touch with Caldey during its Anglican period. When he converted in 1917, Abbot Carlyle congratulated him and offered him aid. Carlyle to Knox, 17 September 1917; 25 September 1917 (Mells, Somerset: Knox Papers).

[92] Mackay to Halifax, 10 November 1910 (Halifax Papers).

[93] Day to Halifax, 16 August 1911 (Halifax Papers).

[94] Carlyle to Halifax, 8 December 1911 (Halifax Papers).

[95] Idem, 22 February 1912 (Halifax Papers).

[96] R. Davidson, "Interview at Lambeth, 6 March 1912, with the Abbot of Caldey" (Caldey: Davidson Papers).

[97] Ibid.

[98] These priests would be exempt from the educational requirements, normally a university degree, and the deacon year spent in a parish. Moreover, they would not be required to use the Book of Common Prayer, and Abbot Carlyle would become their ecclesiastical superior, not the Bishop of St. David's.

[99] Davidson to Gore, 7 March 1912 (Caldey: Davidson Papers).

[100] Carlyle, "Original Interview Notes" (Carlyle Papers; Prinknash Abbey Archives).

[101] Davidson to Gore, 7 March 1912.

[102] Gore to Davidson, l0 April 1912 (Caldey: Davidson Papers).

[103] Gore to Davidson, 19 March 1912 (Caldey: Davidson Papers). In spite of the recommendations of the 1887 Lambeth Conference's report on religious brotherhoods, Caldey had no Episcopal Visitor.

[104] Davidson to Carlyle, 20 May 1912 (Carlyle Papers; Prinknash Abbey Archives).

[105] Carlyle to Davidson, 29 August 1912 (Carlyle Papers; Prinknash Abbey Archives).

[106] Gore to Carlyle, 24 October 1912 (Carlyle Papers; Prinknash Abbey Archives). Carlyle had hoped that Gore would personally visit Caldey, but the Bishop's busy schedule would not permit this plan. Both priests, who were Anglo-Catholics, knew Carlyle and were sympathetic to the Anglican Benedictines.

[107] Carlyle to Stone, 9 January 1913 (Carlyle Papers; Prinknash Abbey Archives).

[108] Stone and Trevelyan to Gore, 21 January 1913 (Stone Papers; Oxford: Pusey House Library).

[109] Ibid.

[110] Gore to Carlyle, 8 February 1913 (Carlyle Papers; Prinknash Abbey Archives).

[111] The ownership of the property was vested in Abbot Carlyle alone. The three established Anglican brotherhoods, the Cowley Fathers, the Society of the Resurrection, and the Society of the Sacred Mission, had legislated that their property would be vested in a trust under the supervision of the Anglican Church. The Established Church always tried to regulate and oversee the property owned by religious brotherhoods. The 1908 Lambeth Conference report on brotherhoods stressed that "provision for due rules as to the possession and disposition of property" should be stipulated in the community's by-laws. "Report of the Committee Appointed in 1897 to Consider the Relations of Religious Communities within the Church to the Episcopate" (Lambeth Conference, 1908) 5.

[112] Gore to Carlyle, 8 February 1913.

[113] Carlyle to Gore, 11 February 1913 (Carlyle Papers: Prinknash Abbey Archives).
[114] Including Abbot Carlyle, there were thirty-one monks on Caldey in 1913. Three Anglican priests did not convert. Denys Prideaux, one of the "faithful remnant," became the founder of a new Anglican monastery at Pershore. The community later moved to Nashdom, Slough.

[115] Carlyle, "Questionnaire," 18 February 1913 (Carlyle Papers; Prinknash Abbey Archives).

[116] Carlyle, "Notes of the Address to the Community of Caldey," 18 February 1913 (Carlyle Papers; Prinknash Abbey Archives).

[117] Carlyle, "Questionnaire."

[118] Davidson to Gore, 24 February 1913 (Caldey: Davidson Papers).

[119] Fowler to Davidson, 11 March 1913 (Caldey: Davidson Papers).

[120] "Home—At Last," *Churchman's Magazine* (April 1913) 110.

[121] *The Church Times* (7 March 1913).

[122] *The ChurchTimes* (28 February 1913).

[123] *Catholic Times* (28 February 1913). During the summer of 1905, the *Catholic Times* printed a series of articles attacking Carlyle's brotherhood. The Anglican monks, according to one report, were guilty of "spreading heresy and error in England, and propagating that last new sect, Catholicism without Rome" *(Catholic Times* [28 July 1905]).

[124] *The Times* (17 March 1913).

CHAPTER VI

RITUALISM IN A GLOUCESTERSHIRE VILLAGE: ANGLICAN MONKS, CLERGYMEN, AND THE PARISHIONERS OF LOWER GUITING

During the last half of the nineteenth century, questionable liturgical actions on the part of some Anglican clergymen and the attempts of some dedicated members of the Church of England to stifle these practices at times resulted in violence and riots. These ecclesiastical comic operas are usually associated with the famous urban parishes and their equally noteworthy clerics. London produced some of the most celebrated cases in this aspect of English ecclesiastical life. Mackonochie, Stanton and Lowder, to name a few, have been venerated as saints by those who welcomed their liturgical innovations. Others saw them as clerical hooligans and outlaws who deserved to be disciplined by their church superiors. St. Alban's, Holborn, and St. Peter's, London Docks, became shibboleths for those Anglicans who appreciated the beauty and significance of elaborate liturgies.

Ritualism, obviously, did not confine itself to the environs of London; Plymouth, Brighton and Leeds also boasted of their ritual priests and churches where elaborate worship took place. The Disraeli government tried to curb the enthusiasm of the ritualists with the force of a parliamentary statute, but the so-called Bishop's Veto, which gave power to the local bishop to override a charge of liturgical irregularity brought against a cleric by a layman, neutralized the force of the 1874 Public Worship Regulation Act. Consequently, some zealous people tried to take church law into their own hands. Outraged individuals and groups sought out parishes which tolerated departures from traditional Protestant formularies. City, borough or village became targets, and no part of the country was spared. Alleged popish practices even attracted an itinerant preacher to the small Gloucestershire parish of Lower Guiting in western England.[1]

Anglican priests accused of introducing practices outlawed by the Reformation and subsequent legislation usually became the target of hatred and attacks. Benjamin Fearnley Carlyle, an unordained and idealistic youth, hardly appeared to be the material that would attract the attention and then scorn of some Anglicans. Yet some Anglicans sensed that he wanted to advance the cause of popery within their church, and eventually they took action against this threat. Born in 1874, Carlyle soon became captivated by the glories of Roman Catholic Benedictine Monasticism through books such as the Rev. Samuel Fox's romantic piece of literature, *Monks and Monasteries,* and visits to Buckfast Abbey, a Roman Catholic monastery in Devon.[2] In 1893, he established a small and short-lived fraternity based on Benedictine principles, and adopted the name "Aelred" as a sign of this youthful commitment to the monastic life. After a bout with "Roman fever" in 1896, he decided to remain in the Anglican Church, and began an affiliation with the Anglican nuns of West Malling, Kent, as a novice. During the same year, he founded a rescue home for boys on the Isle of Dogs in London's East End. His work among the poor lads of the capital's slums certainly did not threaten the spiritual fabric of the Anglican Church, but he did not escape criticism from a local paper. "When the mask of unreality was torn away from the ideal," The *Cubitt Town Protestant Banner* told its readers, the monk "settles down into a concrete agnostic or atheist."[3] And events soon developed which cast Carlyle as a dangerous character in the eyes of some Anglicans.

Aelred Carlyle's close association with another Church of England cleric, who had already been marked as a ritualist, damaged his reputation. In September 1897, the Rev. J. Green,[4] a clergyman who had held the livings of Farmcot and Lower Guiting in Gloucestershire since 1895, wrote to Carlyle and offered him the facilities of the Lower Guiting parish as home for his brotherhood. Green wanted to establish a religious fraternity there, "not an adaptation of the old monastic life, but the old life as we have it set out in the Rule of St. Benedict."[5] For some time he had been searching for the time and place to set up a brotherhood "to train men to work 'homes' [for youth], and this as religious."[6] Carlyle responded enthusiastically to Green's letter and emphasized that "our work here [the Isle of Dogs] lies chiefly among such boys as you are interested in, and I have been longing for two years past for some organization as yours where some of our poor lads might be sent."[7] He also agreed with Green's emphasis on the conventual or religious life: "the monastic system...is indeed the great solution to many social problems."

After a meeting with Green in London, Carlyle accepted the invitation to move and, on September 23rd, he decided to leave the Isle of Dogs "to staff a community in Lower Guiting."[8] Carlyle could not leave London immediately, so he suggested to Green that the Rev. Herbert Drake,[9] then living with Carlyle, should go to Lower Guiting immediately to conduct the Sunday services for the parish. Two associates would accompany Drake to prepare the vicarage for the new monastic quarters.[10] Everything appeared to go smoothly: Drake would act as the new curate; and the Rev. Green agreed to supply food and money for the new monastery. Two other Anglican priests even expressed interest about joining the new brotherhood.[11] The Rev. Drake and two interested candidates arrived at Lower Guiting in early October. Aelred Carlyle appointed Drake as the superior of this so-called Monastery of St. Bernard, but for the time being Carlyle still continued to direct the operations of the new foundation from his base in London.

Some critics, however, believed Herbert Drake's ritualism and alleged Romeward tendencies posed a serious threat to the integrity of the Anglican Church. The Church Association, for example, included him on a list of suspect clergymen whom it believed disregarded ecclesiastical law and worked to introduce popish practices into Anglican liturgies.[12] Drake held membership in the English Church Union and the Confraternity of the Blessed Sacrament, two ritualist societies.[13] But his association with the clergy-dominated Society of the Sacred Cross, which advocated the adoption of some Roman devotions, corporate reunion with Rome, and auricular confession, was more damning. *The Secret History of the Oxford Movement* described the SSC as "...one of the most dangerous of these organizations...[and] the most advanced ritualistic doctrines are taught."[14] *The Disruption of the Church of England,* an expose of ritualism and ritualist clerics, claimed that it represented "the oldest and most mischievous of the ritualist organizations..."[15] According to the Church Association, "its main object is to undo the glorious work of the Reformation."[16]

Carlyle's objective, namely, the establishment of a brotherhood on lines similar to the monastic system, tended to offend the sensitivity of some Anglicans. His tone was militant. "I wish each man to be a law unto himself, keeping his own rule and being responsible to me alone for it," Carlyle told his benefactor, the Rev. J. Green, and "each man will tell me himself how the rule has been kept."[17] The words of Aelred Carlyle shocked some who fought to maintain the purity of the Protestant character of their church which had eliminated monasticism during the Reformation. According to Carlyle: "Our object is to lead the strict religious life and to train men for rescue work, living quietly and unostentatiously, doing well the daily work that God gives us to do." "I must be absolutely true and unswerving to my first principle," he wrote, "that we came into the country to build up a strong community, quite apart from work of any kind at present."[18] He emphasized the non-clerical character of the brotherhood and also minimized any educational requirements for membership since "such restrictions would narrow and weaken our work." But would his new village home and the local bishop welcome the brotherhood and tolerate its activities?

According to Peter Anson, Carlyle's biographer, "Lower Guiting was some three miles distant from Notgrove, the nearest station on the branch line from Kingham to Cheltenham."[19] The Bishop of Gloucester, Charles John Ellicott (1819-1905), was anxious to get a priest to serve the spiritual needs of the parish on a permanent basis. Drake, Carlyle, and the small group of Anglican monks might meet this need. Ellicott later told the members of Lower Guiting that "the cares of this parish have been to me very great indeed and that for a long time."[20] He also expressed his concern over the dilapidated physical condition of the church: "I remember, even in the early days...being anxious as to the neglected state of the parish." Some members of the diocese, however, believed that their bishop was too lenient about liturgical innovators. A number of prominent laymen, for example, later published an open letter to Bishop Ellicott proclaiming their "devotion to the Church of England as Catholic, but yet Protestant against the errors and corruptions of the Roman Communion."[21] The supporters of this petition demanded loyalty to the Book of Common Prayer, a "dignified simplicity of ritual" to distinguish "our Reformed Church from that of Rome," and a strong condemnation of habitual auricular confession "as tending to revive some of the most dangerous abuses of the medieval church." In short, this letter alleged that Ellicott did not take his office of bishop seriously; these Anglicans believed that episcopal leniency took preference over lawful uniformity.

While still in London, Carlyle sensed that problems might develop, and urged caution and restraint. He stressed the need for secrecy to the Rev. J. Green, and decreed that no member of the parish "should come into the enclosure except with Green's permission; and then only to talk about enclosure work."[22] Carlyle also warned about the dangers of ritual experiments: "It is quite wrong that anything should be done by him [the Rev. Herbert Drake] in church to cause an appeal to the Bishop."[23] "How can our work prosper if we reach an episcopal climax within the first few weeks." Despite this prudent and cautious approach, another incident brought the brotherhood notoriety, associated it closely with Roman Catholic practices, and destroyed its anonymity. In February 1898, before

Carlyle arrived in Lower Guiting, a close friend and member of the monastic fraternity, Alfred Northbrook Rose, had been convicted of a felony. And the Protestant press gleefully portrayed Carlyle as a Romanizer and associated his followers with crime.

Rose, also known as Brother Oswald, was found guilty at the Sussex Assize on 14th February, the charge being the theft of valuable books. But this was no ordinary criminal procedure: "behind this simple charge there lurked a bitter ecclesiastical feud...one of the bitterest pieces of religious persecution heard for many years."[24] Sir Edward Marshall Hall, Rose's defense, argued that the Rev. Herbert Drake and Aelred Carlyle brought the charges to punish Rose for selling incriminating evidence to the Church Association.[25] Drake and Carlyle alleged that Rose stole a number of priceless books from Canon C. Deedes of Brighton, and then stored them at the Lower Guiting monastery. In December 1897, Drake broke into Rose's quarters to search for the books, but also found evidence that Rose had sold information concerning the Society of the Sacred Cross, its membership roster, and the minutes of its September meeting. Canon Deedes did instruct his solicitor to bring the charges against Rose, but the press coverage of the trial emphasized the religious and not the legal aspects of the case. The *Westminister Gazette,* for example, ran a story under the heading, "A Monk in Court," and described the religious garb that Carlyle wore in the courtroom.[26] The *Church Review* told its readers that there was more at stake than a question of theft, and questioned the legality of Carlyle's monastic brotherhood: "It is news to me that there are monks in the Church of England,"[27] Other stories also emphasized the monastic aspect.[28]

The court eventually found Rose guilty and sentenced him to three years imprisonment, a harsh punishment, but the allegations and publicity, especially from the Protestant papers, did not stop. Carlyle and his Anglican monks made good news. The *Church Intelligencer* launched a violent attack against Carlyle. The March edition questioned the loyalty of these monks to the Anglican Church. "Can any imagination, however vivid, picture a more complete portrayal of the Church of England...servilely copying the peculiarities of the Roman Church, turning their parsonages into 'cells' for the reception of sham monks."[29] Another article in the same edition pointed out that "there are Church of England persons who crave after the base abuses of Rome...[and are] seeking to reproduce the asceticism and false idea of medieval Christianity."[30] The author described Aelred Carlyle as a "masquerading superior," the brotherhood as "sham Benedictines," and the members as "Ecclesiastical Fenians."

The strongest statements came from *The Rock,* which told its readers that the Rose trial illustrated that "there is a deliberate and persistent attempt...to make monasticism, with all its revolting self-torture, unscriptural and unnatural regulations...a recognized portion of the English Church."[31] "We feel convinced that if the British nation thoroughly realized what was going on it would raise such a storm of indignation that the unclean system would be swept out of the church." Religious communities such as Carlyle's were "unEnglish, sneaking societies" which sought to "destroy the manly frankness of the British character." Finally, both the Protestant Truth Society and the Church Association attacked the outcome of the trial and snickered at the Anglican monks of Lower Guiting.[32] Carlyle and his monastic dreams, therefore, had become suspect, and some believed threatened the integrity and spiritual health of the Anglican Church.

The court trial and the reports about his Anglican monks brought Carlyle some limited and local attention, but his association with the Archbishop of Canterbury marked him as a person who rightly deserved the attention of churchmen and laity who wanted to protect the church against Roman infections. In June 1897, Aelred Carlyle wrote to Archbishop Frederick Temple, and petitioned the primate to sanction his solemn or permanent vows as an Anglican Benedictine monk. Temple chose not to reply immediately, but the young Carlyle persisted. Eventually on 11th February 1898, two days after the conclusion of the Rose trial, Carlyle finally had an interview with Archbishop Temple at Lambeth Palace. According to Carlyle's notes, the Archbishop withheld authorization for his Lower Guiting community for the time being, but did approve Carlyle's petition for vows. "His Grace has given me his sanction and blessing and a special authorization for my profession as a Benedictine," Carlyle wrote to the Rev. J. Green.[33] On 20th February, Carlyle, the Rev. Herbert Drake and another member of the community pronounced vows of stability, conversion and obedience in the presence of the Benedictine nuns and their chaplain at the West Malling convent. This ceremony remained secret for only a short time.

This connection between the new Anglican Benedictines and the Archbishop of Canterbury did not escape the attention of the Church Association, which had just recently pounced on some incriminating statements made by Carlyle at the Rose trial. On 3rd March 1898, the Secretary of the Church Association wrote to Archbishop Temple and asked him to comment on any relationship between himself and Carlyle's monastic brotherhood, especially drawing attention to a remark made by Carlyle that "he was in correspondence with Your Grace with a view to obtaining [the] sanction of your office for the restoration within the Church of England of the monastic order of St. Benedict."[34] The Secretary requested that Temple refute "any intention to act independently...or to incur the responsibility of initiating afresh" any form of conventual life in the Anglican Church. The Archbishop acknowledged this letter, but did not answer the questions. Another one was sent to Lambeth Palace from the office of the Church Association, and again Archbishop Temple chose not to respond. The frustrated Secretary wrote a final letter which expressed the position of the Church Association: "it is evident that the allegation publicly made by Mr. Carlyle that you were in treaty with him for the establishment under your supervision, of a monastic establishment, must be substantially true."[35] This exchange of letters corresponded with the arrival of Aelred Carlyle at St. Bernard's Monastery, Lower Guiting, during the last week of February 1898. By this time, however, some Anglicans saw him as a Roman sympathizer and a traitor to the Anglican Church.

The small community progressed quietly during the next two months. Questions concerning the physical health of the membership, which now numbered three, concerns about food and fuel, and everyday economic problems occupied the time of these Anglican monks. Carlyle's primary objective, however, was to avoid attention and publicity and to receive the blessing and support of Bishop Charles Ellicott. The Rev. Drake, known to the immediate group as Brother Anselm, had already received the episcopal license to officiate at the church services. In spite of this token of approval, Bishop Ellicott continued to take a cautious approach to the existence of the brotherhood within his diocese. "It was the Bishop's expressed wish, that they should not take part in parish matters. They have their life to live and their work apart from the parish."[36] But Carlyle could not escape his recent past, and the allegations of ritualism and Roman Catholic practices soon destroyed the quiet of the Cotswolds.

Soon after Carlyle arrived in Lower Guiting, the Protestant press attacked the honesty and integrity of the small monastic fraternity. In March, the *Church Intelligencer* ran an expose on so-called secret societies within the Church of England, "...which are bent on the restoration of the doctrines and practices which our forefathers designated as 'Popery.'"[37] "The revival of monkery means to bring back the sham 'poverty,' which heaped up wealth and worldly and political power." "Then 'chastity,'" it continued, "was a by-word and a mockery to the worldly, while it proved a snare and an artificial occasion of sin to others." "Their 'obedience'...was a rejection of the natural duties assigned by Providence and the substitution of bondage to a fellow sinner whose behests must be fulfilled..." This article drew attention to Carlyle's monastic foundation at Lower Guiting. It mentioned his correspondence with the Archbishop of

Canterbury concerning monastic vows, questioned the motives behind
Carlyle's intentions in the Rose trial, and argued that the papal banner
already flew over Lower Guiting.

> Here are clergymen already under solemn vows to teach
> the religion of the Thirty-nine Articles, turning their
> parsonages into "cells" for the reception of sham monks,
> and we might add, closing the Sunday School, and
> erecting confessionals without any faculty, though we
> are thankful to add, the villagers at Lower Guiting stay
> away from their Parish Church now that it is trans-
> formed into a Mass-House.

Angry words in the columns of a London paper might not incite any
demonstrations or violence against these monks, but suspicious monks
tinkering with the worship and life of this Gloucestershire parish did bring
hostile threats and mob action.

On his own authority, the Rev. Drake convened the annual parish
vestry meeting on Easter Monday 1898. In the chair, Drake announced that
the vicar, the Rev. J. Green, "had been forbidden to attend by his medical
advisors, and has appointed him, being assistant curate, to act as his
deputy."[38] He then proceeded to ask for nominations to the office of parish
warden. But some parishioners began to question the legality of this
meeting. Could Drake, acting independently of the vestry, convene such
a meeting? One member of the vestry unsuccessfully suggested that the
meeting adjourn. According to a local press account, "at this point two
persons present who had evidently had some refreshment, created a slight
disturbance, but as they and a few friends shortly after left the meeting,
business was concluded with harmony and dispatch."[39] This routine
meeting, consequently, divided the parish into two hostile camps of
Christians.

One disgruntled element took its arguments to the local press, and a
letter soon appeared which questioned the legal status of those recently
elected at the vestry meeting. "Among the thirteen paladins, was there a
rate-payer found? How many were householders? None, we believe, were
Communicants. Some of them are more regular at the Baptist chapel than
at the church."[40] The same letter mentioned the lack of decorum and
proper manners at the past Easter Sunday service. The Rev. Drake, the
writer alleged, had to shoulder the blame. Moreover, the numbers of the
congregation had decreased and Drake had only one candidate for Confir-
mation, yet nine members of the parish approached the rector of nearby

Nauton to prepare them for the sacrament. Concerning the tenor of devotions, "the Vicar's action in re-opening the dilapidated chancel certainly savours very much of spitefulness." Finally, this missive stated that the Rev. Drake did not possess a license from Bishop Ellicott. Defending Drake's actions, a member of the parish replied in a sarcastic and arrogant manner, but failed to answer adequately the charges of impropriety.[41]

Events then took a sudden and unexpected turn, and the centre of attention moved to the diocesan level. Archdeacon Hayward refused to admit to office the recently elected churchwardens. The press gave two reasons for this drastic action: "that the vestry meeting was not legally called"; and "that the newly-elected churchwardens are not parishioners."[42] The point of law rested on the fact that the questionable meeting was not summoned by the vicar, the Rev. J. Green, and the official announcement failed to include the signatures of the two current churchwardens. Another article in the same edition of the *Cheltenham Free Press* re-told the facts surrounding the vestry meeting, noted the actions of the Archdeacon, and also told its readers that "the anti-vicar party were not to enjoy their triumph without a bid for mastery from the other side." Drake and the new churchwardens had sent a letter to Bishop Ellicott protesting the decision of the Archdeacon: "And we submit that the sad action is illegal, inasmuch as the Archdeacon's Court is ministerial and not judicial, as is clear from the fact that the Archdeacon's admission, though necessary, is not sufficient to make the Churchwarden's position clear."[43]

The life and career of the Rev. Herbert Drake, referred to by his monastic name of Father Anselm in the columns of the newspapers, did not escape attention. A brief outline of his priestly biography appeared, but some other dubious aspects also caught the readers' eyes. One article reported that he did not possess the episcopal license, "and the reason that no license was issued was that his stay at Guiting was expected to be of very short duration." The press also commented on his association with the monastic brotherhood. Drake, it reported, "took up residence at the Lower Guiting Monastery of 'The Order of St. Benedict, of the Primitive Observance of the Church of England.'" "This celibate brotherhood," the article continued, "conform [sic] to the three fold vows of 'poverty, chastity and obedience.'" But the same edition also made a startling revelation. Drake had suddenly resigned his parochial duties at Lower Guiting "to undertake similar work" at neighbouring Stroud, "his period of office commencing on the 24th of last month."

The following week Drake confirmed this report in a letter to the press. According to his statement, Bishop Ellicott "desired me to cease officiating there" once it became public knowledge that he was a member of Carlyle's monastic brotherhood.[44] The question of the episcopal license was solved by the Rev. Drake himself: "the Bishop of Gloucester had withdrawn his license without giving any reason." But, he claimed, many of the Lower Guiting parishioners supported his "High Church service...[and] would be most unwilling to return to the former state of things." Drake ended his explanation with a defense of the monastic life and a challenge. "It is almost too late at this time of day to attempt to discredit those who wish to live the religious life—or an Order which, like ours, has worked for more than 40 years under the approval of the highest authorities in our beloved Church of England." Drake, however, continued to live at the parish vicarage with the other Anglican monks.

The Rev. Drake's removal did not calm the waters at Lower Guiting. On 7th May, the living was sequestered. The immediate cause for this action stemmed from the now famous vestry meeting. This action by diocesan officials also prompted the vicar, the Rev. J. Green, to give his views on the subject of that meeting. Green maintained that he could summon a vestry meeting on his authority without obtaining the signature of the churchwardens. Moreover, he announced that if the Archdeacon continued not to sanction the election of the new churchwardens, he would carry on without them. But this did not change the minds of diocesan officials. "The sequestration of living was posted on Saturday week, the reason given being that £154. 18s. 6d., due for repairs to the church at the time Dr. Green was inducted have not been paid to the Governors of Queen Anne's Bounty, as ordered."[45] Legally, all parish matters were now conducted by the old churchwardens, who quickly flexed their ecclesiastical muscle by not providing wine for the Sunday service scheduled to be conducted by the Rev. Green. "It is hardly to be wondered at that such events had a disastrous effect," a local paper added.[46] A disputed vestry meeting and a sequestration divided the parish at Lower Guiting, but accusations of illegal and hated Roman Catholic practices nearly destroyed it.

Carlyle's flaunting of Benedictine monasticism, the existence of a so-called Anglican monastery, and the allegations of ritualism against Drake, Green and the monks stoked the fires of religious passion. A local paper succinctly captured this mood: "since the arrival of the Rev. Green (1895)...there has been constant friction between him and the parishioners on account of the ritualistic practices which are alleged against him."[47] Letters to the press accused him of "teaching 'Transubstantiation,'...[and] that he holds that prayer is for the priest to offer as mediator, and not for the sinner."[48] "For this reason, and in order to carry out the legal obligation, he 'gabbles' through the Morning or Evening Prayer at such a rate as to be unintelligible." Other offenses during the recent Holy Week included: "Mass" twice on Palm Sunday and Easter Sunday, auricular confession, a Good Friday "Meditation preceded by Quiet time, and coloured vestments." The physical condition and upkeep of the church also invited some criticism. The *Cheltenham Free Press* sent a reporter to visit Lower Guiting and he sadly wrote about the ruinous state of the church building. "Entering the wicket of the churchyard, an air of unkemptness and desolation is at once felt," he pointed out, and the "gravestones are in a more than usually battered condition."[49] "Grass and weeds grow unchecked..." He also noted the horrific condition of the chancel, broken glass and holes in the roof. "This May afternoon numbers of sparrows and starlings are busy flying in and out of the gaps, carrying earth-worms and other delicacies to their families within the chancel."

He also detected evidence of ritual irregularities: "the smell of earth predominates with a suspicion of incense"; and "...upon a peg, two embroidered surplices of the kind used by the acolytes of the Roman Catholic service." The newspaper quickly connected these alleged popish practices with Carlyle's brotherhood. The questionable surplices "were worn by two of the brothers, while the harmonium was played by 'Superior Carlyle'...him with shaven head." During the next several weeks, the press continued to repeat the accusations of ritual practices. The familiar story of the vestry meeting and the action of the Archdeacon again found their way into print. Some defended the actions of the Vicar; others roundly condemned the Rev. J. Green and the presence of the Anglican monks. Archbishop Frederick Temple's relationship with the monks also became public knowledge to the villagers; Temple's friendship with Carlyle had already become public knowledge among members of the Church Association.

The *Cheltenham Free Press* printed two letters of protest to the Archbishop of Canterbury from the angry chairman of the Church Association about Temple's association with the monastery. In the first, the chairman reminded Archbishop Temple of Carlyle's statement at the Rose trial when he stated that "he was in correspondence with your Grace with a view of obtaining the sanction of your office for the restoration within the Church of England of the monastic Order of St. Benedict..."[50] The chairman asked Temple to reply to the charge that he supported the introduction of Benedictine monasticism in the Church of England.[51] The letter ended by reminding the Primate that "the revival of monasticism is a matter which deeply concerns the whole Church, and the world-wide experience of its baneful influence...may well excite alarm and distrust."

The Archbishop's terse reply, also printed in the press, merely acknowledged this letter and did not answer the chairman's queries.[52] After another missive asking for "some explicit statement" to calm the anxieties of those loyal churchmen who fear that Lambeth Palace has identified itself with "such a retrograde movement as the re-introduction of monasticism into the Church of England,"[53] Archbishop Temple again chose not to respond. The chairman of the Church Association again replied in print and criticized the fact that Temple had not answered his questions and drew the conclusion that "you were in treaty with him [Carlyle] for the establishment, under your supervision, of a monastic establishment, must be taken as substantially accurate."[54] He ended with a protest against archiepiscopal indifference: "I can...very earnestly protest against the growing habit of bishops taking upon themselves...to alter institutions and traditions of the Established Church, and deplore the fact that your Grace is ready to fasten on our poor betrayed Church evils which from the Reformation at its very outset set us free."

Although the Bishop of Gloucester exerted a heavy hand through the instrument of sequestration and the withdrawal of the Rev. Drake's license, his apparent indifference to the decorum of the Sunday services helped to compound the troubles at Lower Guiting. A large majority of parishioners began to boycott the liturgy. In early June, for example, the Sunday attendance had decreased dramatically. Only eight worshippers, including the vicar and sexton, attended the 10:00 am service.[55] On the following week, the vicar, sexton, one churchwarden, three villagers and three monks attended the early service, and an "unusually good attendance" of thirty-five people attended the afternoon service.[56] The 2nd July edition of a local paper again commented on the dismal showing at Sunday worship,[57] and suggested that ritualism and Roman practices kept the people away from their parish church. One eyewitness commented on the "unleavened wafer and about a teaspoon of a colourless fluid, which smelt and tasted precisely like bad whiskey and water."[58] Moreover, "the chalice was elevated and the monks prostrate before the table." Another angry person wrote a letter to the newspaper which pointed out "that the usual legal vestments for the Holy Communion were not worn at this service..." And another parishioner revealed that he "brought away with me the unleavened wafer, and if that is a sample of ordinary bakers' bread, I should recommend the inhabitants of Lower Guiting to change their baker."

Lower Guiting could not survive this adverse publicity. On 2nd July, a so-called Protestant Van rolled into the village to restore order in the parish. "The disturbances, which appear unavoidable while the present vicar [the Rev. J. Green] holds office, have been renewed this week, when a van belonging to the Church Association and the National Protestant League pitched on the village green."[59] "The *raison d'être* of the crusade," the report continued, "is to carry war into those communities affected by the tendency to Romish ritual apparent in so many quarters of the English Church." Describing his arrival at Lower Guiting nearly six months later, Samuel Bradfield remembered that his van, christened the Hooper Protestant Van, "happened to be placed right near the monastery gate."[60]

Almost immediately, the Rev. J. Green and the Rev. Herbert Drake came out and invited the itinerant lecturer into the makeshift monastery for tea, and he accepted. In the evening, Bradfield gave an "interesting address on Romanism and Ritualism"[61] to a crowd, estimated at 500, which "came out to hear and to show their sympathy with the cause of Protestantism."[62] And Drake tried to express his point of view to this assembly "...from the monastery wall adjoining, but was prevented by interruptions of a verbal nature and even of a more forcible kind."[63] "They did not come to 'apostolic blows and knocks,' but let their pastor understand that...his doctrines were unorthodox, by throwing eggs destined neither to be eaten nor to produce chicken, but simply to exhale a most disagreeable odour."[64] Shouts and jeers also accompanied this protest, "and the parties nearly came to blows."[65] This verbal duel lasted until after midnight, and one of the local papers captured the spirit behind this raucous display: "It is evident that whatever success may have attended the introduction of Ritualism into some of our villages, the people of Lower Guiting will not have it at any price...[and] as they cannot have the old-fashioned Protestant service, they are staying away from the church altogether."[66] On a humourous note, the same story also commented on "the prominent part which eggs of this character have always taken in English controversy, both theological and political."

On the following day, a reporter from the *Cheltenham Chronicle* went to Lower Guiting to interview both parties. Green and the monks declared that they wanted only to welcome "the missioner and express their approval of his work."[67] Some of the villagers, however, told the reporter that the Rev. Green and his liturgical antics were the reason for the van's presence. In the evening, Bradfield gave another address dealing with absolution and confession "as practiced in the Church of Rome and sought to be made universal in the Church of England by 'traitors to their church.'" He also denounced other popish ritual practices. Making reference to his visit to the church on Sunday, third July, the preacher mocked the habit of .".. the communicants putting out their tongue...and Mr. Green (the Vicar) putting the wafer (not bread) on them."[68] When he approached the communion table, Green "brought me a thin bit of something that did not look like bread, and I refused to take it." Voices from the crowd that evening claimed that Green had spoken in favour of confession from his pulpit, and others snickered and made caustic remarks about Drake's monastic practices. It appeared that the mood might turn ugly. The frequent references "to the vicar and the monks caused the crowd to involuntarily turn their eyes towards the monastery gate; but the monks, after their experience of the previous night, evidently thought discretion the better part of valour, and did not show themselves..."[69]

The Bishop Hooper Van, therefore, succeeded in stirring up and agitating the people of Lower Guiting and, for the time being, left the village.[70] For the next two weeks the discontent smouldered, but did not die out. The people of Lower Guiting continued "to resent more strongly than ever the Romanizing elements which these people [Green, Drake and the monks] are endeavouring to introduce into the church and village."[71] And some villagers were not content with angry words. Hooligans broke a window in the monastery building and also destroyed parts of the wall surrounding it. Some threatened the three ritualists with bodily harm, and when Drake appeared in public he was often greeted with cries of "Quack."[72]

Yet the emphasis of the liturgy did not change; the services at Lower Guiting remained so Roman that Samuel Bradfield and the Bishop Hooper Van made a return visit in late July. Bradfield attended the 8:00 am communion service on Sunday, 23rd July, and a number of things that he noticed ran contrary to the letter and spirit of the Book of Common Prayer. "Surrounded by three or four monks and three female communicants," the Rev. Green, who was "clad in a red or scarlet garment with a large cross on his back," mumbled his way through the service.[73] "A bell was rung during the consecration of the Bread and Wine. Water was mixed with the wine. Many times he made the sign of the cross and adored the elements." Bradfield also reported that "he went to the table and saw him putting the wafer on the tongue of a monk who knelt next to me..."

Persistence finally triumphed. During the last week of July, the Rev. J.E. Green departed from Lower Guiting, and "there were no signs of mourning in the village at Dr. Green's removal..."[74] His father, the Rev. J.E. Green from Stroud, performed the services on Sunday and also expressed his disapproval over his son's care of the church and the presence of the Anglican monks. The Hooper Van remained and continued to preach on the village green, "there being an assembly of about 200 persons to hear them last Sunday." With the offending vicar gone, only the monks had to be vanquished. When a reporter sought out the remaining monks for comment, he described their demeanour "as air that a school-boy might have called 'cocky' in the extreme." They refused to comment, but their days at Lower Guiting were quickly drawing to a close. On sixth August, the *Cheltenham Free Press* gleefully announced: "the end has come...no longer is there a 'Monastery of St. Benedict' at Lower Guiting."[75] Empty packing crates outside the monastery had hinted at a departure for over a fortnight. Watched over by the police who expected some trouble, the villagers assembled, "and accordingly a supply of catcalls, whistles and other instruments of music (?) were collected and put into use, probably to the...annoyance of the rest of the place than of the vicarage..." According to one report, "...the villagers made their removal an occasion for public rejoicing, and on Thursday evening the village green was thronged with a joyful crowd, who feasted and held high revelry."[76]

Shortly after their departure, the Bishop of Gloucester, Charles Ellicott visited Lower Guiting and tried to heal the wounds and division. On Sunday, 14th August, he preached to the parish. The bishop confessed that he had tried to meet the spiritual needs of Lower Guiting and had appointed clerics whom he trusted to fulfill this charge. But for numerous reasons, his choices had failed in their spiritual tasks. Bishop Ellicott apologized: "That I have sympathized with you very deeply my presence here will show. An old man, now eighty years of age, had come amongst you to express, by his presence and words, how thoroughly I sympathized with you in the past."[77] Ellicott promised clerical help and the necessary funds to repair the church: "so that the first work to be done is to make it possible for Holy Communion to be administered."

The Rev. Herbert Drake and the Rev. J. Green, the two clerics who drew the wrath of suspicious Anglicans because of their popish rituals, remained loyal to the Anglican Church and continued to serve in parishes throughout England.[78] Aelred Carlyle, the self-proclaimed superior of the Anglican monks at Lower Guiting, continued to pursue his monastic dream and eventually came under the patronage of Lord Halifax. For nearly four years his struggling community of Anglican monks lived on Halifax's estate in Yorkshire. In 1906, Carlyle purchased Caldey Island, South Wales, and the community grew to approximately thirty monks. In 1913, Carlyle and these monks received national attention when they converted to Roman Catholicism. After a career as a monk as missionary, he died in 1955.

Notes

[1] For a general overview, see R. Kollar, "The Opposition to Ritualism in Victorian England," *Irish Theological Quarterly*, January 1985. See John Shelton Reed, "'Ritualism Rampart in East London': Anglo-Catholicism and the Urban Poor," *Victorian Studies* 31 (Spring 1988). Reed's article also contains an excellent bibliography dealing with the history of the ritual movement, biographies of the important personalities, and the descriptions of the leading ritualist societies.

[2] For biographies of Aelred Carlyle and his attempts to introduce Benedictine monasticism in the Anglican Church see: P. Anson, *Abbot Extraordinary* (New York: Sheed and Ward, 1958); P. Anson, *The Benedictines of Caldey* (Gloucester: Prinknash Abbey, 1944); and R. Kollar, "Abbot Aelred Carlyle and the Monks of Caldey: Anglo-Catholicism in the Church of England, 1895-1913" (Ph.D. diss. University of Maryland, 1981).

[3] *The Cubitt Town Protestant Banner,* July 1897.

[4] *Crockford's Clerical Directory,* 1897.

[5] Reynolds to Green, 31st August 1897, Carlyle Papers, Elmore Abbey Archives, Newbury, Berkshire. The Rev. A.R. Reynolds was an Anglican Clergyman at Darlington. Both he and Green had corresponded with each other concerning the necessity of establishing monasticism within the Anglican Church.

[6] Green to Reynolds, 4th September 1897, EAA.

[7] Carlyle to Green, 8th September 1897, EAA.

[8] Green to Drake, 23rd September 1897, EAA.

[9] *Crockford's Clerical Directory,* 1897.

[10] Carlyle to Green, 27th September 1897, EAA.

[11] Carlyle to Green, 5th October 1897, EAA. Neither of these clerics joined Carlyle's brotherhood.

[12] *The Disruption of the Church of England by More Than 9,000 Clergymen Who Are Helping the Romeward Movement in the National Church,* (London: Church Association Press, 1906) 40. The Church Association was founded in 1865 to preserve the Protestant character of the Anglican Church against ritualism and ideas associated with Roman Catholic thought and practice.

[13] The English Church Union was founded in 1860 to promote the cause of ritualism, especially the so-called Six Points: eastward position, eucharistic vestments, the mixing of water and wine in the chalice, altar lights, unleavened bread, and the use of incense. It also advocated reunion with Rome and sought to protect ritualists from attacks by the evangelical wing of the Established Church. The Confraternity of the Blessed Sacrament advocated liturgical innovations which some believed were more appropriate in a Roman Catholic sacrificial mass.

[14] Walter Walsh, *The Secret History of the Oxford Movement* (London: Chas. J. Thynne 1898), 46, 49.

[15] *The Disruption of the Church of England,* p. viii.

[16] "Secret Societies," *Church Association Tracts,* 1881, 2-3.

[17] Carlyle to Green, 19th October 1897, EAA.

[18] Carlyle to Green, 4th December 1897, EAA.

[19] P. Anson, *Abbot Extraordinary,* 57. The population of the village had declined steadily during the last two decades of the nineteenth century. It dropped from 619 inhabitants in 1881 to 428 in 1891. The 1901 census showed 348 people living in Lower Guiting. Between 1895-1898 the parish register recorded 20 baptisms, 10 marriages and 12 burials. "The Census for Gloucestershire," 1881, 1891, 1901, Guildhall Library, London; G.B. Sharp, "Parish Register, 1560-1916," GDR 395, Gloucester County Record Office, Gloucester.

[20] "Extract from the Bishop's Sermon, at Lower Guiting, August 14, 1898," Prinknash Abbey Archives, Cranham, Gloucester.

[21] "To the Right Reverend Charles John, Lord Bishop of Gloucester," D 873 F51, printed in *Gloucester Journal,* 11th March 1899, Gloucester County Record Office.

[22] Carlyle to Green, 19th October 1897, EAA.

[23] Carlyle to Green, 14th December 1897, EAA.

[24] E. Marjoribanks, *The Life of Sir Edward Marshall Hall* (London: Victor Gollancz, 1929), 110.

[25] Christine Brook-Rose, the defendant's granddaughter, has written a fictional account of this trial. She believes, as did Marshall-Hall, that the trial was an attempt to silence or to punish her grandfather. See C. Brooke-Rose, *The Dear Deceit* (London: Secker and Warburg, 1960).

[26] *Westminster Gazette,* 28th January 1898.

[27] *Church Review,* 3rd February 1898.

[28] For example: "A Benedictine 'Sell': Anglican Monks in a Gloucestershire Vicarage" (*The Star,* 5th February 1898); "Remarkable Case at Brighton: Charges Against a Monk" (*Sussex Daily News,* 28th January 1898); and "Revelations of Anglican Monkery" (*Church Intelligencer,* June 1898).

[29] "Revelations of Anglican Monkery," *Church Intelligencer,* March 1898.

[30] "Secret Societies in the Church of England," *Church Intelligencer,* March 1898.

[31] "Was It Spite," *The Rock,* February 1898.

[32] *The Voice of Truth,* March 1898; Church Association Annual Report, 1898, 23.

[33] Carlyle to Green, 15th February 1898, EAA.

[34] Cobham to Temple, 3rd March 1898, Temple Papers, vol. 18, Lambeth Palace Library, London.

[35] Cobham to Temple, 17th May 1898, Temple Papers, vol. 10, LPL.

[36] *Cheltenham Free Press,* 14th May 1898.

[37] *Church Intelligencer,* March 1898.

[38] *Cheltenham Free Press,* 16th April 1898.

[39] Ibid.

[40] *Cheltenham Free Press,* 23rd April 1898.

[41] *Cheltenham Free Press,* 30th April 1898.

[42] *Cheltenham Free Press,* 7th May 1898.

[43] Ibid.

[44] *Cheltenham Free Press,* 14th May 1898.

[45] *Cheltenham Examiner*, 21st May 1898. See "Benefice of Lower Guiting," 7th May 1898, D 16/3/14. Gloucester Diocesan Archives. The sequestration was not relaxed until 20th March 1904.

[46] Ibid.

[47] *Cheltenham Examiner*, 21st May 1898.

[48] *Cheltenham Free Press*, 21st May 1898.

[49] Ibid.

[50] Cobham to Temple, 3rd March 1898, vol. 10, Temple Papers, LPL. Also printed in *Cheltenham Free Press*, 4th June 1898.

[51] Cobham to Temple, 30th March 1898, vol. 10, Temple Papers, LPL. Also printed in *Cheltenham Free Press*, 4th June 1898.

[52] Temple to Cobham, 5th March 1898, vol. 10, Temple Papers, LPL. Also printed in *Cheltenham Free Press*, 4th June 1898

[53] Cobham to Temple, 30th March 1898, vol. 10, Temple Papers, LPL. Also printed in *Cheltenham Free Press*, 4th June 1898.

[54] Cobham to Temple, 17th May 1898, vol. 10, Temple Papers, LPL. Also printed in *Cheltenham Free Press*, 4th June 1898.

[55] *Cheltenham Free Press*, 4th June 1898.

[56] *Cheltenham Free Press*, 11th June 1898.

[57] *Cheltenham Free Press*, 2nd July 1898. According to this report, ten people attended the early Sunday service, and approximately thirty, the late morning service.

[58] Ibid.

[59] Ibid.

[60] *Church Intelligencer*, January 1899.

[61] *Cheltenham Mercury*, 2nd July 1898.

[62] *Church Intelligencer*, January 1899.

[63] *Cheltenham Free Press*, 2nd July 1898.

[64] *Cheltenham Chronicle*, 6th July 1898.

[65] *Cheltenham Chronicle*, 8th July 1898.

[66] *Cheltenham Chronicle*, 6th July 1898.

[67] *Cheltenham Chronicle*, 8th July 1898.

[68] *Cheltenham Free Press*, 9th July 1898.

[69] *Cheltenham Chronicle*, 8th July 1898.

[70] The preacher and his van also paid visits at Cold Aston, Elmstone Hardwicke, Uckington, Burton-on-the-Trent, Lower Slaughter, Middleton Scriven, Deauxhill, Cretton, Northleach, Shepscombe, Bussage, Uley, and Chalford. During the last six months of 1889, Bradfield gave 123 addresses, travelled 886 miles, and visited approximately 75 villages. *Church Intelligencer*, January 1899.

[71] *Gloucester Journal*, 16th July 1898.

[72] Ibid.

[73] *Church Intelligencer*, January 1899.

[74] *Cheltenham Free Press,* 30th July 1898.

[75] *Cheltenham Free Press,* 6th August 1898.

[76] Ibid.

[77] "Extract from the Bishop's Sermon, at Lower Guiting, August 14, 1898," PAA.

[78] See *Crockford's Clerical Directory* for their subsequent appointments. There is no additional information concerning their involvement with ritualism or with any anti-ritual protests.

CHAPTER VII

LORD HALIFAX AND MONASTICISM
IN THE CHURCH OF ENGLAND

Lord Halifax is primarily remembered for his dedication to ecumenism. Negotiations with the Vatican concerning the validity of Anglican orders and the pioneering conversations with Cardinal Mercier are examples of his efforts to bring unity and peace to Christendom. Believing that certain practices, devotions, and customs were the inheritance of all Christians, he sought to introduce into the Church of England some of those common elements. One, absent since the sixteenth century, was Benedictine monasticism. Not only did the Anglican church have the right to claim monastic life as part of its tradition, he insisted, but Benedictine life in the Church of England might invigorate a structure many believed was static.

Thus, Lord Halifax became the patron of Aelred Carlyle and his attempt to reintroduce monasticism into the established church. Carlyle had enjoyed some early success and had also received a degree of episcopal sanction. Consequently, Halifax saw Carlyle as the person to fill the vacuum created by the Reformation. Although he composed no tract or lengthy arrangements for Anglican monasticism, Lord Halifax's public backing of Carlyle gave credibility to the undertaking. Halifax committed his prestige, reputation, and financial backing to the struggling Anglican monastery. His correspondence with Carlyle, articles in the Anglo-Catholic press, and the fatherly advice he extended to the young Anglican abbot demonstrate his dedication to the success of his dream of reintroducing monasticism into the Church of England.

Charles Lindley Wood, second Viscount Halifax (1839-1934), devoted his entire life to the promotion of the Anglo-Catholic revival in the Church of England. Halifax's chief goal was the reunion of the Anglican and Roman churches, and although he regularly attended the House of Lords, he took little interest in politics. Unfailingly he defended high church principles and resisted all attempts on the part of evangelicals to prohibit catholic teaching and worship in the Anglican church. The panacea for the problems of the established church, he believed, was the recovery of the ancient catholic faith.[1] His ecclesiology was pure Tractarian: "What I suggest is that the Church of England is part of a whole, the part is subject to the whole." In certain areas of doctrine and devotion, therefore, all Christians owed their allegiance to the catholic faith rather than to the Anglican church. The ultimate authority was the conscience of the universal church, the Roman and Greek included, and one could correctly appeal to this catholic or universal authority over the precepts of the local English church. According to Halifax, "there might be devotional and doctrinal customs common to the whole church which in later formularies of the English Church might not be explicitly recognized, but which would be implicitly recognized by the Church of England.[2] In Halifax's private chapel at Hickleton, Yorkshire, for example, Mass replaced Matins as the principal service on Sunday morning, and the liturgy of the First Prayer Book of Edward VI was adopted by permission of the Archbishop of York.[3]

His greatest accomplishment, however, was the control he exercised over the English Church Union, serving as president from 1868 until 1921.[4] Beside defending Anglo-Catholic priests at ritualist trials, he used his position to promote reunion with Rome by encouraging a reconsideration of the validity of Anglican orders on the part of the Vatican. Although that campaign ended in failure, "his authority among Anglo-Catholics,...not always unquestioned, was for a layman unrivaled."[5]

His high church theology also influenced his lifelong interest in the revival of Benedictine monasticism in the Anglican church. "It is the recovery of a great principle, for lack of which the Catholic revival had been incomplete.[6] He had previously helped to establish the Cowley Fathers and supported the Community of the Resurrection, two recognized religious orders in the established church. He also visited the self-styled pioneer of Anglican Benedictinism, Fr. Ignatius Lyne, but the latter's erratic personality and unauthorized lifestyle repelled Halifax.[7] However, the courage and enthusiasm of a young ex-medical student, Aelred Carlyle, for the revival of the monastic system in the established church impressed the viscount.[8] Moreover, Carlyle had received the sanction of Archbishop Frederick Temple for his work.

It is not known when Lord Halifax became acquainted with Carlyle, but in 1901 there were rumors that Halifax was seriously weighing the possibility of buying a medieval monastic site to donate to Carlyle. Consequently, Carlyle wrote Lord Halifax and asked for funds to purchase and develop Caldey Island, South Wales.[9] Halifax responded, but instead offered the Anglican monks a haven in Yorkshire. Carlyle preferred Caldey. In September 1901 he met Lord Halifax to discuss the future of the Benedictines. Halifax heightened Carlyle's hopes about the purchase of Caldey Island and promised to send a representative of the English Church Union to investigate the possibility of a transaction. Believing his brotherhood must disband if Caldey could not be bought, Carlyle appealed to the viscount's devotion to monastic life. "There seems nothing to be done if we cannot obtain the money except a 'dissolution' and this would be very hard for we have eight men and every prospect of a steady income." Without Halifax's help, the experiment would surely fail. "If we have to leave here, it must mean either an end of our little work at its most promising stage or beginning it all over again under very altered conditions."[10] By January, however, it was clear that Lord Halifax could not raise the money to purchase Caldey. Carlyle, consequently, accepted Halifax's previous offer of refuge at the viscount's estate in Yorkshire. "If your kind offer of Painsthorpe is still open," he wrote Halifax, "we could...get at least all of our food out of the land." Moreover, he informed Fr. Kelly of the Society of the Sacred Mission that "we shall be in a secure position under Lord Halifax's protection."[11]

On 5 March 1902 Aelred Carlyle and eight monks moved to Painsthorpe and occupied a dwelling in the parish of Kirby Underdale, which Lord Halifax provided rent free. This offered Carlyle a favorable environment to experiment with religious life. The vicar, Rev. W.R. Shepherd, encouraged him to participate fully in the life of the parish. "I feel sure that your presence among us will have a very important bearing on the work of the Church, not only in this parish, but in the district around," he wrote Carlyle.[12] Consequently, members of the brotherhood conducted church services and taught in the Sunday School. Their other work consisted in caring for the sick and homeless, operating a guest house, printing, metal work, and vestment making.[13]

Despite this comfortable working relationship, the accomplishments and success of the Anglican monks of Painsthorpe depended on the good will of Lord Halifax. Animated by his Tractarian view of the essential unity of Christianity and the continuity between the contemporary Church of England and pre-Reformation Christendom, Lord Halifax enthusiastically supported the Benedictine revival on his estate. He reminded Carlyle, "Your call was to raise up the old waste places and to build up again a Benedictine community in the ancient *Ecclesia Anglicana* in communion with Canterbury." Halifax also tried to convince fellow Anglo-Catholics that they "must rally around Abbot Aelred, who in the sphere of religious life, has been enabled by the grace of God to win a position for the

Benedictine Order" in the Anglican church. The goal of Benedictine life in England was the "recovery of a great principle, for the lack of which the Catholic revival has been incomplete."[14]

A strong spirit of romanticism and the recognition of the possible benefits flowing from monastic social work also strengthened the viscount's commitment. Lord Halifax dreamed of Painsthorpe as a catalyst in "a revival, with all the accessories of place and scenery amid our Yorkshire hills and dales, of the old monastic life which in the past gave us Fountains, Rievaulx and Bolton."[15] Work with the poor and outcasts also occupied an important place in this renaissance of Benedictine life. "In the revival of Religious Life for men...is to be found the true solution of the many social problems which perplex the present generation." According to Halifax, the Anglican monk would "enkindle the flames of spiritual endeavour, and move those mountains which...appear to present insuperable obstacles to any, even the best considered plans for social reform." Painsthorpe would become "the nucleus of such an endeavour which, if developed, will in time generate a spiritual force calculated to deal with these great problems."[16]

The romantic spirit of Carlyle's monasticism, the Latin devotions, and the "simple and primitive strictness" of their obedience to the Rule of Saint Benedict, captivated the viscount; but in addition to this emotional appeal, he also endorsed Carlyle's brotherhood because "they have the imprimatur and the authority of the Archbishop of Canterbury."[17] Halifax, therefore, put his reputation behind Carlyle's brotherhood. "I think Fr. Aelred and his people...so far as I can judge, are perfectly simple," Halifax informed Lord Stanmore in October 1903.[18]

Aelred Carlyle had arrived in Yorkshire as an unordained monk, but Lord Halifax hastened to correct that. Carlyle must have credentials as an Anglican clergyman. The archbishop of York, William Maclagan, had earlier informed Halifax that he would gladly welcome the monks in York, but he remained uncommitted and anxious about extending any episcopal favor to Carlyle.[19] On the suggestion of Lord Halifax, however, Maclagan permitted Bishop Charles Grafton, visiting from Fond du Lac, Wisconsin, to install Aelred Carlyle as the first abbot in the Church of England since the Reformation. On 30 October 1903 Grafton blessed Carlyle as abbot of Painsthorpe. Halifax witnessed the ceremony and testified that Archbishop Maclagan permitted the installation. He recorded that during "a most impressive ceremony...the Bishop of Fond du Lac, with the Archbishop of York's permission blessed Fr. Aelred and installed him as Abbot."[20] Two years later, the same American prelate ordained Carlyle a priest in a service conducted at Fond du Lac on 15 November 1905.[21]

Halifax was becoming greatly impressed with Carlyle's determination and stability, and the foundation showed numerous signs of success. "So many novices are applying," Halifax informed a friend, "that we must beg, borrow or steal some £2,000 to provide accommodation."[22] Carlyle naturally expected the needed capital, but Halifax was not able to procure the needed funds for the abbot to expand his monastery. Halifax informed him that "it is evidently quite impossible for me to borrow £500 at present for your purposes, nor do I see when I should be likely to be able to do so."[23]

Because of Halifax's public support, the Anglo-Catholic press began to praise the revival at Painsthorpe. The official publication of the English Church Union, the *Church Union Gazette,* commented that the brotherhood was "equally loyal to their spiritual mother, the Church of England, and their spiritual father, Saint Benedict." Moreover, "the most important and encouraging feature of this new venture of faith [is] the fact that this revival of the Benedictine rule in the Church of England is *recognized* by authority." The Guild of Saint Alban described Painsthorpe as resolute in purpose and mature in vision, a community "that has reasonable hopes of stability and continuance...and has not the slightest connection with similar attempts by members of our communion whose reputation was not encouraging to those whose interest in the revival was real." Halifax's monks were authentic Benedictines. Consequently, the guild urged Anglo-Catholics to support "the Order to which the English Church owes...almost her very life and existence."[24]

Not all the publicity, however, was complimentary. The Protestant or low church press saw the Anglican brotherhood as a threat to the established church. *The English Churchman* inveighed against the foundation and warned its readers that "the Painsthorpe 'Benedictines' carry on their propagandist operations in parishes under Ritualist incumbents. Because of the monks' high church liturgies, M.W.B. Etches, Protestant Parliamentary Agent to the Church Association and National Protestant League, seriously questioned their loyalty to the Church of England. The Church Association, consequently, condemned the "new peril from the growth of monkery at...Painsthorpe." A pamphlet, *Playing at Monks: A Day at Painsthorpe Priory,* also satirized the Romish devotions of the Anglican monks.[25]

In June 1904 John Kensit, the fiery evangelical preacher, mounted a campaign against Halifax's monks.[26] According to Kensit, "we have now the spectacle of a number of young men professing to be adherents of the Church of England backed up by Lord Halifax, leader of the ritualist movement." As president of the English Church Union, Halifax was a frequent target of the Church Association. In 1900, for example, some sympathizers vandalized the family cemetery and desecrated a cross which he had erected in memory of his dead sons. In July 1904 two "preachers" arrived at Painsthorpe and commenced their attack against the monks at an open air meeting. "After a short opening hymn, prayer and chapter from the Bible, one of them preached a violent antinomian sermon" and denounced "the poor deluded clergy and monks...." The Painsthorpe villagers showed little sympathy. Not more than twenty listened to the "preachers" mock the Anglican monks, "who, during the meeting, distributed as an antidote to the strange teaching, various leaflets" which criticized the methods and aims of Kensit's evangelical crusade.[27] Failing to arouse the Yorkshire villagers, the "preachers" left immediately.

Although Lord Halifax wanted Carlyle to remain at Painsthorpe indefinitely, the Anglican abbot dreamed of moving his monastery back to Caldey. In April 1906 Abbot Aelred Carlyle informed Lord Halifax that he had "received a generous offer from a layman interested in our community...which might make it possible for us to acquire Caldey as our permanent freehold...."Although he was sympathetic to Carlyle's decision, Lord Halifax was disappointed; his dream for a monastic revival in Yorkshire was shattered. "You well understand with what very mixed feelings I have received your letter about Caldey," Halifax told the abbot, since "it has been a greatest happiness seeing the community there [Painsthorpe], and I had hoped you might have taken root in our Yorkshire woods." Nevertheless, he expressed his good wishes for the eventual success of Caldey. "I do also entertain the hope that in the days to come the monks of Caldey may be able to extend their borders and perhaps return to Painsthorpe, and to establish a cell there in connection with the Mother House."[28]

After the purchase of Caldey Island, the viscount supported Carlyle's action in the columns of the high church newspaper, *The Church Times.* "I have known Abbot Aelred since he began his work...and I have observed the wise and constant course he has followed...how well and truly he has laid the foundations of that which, I feel confident, will prove to be a lasting structure fraught with blessings...." He identified Carlyle's brotherhood with the Celtic monastic tradition which had flourished centuries earlier on the island before the "cataclysm" of the Reformation. Halifax rejoiced "that Caldey, of all places in the kingdom, comes back to the Benedictine." The islanders "will once more be brought within the pale of the Catholic Church, and this through the return of the Sons of Saint Benedict."[29]

After a sad farewell to Lord and Lady Halifax, the brotherhood departed.[30] On 19 October Abbot Carlyle and 19 Anglican Benedictine monks arrived on Caldey Island. Lord Halifax, however, remained Carlyle's most enthusiastic patron. His visit to Caldey in July 1908 further strengthened his devotion to the Anglican Benedictines. The viscount described with great excitement his sojourn on Caldey. "I must tell you about Caldey; it was delightful...a paradise...very comfortable arrangements." "The liturgy was very well sung and most moving...If Caldey did not belong to the monks I would give anything to have it myself...." In addition to friendly conversations with the abbot and explorations of the island, the high church liturgy also pleased him immensely. "At 6:30 Evensong in the old church and then Exposition of the Blessed Sacrament with intercessions and Compline in the monastery chapel. It was really the chief dream of my life realized." In October 1908 he told Athelstan Riley, a prominent Anglo-Catholic layman, that "Caldey and the Abbot appeal to all things I care for very much."[31]

But the relations between Lord Halifax and Abbot Carlyle did not remain calm. Carlyle believed that Halifax would be the paymaster for a £30,000 building scheme on the island. But Halifax, much to the disappointment of Carlyle, agreed only to pay the interest on the mortgage, about £200 per annum. This arrangement continued until the end of 1910.[32] More serious, however, were stories about the abbot's extravagant and pompous lifestyle. The luxury of the abbot's quarters, a richly furnished monastery, the services of a private yacht, and a chauffeur-driven Daimler offended many loyal Anglo-Catholic supporters who reported their displeasure to Halifax. It was eventually a series of vacations in France, Genoa, Pisa, and Florence that disillusioned Halifax.[33] Consequently, he wrote and scolded Carlyle for his irresponsible behavior. Halifax warned him that such actions attracted attention and became the subject of much gossip in ecclesiastical circles. "Such a position as you hold and such opportunities as have been given to you are a great gift, but they are also a great danger." The viscount recognized the pressures and demands made upon the abbot, but he could not condone his travels and foreign holidays. "Is it quite consistent," Halifax queried, "with the idea of your life to be preaching missions and energizing all over the country?"[34] Carlyle remained insensitive to this rebuke and defended his actions. Wealth, he believed, was not necessarily incongruous with religious life. Stories, especially concerning his holidays, were the products of idle gossip.

It was not Abbot Carlyle's ostentatious living, however, that distressed Lord Halifax the most, but his flirtations with Rome and his arrogant threats to convert. By the summer of 1911 some of the abbot's statements and actions indicated that conversion to Rome was imminent.

Among others, Rev. H.F.B. Mackay, Rev. H.P. Denison, and E.H. Day informed Lord Halifax that stories attributed to Carlyle indicated that the abbot was on the verge of conversion.

Prompted by the fears of other Anglo-Catholics about Carlyle's impending secession to Rome, Halifax composed a long letter to the abbot pleading with him to remain in the established church. "My very dear I am troubled about you. You have the opportunity of doing much for the restoration of the Catholic Faith in England, and for winning back for the Church of England all that is here. Such a work is the work above all others which is needed in the interests and for the future welfare of Christendom at large." He reminded Carlyle that "many hearts are drawn towards you, you have kindled much enthusiasm...and you have seemed in your own personal work to be realizing much that responds to their deepest hopes and most cherished wishes." "If you fail them," Halifax warned, "the mischief will be great and irremediable, the disappointment will be cruel...it will be the history of another opportunity thrown away, of broken hopes...." Halifax pleaded with Carlyle, "Ask yourself whether scandals, grievous as they may be, are not matched by scandals as serious...in other communions." "Splendid as the Roman Catholic is on its devotional and self-denying side and its witness to the Faith," Halifax concluded, "can we shut our eyes to the fact that in much of its working and centralization it is the revival of the old Roman Empire in a Christianized form?"[35]

Abbot Carlyle responded with two letters. In the first he defended Caldey against suggestions of sedition and disloyalty. As abbot, he had no control over the conversations of guests. "It is quite impossible that certain faults which are very noticeable in the Church today...of ecclesiastical gossip and discontented criticism of superiors...should be altogether suppressed by those who come to the Guest House." However, it was not the policy of Caldey to encourage such discussion. Carlyle's second letter dealt exclusively with the alleged Roman problem. He told Halifax that he was "certainly not in the least unsettled in the way that is usually understood," and he was "in communication with no Roman authority whatsoever." He attributed such reports to cruel gossip. But Abbot Carlyle did admit that a future conversion was not out of the question. He told Lord Halifax that he was experiencing difficulties and frustrations as an Anglican, and explained that some decisions must be made. "I also feel that no action is worth taking unless what is done is going to tend towards Catholic Unity, i.e., with the Roman Church, and not for the upholding of an insular policy which becomes more and more self satisfied." Therefore, Carlyle queried, "Can there be any true catholicism without the Papacy?"[36]

To assure Carlyle of Anglo-Catholic support, Halifax invited him along with other influential Anglicans to attend a meeting at Hickleton in August 1911. Lord Halifax chaired the meeting and set the theme: "the Catholic Revival must go forward...Churchmen throughout the country have to be led, and it is our business...to supply that leading."[37] Carlyle's notes reveal that some members were anxious to prevent the rumored conversion of Caldey. Halifax assumed the burden of convincing the abbot to remain in the Anglican church. The Church of England, according to Halifax, was "a severed limb and must be brought back by us to its proper relation with the whole body of Christ which is the Church"; but conversion was outrageous. Halifax told the abbot that "from every point of view the submission of the community at that moment would be disastrous." On the other hand, "by waiting for a time in faithful adherence to the Catholic Faith in the Church of England, much good might ultimately accrue to the cause of Reunion with the Holy See—not only for the community itself, but for the Church at large."[38]

Halifax's intervention temporarily halted Carlyle's drift toward Rome, but by December there was a recrudescence of troubles on Caldey. Although many urged him to save Caldey from disaster, Halifax did not act until February 1912, when he questioned Abbot Carlyle about the validity of certain stories which indicated that the Anglican community was ready to convert. Carlyle told Halifax that "we have to consider whether or not we can safely and rightly continue in our allegiance to the Church of England." Moreover, the abbot informed Halifax that he had already arranged an interview with the archbishop of Canterbury, Randall Davidson, to discuss his position in the Anglican church. Halifax sensed disaster and appealed to Carlyle's conscience. He stressed Abbot Carlyle's importance as a pioneer in the re-establishment of religious life in the Church of England. "There could have been no call or need to build up a Benedictine Community in the Roman Communion." He also questioned the wisdom of approaching Archbishop Davidson. "The ecclesiastical authorities only want to leave you alone, what they don't want...is to be made to give definite opinions on matters they don't want to do...." Two days later Halifax wrote again and told Carlyle that "it will be a bitter disappointment to all those who have been encouraged to hope you were destined to restore the observance of the Benedictine Rule...." Carlyle replied briefly that his community was indeed seriously considering conversion. Halifax's response was blunt but conciliatory. "We desire to restore the desolations of former generations and to build up the old waste places. We start on our enterprise full of enthusiasm, and then we find out how much there is to restore, what scandals exist, how little our ideals are realized in fact."

Finally, Halifax implored Carlyle to remain in the church, and pointed out the harm which a secession to Rome would produce.[39]

Lord Halifax feared that Carlyle might lead his community out of the Anglican church, but he hoped that the abbot's anxiety would eventually pass. Halifax also believed that the scheduled meeting between Carlyle and the archbishop of Canterbury might produce an unwelcome confrontation between the primate and the Anglican abbot. On 28 February, therefore, Lord Halifax had an audience with Archbishop Davidson and warned him that Abbot Carlyle might be searching for an occasion or excuse to convert to Roman Catholicism. Following this meeting, Halifax sent Davidson a confidential letter which urged the archbishop not to offend Carlyle. Halifax stressed the great influence Abbot Carlyle exerted in the Anglican church and his skills as a preacher. In spite of this, Halifax confessed that "with all this he had been too successful for his own good..., which hardly diminishes the disappointment and mischief which will ensue if he does transfer his obedience to the Roman Communion." He also advised Davidson to tell Carlyle that he desired "to do all that can properly be done to further such a work," but on the other hand, "all Religious Communities had to prove their worth before they received the final sanction of Ecclesiastical Authority." The archbishop should recommend that Carlyle "go on perfecting the religious life in himself and in his community...."[40]

The result of the dreaded meeting between Carlyle and Davidson, which took place on 6 March 1912, was the proposal that Charles Gore, the bishop of Oxford, should study the Benedictine life on Caldey and, as the official episcopal visitor, suggest areas for change or improvement.[41] Some Anglicans continued to argue that Caldey must be saved. Anglo-Catholics such as Rev. R. L. Langford-James and Fr. Puller of the Cowley Fathers visited Caldey, encouraged the abbot, and reported their impressions back to Halifax: Caldey might still be secured for the established church.[42] But by the spring of 1912 Lord Halifax was probably convinced that his dream of Anglican monasticism was being shattered by Abbot Carlyle's love affair with Roman Catholicism. Moreover, Halifax believed that the scandal of Carlyle's departure must not be allowed to blacken the future of monasticism in the Anglican church.

Even at this late hour Halifax tried to salvage the Benedictines of Caldey for the established church. As the defection became imminent, he appealed to Carlyle to remain steadfast in the Anglican church. "It was inconsistent," he urged, "to be discouraged by scandals or setbacks of the existence of which they had all been aware when the enterprise began." Halifax even wrote to Bishop Gore and offered to serve as a mediator. "I have just seen a correspondence between the Abbot of Caldey and yourself which makes me very unhappy," he informed Gore, "and it can have but one result and will supply the Abbot with the chance he has *perhaps* been looking for...."[43]

But on 18 February 1913 the inevitable happened. Abbot Carlyle and the majority of his monks felt unable to accept a list of demands put forth by Bishop Gore, and consequently the abbot announced that he was leading the monks out of the Anglican communion.[44] Like Bishop Gore, Lord Halifax maintained that the abbot had staged the confrontation with the Anglican authorities. Halifax informed a friend that "the Bishop of Oxford's letter has given the Abbot just the excuse he was perhaps looking for...."Although the viscount admitted that he "had not been happy...for some time" with Carlyle, he nevertheless lamented Gore's uncompromising actions which "would go a long way to justify the Abbot's decision...."[45]

Yet Lord Halifax did not abandon Abbot Carlyle. Although saddened by the loss, his dream of Anglican monasticism would not be compromised or hurt by the departure of one man. Moreover, it was not the inability of Benedictinism to graft itself onto the fibre of the established church, but the intransigence of Bishop Gore which pushed the abbot out of the church. As soon as the Caldey community was formally accepted into the Roman church on 5 March, Halifax unleashed his anger against Gore in a diatribe published in *The Church Times*. He ridiculed the position "that it is the duty of clergy and laity alike to submit unreservedly without any 'bargaining' to any direction any individual Bishop may choose to give once his right to intervene has been accepted." Halifax argued that this philosophy was usually "associated with ultramontane principles...." "Mischievous among our neighbours, are they not mischievous when pressed into the service of the Church of England, and ridiculous to boot?" Thus, Abbot Carlyle was justified in his action by an appeal to catholic authority. Halifax also warned the readers that the "great mass of English Churchmen...will not accept in regard to themselves, or the worship of the Church they love so well, the principles which seem to have determined the action of authority in relation to the Abbot and Community of Caldey."[46]

The Caldey secession was a severe blow to the integrity of the Catholic movement. Carlyle's departure also threatened the future of Benedictine monasticism in the Anglican church. Lord Halifax responded to the danger in two ways. In the first place, he convened a meeting to solve a dilemma which grew out of the conversion: could the Caldey monks, now Roman Catholic, claim money and capital previously donated by Anglicans? The viscount informed the prospective participants "that there are many who may have given, and probably did give money to Caldey, who would not have done so had they supposed that the community was likely to be transferred to the Roman obedience."[47] A prolonged court battle would have injured the Anglo-Catholic reputation; but the unanimous report softened any criticism. Urged by Halifax, Carlyle agreed to pay the Anglican church £3000 and to return the property at Pershore, Worcestershire, which had been donated to the abbot. On the other hand, the ownership of Caldey Island and funds given to Carlyle while an Anglican were to remain rightfully his. Pershore dictated Lord Halifax's second reaction. The owner immediately bequeathed the property to "the faithful remnant," those few monks who refused to convert with Carlyle, for the purpose of continuing monastic life in the Anglican church. Lord Halifax again lent his name and prestige to this project. Benedictinism in the church, he still believed, was an integral and important aspect of the faith. This venture proved more successful. Denys Prideaux, a former member of the Caldey community, took charge of the observance of Anglican Benedictinism in Worcestershire. In 1926 these Anglican monks left Pershore and settled at Nashdom near Slough.

Notes

[1] *Dictionary of National Biography*, s.v. "Wood, Sir Charles Lindley"; Anselm Bolton, *A Catholic Memoir of Lord Halifax and Cardinal Mercier* (London, 1935); J.G. Lockhart, *Charles Viscount Halifax* (London, 1936), p. 192; Sidney Dark, *Lord Halifax* (Oxford, 1934), p. 10.

[2] *The English Churchman and St. James Chronicle,* 30 August 1906.

[3] Lockhart, *Charles Viscount Halifax,* p. 93.

[4] For a history of the English Church Union see George Roberts, *The History of the English Church Union, 1859-1894* (London, 1895); and idem, *Rules of the English Church Union* (London, 1860). The English Church Union was the result of the amalgamation of numerous church unions and church protection societies in 1860. It championed the Anglo-Catholic position within the Anglican church. Among other things, it campaigned for catholic liturgies, rapprochement between Rome and Canterbury, and the recognition of the validity of Anglican Orders by the Vatican.

[5] *Dictionary of National Biography,* s.v.

[6] *The Church Times* (London), 17 August 1906.

[7] Lockhart, pp. 203-204.

[8] For biographies of Aelred Carlyle see Peter Anson, *Abbot Extraordinary* (New York, 1958); idem, *Benedictines of Caldey* (Gloucester, 1944); and Rene Kollar, "Abbot Aelred Carlyle and the Monks of Caldey Island: Anglo-Catholicism in the Church of England" (Ph.D. diss., University of Maryland, 1981).

[9] "Caldey Abbey Journal," 1 April 1901, Carlyle Papers, Prinknash Abbey Archives, Gloucester.

[10] Carlyle to Halifax, 18 December 1901, Halifax Papers, The Borthwick Institute of Historical Research, York.

[11] Carlyle to Halifax, 20 January 1902, Halifax Papers; Carlyle to Kelly, 5 February 1902, Kelly Papers, Society of the Sacred Mission Archives, Willen, Milton Keynes.

[12] Shepherd to Carlyle, 18 February 1902, Carlyle Papers.

[13] *A Benedictine Revival in the Church of England* (Mildenhall, 1903), pp. 23-25.

[14] Halifax to Carlyle, 7 February 1912, Halifax Papers; *The Church Times,* 17 August 1906.

[15] Halifax to Carlyle, 25 May 1902, Carlyle Papers.

[16] Quoted in *A Benedictine Revival, p. 7.*

[17] Ibid. The original document from Archbishop Frederick Temple is either misplaced or lost. Reproductions appeared in *A Benedictine Revival,* p. 21, and "Notes on the History of the Community," *Pax,* March 1905, p. 81.

[18] Halifax to Stanmore, October 1903, Halifax Papers.

[19] "Caldey Abbey Journal," 15 August 1902.

[20] Halifax to Hill, 31 October 1903, Halifax Papers.

[21] This ordination took place with the written permission of Archbishop Maclagan.

[22] Halifax to Hill, 31 October 1903, Halifax Papers.

[23] Halifax to Carlyle, 13 January 1904, Halifax Papers.

[24] *Church Union Gazette,* December 1903; "A Revival of Benedictine Life," *The Guildsman,* November 1902, p. 161; "The Benedictine Revival in the Church of England," *The Guildsman,* March 1906, p. 33.

[25] *The English Churchman and St. James Chronicle,* 15 October 1903; *The Record,* 23 October 1903; *Church Association Annual Report,* 1903; *Playing at Monks: A Day at Painsthorpe Priory* (London, 1904).

[26] John Kensit (1853-1902) was the leader of the extreme element of the Protestant party. In 1898 he organized the "Wickliffite" itinerant preachers to denounce ritualism. See *Dictionary of National Biography,* s.v. "Kensit, John"; and J.C. Wilcox, *John Kensit: Reformer and Martyr* (London, 1902).

[27] *Yorkshire Herald* (York), 21 June 1904; Lockhart, p. 135; *The Tablet* (London), 6 August 1904; *The Church Times,* 22 July 1904.

[28] Carlyle to Halifax, 17 April 1906, Halifax Papers; Halifax to Carlyle, 26 July 1906, Carlyle Papers.

[29] *The Church Times,* 17 August 1906.

[30] Carlyle to Halifax, 22 October 1906, Halifax Papers.

[31] Halifax to Edward, 20 July 1908; Halifax to Agnes, 20 July 1908; Halifax to Riley, October 1908, Halifax Papers.

[32] "Book of Benefactors," Prinknash Abbey Archives.

[33] Brother Aidan to Wilfred Upson, 2 April 1911, Carlyle Papers.

[34] Halifax to Carlyle, June 1911, Halifax Papers.

[35] Ibid.

[36] Carlyle to Halifax, June 1911; Carlyle to Halifax, 24 July 1911, Halifax Papers.

[37] "A Conference of the Clergy and Laity at Hickleton, August 1911," Riley Papers, Lambeth Palace Library, London.

[38] "Notes of Hickleton Conference," printed in Anson, *Benedictines of Caldey,* pp. 136-141.

[39] Halifax to Carlyle, 9 February 1912; Carlyle to Halifax, 2 February 1912; Halifax to Carlyle, 7 February 1912, 9 February 1912, 14 February 1912, Halifax Papers.

[40] Halifax to Davidson, 29 February 1912, Halifax Papers; Halifax to Carlyle, 14 February 1913, printed in Lockhart, p. 211.

[41] Davidson to Carlyle, 20 May 1912, Carlyle Papers.

[42] Langford-James to Halifax, 18 February 1912, Halifax Papers; Puller to Halifax, 12 March 1912, Halifax Papers.

[43] Halifax to Gore, 15 February 1913, printed in Lockhart, p. 211.

[44] Bishop Gore demanded the following changes: the property of Caldey must be legally secured to the Church of England; the Book of Common Prayer must be used exclusively; the doctrines of the Immaculate Conception and Assumption must be abandoned; and Benediction, Reservation of the Blessed Sacrament, and exposition of relics must be curtailed. Gore to Carlyle, 8 February 1913, Carlyle Papers.

[45] Halifax to Darwell Stone, 24 February 1913, 22 February 1913, Stone Papers, Pusey House Library, Oxford.

[46] *The Church Times,* 7 March 1913.

[47] Halifax, "Caldey Enquiry," July 1913, Halifax Papers. The membership of the committee included Lord Halifax, Lord Balfour of Burleigh, the Duke of Norfolk, the Roman Catholic bishop of Menevia, Francis Mostyn, and Athelstan Riley.

CHAPTER VIII

PAX: AN EARLY ECUMENICAL JOURNAL

In the summer 1983 edition of *Pax*, the publication of the Benedictine monks of Prinknash Abbey near Gloucester, the editor announced that the format of this journal would soon change. 'A circulation of one thousand is generally considered to be the minimum acceptable,' the statement read, 'but our mailing list now totals no more than 393 addresses of which only 276 are those of private individual subscribers.'[1] The editor explained that 'the considerable effort involved in producing PAX as a well-written, accurate and informative magazine is out of proportion to the effect that can be achieved.' Other journals now discuss issues which *Pax* had addressed in its infancy, especially ecumenism and Anglo-Catholicism. 'We can look back with satisfaction on the service given to the Church when the liturgical and ecumenical movements were starting,' and of our original aims, the editor concluded, 'we are left with one: to keep our friends in touch with the Community.' From its first edition in 1904, *Pax* had published stories and essays dealing with the revival of Benedictine life in the Church of England under the leadership of Abbot Aelred Carlyle, and it successfully kept its readers aware of the daily activities of the monks at Painsthorpe in Yorkshire and later on Caldey Island, South Wales. But *Pax* represented more than an informative newsletter. The early articles and columns of the publication presented compelling essays and arguments which dealt with catholicity, the need for unity in Christendom, and the similarities shared by all Christians. In its attempt to justify and explain Carlyle's Anglican Benedictines, therefore, *Pax* soon became a pioneer in the literature of the ecumenical movement and a harbinger of the numerous periodicals, journals, and books of this genre which appeared during the century.

Abbot Aelred Carlyle (1874-1955), the founder of *Pax*, had struggled to re-establish Benedictine monasticism in the Church of England.[2] As early as 1891, he believed that it was his vocation to live as a Benedictine monk, and by 1895, Carlyle had even composed a set of rules and regulations for his future monastic brotherhood. After a series of short-lived and unsuccessful attempts to found a Benedictine settlement in London, Gloucestershire, Newton Abbot, and Wales, he attracted the attention of Lord Halifax, who invited Carlyle and a handful of monks to live at his estate in Yorkshire. By this time, Carlyle could also boast that his monastic dream enjoyed the blessing and sanction of the Archbishop of Canterbury, Frederick Temple. In 1898, Temple had permitted Carlyle to pronounce solemn vows as an Anglican Benedictine monk, and four years later, the same Primate signed a 'Charter' which authorized the establishment and lifestyle of Aelred Carlyle's brotherhood.[3] After ordination by Bishop Charles Grafton in America (1904), Carlyle remained in Yorkshire a short time before leaving for Caldey Island, which he had recently purchased. On this picturesque and romantic island, the Anglican Abbot's search for stability appeared to be successful.

The membership of the community grew, wealthy patrons contributed to the upkeep of the monks, and prominent members of the English Church Union publicly supported and encouraged Carlyle's dream. The liturgy and devotions of this brotherhood, however, soon attracted the attention of some Anglicans who complained that the Benedictines of Caldey had abandoned some teachings of the Anglican Church and had adopted certain distasteful Roman Catholic practices. In response, Carlyle repeatedly proclaimed his loyalty to the Established Church, but also argued that Benedictine monasteries transcended the chaos and disruptiveness of sixteenth century England; monasticism, along with its liturgies and devotions, constituted the inheritance of all Christians, not just Roman Catholics. 'Our position in the Church of England is,' he maintained, 'that of Catholics separated from the rest of Western Christendom by the events of the Reformation.'[4] Moreover, he was convinced 'that it was through no personal fault of our own that we are separated from the communion of the Latin Church.'[5] Consequently, the liturgy, customs, and devotions of the Anglican monks of Caldey corresponded to practices found in any Roman Catholic monastery.

On Caldey, the Benedictine ritual and breviary replaced the Book of Common Prayer. Exposition of the Blessed Sacrament, Reservation, Eucharistic processions, and the veneration of relics composed an essential part of the Anglican monks' liturgical life. The Caldey Benedictines also celebrated the feasts of the Assumption and the Immaculate Conception, and Carlyle's devotion to the Blessed Virgin and cult of the saints was well known. When critics accused him of introducing questionable Roman Catholic practices into an Anglican brotherhood, he replied that Benedictine monasticism tolerated no division between Rome and Canterbury;

Benedictinism contained certain devotions and liturgies common to all Christians. In 1913, Carlyle stubbornly refused to submit to the wishes of Charles Gore, Bishop of Oxford, who demanded that the Abbot abandon some of the more obvious Roman practices. Carlyle and a majority of his monks, therefore, converted to Roman Catholicism. At this time, subscriptions to *Pax* numbered over one thousand. During his career as an Anglican Abbot, *Pax* became a mouthpiece for the movement toward Christian unity and an ecumenical approach to monastic life. Readers were introduced to the daily life and struggles of these novel Anglican monks, and moreover, the columns of *Pax* presented arguments in favour of a Benedictine monasticism which was catholic, universal, and nondenominational.

In September 1904, the Anglican Benedictine community of Painsthorpe in Yorkshire published the first issue of *Pax*. The editorial explained that it had become difficult for the brotherhood to keep in touch with those who supported the Benedictine revival, and consequently 'we have come to the point reached by so many Communities, when a magazine becomes a necessity.'[6] The editor promised that each quarter *Pax* would 'give such news of the life and work of the Community as may seem likely to interest our friends.'[7] 'These will be papers on spiritual life, which we hope may be of service, and articles on various subjects of interest to Church people.' Significance could also be found in the name of the new journal: 'the title to the present publication is not, then, due to fancy or caprice, but has been adopted because it represents the spirit which those fighting under the rule of S. Benedict desire to cultivate in themselves and to propagate among others.'[8] Its thrust and spirit, therefore, was ecumenical and dedicated to peaceful religious co-existence; the constant bickerings and feuds among Christians must cease. The contents of the first issue of *Pax* mirrored what the public could expect in later editions: an article on mortification, which stated 'that true happiness is only to be found in a mortified, self-restrained, penitent life, and a new and truer vigour will be infused into the Catholic movement in England';[9] a section on the early history of Carlyle's brotherhood, which emphasized the founder's fervent dedication to the monastic tradition; and a brief sketch of the life of St. Benedict. Finally, 'Chantries and Chantry Priests' traced the origin and history of chantries, and condemned the mindless and destructive action of the Reformers taken against this venerable institution:

> The Chantry Priests, have, as a body, often been harshly judged, often condemned. But with greater justice,

surely, should we respect the memory of men who in poverty and obscurity laboured in the fulfillment of duties imposed on them by the devotion of their times, humbly and patiently serving God in their generation.[10]

In the following issues of *Pax,* Abbot Carlyle adroitly portrayed the struggles and activities of his Anglican foundation. His monks were not anomalous and their liturgy did not merely mimic Roman Catholic practices. The Caldey monk, as his Roman counterpart, enjoyed the common, catholic heritage of Benedictine monasticism. By describing the daily life and work of his monastery, Carlyle hoped to demonstrate that Benedictinism bridged the chasm opened by the Henrican reforms and provided the balm to heal the wounds of hatred and persecution. In March 1905, Abbot Carlyle founded the Confraternity of the Order of St. Benedict, and *Pax* explained that this lay fraternity would help to forge a strong bond between the monks and local chapters established in sympathetic parishes. 'By associating themselves with the Order, our friends are banded together for the purpose of uniting their prayers and good works with those of the monastic brethren.'[11] Organized on the local level and 'under the immediate direction of the parochial clergy,'[12] sympathetic lecturers chronicled the growth of Carlyle's monastic revival. Abbot Carlyle, who was encouraged by the growth of his Yorkshire community, soon established a branch house in Birmingham to work among the city's youth. Under the patronage of the Bishop of Birmingham, St. Benet's Home for Boys extended to the poor and lonely urban youngsters the benefits of a happy home life, and at the same time, worked to train and equip its members to become productive and educated citizens. But the death of the monk in charge soon ended this apostolate. *Pax,* however, told its readers that Benedictinism could minister 'to the little heathen of our great cities whose houses have never been homes to them,' and following the example of the Settlement House Movement, monks might some day establish an urban brotherhood, which would live according to Benedictine principles. Encouraged by the support of the High Church party and the growth in membership of the Painsthorpe brotherhood, Abbot Carlyle began to publicize his dream of a grandiose monastery in Yorkshire.

Pax, therefore, chided its readers that it was their responsibility to give financial support to the revival of Benedictine life in the Established Church. '*We* have the men, and if our work is to grow as it should we must be able to take more. *You* have the money and can give us room for the men if you wish.'[13] Carlyle believed that his goal of £3000 did not represent a large sum, and he hoped that '...those who have written...letters of sympathy and encouragement...will express their sympathy in a tangible form now.' In addition to £3000, he also requested an additional £250 for a printing press, garden supplies, coal, and clothing for the monks. Carlyle's building programme, however, conflicted with the reports of the poverty endured by his monks. The work of the community, e.g., vestment making, dog breeding, and gimp making, could not provide even the daily necessities for the community. Prospective postulants were required 'to be free from engagements of debt...and are expected to defray the expenses of their novitiate.'[14] *Pax* sought donations of 'a little tea, or a parcel of groceries, etc., for the monks.'[15] Gifts of flannel shirts, coal, vegetables, and seeds were acknowledged monthly. By February 1906, only £7 had been pledged toward the goal of £3,000.[16] Consequently, the new monastery was postponed and the increasing membership was lodged in used railway carriages.[17] During its days as an Anglican journal, *Pax* continued to plead for money, but the dismal and disappointing results failed to dampen Carlyle's enthusiasm, energy, or vision.

In 1906, *Pax* proudly announced that on 19 October Abbot Aelred Carlyle and nineteen Anglican monks had left Painsthorpe to take possession of Caldey Island. *Pax* emphasized the drama of the move and pointed out the continuity between Carlyle's arrival on Caldey and that of the early missionary monks sent to Britain. 'The rain had ceased,' Abbot Carlyle told the readers of *Pax,* and 'the wind had dropped and the sun began to shine propitiously.'[18] On the island, flags were flying, bells rung, and the curious islanders assembled to greet the monks on the beach. After the Anglican Benedictines had disembarked, 'a solemn procession was formed...and the Abbot in pontificals, with pastoral staff in hand, attended by deacon and sub-deacon...moved slowly up to the little village chanting...the antiphon sung by St. Augustine and his monks at their first entry into England.'[19] Abbot Carlyle's joy was exuberant and his optimism high: 'our life began at Caldey, when our life at Painsthorpe ceased; and all goes on here as it did there, and as it does in every Benedictine house the world over.'[20] If Caldey represented a new Isle of Thanet, then *Pax* must show other similarities between Carlyle's brotherhood and the monasteries of pre-Reformation England.

Abbot Carlyle quickly created the climate and environment of a medieval monastic manor. From the beginning, the Abbot fostered a close relationship between the Benedictine monks and the islanders. 'Cut off in so large a measure from the outside world the inhabitants are dependent on each other for nearly everything; and indeed we do wish to be like one Christian family, bearing with each other's faults and difficulties.'[21] Carlyle, therefore, staffed the village school with his monks. According to the Abbot, 'two oblate Brothers teach the children, and they all assemble in the church close by for prayers at the beginning and end of their daily work.'[22] The monastery conducted the services at the village church, and Carlyle confessed that he was anxious 'for our little church to be a model of what a village church should be.'[23] Throughout the year, Abbot Carlyle designated certain days as special island holidays. At Christmas, for example, monks and villagers sponsored a series of social gatherings. In 1911, a Bethlehem tableau was staged, and in January 1913, a series of skits, songs, and dances were performed. Like his Roman Catholic predecessors, the reception of guests constituted an important apostolate for Carlyle: 'the Guest House means much to us, as to those who come to stay with us.'[24] 'Though the two houses are apart, and the guests come in touch with the Abbot and Guest-Master,' he continued, 'yet the spiritual links are felt and the gain is mutual.' The guests ate their meals separately, and Abbot Carlyle invited them to attend the full schedule of the monks' devotions and to meet with him for conferences.[25] Silence was encouraged, but lively discussions on theology and the condition of the Anglican Church became an important part of the life at the Caldey Guest House. In addition to reporting the hardships and achievements of the Anglican brotherhood and portraying it as any other Benedictine monastery, the columns of *Pax* also provided convincing theological arguments in favour of a catholic, universal, and ecumenical approach to Benedictinism.

Scholars and clerics contributed to *Pax* numerous articles dealing with varied aspects of Benedictine monasticism.[26] Some attempted to demonstrate that Carlyle's Anglican monastery could boast of a pure monastic pedigree and membership in a common Benedictine family. When the monks sailed to take possession of Caldey Island in 1906, *Pax* pointed out that the Anglicans were part of a hallowed Welsh tradition: 'For a thousand years and more has the Island been the home of monks; first of Celtic, then of the Benedictine Rule.'[27] Another article associated Caldey with Iona, Lindisfarne, and Patmos.[28] The Henrican Revolution, however, was singled out for special scorn. In an essay, 'The Dissolution in England,' the author spoke of the 'dirty work' of Cromwell's agents and the 'hostile evidence' gathered against the English houses.[29] Consequently, 'the Dissolution left the nation infinitely poorer, economically, religiously, socially.'[30] Moreover, English Christians should rejoice in their monastic history and heritage. 'It will only be when "the Judgment is set and the books open," that we shall be able to perceive the wondrous extent that Monastic prayers have exerted upon the lives of English men and the events of English history.'[31] *Pax* also tried to silence critics who complained that Abbot Carlyle was a Romanizer. When some individuals questioned the use of the Roman monastic breviary, *Pax* told its readers that this rite was not exclusively Roman. 'Here we have an office, many features of which, certainly, have been suggested by the Roman Office,' the article noted, 'but which taken as a whole is distinctly the creation of the mind of St. Benedict.'[32] In an attempt to dampen the Protestant element in Britain's ecclesiastical history, one author maintained that most Britons were 'inclined to lose sight of the Catholicity of the English Prayer Book and to forget the trend of the final Revision of 1662, which of express intent omitted many anti-Catholic features that had crept in at earlier dates, and restored the Catholic tone which had been abandoned.'[33] The writings of Abbot Carlyle and one of his monks, Denys Prideaux, however, dominated the pages of *Pax*.

Between 1904 and 1913, Abbot Carlyle formulated a theology of monastic life for his Anglican brotherhood, and *Pax* popularized this vision. Carlyle was not a creative theologian, but he was gifted in picking and choosing elements of traditional Christian thought and then constructing a coherent statement from these different sources. Two common elements emerged in Carlyle's theory of monasticism. His grasp and understanding of Roman Catholic scholarship was apparent, and he skillfully utilized what appealed to him. Secondly, the High Church emphasis on catholicity and continuity formed an essential part of his theology. According to Carlyle, monastic life was not limited to Roman Catholicism, but the tradition of conventual life transcended the squabbles of the Reformation. Consequently, the Anglican Church could legitimately claim Benedictinism as a part of its Catholic heritage. 'Our Purpose and Method,'[34] which was serialized in *Pax,* a few other sentences from the community's journal, and speeches given during fund raising tours form the bulk of his thought. In spite of some inconsistencies, Carlyle's theory of monastic life was important. It represented an early attempt to reconcile Roman Catholic monasticism with the High Church desire and quest for unity.

The basis of Carlyle's theology was 'a really innocent and ardent desire to possess something in our Church which was lacking; and as it did not then exist, I set out to establish it.'[35] 'I saw a Revival of the Spiritual Life spreading through Europe with here and there men waiting and longing for the opportunity of withdrawing themselves from the hurried life of the day, to seek the peace and regulated discipline of the cloister.'[36] The purpose behind Caldey, he wrote in *Pax,* was the highest possible because 'it is a Response to the call of Almighty God to live in eternal relations with Him, and through Him, with men and all things.'[37] 'The service of the Creator must obviously be the end and purpose of the creature.' Consequently, 'one's vocation is the call of God to the individual soul...in the realization of the simple fact that we are His creatures, over whom God has an absolute and inalienable right.'[38] Carlyle argued that everyone should rejoice in their specific vocation, and therefore no vocation was better than another. 'In the sight of God the good Religious is of himself no better than the good secular, the good priest no better than the good business man.'[39] Abbot Carlyle also stressed that the essence of religious life could be found in the Incarnation, that is, the 'true Nature of God who is Perfect Love, [and] the nature of Man, whose soul is made in the image of God by creation, who is renewed by Redemption by Jesus the Son of God, and dedicated in Sanctification by the Holy Spirit of God.'[40] By creation, redemption, and sanctification, Carlyle believed that 'we are entirely God's and our souls, being formed after His likeness, possess in a certain measure His attributes.'[41] Monastic life called one to return to these basic Christian principles.

Based on the Incarnation, Benedictinism demanded some personal sacrifice on the part of the monk. Carlyle told the readers of *Pax* that religious life signified 'the drawing up of the Natural into the Supernatural, and it strives to make the whole of life a consistent, cheerful, and beautiful thing. The Benedictine Religious Life means a total self-committal to God and His service...'[42] Carlyle spoke of a monastic vocation in terms of a serious call to emulate the principles of the primitive Christian community. 'It is not the idle dream of sentimentalists tired of life in the world, striving to do something extraordinary in order to bring themselves into notice, but it *is* the downright conviction of doing God's will.'[43] For Carlyle, this meant following the precepts of St. Benedict in their strict and literal sense. 'In this we [on Caldey], in common with many others elsewhere, find our vocation to live in Community under the Holy Rule of St. Benedict.[44] Regretfully, the observance of Benedict's Rule had been absent from England for too long. Abbot Carlyle wrote in *Pax* that 'as the Catholic Church in all ages has possessed her religious Communities, so now after her long sleep, the Church in England, roused at last to the realization of her Catholic heritage, would awake to the fact that she alone in Catholic Christendom possessed few Religious Houses for men...'[45] As representatives of the Anglican Church, religious communities would also stand in striking contrast to the crass materialism of the times. 'If we are agreed about the spirit of the age, it must also be agreed that a contradiction is needed, and as a concrete example of this contradiction we advocate the quiet life of Religious Communities.'[46]

Although he had earlier experimented with parish work in Birmingham, Abbot Carlyle had always favoured the contemplative spirit, and the seclusion and isolation of Caldey offered the first opportunity to experiment with a cloistered monastery. 'Our Ideal from the beginning of this work was to found a Religious Community strictly contemplative in character, that should be bound to the full observance of the Benedictine Rule.'[47] Carlyle's initial success and popularity was due largely to the support of church officials and friendly patrons because of his avowed dedication to social work. Consequently, Abbot Carlyle had to justify his change in emphasis from an active to a cloistered community in *Pax*.

> We have a profound conviction that this work of the
> Revival of the Contemplative Life is really needed today:
> and this conviction is being daily confirmed by the way
> in which the work is growing amidst much difficulty and
> contradiction, and the unconscious opposition of those
> who have not grasped the principles of the life.[48]

He believed that 'there is plenty of activity in the Church of England,' and the monks of Caldey can supplement this work, 'supporting it with our prayers...like Moses of old on the Mount with hands upheld in intercession for those who are actively engaged in the noble and trying work of meeting the enemy in the field.'[49]

Abbot Carlyle argued that the utility or worth of the contemplative monk can be understood only in terms of prayer, that is, 'the primary work of our Community at Caldey is *Prayer*.'[50] Thus at Caldey the main idea of our life is the Service of God: and this idea of service finds its expression in the careful and solemn recitation of the Divine Office.'[51] Although he did admit the possibility of conducting retreats for the clergy on Caldey,[52] it was primarily through prayer and example that the monk would demonstrate the joy and the power of the contemplative life. The activity of numerous clergymen and the increasing social consciousness of the Edwardian bishops did not exclude the need for a contemplative witness within the Church of England. Abbot Carlyle pointed out in *Pax* that 'Our Lord's preparation of thirty years for his three years ministry contrasts sharply with the way in which so many of our clergy plunge from an all too thoughtless University career into the sacred ministry of Christ's Church and hasten to convert the souls of their fellow-men.'[53] The ultimate goal of all prayer was the intense personal relationship which one's soul enjoyed with God. For Carlyle, the monk 'gradually draws himself and retires into the inmost recesses of his heart, there to take knowledge of himself...and to converse with God.'[54] Moreover, dedication to the reunion movement represented an important aspect of the contemplative Caldey monk.

From his early student days, Abbot Carlyle never viewed English religious life in terms of Anglican versus Roman. He believed that the English Church enjoyed membership in the universal catholic church, and consequently, Benedictine life was as much Anglican as Roman Catholic. Carlyle succinctly stated this view in *Pax:* 'Communities such as ours have ever existed in the Catholic Church, and we believe that such a life is needed to secure the spiritual balance which the one-sided development of the present day renders us in danger of losing.'[55] A proponent of the validity of Anglican Orders, Carlyle emphasized the historical connection between Rome and the Church of England, that is, historically the Caldey monks were in continuity with the pre-Reformation Catholic Church. Throughout his Anglican career, he constantly appealed to 'the Catholic and Universal Church' in questions of doctrine and practice. 'Our position in the Church of England,' he wrote Brother Denys Prideaux, 'is that of Catholics separated from the rest of Western Christendom by the events of the Reformation.'[56] Carlyle told his followers that 'we are simply Benedictines living in the Communion of the English Church fully persuaded that she is an integral part of the Catholic Church.'[57] Moreover, one should not view Anglican monastic life as an experiment 'for it is a return to the First Principles of Primitive Christianity.'[58] Since considerable doubt existed in the minds of some as to the legitimate and valid existence of Benedictine Communities apart from the jurisdiction of the Holy See, Carlyle argued that monasticism was not the private property of Rome. 'In all ages and provinces of the Church,' *Pax* announced, 'men and women have been found ready to yield themselves to the exclusive service of Almighty God.'[59]

The readers of *Pax* learned that the monastic life was ready and eager to flourish again in the Anglican Church. 'In these days of infidelity and sin,' Carlyle wrote, 'the Monasteries shall be once more, as of old, the bulwarks of the Church, to preserve her faith and her love in the perils that are close upon us.'[60] The reason for Carlyle's optimism rested with the spirit and flexibility of the Benedictine constitution. Although the Reformation, 'that dark place in our religious history which tells of the destruction of those glorious religious houses of the past...,'[61] had destroyed the monastic system in England, Benedictine monasticism could not remain extinguished forever. Carlyle told his supporters that the 'secret of the influence and vitality of this Rule is to be found in its intense realization of human nature and the needs of the soul.'[62] Moreover, the eventual success of Benedictinism in England can be discovered in 'its practical adaptability to all the various changes in manners, in customs, and nations as the ages flow on...' In addition to Aelred Carlyle's writings on Benedictine life, *Pax* also published a series of essays written by one of his monks. Like the Abbot, Denys Prideaux argued for the universality and catholicity of Benedictine monasticism.

Brother Denys Prideaux[63] skillfully sketched out a theology of Benedictine life which was not limited to or hampered by allegiance to Rome. The object of Prideaux's essays in *Pax* was 'to give a short and simple account of the Catholicity of Benedictinism...of the fact that Benedictinism — the Holy Rule of S. Benedict, his form of monasticism, and the title "Benedictine" — is part of the heritage of the whole Catholic Church.'[64] Prideaux pointed out that 'Christ founded *One* Church,' but 'divisions have marred the oneness of the Church.' Like the Tractarians, this age of peace and unity represented a lost ideal: 'To the period of the unimpaired oneness...the English Church appeals back, and holds to be Catholic all that is the witness of the Holy Spirit in the church and the witness of the Holy Spirit in the Scriptures, as interpreted by this one Church.' During this era, Benedictine monasticism flourished, and 'hence the Monastic system is part of the heritage of the Catholic Church.' Because of this association, Prideaux reasoned, '...the Holy Rule of S. Benedict not only has the sanction of this period, but is also used in some form by every Communion of the Catholic Church today.' But the universality of appeal and practice of Benedictinism has disappeared, and Prideaux, in explaining this unfortunate development to the readers of *Pax,* distinguished between two forms or types of Benedictinism: 'the *original* or Catholic form, and the *later* or Papal-Catholic form.'[65]

In its original and catholic state, Benedictine monasticism 'was a State of Life lived under the sanction of the Diocesan...whether he himself was a Benedictine or not.'[66] Each monastery constituted an independent unit: no formal bond or union with any other monastery existed; no centralized government with its attendant superior general, general chapters, and visitations had developed; and the only link between the Benedictine religious houses was simply the *Holy Rule*. This, the readers of *Pax,* were told, represented the 'original and Catholic form, that is, as it existed in the Early Church, and continued to exist, with hardly an exception, till Christendom was divided.'[67] But unfortunately this pure state became an 'Order' in the sense 'of a Federation or Close Corporation with a line of succession.' This Close Corporation, according to Prideaux, exhibited several characteristics: it did not develop with Benedictinism, but was imposed upon it by an outside agent; it was enforced on the original and catholic organization 'by the Church of Rome on the grounds that she alone constitutes the Catholic Church and has, therefore, the monopoly of the Monastic System of the Early Church;'[68] and finally, the Close Corporation received the sanction and approbation of the pope, 'without which it could not have been established.' Prideaux argued that as a result of this interference 'the Federation or Close Corporation Form of Benedictinism, the Papal-Catholic Form' was born.

Brother Denys maintained that the federalizing tendency might have been a matter of convenience, and he pointed out the early attempts of Aniane in Languedoc, the Abbey of Cornelimünster, and the Emperor Charlemagne. As a result of the Cluniac Reforms, however, centralization became policy, and eventually this 'system of a feudal hierarchy in monasticism reached its full development in the Monastery of Cîteaux' in the twelfth century.[69] At this point in monastic history, the popes began to direct, control, and manipulate the new Benedictine federation. This, Prideaux wrote in *Pax*, developed alongside with the growth of papal power and 'the Papalizing of Europe.' However, the author cautioned, direction and legislation from Rome 'are particular and not of the *essence* of Benedictinism.'[70] 'For, in principle, the title "Benedictine" belongs to the whole Catholic Church, however Rome may have monopolized it.'[71] If the Holy See claimed the prerogative to impose her wishes on the entire church, this represented an 'infringement of the rights of the whole Catholic Church,' and therefore was not binding.[72] This Federation or Corporation Form, moreover, depended 'strictly on the Papal theory which has never received the Oecumenical consent of the whole Catholic Church.'

Although eventually tainted by the growth of papal pretensions, Catholic Benedictinism formed an essential part of the primitive and undivided Christian community. According to this argument, 'the English Church, both as being Catholic and by virtue of her appeal to the Early Undivided Church, possesses this original independent Benedictinism as part of her Catholic heritage...'[73] Unlike the Dominicans, Franciscans, Cistercians or Jesuits, which were created by the Roman Church, the Benedictine Order appealed to a higher authority: 'Benedictinism is Catholic.'[74] Carlyle's Anglican Benedictinism, therefore, represented 'a return to the original constitution of S. Benedict...[before] the original System of the Founder had been perverted by the Pope...'[75] Benedictine monasticism, Prideaux forcefully maintained, represented the common property of all Christians, and an urgency existed which cried out for the resuscitation of this inheritance in the Anglican Church.

Pax reported that the Benedictine system could exert a profound and practical influence on English Christianity. Even with the emphasis on social concern and the missionary activity of the clergy in urban slums, Prideaux, like Abbot Carlyle, believed that contemplative Benedictinism represented 'the key to all else, the only source of true beneficence and a permanently effective activity.'[76] The English must learn, Prideaux wrote, to balance activity and prayer; the 'Monastic Life is but the survival of the Primitive Christian life.' Christianity, therefore, will only become the Body of Christ and re-capture its original unity of spirit and purpose 'in so far as she makes evident His *completeness* and gives a balanced expression *to every* side of His Incarnate Person.'[77] The monk's life of retreat should not be seen as selfishness, idleness, or cowardice, but 'the law of seclusion has its work, its fruitage in the Organism of the Body, the Church.' The Benedictine's schedule of prayer could become the catalyst for Christian unity and catholicity. 'Of this Life of Prayer and Contemplation,' Prideaux reasoned, 'Benedictinism has a special claim upon us by its adaptability and as being part of the Catholic heritage handed down to us from the Early Church, and the nursery of our English Communion.'[78] Contemplation and prayer, consequently, symbolized the creative and unifying power of Christianity.

In the columns of *Pax,* Denys Prideaux also attempted to formulate answers to the following questions dealing with Benedictine monasticism: what is the purpose of religious life; and what was St. Benedict's conception of monastic or conventual life? Religious life, Prideaux argued, captured 'an inherent part of human nature'[79] and represented the quest for the unity, universality, and concord of the early church. 'Monastic Life is but the survival of primitive Christian Life; and the acute distinction that the Middle Ages drew between the monk and the ordinary Christian...rests really upon a half truth.' Unity and harmony constituted the *raison d'être* of Benedictinism: 'the aim of the Monastic Life...consists in offering to God...one's best self in body, mind and soul — that harmony of being where all is duly ordered.'[80] 'Without this holy proportionalness,' he continued, 'a disintegration of the Self ensues, that sooner or later either dries up or poisons the springs of prayer, which are the sources both of true personality and Religious Unity.' Monasticism, therefore, offered a cure for the regrettable fragmentation of Christianity; Benedictinism might become the panacea for religious diversity. 'Balance — the harmony of the natural and the spiritual self resulting in unity of being — this...is the root purpose of the Holy Rule of S. Benedict.'[81] The Benedictine revival under Aelred Carlyle, Prideaux maintained, enjoyed a profound and significant vocation: 'it still has an active work to do for personal religion and Reunion...but also it may be, as a balancing and completing factor in the culmination of our Christianity.'[82]

In February 1913, Abbot Carlyle's dream had been destroyed by Bishop Gore's desire to reform the Caldey community. A brotherhood which advocated reunion within Christendom, appealed to the catholicity and unity of the early Christians, and saw nothing compromising in adapting rites and liturgical practices usually associated with Roman Catholicism, seemed to many Anglicans as a betrayal of their faith. Carlyle's conversion to Rome destroyed his unique vision of Benedictine monasticism as a possible formula to heal the divisions in Christianity. Benedictinism, he believed, was the heritage of all Christians, and it emulated the catholicity of the primitive Christian communities. Moreover, Benedictinism transcended the ruptures of the Reformation and proclaimed religious unity as its goal. The publication of the Anglican Benedictines, *Pax,* became a forum for the dissemination of these principles. In its pages, the subscribers were treated to articles and essays which championed unity and a theory of Benedictinism based on catholicity and continuity with the pre-Reformation Christendom.

With the secession to Roman Catholicism, *Pax* ceased to be the vocal platform for the reunion movement as it was during its Anglican days. A necessity to demonstrate the authenticity and sincerity of the monks' conversion and the amount of space devoted to financial appeals changed the early character and approach of the journal. Caldey also lost its premier theologian and advocate for the 'original' or 'catholic' monastic system: with a few other monks, Denys Prideaux refused to convert to Roman Catholicism. Under his leadership, Benedictinism continued to exist in the Anglican Church first at Pershore and later at Nashdom, where the monks moved in 1926.

The issues raised by the early editions of *Pax* pose some provocative and stimulating questions for those who currently search for Christian unity. Living the Gospel message on a daily basis, brotherhoods and sisterhoods may become the instruments to explore the reasons behind the differences which exist between the creeds, but also and more importantly, to stress the similarities, the common dedication to Christ, and the importance of Scripture. Benedictine monasticism, or any community founded on monastic principles, is a powerful ingredient in ecumenical discussions. Appeals to the spirit of the primitive Christian community and the writings of Benedict may defuse the emotions and suspicions which originated with the reforming movements of the sixteenth century. The 'original' or 'catholic' picture of monasticism depicted by *Pax* early in the century may be the modern medicine to heal the wounds opened by the Reformation. The pages of *Pax,* therefore, deserve scrutiny by those dedicated to the reality of a unified Christendom. Will it prove to have been a prophetic journal in the field of ecumenical research and scholarship?

Notes

[1] 'Last Lap: A Statement by the Editor,' *Pax*, Spring 1983, p. 54.

[2] For the life of Abbot Carlyle and the Benedictine revival in the Anglican Church see Peter Anson, *Abbot Extraordinary* (New York: Sheed and Ward, 1958); *Benedictines of Caldey Island* (Gloucester: Prinknash Abbey, 1944).

[3] A reproduction of the 'Charter' appeared in 'Notes on the History of the Community,' *Pax*, March 1905, p. 81.

[4] A. Carlyle to D. Prideaux, 6 November 1912, Carlyle Papers, Prinknash Abbey Archives.

[5] Quoted in P. Anson, *Benedictines of Caldey Island*, p. 139.

[6] 'Pax,' *Pax*, September 1904, p. 3.

[7] Ibid., p. 4.

[8] Ibid.

[9] 'Some Aspects of Christian Life,' *Pax*, September 1904, p. 6.

[10] 'Chantries and Chantry-Priests,' *Pax*, September 1904, p. 26.

[11] 'The Confraternity of the Order of St. Benedict,' *Pax*, March 1905, p. 106. By 1913, the Confraternity numbered over one thousand members.

[12] 'Community Letter,' *Pax*, September 1905, p. 187.

[13] 'Community Letter,' *Pax*, December 1904, p. 40.

[14] 'Community Letter,' *Pax*, September 1904, p. 25.

[15] 'Community Letter,' *Pax*, March 1905, p. 317.

[16] 'General Fund,' *Pax*, March 1906, p. 103.

[17] 'Fasciculi,' *Pax*, December 1905, p. 242.

[18] 'Our Home-Coming,' *Pax*, Christmas 1906, p. 63.

[19] Ibid., p. 65.

[20] Ibid.

[21] Ibid.

[22] 'Community Letter,' *Pax*, December 1907, p. 338.

[23] 'Community Letter,' *Pax*, September 1908, p. 30.

[24] 'The Guest House,' *Pax*, Michaelmas 1906, p. 36.

[25] 'The Guest House,' *Pax*, March 1907, p. 152.

[26] The scope of these articles included: 'S. Benedict of Nursia,' *Pax*, Sept. 1904, pp. 12-13; G.C. Joyce, 'Monastic Life in Medieval England,' *Pax*, March 1905, pp. 94-104; Bro. Chad, 'Monasticism: Origin in the East,' *Pax*, Sept. 1905, pp. 191-201; F.W. Woodhouse, 'Monasticism: Development in the West,' *Pax*, Dec. 1905, pp. 245-255; W.G. Cruft, 'Monasticism: The Influence in England,' *Pax*, March 1906, pp. 268-281; E.H. Day, 'The Dissolution in England,' *Pax*, August 1906, pp. 340-353; P.H. Droosten, 'The Desolation of Three Hundred Years,' *Pax*, Michaelmas 1906, pp. 18-32; Rev. E. Rogers, 'The Recovery of Community Life for Men,' *Pax*, March 1907, pp. 129-142; Bro. Denys, 'Cassiodorus, S. Benedict and S. Gregory the Great,' *Pax*, September 1909, pp. 3-17; and the series on 'Benedictinism' by Bro. Denys, *Pax*, December 1910-March 1911.

[27] 'Our Return to Caldey,' *Pax*, August 1906, p. 324.

[28] 'The Isle of Caldey,' *Pax*, August 1906, p. 338.

[29] E.H. Day, 'The Dissolution in England,' *Pax*, August 1906, p. 343.

[30] Ibid., p. 350

[31] W.G. Cruft, 'Monasticism: The Influence in England,' *Pax*, March 1906, p. 281.

[32] A. Barley, 'The Monastic Brewery,' *Pax*, March 1908, p. 393.

[33] C. Atchley, 'The Catholicity of the Book of Common Prayer,' *Pax*, September 1909, p. 40.

[34] The essay 'Our Purpose and Method' appeared in *Pax*, September 1905, pp. 158-172; December 1905, pp. 211-227; and August 1906, pp. 357-368. The work contains copious and lengthy quotations from such traditional authorities as St. Thomas Aquinas, St. Anselm, Suarez, Bossuet, Thomas à Kempis, Montalambert, Maturin, Conan Doyle, Fr. Hugh Benson and Abbot Columba Marmion.

[35] A. Carlyle to P. Anson, 21 January 1938, Carlyle Papers, Pluscarden Abbey Archives.

[36] 'Our Purpose and Method,' *Pax*, December 1905, p. 220.

[37] 'Our Purpose and Method,' *Pax*, September 1905, p. 159.

[38] Ibid.

[39] Ibid., p. 160.

[40] Ibid., p. 161.

[41] Ibid.

[42] 'Community Letter,' *Pax*, March 1911, p. 194.

[43] 'Our Purpose and Method,' *Pax*, September 1905, p. 167.

[44] Ibid., p. 162.

[45] 'Our Purpose and Method,' *Pax*, December 1905, p. 221.

[46] 'Our Purpose and Method,' *Pax*, September 1905, p.169.

[47] 'Community Letter,' *Pax*, September 1911, p. 384.

[48] 'Community Letter,' *Pax*, September 1910, p. 21.

[49] 'Our Purpose and Method,' *Pax*, December 1905, p. 211.

[50] 'Our Purpose and Method,' *Pax*, September 1905, p. 170.

[51] 'Community Letter,' *Pax*, March 1911, p. 192.

[52] 'Community Letter,' *Pax*, March 1909, p. 185.

[53] 'Our Purpose and Method,' *Pax*, September 1905, p. 169.

[54] 'Community Letter,' *Pax*, March 1909, p. 181.

[55] 'Our Purpose and Method,' *Pax*, September 1905, p. 176.

[56] A. Carlyle to D. Prideaux, 6 November 1912, Prinknash Abbey Archives.

[57] 'Our Purpose and Method,' *Pax*, August 1906, p. 368.

[58] 'Our Purpose and Method,' *Pax*, September 1905, p. 167.

[59] Ibid., p. 164.

[60] Ibid.

[61] Ibid., p. 171.

[62] 'Our Purpose and Method,' *Pax*, December 1905, p. 214.

[63] Denys Prideaux (1864-1913) was an ordained Anglican priest who joined Caldey as an Oblate in 1907. A university trained theologian and linguist, he frequently contributed scholarly articles and book reviews to *Pax*. See A. Hughes, *The Rivers of The Flood: A Personal Account of the Catholic Movement in the 20th Century* (London: The Faith Press, 1963); *Church Quarterly Review,* December 1952, pp. 46-54; *The Jubilee Book of The Benedictines of Nashdom* (London: The Faith Press, 1964).

[64] 'Benedictinism: Catholic,' *Pax*, December 1910, p. 104.

[65] Ibid., p. 105.

[66] Ibid., p. 106.

[67] Ibid., pp. 107-108.

[68] Ibid., p. 108.

[69] Ibid., p. 109.

[70] Ibid., p. 110.

[71] 'Benedictinism: Nature,' *Pax*, June 1911, p. 288.

[72] 'Benedictinism: Catholic,' *Pax*, December 1910, p. 110.

[73] Ibid., p. 112.

[74] Ibid., p. 113.

[75] 'Benedictinism: Nature,' *Pax*, June 1911, p. 288.

[76] 'Benedictinism: Need,' *Pax*, March 1911, p. 198.

[77] Ibid., p. 200.

[78] Ibid., p. 205.

[79] 'Benedictinism: Nature,' *Pax*, June 1911, p. 295.

[80] Ibid., p. 296.

[81] 'Benedictinism: Nature,' *Pax*, December 1911, p. 484.

[82] Ibid., p. 497.

CHAPTER IX

THE CALDEY MONKS AND THE CATHOLIC PRESS, 1905-1913

Aelred Carlyle (1874-1955) devoted his entire life as an Anglican to the establishment of Benedictine monasticism in the Church of England. Monastic life had attracted him early: as a medical student in London he joined a brotherhood in 1893; he often visited Buckfast Abbey, where he almost converted to Roman Catholicism; and in 1898 he took private vows of poverty, chastity and obedience according to the Rule of Saint Benedict. In the same year, the Archbishop of Canterbury, Frederick Temple, sanctioned his solemn profession as an Anglican Benedictine monk. Four years later, Temple also signed a charter which commissioned Carlyle to found an Anglican monastery and appointed him as its abbot. With the approbation of William Maclagan, the Archbishop of York, Bishop Charles Grafton ordained him a priest on 15 November 1904, in his American diocese of Fond du Lac. Along with archiepiscopal sanction and orders, Carlyle also enjoyed the patronage of Lord Halifax, the prominent Anglo-Catholic. In 1902, Carlyle accepted Halifax's invitation to settle at his estate at Painsthorpe in Yorkshire.

Because of Halifax's support, the backing of the Anglo-Catholic party, and Carlyle's official standing within the Anglican Church, Painsthorpe quickly attracted members. But to many English Roman Catholics, this 'playing at monk' must be exposed as ludicrous. During the first years of the monastery's existence in Yorkshire, the Roman Catholic press did not specifically deal with Carlyle's monks. Anglo-Catholics, however, were ridiculed, and the Catholic papers lashed out against Anglican clergymen who emulated Roman practices. In 1905, the *Catholic Times* published a sympathetic article about the Painsthorpe Benedictines, the start of a rancorous controversy which continued for months.

The author, James McFall, a Roman Catholic from Belfast, recounted the highlights of his visit to Painsthorpe. Expecting to find an Anglican brotherhood, he 'was agreeably disappointed...to find instead a very anti-

Protestant one..., so thoroughly attached to Catholic practices, ritual, liturgy and monastic usage that I almost found it difficult at times to remember that I was not in a Roman Catholic monastery at all.' The Marian devotions 'would make the heart of a good Catholic glad,' and 'the word Protestant makes these monks "wince," for to them it was the blight that destroyed all that was Catholic in their Church.' Liturgically, 'everything was in strict harmony with Catholic usage and practices...[and] they are able to keep up this ancient custom as well as lavish an extraordinary display of beauty and magnificence on the monastic ceremonial in their Church.'[1] Embracing a richly carved crozier and wearing a jewelled pectoral cross, the Abbot presided from his throne. Otherwise the life was frugal: vegetarianism and harsh straw pallets for beds were the rule.

Angry Roman Catholics, however, protested that the Painsthorpe brothers were not real monks, but heretics mimicking practices which were exclusively Roman. 'It is absolutely necessary for them to be in communion with the See of Rome' was the common response. *Catholicus* called them 'a somewhat unpleasant species of masquerade.' Another correspondent complained that 'they lack...the spirit of submission to properly constituted authority.' A third remarked: 'How do the scenes of ornate ritual...differ from those which could be produced in a series of religious tableaux artistically staged at one of our theatres?' The Painsthorpe brotherhood was a 'parody of religious life,' 'so grave and shocking a sacrilege,' and the 'monks' were guilty of 'spreading heresy and error in England and propagating that last new sect, Catholicism without Rome.' Roman Catholic support of this community would, moreover, hinder the conversion of England because it would 'make people contented with Anglicanism..., retard their reception into the Church' and 'keep back souls from the Catholic Church by offering them a substitute...that sufficiently resembles the real thing to deceive the simple or those willing to be deceived.' The official position of the *Catholic Times* was also very critical of Carlyle's brotherhood. 'We cannot be too clear or too firm in exposing false tenets and dangerous errors, and this duty is all the more incumbent upon us in the case of the leaders of ritualism.'[2]

Some Roman Catholics, however, deplored the uncharitable and abusive treatment of Carlyle. Dom Bede Camm, a monk of Erdington, near Birmingham, protested against the prejudice of the correspondents in the *Catholic Times*. 'If only Catholics could realize the immense harm they do by rash and unkind judgments outside the Fold.' Although it was impossible to recognize any Catholicism outside of Rome, he advised Roman Catholics to 'keep silent and pray...To rail at people because they have not got it is rather like mocking a blind man because he cannot see.' Another monk of Erdington, John Chapman, claimed that such acrimony prevented conversion, and a sympathetic layman pleaded that 'it is our duty to pray for them but not abuse them.'[3]

Aelred Carlyle deprecated the controversy, but he did not abandon his claim to Catholicism and the common heritage of Benedictinism. 'The correspondence in itself can do us no harm,' he wrote to Bede Camm, 'but the whole question of religious controversy should be so sacred that I am sorry to think that the *Catholic Times* can open its columns to amuse itself at our expense.'[4] He believed that 'no good purpose can be served by such cheap advertisement,' but he refused to compromise his Anglo-Catholic principles. 'I cannot agree with you,' he told Camm; 'the Rule of our Holy Father (believing as we do that we belong to the Catholic Church) is as much ours as yours.'[5] Carlyle confessed that McFall had written the article without his knowledge, and consequently 'he confused those Catholic doctrines and practices which we of right inherit from our forefathers with those more modern developments which are peculiar to his own communion.' Moreover, the Catholic Church is 'rightly represented in this land by the Church of England; were we not certain of this...we should long ago have submitted to Rome.'[6]

Carlyle's Painsthorpe monastery attracted so much attention and support that in 1906 he was able to purchase Caldey Island as the new home for his Anglican Benedictines. The secular press greeted this move with enthusiastic reports and pictorial essays. The Anglo-Catholic press told its readers that they could be proud that monasticism was firmly planted in the Anglican Church. The Roman Catholic press, however, feared Carlyle's new-found fame and claim to the heritage of medieval monasticism. The *Catholic Times* scorned Lord Halifax's equation of the Caldey foundation with Benedictine monasticism. 'But should not Lord Halifax frankly acknowledge that no one can be a Benedictine monk without observing the principles of St. Benedict, chief amongst which was dutiful homage to the See of Rome?'[7] *The Universe* quoted an anonymous article which described Carlyle's move to Caldey as 'childish nonsense for a few unauthorized imitators and amateurs to pose as Benedictines.'[8] The strongest denunciation, however, appeared in *The Tablet*. As in the 1905 controversy, it ridiculed Carlyle's High Church practices and insisted that Benedictinism had no validity *extra Romam*. 'Certain grave questions arise out of the title "Benedictine" which these jealous monks have assumed.' Some Anglo-Catholics believe 'that by a restoration here and there...the Church of England will gradually establish and make good her claim...to be part and parcel of the visible Church of Christ.' Benedictine monasticism was the exclusive property of Rome. The article also cautioned unknowing Roman Catholics against the 'veering wind of Anglican doctrine...and changing gust of Anglican practice' and warned against the 'discordant jangling of sects' which emulate Roman practices. The story concluded that 'the presence of monks and nuns..., the use of high ritual...and all the other things hotly debated by Episcopalians do not in any way change the ecclesiastical position of the Church of England.'[9]

Nonetheless, Caldey Island flourished and quickly became a paradise for Anglo-Catholics who wanted to delight in the life of a pre-Reformation Benedictine monastery. On Caldey, there was Reservation of the Blessed Sacrament, Benediction, and devotions to the Blessed Virgin. Carlyle favoured the Roman Catholic monastic breviary and refused to use the Book of Common Prayer. Caldey Island was Roman in letter and spirit. But the Roman Catholic press continued to accentuate its anomalous position. The *Catholic Times* scorned an article in the Caldey periodical *Pax* which defended a catholic or universal interpretation of the Church and condemned 'the unhappy divisions of Christendom.'[10] It was an absolute misrepresentation, the Roman paper argued, 'to state that the Anglican and Orthodox "Pews"...have been set up inside the Church; on the contrary, every division, every sect, every rival church, has been deliberately established outside and in opposition to the one original Catholic Church.' In conclusion, the article dismissed all Carlyle's attempts to minimize the differences between Rome and Canterbury, and proudly declared that 'the Church itself is not divided, it is One.'[11] *The Tablet* tried to avoid any reference to Caldey from curious readers.[12] Some Roman Catholics even ridiculed the Caldey monks in public.[13] On 7 January 1910, the *Catholic Times* implored the Anglican monks to 'either abandon the pretence of being followers of St. Benedict or enter the Catholic Church of which he was such a distinguished ornament and benefactor.'[14]

In February 1913, however, Abbot Aelred Carlyle and the majority of his monks announced that they were leaving the Anglican Church and seeking admission into the Roman Catholic Church. The reason for the conversion was a list of demands drawn up by the Bishop of Oxford, Charles Gore, which would have eliminated some of Caldey's more pronounced Romish practices and regularized its questionable status within the Church of England. According to Bishop Gore, the Anglican Benedictines must abandon Reservation of the Blessed Sacrament, Exposition and the doctrine of the Immaculate Conception, vest the community's property in the Established Church, and promise to use exclusively the Book of Common Prayer. Carlyle refused and renounced the Church of England. A change in the Roman Catholic estimation of him and his monastery appeared immediately. The press which earlier had vilified him as a fool and knave now portrayed him as a man of deep spirituality, an heroic pioneer, a martyr sacrificed by the prejudices of the Anglican Church. Bishops and abbots flocked to Caldey to comfort him. Hopefully, this secession would induce others to follow the Caldey monks to Rome.

After his decision, Carlyle immediately wrote to Dom Bede Camm, and advised him to 'start for Caldey as soon as possible; we need your help and advice.'[15] Two days later, he informed Dom Bede that the community were certain they were following the will of God in going to Rome. 'You are the first Catholic priest to whom I have written, and I feel that we cannot turn to anyone better qualified to assist us. I have...ceased to minister as an Anglican and we wait now for your arrival.'[16] Bede Camm was overjoyed and immediately set out for Caldey.

He arrived there on 26 February and began to prepare for the corporate submission of the monks. His first impression of the community was positive. 'They were most of them quite young, and they were evidently trying their best to be real monks...I was impressed by their solid piety, and the signs they gave of a real vocation.'[17] He informed the Roman Catholic Bishop of Newport, John Hedley, that 'God has indeed wrought wonders here...What amazes me so much is their faith and devotion. They might have been Catholics for years.'[18] The Abbot of Downside[19] and Dom Bede's superior, Columba Marmion,[20] the Abbot of Maredsous, agreed to attend the ceremony. Francis Mostyn, the Bishop of Menevia,[21] consented to receive the monks into the Roman Catholic Church on 5 March. In the meantime, Dom Bede warned the community that they must be willing to make some necessary modifications. Moreover, they must continue to support the Abbot 'for his noble spirit of self-forgetful love' and 'help him by accepting loyally the changes that are necessary.'[22] On 5 March 1913, in the presence of Bishop Mostyn and other Benedictine Abbots, Carlyle and twenty Caldey monks were formally received into the Roman Catholic Church.[23]

Cardinal Merry Del Val conveyed the best wishes of the Vatican and telegraphed the monks that the 'Holy Father affectionately blesses new converts on their reception into the Fold and prays God to grant them the abundance of every grace.'[24] The Archbishop of Westminster, Cardinal Bourne, sent his 'heartfelt blessing to the Abbot and community' and told Abbot Marmion that 'the news about Caldey has given great joy to everyone.'[25] Bishop Mostyn was 'astonished at the genuine piety, nay holiness, of these good people,' and maintained that 'the wonder would have been if these people had *not* come into the Church.'[26] Marmion told a nun that 'the conversions at Caldey are a great consolation, but also an increase of responsibility, work and correspondence for me.... They are beautiful souls, very simple, and several of them are very close to God and far advanced in contemplation.'[27] The English Benedictines also revelled at the events on Caldey. The Abbot of Downside, Cuthbert Butler, believed that everything necessary to ensure the success of Caldey must be done.[28] He hoped that 'God's work may be brought to a happy issue,' and told Camm that 'it is indeed a great thing — probably the greatest work of your life.'[29] The President of the English Benedictine Congregation and future Cardinal, Aidan Gasquet, congratulated Carlyle and told him that he viewed the conversion and the Abbot's 'determination to seek admission into the Catholic Church...as the powerful working of the Holy Spirit.'[30] Gasquet also assured Camm that 'anything I can do about Caldey in Rome I shall be glad to attempt.'[31] This same spirit appeared in the English and foreign Roman Catholic press.

The Jesuit publication, *The Month*, referred to the Caldey conversion as a 'remarkable story.' The monks did not act like 'sulking children' or 'claim to be a law to themselves,' as their Anglican detractors claimed, but 'they showed a true anxiety to place themselves under Catholic authority.' The article concluded that they 'were acting in strict conformity with their professed principles...and sought to place themselves under a true Catholic authority.'[32] The *Catholic Herald* joyfully announced the news of the conversion[33] and kept its readers informed with reports on Carlyle's reconciliation with Rome.[34] The Salford diocesan paper reprinted Camm's account of the conversion[35] and argued that the property belonged to the Roman Church.[36]

The *Catholic Times*, which had described Carlyle as a fraud and hypocrite in 1905, now described the conversion as a 'gallant attempt' which exhibited 'real moral courage.' A leading article on 28 February portrayed him as a 'man of ability and strong character [who] hoped to familiarize Anglicans with Benedictine traditions.' The next edition emphasized the patronage of Anglican bishops which Caldey enjoyed and continued to describe Carlyle as 'a man of deep spiritual purpose.' 'Certainly it seemed that this struggling community was visibly blessed and protected by Almighty God.' Reacting to charges of abbatial dishonesty, the *Catholic Times* declared that the monks 'may have had their eyes opened to the true facts of their position and may have resolved to join that Church which alone upholds the fulness of Christian doctrine.' Another article told the High Church Anglicans that 'it was a courageous act' and that 'to return to the pre-Reformation means to enter on the path to Rome...The only place for Benedictine monks, as followers of a Catholic Saint most faithful to the Pope,...is the Catholic Church.' By forsaking the Established Church, moreover, the monks were 'poorer than they were in the Church of England.' On 4 April, the paper appealed to loyal Roman Catholics for money to support the monks, who had forfeited an estimated £20,000 of promised aid as a result of the secession. On 15 March and later, it scoffed at the disunity of the Anglican Church and the illogical position of the Anglo-Catholic movement, urging Anglicans to abandon their Church and follow Caldey's path to Rome. A May edition dealt with the 'Anglican advance towards the Catholic Church' and the insecurity of the Anglo-Catholics. Consequently, 'there is no doubt that the conversion of the monks of Caldey was a severe blow to High Churchmen.'[37]

Prior to the conversion, *The Universe* had published scurrilous attacks on the Anglo-Catholic party and printed a series of articles enticing people to convert.[38] The first announcement of the events of Caldey was followed a week later with a cover-page pictorial essay dealing with the island, the Abbey, and Abbot Carlyle.[39] The editorial gloried 'in the fact that some sixty-odd erstwhile members of the Church of England have found their true home in communion with Rome.' The 14 March edition stated that 'the inevitable has happened to the monks of Caldey.... Their purity of motive, sincerity of life and true conception of spiritual ideals made the end of their experiment all but certain.'[40] The revival was doomed to failure when it came into conflict with 'an Establishment the root and centre of which is compromise with incompatibilities.' The article contrasted the unity and peace of the Roman Church with the chaos of the Anglican Church, 'the city of confusion.' The conversion of the Caldey monks, therefore, was motivated by 'pure conformity to the Will of God...pure intention and good faith, and the singleness of purpose [which] led them along the way of peace and liberty.'[41]

Throughout the following months, *The Universe* informed its readers of events on Caldey, attacked those Anglicans who demanded that the monks return the island to the Church, appealed for funds to maintain the monastery,[42] and reported all progress concerning Caldey's adoption of Roman Catholicism.[43] The paper also used the example of Caldey to tempt others to secede and to ridicule the Anglican Church. 'But certain Anglicans have conceived a fantastic society in the clouds, without a visible centre, without unity in doctrine...without historical continuity from Christ, without any credentials to show their mission to the world.' 'The Protestant Church is full of the strongest anomalies,' one article declared, and another characterized the Anglican claim to catholicity as 'a source of amusement.'[44]

The Tablet printed two articles by Camm which described the conversion and reception in glowing terms. It also published extracts from the correspondence between Abbot Carlyle and Bishop Gore and defended the right of the monks to retain ownership of the island. Carlyle's career was portrayed as an 'heroic effort to graft the spirit of monasticism upon the tree of Anglicanism,' and the Abbot was described as 'a pious young medical student.' *The Tablet* also acquainted the public with every aspect of the new converts' first months as Roman Catholics. The secession became a useful apologetic device. An article stated that the example of the Caldey monks demonstrated 'that the claims of Rome are not to be found only in dim confines of thought, but may confront a man's life wherever he determines to live it.' True religious life could only be lived in communion with Rome. 'A man of resolve has but to take up any line of spiritual life wholeheartedly, and in a short time Rome will be in sight.' The apparent discord in the Anglican Church was also exploited. A July article claimed that 'if the Church of England really holds Catholic truths, she is the wickedest institution that ever appeared on earth.' The same essay also described the Anglo-Catholic movement as 'so sad, so perverse, so self-torturing, so unworthy; so foolish even, and useless.' Roman Catholics were urged to help by contributing to a fund to sustain the Caldey monks, who suffered financially by the desertion of their Anglican friends.[45]

Members of the English Benedictine Congregation entertained definite plans about Caldey's future in the Roman Catholic Church. Abbot Butler believed it was imperative that the monks remain together as a community and join the English Benedictine Congregation. He instructed Camm to 'do what is necessary for Caldey...and to stay there as long as may be needful.'[46] Butler hoped that 'it may be arranged to keep the Community together, and to turn them into a Catholic Benedictine Abbey *in toto.*' For the time being, 'it will be necessary for at least about six Benedictines to live there among them—Superior, Novice-Master...for at least a year.' But they must become English Benedictines. 'I hope things may be so arranged that the Abbey will remain English and not be tacked on to any foreign Congr[egation].' Butler desired that 'the English Congr[egation] will gradually come to embrace all Black Monk Monasteries in England, without spoiling their observance and life.'[47]

Aidan Gasquet, the Abbot President of the English Congregation, had his own plans. He informed Carlyle that he hoped 'nothing will prevent your keeping together as a community.' Moreover, 'it may be useful, and perhaps necessary, that for a time, some of your members should go and live in our monasteries and that you should have some Benedictines with you at Caldey.'[48] Gasquet was adamant that 'they must keep up Caldey...[and] they must not hitch on to any other body but the English

Congregation.... I trust that whatever happens the community will manage to keep together,' and therefore it might be prudent that 'they have some of their members in other monasteries for a time and that some OSB (real) come and guide them at Caldey.'[49] Abbot Gasquet recognized the influence which Abbot Marmion of the Beuronese Congregation exercised on Carlyle, but he did not believe 'there is any danger of the Beuron people being able to work their will in Rome.' Caldey must not be affiliated with a foreign congregation; this 'would be fatal.' 'If possible let them be under the Bishop with the monastic Visitor you speak about.'[50] Even Abbot Marmion believed Caldey would join the English Congregation. He told Bede Camm that 'it appears that Br. Aelred is going to place Caldey under D. Gasquet and the E.B.C.... Be it so.'[51]

At the end of April, Abbot Gasquet had presented Abbot Carlyle's petition to the Sacred Congregation of Religious and informed John Chapman that it was 'absolutely sure to secure immediately' a favourable reply. According to Gasquet, the Secretary of the Congregation 'promised to expedite the document.' The guarantee of the jurisdiction and authority of Bishop Mostyn over the affairs of Caldey was the essential point. 'I suggested that he [the Secretary] had better give the Bishop full powers to act in every necessary way without having to have recourse to the Holy See as anything in the way of a difficulty crops up.'[52] Gasquet believed that any dispensations depended on the power being vested in the Bishop of Menevia, but Abbot Marmion and Carlyle, who had recently arrived in Rome, suddenly rejected any control by Bishop Mostyn. 'Neither the Abbot nor Aelred made any remark about the Bishop's report,' Gasquet wrote to Camm, 'except they consider it a mistake to place Caldey under the Bishop for ten years.'[53] 'They suggest I hold the petition back.' Gasquet argued 'that it was the obvious course for a time' and pointed out that the idea originated with Carlyle. He also remarked that Abbot Marmion 'appears to be quite charmed with the Abbot Aelred, who I must confess has not made a very good impression on me.'[54] Gasquet believed the problem revolved around the question of authority, and informed Camm that he had 'no doubt that what Abbot M[armion] wished for was that he should have been appointed superior, and this has been avoided.' Gasquet prophetically predicted, 'There are many rocks ahead.' In spite of Carlyle's objection, the Bishop of Menevia will be given 'full faculties to act.'[55]

On 16 May, Marmion and Carlyle had a private audience with Pope Pius X, who spoke of 'the great favour and grace received by the Abbot and monks of Caldey.' Marmion told the Pope that the conversion was due to the monks' liturgical training. The Pope agreed, but added 'that it was miraculous.'[56] During the audience, Carlyle presented his formal petition, which emphasized that Carlyle was 'the founder and superior' of the monastery and how 'he himself shaped and directed the monks...and led almost all of them into the bosom of the True Church.'[57] It also stated that the community wished to continue a monastic observance 'under the jurisdiction of the Bishop of Menevia and under the instruction of two monks of the Monastery of Maredsous.'[58] Carlyle argued that 'it is of very great importance to the Catholic Church in England that this community, now it is converted, should proceed without a defection and should bring day by day greater fruits of holiness.'

'On account of circumstances which are rather special,' Carlyle requested the following dispensations: permission to complete a canonical novitiate at Maredsous and 'receive all necessary and suitable dispensations'; after this, to be allowed to profess Solemn Vows immediately instead of undergoing any probation period; and, on the recommendation of Abbot Marmion, 'to receive Holy Orders as soon as possible,' and soon afterwards be blessed as Abbot of Caldey.[59] Abbot Marmion urged the Pope to grant the necessary dispensations, 'for example and edification of Christians,'[60] and Pius X agreed. 'We accord the most ample faculties and all dispensations, in order that he may be ordained immediately after his novitiate, and not only for him but also for those of Caldey.'[61] Consequently, the Sacred Congregation for Religious granted Bishop Mostyn the faculties to carry out the wishes of the Pope.[62]

In August, Bishop Mostyn issued the official announcement on the status of Caldey. He emphasized that 'the Holy See now recognizes [Caldey] as a canonically established Monastery with a novitiate.' The life at Caldey 'has been approved by the Supreme Authority, and therefore in this regard all will continue as before.' Mostyn also revealed that he had been 'given jurisdiction over the community for a period of ten years' and announced the appointment of John Chapman as temporary superior and Camm as novice master. Because of the gracious dispensations from the Vatican, Carlyle would return in a year as a priest and legitimate Abbot of Caldey.[63] Although pleased, little expression of enthusiasm on the part of English Catholics appeared. There were, however, some hints of disapproval or jealousy from other English monks. Abbot Cummins of Ampleforth complained that 'on the conversion...the provisions of Canon Law and the traditions of the Benedictine Order were largely dispensed on their behalf.' He also remarked that 'the community, with no constitution and no traditions, with little knowledge of Canon Law or Theology, and with little supervision, were not affiliated to any monastic congregation, but were kept under the immediate jurisdiction of the Holy See delegated to a distant Ordinary.'[64]

Carlyle's career remained turbulent despite the ease of his reception into the Roman communion. The outbreak of the Great War had serious consequences for the Caldey monks: the island's labour force left to fight on the Continent; and all hope to develop any trade or industry vanished. Economically, Caldey was far from secure, and the Roman Catholic press appealed to the conscience of English Catholics to save the island. But financial disasters continued to plague the community. A growing debt and ill health forced Carlyle to resign as superior of the monastery in 1921. Soon afterwards, he went to Canada and worked as a missionary. In 1951, he returned to Prinknash Abbey, where the Caldey community had moved in 1928. On 14 October 1955, he died, and was buried in the crypt of the abbey church.

Notes

[1] *Catholic Times,* 23 June 1905.

[2] *Catholic Times,* 30 June 1905; 14 July 1905; 21 July 1905; 28 July 1905; 18 August 1905; 1 September 1905.

[3] *Catholic Times,* 21 July 1905; 18 August 1905; 21 July 1905. Bede Camm was a convert to Roman Catholicism. St. Thomas, Erdington, was a foundation of Maredsous Abbey, Belgium. Canonically, Dom Bede was a member of the Belgian monastery and under obedience to its superior, Abbot Columba Marmion. In 1913, Dom Bede transferred his stability to St. Gregory's Abbey, Downside. See B. Camm, *Anglican Memoirs* (London: Burns, Oates, Washbourne, 1935).

[4] A. Carlyle to B. Camm, 24 July 1905, Camm Papers, Downside Abbey Archives, Somerset.

[5] A. Carlyle to B. Camm, 24 July 1905, DAA.

[6] *Catholic Times,* 14 July 1905.

[7] *Catholic Times,* 24 August 1906.

[8] *The Universe,* 31 August 1906.

[9] *The Tablet,* 8 September 1906.

[10] 'My Pew: A Parable,' *Pax,* March 1908, pp. 418-423. Allegorical in nature, each 'pew' represented a church in divided Christendom. Although they were divided, the article argued for the fundamental unity of all Christians.

[11] *Catholic Times,* 29 May 1908.

[12] *The Tablet,* 5 February 1910.

[13] A. Carlyle to P. Anson, 25 April 1910, Carlyle Papers, Pluscarden Abbey Archives, Elgin, Scotland.

[14] *Catholic Times,* 7 January 1910.

[15] A. Carlyle to B. Camm, 22 February 1913, printed in B. Camm, *The Power of Prayer Shown in the Conversion at Caldey and St. Brides: A Paper Read at the 4th National Congress at Plymouth,* July 1913, private printing, DAA. It was Dom Bede's personal opinion that the conversions were miraculous. He pointed out that a nun had received a vision in 1907 which foreshadowed the secession.

[16] A. Carlyle to B. Camm, 24 February 1913, printed in B. Camm, *The Call of Caldey* (London: Burns, Oates, Washbourne, 1937), p. 20.

[17] Ibid., p. 25.

[18] B. Camm to Hedley, 18 March 1913, Hedley Papers, Cardiff Diocesan Archives, Cardiff.

[19] Abbot Cuthbert Butler, O.S.B.

[20] Abbot Marmion was the Irish-born Abbot of Maredsous Abbey and Dom Bede's superior. By 1913, Abbot Marmion was a recognized authority on spirituality and an acclaimed religious writer. He had also conducted retreats for the priests of the Dioceses of Westminster and Southwark. See Benedictine Studies, *The English Letters of Abbot Marmion 1858-1923* (Dublin: Helicon, 1962); *New Catholic Encyclopedia,* s.v. 'Columba Marmion'; R. Thibaut, *Abbot Columba Marmion* (London: Sands Co., 1932).

[21] Caldey was located in the Roman Catholic Diocese of Menevia.

[22] 'Sermon Preached at Caldey,' 2 March 1913, Camm Papers, DAA.

[23] According to the calculations of Dom Gregory Fournier, a monk of Maredsous Abbey, six monks who signed the 28 February protest to Bishop Gore did not become Roman Catholic on 5 March. Out of the twenty-two monks who were received, only thirteen including the Abbot were professed as monks in 1914. The programme of the reception ceremony is part of the Camm Papers at Downside. The Bishop baptized the monks conditionally and sacramental absolution was given. Details of the reception appeared in *The Tablet,* 15 March 1913, and *The Universe,* 14 March 1913.

[24] Printed in *The Universe,* 7 March 1913. The Cardinal's mother was English, and he had become one of the most powerful Cardinals in Rome. In 1913, he was Secretary of State for the Vatican.

[25] Bourne to Marmion, 9 March 1913, Carlyle Papers, Prinknash Abbey Archives, Gloucester.

[26] Mostyn to ?, 25 March 1913, Mostyn Papers, Menevia Diocese Archives, Wrexham, Clwyd. This is the only reference to Caldey in the Menevia Archives. There is mention of a 'Caldey File,' but this is either misplaced or lost. Bishop Mostyn's earlier papers are deposited at Cardiff, but a search of these papers revealed nothing.

[27] Marmion to Sister, 26 March 1913, printed in Benedictine Studies, *The English Letters of Abbot Marmion 1858-1923,* p. 193.

[28] C. Butler to B. Camm, 23 February 1913, Butler Papers, DAA.

[29] C. Butler to B. Camm, 28 February 1913, Butler Papers, DAA.

[30] A. Gasquet to A. Carlyle, 3 March 1913, Gasquet Papers, DAA.

[31] A. Gasquet to B. Camm, 18 March 1913, Gasquet Papers, DAA.

[32] 'The Benedictines of Caldey,' *The Month,* April 1913, pp. 408, 410, 412.

[33] *Catholic Herald* (London), 7 March 1913.

[34] *Catholic Herald,* 27 September 1913.

[35] *The Harvest* (Manchester), March 1913.

[36] *The Harvest,* April 1913.

[37] *Catholic Times,* 28 February 1913; 7 March 1913; 21 March 1913; 4 April 1913; 15 March 1913; 30 May 1913; 25 October 1913; 30 May 1913.

[38] *The Universe,* 3 January 1913; 10 January 1913; 24 January 1913; 7 February 1913; 14 February 1913.

[39] *The Universe,* 28 February 1913; 7 March 1913.

[40] In addition to the monks, approximately forty islanders also converted.

[41] *The Universe,* 7 March 1913; 14 March 1913.

[42] *The Universe,* 14 March 1913; 3 May 1913; 28 March 1913.

[43] *The Universe,* 25 April 1913; 23 May 1913; 30 May 1912; 27 June 1913; 25 July 1913.

[44] *The Universe,* 11 April 1913; 20 March 1913; 11 April 1913.

[45] *The Tablet,* 8 March 1913; 22 March 1913; 5 April 1913; 8 March 1913; 22 March 1913; 31 May 1913; 7 June 1913; 21 June 1913; 2 September 1913; 27 September 1913; 24 May 1913; 26 July 1913; 29 March 1913.

[46] C. Butler to B. Camm, 23 February 1913, Butler Papers, DAA.

[47] C, Butler to B. Camm, 28 February 1913, Butler Papers, DAA.

[48] A. Gasquet to A. Carlyle, 3 March 1913, Gasquet Papers, DAA.

[49] A. Gasquet to C. Butler, 3 March 1913, Gasquet Papers, DAA.

[50] A. Gasquet to B. Camm, 18 March 1913, Gasquet Papers, DAA.

[51] C. Marmion to B. Camm, 21 April 1913, printed in Benedictine Studies, *The English Letters of Abbot Marmion 1858-1923,* p. 106.

[52] A. Gasquet to J. Chapman, 29 April 1913, Gasquet Papers, DAA.

[53] A. Gasquet to B. Camm, 5 May 1913, Gasquet Papers, DAA.

[54] A. Gasquet to B. Camm, 5 May 1913, Gasquet Papers, DAA.

[55] Gasquet to Camm, 28 May 1913, Gasquet Papers, DAA.

[56] 'Private Report Written by Abbot Marmion After His Audience With Pius X,' 16 May 1913, Chapman Papers, Maredsous Abbey Archives, Denée, Belgium.

[57] 'Petition of Aelred Carlyle,' 11 May 1913, Camm Papers, DAA.

[58] John Chapman had convinced Carlyle that his only hope for favours and dispensations depended on the suzerainty of the Bishop of Menevia.

[59] 'Petition of Aelred Carlyle,' 11 May 1913, Camm Papers, DAA.

[60] 'Petition of Abbot Marmion,' Document 2479/13, Caldey-Prinknash Papers, Office of the Abbot Primate, Sant' Anselmo, Rome.

[61] 'Private Report Written By Abbot Marmion After His Audience With Pius X, 16 May 1913,' Chapman Papers, MAA.

[62] 'Decree of the Sacred Congregation for Religious,' 31 May 1913, Caldey-Prinknash Papers, Office of the Abbot Primate, Rome. The files of the Sacred Congregation for Religious on the Caldey conversion were moved to the archives of the Congregation for the Doctrine of the Faith (the old Holy Office). This Congregation would not permit research into the Caldey Papers.

[63] 'Statement as to the Abbey and Community at Caldey by the Bishop of Menevia,' *Pax,* August 1913, p. 307.

[64] Cummins to Laurentes (The Cardinal Prefect, Congregation For Religious), 1921, Cummins Papers, Ampleforth Abbey Archives, Yorkshire.

CHAPTER X

WESTMINSTER CATHEDRAL: FROM DREAM TO REALITY

1. Catholicism in England from the Reformation

The Henrician Reformation radically transformed the social and religious life of England, and for at least two centuries many stereotyped Roman Catholicism as a threat to the integrity and security of the realm. The Roman Catholic Church, however, had come under attack from many sources prior to the reign of Henry VIII; a desire to correct ecclesiastical abuses had been voiced before the Reformation Parliament assembled in 1529. The problem of church appointments to English posts by Roman officials and appeals to ecclesiastical courts in Rome had constantly plagued church-state relationships. During the fourteenth century, the Statutes of Praemunire and Provisors attempted to limit the pretensions of the Roman Church which had been growing since the time of Henry II. In the areas of theological speculation and ecclesiastical practice, some pious and brave individuals seriously questioned the accepted norms and interpretations provided by the Roman Church. With its emphasis on the importance of a direct and personal experience of God, mysticism turned the eyes of its followers heavenward and helped to undercut both the role of the priest as mediator and the claim of the institutional church as the exclusive dispensor of salvation. Some of the writings of the Oxford don, John Wycliffe (c.1329-1384) anticipated many of the programmes advanced by the later reformers: the need for the bible in the vernacular; doubt concerning the doctrine of transubstantiation; the propriety of ecclesiastical ownership of property; the priority of sacred scripture; the need to reform the scandalously lax lives of monks and nuns; and questions concerning the superstitious character of relics, pilgrimages, and the cult of the saints.

Not surprisingly, ecclesiastical abuses and scandals attracted much attention. In *The Canterbury Tales,* for example, Geoffrey Chaucer's lively vignettes portrayed churchmen and churchwomen still strongly attached to the lures and enjoyments of the world which they had vowed to renounce. Another fourteenth century piece of literature, *Piers Plowman,* written by William Langland, castigated the wealth and extravagances of an institutional church dedicated to poverty. The humanists and students of the 'new learning' also recognized some of the shortcomings and hoped to correct them by poking fun through satire. Erasmus (c. 1469-1536), whose 'sensible and scholarly nose was otherwise offended by the stink of corruption,'[1] became one of the chief representatives of this school of thought. His works, especially *The Praise of Folly* and *The Colloquies,* captured a wide audience and exerted a great influence throughout Europe. 'More than any single man, he lowered the European reputation of popes and clergy, monks and friars, and (above all) of the theologians.'[2] At the dawn of the sixteenth century, therefore, the complaints and critiques against the Roman Catholic Church seemed innumerable and even insurmountable: the immoral or luxurious lifestyle of nuns and clerics; the benefit of clergy; sanctuary; mortuary fees; and the wide-reaching claims of the clerical courts. Reform was long overdue, and 'like Erasmus, many educated men would have preferred the Church to be ridiculed into good sense and efficiency and purity of life. But a man who is holding property will not be mocked out of it.'[3]

Unlike the reforming movements on the continent, the English Reformation was an act of state. The King in Parliament reversed centuries of custom, tinkered with the liturgy and, of course, revolutionized the relationship of England to the Pope in Rome. Henry VIII had agonized over ways to save his kingdom from the chaos and upheavals associated with the War of the Roses, and a male heir became an urgent necessity to give stability to his dynasty. Moreover, Henry tried to resist radical changes in religious practices or in doctrine. Innovations in the area of religion could not remain isolated from the demands of political expediency.

Henry's Spanish queen, Catherine of Aragon, had grown old and sterile, and he had already cast fond eyes on Ann Boleyn, but the chances of a papal annulment seemed remote if not impossible — not least because Catherine's nephew, the Emperor Charles V, had sacked Rome and held the Pope under house arrest! Frustrated and eager to re-marry, Henry dismissed Cardinal Wolsey, who was unsuccessful in obtaining the necessary divorce from Rome and even failed in having the case heard in England, and summoned Parliament in 1529. So reform of the Roman Catholic Church commenced.

A series of statutes attacked the traditional privileges of the Church and transformed England into a unitary national state. The Convocations of Canterbury and York paid fines of approximately £118,000 for alleged violations of the *Statute of Praemunire*. In 1532, the *Act of Submission of the Clergy* prohibited enactment of any new ecclesiastical laws without royal permission, and the Church also agreed to submit the existing canons to a committee of laymen and clerics for review and possible revision. The economic aspects also crept into the legislation: annates or first fruits were no longer paid to Rome, but instead went to the Crown's coffers. The *Act in Restraint of Appeals* (1534) abolished appeals from England to Rome. Henry divorced his wife and married his mistress, Ann Boleyn, in 1533, and so Catherine was denied access to the ecclesiastical courts in Rome. More importantly, the *Act in Restraint of Appeals* also signaled the advent of a new national and independent state. According to the preamble,

> by divers sundry old authentic histories and chronicles it is manifestly declared and expressed, that this realm of England is an empire...governed by one supreme head and king...unto whom a body politic, composed of all sorts and degrees of people, divided in terms, and by names of spirituality and temporality, be bounden and august to bear, next to God, a natural and humble obedience.

Consequently, the *Act of Supremacy* (1534) declared that the king was now the supreme head of the Church of England. With the exceptions of Thomas More and John Fisher, acts of heroism and displays of loyalty to Roman Catholicism were rare. The momentum of reform continued, and monastic houses became the next victims of Henry's policies.

On the eve of the Reformation, approximately eight hundred religious houses of various sizes and wealth dotted the English countryside. For some time the monasteries had failed to contribute significantly to the religious or intellectual climate of England, but on the other hand they were not the dens of licentiousness and drunkenness which some critics claimed. Rather, they had grown complaisant, and the small number of monks was out of proportion to their vast wealth: '...for the most part the monasteries were neither fervent nor disgraceful. They were pleasant, half-secularized clubs for common and comfortable living. Some of the smaller were little more than farms.'[4] The monasteries caught the keen eye of Henry VIII for two reasons: their wealth would greatly enrich the royal purse; and, as enclaves of loyal Roman Catholics, they might easily become seedbeds of sedition. Consequently, the monasteries must be suppressed and their extensive lands become royal property.

The first hint of a national policy had already appeared between 1524 and 1529, when Cardinal Wolsey suppressed a number of the smaller monasteries to fund and endow colleges at Oxford and at his home town of Ipswich. In 1535, the Crown ordered an evaluation of the worth of the English houses, the *Valor Ecclesiasticus;* the stage was set for the anti-monastic campaign. 'Hence, when in 1535 the great visitation of the monasteries was undertaken under the supervision of Thomas Cromwell, the King's Vicar-General for ecclesiastical affairs,' Powicke remarked, 'the Crown had already in its possession a survey of monastic wealth and was using for the material control of the whole Church all the machinery of government, all the experience acquired by the exchequer and chancery during the previous centuries.'[5] In January 1536, Parliament set the quantitative definition of laxity and sin for English monasteries at £200 per annum, and dissolved those houses which failed to meet this standard. A Court of Augmentation was quickly created to facilitate the transfer of the monastic property to the Crown. The so-called 'greater monasteries' caught the attention of Henry's officials in 1537, and visitants were dispatched to convince these houses to dissolve themselves. Most offered no resistance to the King's wishes. 'Persuasion was seldom difficult, partly because everywhere it was rumoured that soon they would all be sup-pressed, partly because some houses already found difficulty in continu-ing.'[6] Finally, a parliamentary act of 1539 declared that all monastic property surrendered after 1536 legally belonged to the Crown. The Henrician monks did not embrace the martyr's mantle, and they passively accepted their fate along with their pensions. A few individuals, however, questioned the royal policy; the Abbots of Colchester, Reading, and Glastonbury all protested, and were executed in 1539. Among other things, the short-lived Pilgrimage of Grace (1536-37) also reacted against the suppression of the smaller northern monasteries.

After Henry VIII's death in 1547, the course of the Reformation and the status of English Roman Catholics became confused. During Edward VI's reign (1547-1553), a more radical Protestant theology replaced Henry's conservatism: clergy were permitted to marry; images and statues destroyed; and chantries abolished. More radical than its 1549 counterpart, the *Prayer Book* of 1552 and the accompanying *Act of Uniformity* brought the English Reformation closer to continental practices. Then came an abrupt change: Mary Tudor succeeded her brother to the throne in 1553; the main objective of the reign being the restoration of Roman Catholi-cism. Mary presided over the repeal of the laws passed during the previous two reigns against the old religion, and in 1554 Reginald Pole absolved members of Parliament from their sins of schism. Moreover, the Queen re-established a monastery at Westminster, but the experiment did not survive the reign of her sister Elizabeth, who dissolved the community within two decades after her accession. Although the monastic lands were not returned to the Roman Church, Mary's brief reign did not endear Catholicism to her countrymen. Her marriage to Philip, King of Spain, the loss of Calais, and the needless burnings of Smithfield, turned Catholicism into a feared and hated religion. John Foxe made it certain that people would never forget the fiendish and cruel deeds of this Roman Catholic monarch. Unmourned and childless, Mary died on 17 November 1558, and was succeeded by her half-sister Elizabeth, the daughter of Ann Boleyn.

Elizabeth (1558-1603) tried to steer English religious life back to the days of her father and consequently tolerated some aspects of Roman Catholicism, but like Henry she rejected papal authority. During the first year of her reign, the *Act of Supremacy* declared Elizabeth the Supreme Governor of the Church of England, and later the *Act of Uniformity* required that all church and state officials must swear an oath of allegiance. This Act also stipulated that her clergy must conduct services according to *The Book of Common Prayer,* and a graduated penalty of imprisonment was imposed on those who refused. After the third conviction, for example, the guilty cleric faced the possibility of life imprisonment. Moreover, it became an offence to hear a Roman Catholic mass, and attendance at Anglican services was made mandatory.

Elizabeth wanted a compromise, and would tolerate no extremes. Both the Puritans returning home from exile on the continent and those who clung to the old order were subjected to restrictive legislation. But a series of domestic and external events—for example, the Northern Rebellion of 1569, the papal excommunication of Elizabeth in 1570, the Ridolfi plot, the intrigues of Mary Queen of Scots, and finally the Armada— especially marked the Roman Catholic as a potential traitor. And Parliament responded to this Catholic threat with a series of statutes. To declare the Queen a heretic or schismatic, or to convert or be converted to Roman Catholicism, carried the charge of treason. The penalties for attending mass or missing its Anglican counterpart were also increased. Harbouring recusants (that is, those who refused to attend Anglican services), became a crime, and convicted recusants were required to possess a license to journey more than five miles from their home. The increasing flow of continentally trained priests and Jesuits into Anglican England produced the so-called 'act that made martyrs': it was a treasonable act for a native Englishman to return to his country unless he registered or declared himself within forty-eight hours of his arrival. Moreover, any person who assisted or helped a priest could be subjected to the same punishment; 'priest holes,' consequently, became an accepted part of the architecture of many Roman Catholic homes.

These laws, however, were never applied consistently or even rigorously. In some parts of the country, leniency muted the full force of law, and it appears that these penal laws were enforced most stringently when Parliament was in session. The demands of the Puritans for a presbyterian system may have posed a more serious threat to the security of the realm, but the animosity against Catholicism remained the stronger current in English life. During the reigns of Henry VIII and Elizabeth I approximately one hundred and sixty-four priests, including such luminaries as Edmund Campion and Richard Gwyn, were executed. Under the reign of Mary Tudor over two hundred and seventy-three of their countrymen were also executed. By the end of the sixteenth century, therefore, the civil and religious rights of English Roman Catholics had been curtailed. They had become second-class citizens, potential traitors, and superstitious people who owed a higher allegiance to a foreign, and at times hostile, Pope in Rome.

This reforming fever soon spread over the border into Scotland, where the corrupt fabric of the Roman Catholic Church had also been recognized. The burning of the 'heretic' George Wishart on the authority of David, Cardinal Beaton, and the subsequent murder of the Cardinal, demonstrated the intensity of the hatred boiling beneath the surface of Scottish life. The presence of the French and the real possibility of Scotland becoming a Roman Catholic satellite prompted Queen Elizabeth to quick and drastic action. She supported the 'Congregation of the Lord' with men and money, and eventually these Scottish leaders expelled the French and deposed the French Regent, Mary of Guise, in 1560. This political revolution heralded the beginning of the reformation of the Roman Catholic Church in Scotland. The Scottish Parliament outlawed the mass and prescribed the death penalty for the third offence. The Parliament renounced the authority of the Pope, and John Knox's *Confession of Faith* and *Book of Discipline* - Calvinistic in doctrine and liturgy—were adopted. Scottish monasteries were pillaged, and religious life became impossible through harsh legislation against the mass. The northern reformers set up the Scottish General Assembly and authorized *The Book of Common Order,* which was based on the Geneva model. The *Concordat of Leith* (1572) declared that all individuals who held ecclesiastical benefices had to subscribe to the articles of religion contained in *The Westminster Confession of Faith* and had to swear an oath affirming the Monarch's supreme authority. No

Roman Catholic protest broke out in Scotland such as the Pilgrimage of Grace or the Northern Rebellion; even the return of Queen Mary in 1561 failed to galvanize support for the old religion. Her son James Stuart's religious preferences confused many.

English Catholics expected much when the Scottish King, James VI, succeeded Elizabeth in 1603 as James I of England. Some of James I's public statements, his flirtations with Spain, and the Catholicism of his wife, Anne of Denmark, seemed to augur well for the future of English Catholicism. But the imprudent, zealous, and rash actions of some again linked their faith with treason and disloyalty. Roman Catholics were clearly implicated in the Bye Plot (1603), and Catholic priests and laymen emerged as ring-leaders in the Gunpowder Plot (1605). Several Jesuits, including their Superior in England, Henry Garnet, suffered the fate of traitors. Consequently, the government began to prepare new legislation to tighten up the Elizabethan penal laws: Roman Catholics were excluded from certain professions such as law and medicine, and barred from holding commissions in the army and navy; their movements within the country were severely curtailed; a sacramental test was now demanded; and an oath of allegiance which declared that 'the pope, neither of himself, nor by any authority of the church or see of Rome...hath any power or authority to depose the king' was required. Although the force of these laws was applied with unequal severity throughout the country, and some Roman Catholics even dared to practice their faith openly, the stigma of disloyalty still survived. The news that Prince Charles and the Earl of Buckingham had failed to cement a marriage agreement with Roman Catholic Spain sparked bonfires and rejoicing in London, and demonstrated the intensity of the suspicion of many Englishmen towards Roman Catholicism. In Scotland, the earlier penal laws against Catholics were also strengthened and new measures passed; for example, laws against hiding priests and a prohibition against Scottish children being sent to Catholic colleges or to the continent were enacted.

English Catholics again anticipated the beginning of a new era of freedom and a relaxation of prohibitive legislation with the accession of Charles I, and with few exceptions the machinery of the penal laws did slow down. The public displays of Roman Catholicism by Queen Henrietta Maria, whose retinue included a bishop and several French priests, encouraged Catholics to practice their faith openly, if discreetly. The stormy relations between the Crown and Parliament dwarfed the urgency to enforce the legal restrictions against Catholics. When the Civil War finally erupted, some leading Roman Catholics supported the claims of the Stuart dynasty, although both sides in the conflict continued to collect fines against Catholics as a way to increase the size of their war chests! The victorious Puritans relaxed laws dealing with mandatory church attendance, but restrictions against Roman Catholics, who still aroused their suspicion, were not lightened. During the Interregnum, moreover, many English associated the papists with the royal cause.

When the third Stuart, Charles II, landed at Dover in 1660, many Catholics again believed that the new monarch would look favourably on their religion. Some of his statements from the continent, the *Declaration of Breda,* the secret Treaty of Dover with France and his marriage to Catherine of Braganza, all raised Catholic expectations and hopes, but the legislation from his Protestant Parliament represented a victory for the Anglicans against Roman Catholicism and the various Puritan sects which flourished during the previous decades. The Clarendon Code, a series of statutes aimed at the Nonconformists, also curtailed the civil and religious liberties of England's Catholic community: the *Corporation Act* (1661) required municipal office holders to take the Anglican sacrament yearly; the *Act of Uniformity* (1662) demanded that clergymen use the Prayer Book, which was modified in 1660 for religious services; the *Five Mile Act* (1665) excluded dissenters from teaching and prohibited them from coming within five miles of a town; and the *Conventicle Act* (1664) limited attendance at non-Anglican services to four. Charles' open espousal of Roman Catholicism, his intention to suspend several laws against the papists and the haunting fear that James, the King's Catholic brother, might spawn a Roman dynasty, drove the loyal Anglicans in the House of Commons to seek new repressive measures. The *Test Act* (1673), consequently, required all who held civil or military office to receive the Anglican sacrament, to swear oaths of loyalty and allegiance to the Crown, and to make a declaration against transubstantiation which stated, '...I do not believe that there is any transubstantiation in the Sacrament of the Lord's Supper, or in the elements of bread and wine, at or after the consecration thereof by any person whatsoever.' Finally the *Test Act* (1678) excluded all Roman Catholics from Parliament.

Moreover, Roman Catholicism did not fare well outside the walls of the Anglican-controlled House of Commons. Some blamed the London fire of 1666 on the city's Catholics, but 'the Popish Plot' had more serious implications. Titus Oates, a rogue and consummate liar and a former Anabaptist, had converted to Catholicism but after a chequered career he turned to the Church of England. In 1678, he started a national panic by announcing that he had uncovered the plot which aimed to assassinate Charles II and place his Roman Catholic brother on the throne. The Society of Jesus, of course, emerged as the chief conspirators. The panic lasted until 1681, and unleashed a tide of hatred and cries for vengeance against Roman Catholics. Many were imprisoned, and numerous Catholics executed for their alleged involvement in the plot. Oliver Plunket, the Archbishop of Armagh, was one of them, and became the last priest executed at Tyburn for his religion.

Much to the embarrassment and disgust of his co-religious, who wanted to practice their faith quietly and unobtrusively, the Roman Catholic James II, who converted in 1670 and succeeded his brother in 1685, flaunted his religion. (Parliament had sought to exclude him from the throne, but without success.) James appointed Roman Catholics to positions in the government, the army and universities. To the sensitive and suspicious Anglican, this appeared as another plot to re-introduce Catholicism by royal fiat, which must be resisted. In 1687, the King rashly issued a *Declaration of Indulgence* which proclaimed religious liberty throughout the kingdom and suspended the operation of the penal laws against Catholics. The birth of a male heir transformed the possibility of a Roman Catholic dynasty into a reality, and so began the process known as the Glorious Revolution. William of Orange accepted the crown in defense of the country's religious and constitutional liberties, and became joint monarch with his wife Mary; James fled into exile. Fearing reprisals from this thoroughly Protestant prince, many English Catholics also fled to the continent, but William and Mary (daughter of James II) used statute law and not the gallows to defend the Anglican establishment of their country. Acts of Parliament strengthened the exclusion of Catholics from certain areas of the legal profession and required Roman Catholics to register their property, which was more heavily taxed than non-Catholic land.

Concessions were made, however, to the Protestant Dissenters. In an attempt to unite all Nonconformists in opposition to James II the *Toleration Act* of 1689 granted them some religious freedom. With their emergence Roman Catholics also began to be accepted as responsible citizens. Accusations that some Catholics had actively supported the 1715 rising failed to ignite the fires of hatred as such a charge would earlier have done. And some Catholic priests did offer mass for the success of the 1745 Rebellion, but the Stuart magic had worn thin with English Catholics and large numbers failed to flock to the Stuart standard; so died the cause of Prince Charles.

With the Hanoverians came real signs of relaxation, and gradually Roman Catholics began to gain religious and civil parity with other denominations. In 1778, Catholics could own property provided that they took an oath—but one which did not involve a denial or rejection of their religious beliefs, and the harsh penalties for operating Catholic schools were relaxed. This legislation, however, occasioned the last great outburst of anti-Catholic hatred. Armed with a petition demanding the repeal of the 1778 *Relief Act,* and leading a large and angry 'no popery' mob, Lord George Gordon approached the Parliament buildings at Westminster during the summer of 1780. Some rioting and looting broke out, and the military had to dislodge the protesters who had by then taken control of the City of London.

In spite of this and other isolated outbursts, the government continued to repeal the restrictive laws; English Roman Catholics had proved their loyalty over the centuries, and their patriotism should be rewarded. By 1791, they were considered safe. Consequently, 'Catholics who took the oath of allegiance were free from disabilities relating to education, property, and the practice of law. Catholic peers were given the right of access to the king; they were permitted attendance at religious services and were allowed to enter religious orders.'[7] These rights were also extended to Irish and Scottish Catholics. In 1817, commissions to all ranks of the army and navy were opened to Catholics. Catholicism, therefore, had survived the attacks of the Reformation and the restrictions of the penal laws and, indeed, 'maintained its continuity through an age of unprecedented upheaval.'[8] John Bossy interpreted the struggles of the post-Reformation Catholic Church in England not as a 'process of continuous decline reaching its nadir in the eighteenth century, but as a patient and continuous process of construction from small beginnings in which the eighteenth century represents a phase of modest progress and of careful preparation for the future.'[9] Moreover, the early years of the nineteenth century represented a 'take-off' period for English Catholics. One of the crucial and emotional debates of these years concerned the rights of Catholics to sit in Parliament.

The story of Catholic emancipation was intimately connected with England's stormy and troublesome relationship with Ireland. Pitt's desire to unite the Parliaments of England and Ireland resulted in the *Act of Union* of 1800. To secure the support of the Irish members for the abolition of their assembly, the Prime Minister hinted at the possibility of Catholic emancipation. But Pitt's bill, drafted in 1801, floundered because of George III's belief that his assent would violate the provisions of his coronation oath. The campaign for Catholic emancipation, however, did not die. It did attract some support in England, but the lingering fear and suspicion of Roman Catholicism meant that any act must contain some securities to protect the Anglican state. The most important of which concerned the right of the English government to exercise a veto on ecclesiastical appointments by Rome. Meanwhile, personalities and events in Ireland continued to act as catalysts. The English hierarchy agreed to the compromise of a veto, but Daniel O'Connell and the Irish bishops successfully argued that this concession would destroy the independence of the Catholic Church. The charismatic O'Connell used the Catholic Association and the funds from Catholic rents to campaign throughout Ireland for emancipation. His electoral victory over Vesey Fitzgerald in County Clare during July 1828 forced Wellington, the Prime Minister, and Robert Peel to retract their earlier opposition to Catholic emancipation.

The earlier repeal of the *Test* and *Corporation Acts* in 1828 provided a precedent for this concession to Catholics, but the prospect of a civil war in Ireland if O'Connell did not take his seat finally pushed the Tories to concede. Wellington's threat of resignation forced George IV to withdraw his opposition to the bill. Despite protests from organizations such as the Brunswick Clubs that the English constitution was in danger, the *Catholic Emancipation Act* received the royal assent in 1829. Roman Catholics were again admitted to most public offices, save those of the Lord Chancellor, Keeper of the Great Seal, Lord Lieutenant of Ireland, and the High Commissioner of the Church of Scotland. Other securities were included to safeguard the established church. Catholic bishops, for example, were forbidden to take a title of a see already claimed by the Anglican hierarchy. The Act also outlawed public religious services conducted by Roman Catholics. A clause which sought to strangle the growth of the Jesuits and other religious orders was more rhetoric than forcible in law. Finally, Roman Catholics elected to Parliament had to swear an oath that they would not subvert the established church. Fearing that Irish Catholics might swamp the House of Commons, and also hoping to preserve the Protestant ascendancy in Ireland, the Act radically altered the Irish franchise: the voting qualification was raised from the traditional forty shillings to a prohibitive £10.

With very few exceptions, English Roman Catholics had finally reclaimed their birthright, after centuries of being penalized for their faith. Many believed that Rome should also recognize their vitality, stability and accomplishments, and re-establish the hierarchy in England. The question of ecclesiastical authority in England had always presented a problem for Rome. When it became apparent that the reformers could not succeed in expunging Roman Catholicism from English soil, the Pope appointed a cleric in 1598 with the title of Archpriest to govern the secular priests in the country. But the traditional jealousy between the secular and religious priests soon erupted. According to the secular clergy, George Blackwell the first Archpriest, favouring the Jesuits, ignored them, and jeopardized the interests of English Catholicism because of his pro-Jesuit policies. Consequently, a group of secular priests, the Appellants, wrote to Rome in 1599 and asked for Blackwell's removal.

The controversy lasted for years and saw several Archpriests trying to govern and administer English Catholicism. In 1623, Rome experimented with the appointment of William Bishop as Vicar Apostolic. Some problems arose, and the feud between the seculars and religious continued to divide Catholicism. In 1685, John Lyburn was appointed Vicar Apostolic, and after three years the country was divided into four geographic districts: London, Midland, Northern, and Western. Rome increased the number of Vicars Apostolic to eight in 1840, many Catholics beginning to regard this institution as a temporary arrangement until Rome could reconstitute an English hierarchy. Scottish interests were initially supervised by the Archpriest in England. Some Scots, however, worked to free the Catholic Church in Scotland from authority south of the border, and several proposals were discussed. Finally, on 16 March 1694, Pope Innocent XII appointed Thomas Nicolson as the first Vicar Apostolic in Scotland. Like its English counterpart, the Scottish institution increased in numbers until there were three districts in 1827.

By the middle of the nineteenth century, English Roman Catholics demanded their freedom and independence from the Propaganda in Rome. England should no longer be regarded in Roman eyes as missionary territory; it must, therefore, have a proper hierarchy. The Vicars Apostolic and the clergy desired the re-establishment of a hierarchy, but for different and conflicting reasons. 'While the vicars apostolic wanted a hierarchy because they wanted freedom from Rome, their clergy wanted a hierarchy to secure more freedom from vicars-apostolic.'[10] Under the missionary set-up, for example, priests could be moved from place to place at the whim of the Vicar Apostolic. Rome, however, refused to act on these requests, part of the reason for which can be found in the arguments of Cardinal Acton, who told Roman authorities that a hierarchy would destroy the fragile structure of English Catholicism. After his death in 1847 the last obstacle was removed.

The long awaited creation of an English hierarchy was scheduled for late 1847, but the plan was suddenly postponed. Rome's sensitivity to conditions in England and the history of Catholicism in the country asserted themselves. Certain prerequisites must be met before the establishment of the hierarchy: a Whig government must be in power; Parliament must be in recess; and the new Catholic dioceses must avoid those ancient titles associated with the established church. The year 1850 was optimum, but 'the actual timing proved nothing less than tragic.'[11] Because of John Henry Newman's recent conversion (in 1845) and the scandal caused by the Gorham case of 1850, many Anglicans believed that the restoration of a Catholic hierarchy constituted nothing less than a frontal attack on the established church. In September 1850, however, Pope Pius IX issued the brief which established thirteen sees in England, and shortly afterwards he created Nicholas Wiseman Cardinal Archbishop of Westminster.

This papal action, the new Cardinal's pastoral *Out of the Flaminian Gate,* and his inopportune rhetoric, occasioned a harsh rebuke in *The Times,* some no-popery riots, and Lord John Russell's fiery 'Durham Letter.' But the energy and intensity of this reaction could not be sustained. The government's ill-timed and unfortunate *Ecclesiastical Titles Act* (1851) attacked 'Papal Aggression' by making the creation of territorial titles illegal. This law, however, was a dead letter and a sham, and was repealed by Gladstone in 1871. In 1878, Pope Leo XIII re-established the Roman Catholic hierarchy in Scotland.

Newman's comment about English Roman Catholicism's 'second spring' captured the euphoria and self-confidence of Catholics in England. Despite some real tensions within Catholicism, for example, the increasing strength of the clergy in church affairs at the expense of the laity, the triumph of Ultramontanism over the traditional Catholic spirit, and the challenge to old and accepted ways by the increasing number of converts to Catholicism, it had successfully survived centuries of persecution and legal disabilities, and had even regained some of its lost status. Notable converts, such as Newman, Manning, and Lord Ripon, added to the respectability and vitality of the faith. The number of churches, schools and convents increased. Religious orders flourished. Catholic clergy shed their timidity and began to take an active part in educational and social reforms. English Roman Catholicism had a right to be proud of its achievements: only a temple or a shrine could adequately capture this buoyancy and sense of accomplishment.

2. A Cathedral for Westminster

A cathedral in central London, many English Catholics agreed, was needed not only to provide a place of worship for the faithful of the metropolis, but also to provide a visible monument to the respectability and achievements of their religion. 'The outward symbol of this ability to build well and expensively was Westminster Cathedral.'[12] Moreover, some Roman Catholics wanted a permanent monument to their first archbishop of the industrial age, Nicholas Wiseman. His successor,

Cardinal Henry Manning, saw other priorities, and his dedication to the eradication of poverty in London meant that a new cathedral might have to be sacrificed. Manning believed that 'the work of saving these children was his first duty, the first duty of the Catholics of London.'[13]As he remarked elsewhere, 'Could I leave 20,000 children without education and drain my friends to pile up stones and bricks?'[14] Cathedral-building represented an expensive relic associated with medieval civilizations: 'I have been content with my Old Sarum and my Selsey. The days of Salisbury and Chichester are to come.'[15] Purcell captured Archbishop Manning's thoughts on a new cathedral:

> A memorial church to Cardinal Wiseman belonged to the past, but the saving of Catholic children from the Protestant workhouses or reformatories, where their faith would be lost, belonged to the present and the future, and he made this saving work the primary end and aim of his labours.[16]

Although Cardinal Manning discouraged building an 'arch of triumph before the battle was won,'[17]and openly acknowledged the urgent need to educate the children of his archdiocese, he nonetheless recognized that a cathedral had to be constructed in the future.

In 1867, Manning purchased some property in Carlisle Place for £16,500, and began to discuss plans for a cathedral to be built on a modest scale.[18]When he acquired another nearby piece of property, his vision also began to expand: the future cathedral must now be patterned along the lines of Cologne Cathedral. But Cardinal Manning lacked the funds to flesh-out his dream. In 1882 a promise from a wealthy layman to finance the cathedral failed to materialize, but even though the funds eluded him, Manning did not abandon hope. A year later, the Cardinal again demonstrated his support for a Roman Catholic cathedral in central London. 'Opposite the windows of his residence and adjoining the land he had already purchased, stood the Middlesex County Prison of Tothill fields';[19]Cardinal Manning found out that the site was for sale. He believed that the four-acre property would prove to be a better investment for the future cathedral than the land he had previously bought. Consequently, he sold the old site, collected another £20,000, and took out a mortgage to acquire the grounds of the former prison for approximately £115,000. But Cardinal Manning could never scrape together enough money to begin the actual construction; accordingly his successor at Westminster, Herbert Vaughan, accepted the challenge.

'Like Manning's, Vaughan's reputation has rather suffered at the hands of subsequent assessors of his work.'[20]As a result of this, the personality of Herbert Vaughan emerges as a humourless administrator, an individual more at home with fund-raising drives, immersed in the world of debits and credits rather than in a ministry of personal contacts and relationships. The stereotype of Cardinal Vaughan sounds brutal: '...a man who was coldly efficient, a nuts-and-bolts administrator, too distant to be likable.'[21]These opinions, however, do contain some elements of truth. Vaughan was a scrupulous and skillful administrator and organizer. Suffocated by the administrative responsibilities at Salford, and then at Westminster, and also because of ill-health, Vaughan never enjoyed popularity with his priests who thought that their spiritual leader was cool and aloof. But this caricature is too harsh. The needs of people, as well as the cost of bricks and mortar, also consumed Cardinal Vaughan's time and energy.

Herbert Alfred Vaughan was born into an old established Roman Catholic family on 15 April 1832, in Gloucester. His mother, a convert, prayed that all her children would become priests or enter the convent. And it appears that her prayers were answered: six of her eight sons became priests, and four of her daughters became nuns. Herbert, the eldest son, experienced England's religious orders early in life. For the five years between 1841 and 1846 young Vaughan was educated at Stonyhurst; subsequently at another Jesuit school in Belgium. But he also had close contacts with the Benedictines. He spent a year as a student with the monks at Downside Abbey and his brother Joseph eventually joined the Benedictines of that house. In 1851, Herbert Vaughan went to Rome to continue his studies for the priesthood, being ordained in October 1854. It was in Italy that his close friendship began with the recent convert from Anglicanism, Henry Manning, which would later influence his career in the church.

On his return to England, Vaughan went to St. Edmund's, Ware, where he served as vice-president, later joining Manning's Oblates. Four years later, he resigned this post because of ecclesiastical in-fighting which resulted in the departure of the Oblates from St. Edmund's. A desire to minister to the world's heathen population soon grew into an obsession with the young and idealistic cleric, and for nearly two years (1863-1865) Vaughan traveled throughout North and South America trying to raise enough money to establish a college in England to train foreign missionaries. The trip proved successful, and patrons promised more money after his return to England in July 1865. A year later, St. Joseph's College, Mill Hill, opened its doors. In November 1871, Vaughan triumphantly accompanied several Mill Hill Missionaries to America, where they began work among that country's black population.

But Vaughan was not destined to direct grand missionary projects. Manning, who became Archbishop of Westminster in 1865, chose Herbert Vaughan as the new Bishop of Salford. Unknown in the North, Vaughan owed this appointment to his long friendship with the Cardinal because 'by this time all appointments to the English hierarchy had effectively become Manning's appointments.'[22] Vaughan's accomplishments at Salford were noteworthy: a pastoral seminary to prepare priests for work in the cities; annual diocesan synods which, among other duties, co-ordinated various fund-raising programs; and the creation of numerous new parishes, to name but a few.[23] Bishop Vaughan went to Rome and argued for the rights of bishops against the Jesuits, who claimed certain exemptions from episcopal supervision and opened a grammar school in Manchester without Vaughan's permission. His influence helped to produce *Romanos Pontifices* (1881) which upheld the rights of his fellow bishops against the Jesuits. Alarmed by the so-called 'leakage' which drained children from the Roman faith, Bishop Vaughan founded the Catholic Protection and Rescue Society in 1886 'to save the children by providing alternative social relief from that given by the workhouses and the Protestant philanthropic bodies.'[24] Vaughan established soup kitchens, night shelters, and encouraged numerous other schemes for the poor in his diocese. He also attacked the problem of drink by advocating a reduction in the licenses given to public houses.

If Vaughan's appointment to Salford caused some consternation in Roman Catholic circles, the announcement in 1892 that he would succeed his friend at Westminster was generally expected, and it met with the approval of the English bishops. A year later he was created a Cardinal. In addition to his administrative skills, his accomplishments as Archbishop of Westminster matched his impressive achievements in the North. Catholic education still remained one of his favorite projects. Archbishop Vaughan closed down the diocesan seminary at Hammersmith, but he actively supported the establishment of a central one at New Oscott in the Midlands to serve several dioceses; it opened in 1893. Vaughan had approved the ban on Roman Catholics going to Oxford and Cambridge, but he eventually changed his mind and persuaded the other English bishops to approach Rome and petition to have the prohibition lifted, which was done in 1895. He also campaigned for the 1902 *Education Act,* which acknowledged the rights of denominational schools to government support. In the area of theology and ecclesiastical policy, Cardinal Vaughan became the outspoken critic of the reunion movement, and against the efforts of Anglo-Catholics and some Roman Catholics to have Anglican orders declared valid. It was through his efforts in England and Rome that Anglican orders were declared 'null and void' in 1896. In the opinion of some, however, the construction of Westminster Cathedral ranked as his greatest single achievement.

When Vaughan[25] became Archbishop of Westminster in 1892, he brought to his large urban archdiocese a sense of triumphalism, loyalty to Rome, and a commitment to educational and financial reforms. But dedication to the construction of a new cathedral also coloured his tenure in office: '...he immediately decided as his major project, to build a cathedral which would be a liturgical, pastoral and intellectual center for English Catholicism.'[26] The overdue recognition for the progress of Roman Catholics in Britain was the motivation, and 'the building of Westminster Cathedral was both symbolic of his general attitude as well as an example of his administrative ability.'[27] According to his biographer, Vaughan wanted a 'Cathedral which should be the head and heart of the life of the Church in England, and the vivifying centre of its spirit and worship.' Moreover, 'it was to be the home of a companionship of priests, the example of whose lives should colour all the ideals and activities of the diocese.'[28] This new church must necessarily become the spiritual centre of England. Lecturers would address the faithful, meeting-space would be available for clubs, and dedicated clergy would minister to the special needs of the London area. Because of his untiring efforts and the financial contributions of numerous eager Roman Catholics, Westminster Cathedral emerged from dream to reality.

The construction of this cathedral became one of Vaughan's top priorities. According to one of his biographers, 'Cardinal Vaughan told his cousin at St. Pancras when he arrived in London from Salford as Archbishop-elect, his biggest project was to build a cathedral in Westminster.'[29] The property for the cathedral had been secured, some money already collected or pledged, and numerous influential Roman Catholics had openly endorsed the scheme, but Vaughan realized that his building project might invite some criticism. Cardinal Manning had already wrestled with the strong emotional critique which haunted Vaughan: money lavished on a church robbed the poor, and should be given instead to a charitable organization. But other voices of opposition also confronted Cardinal Vaughan. Some argued that the age of cathedrals belonged to the Middle Ages, while others maintained that the project failed to capture the imagination of the rank and file of Roman Catholics needed to finance the construction of this grand church. Some sceptics observed that the undertaking might prove an embarrassment to English Catholics rather than a proud symbol of accomplishment. They doubted the Cardinal's ability to complete the project, and believed that an unfinished folly, not a proper cathedral, would greet Londoners in Victoria Street.

In spite of these misgivings, Cardinal Vaughan did not waver. He used the Catholic press to drum up support and began a fund-raising drive. In 1894, J F Bentley was named as the architect, and immediately set out for Italy to study firsthand the country's numerous churches and basilicas. The design had also been chosen: it was to be in the Byzantine tradition. Several reasons contributed to this decision. Unlike the more popular and ubiquitous Gothic, a Byzantine church did not have to be completed in sections; the shell could be finished first, and then attention could be focused on interior decorations.[30] More importantly, the Byzantine style was cheaper to construct than its Gothic or Baroque counterparts. Success shined on Cardinal Vaughan's efforts, and the first important stage of construction began in the summer of 1895.

With pomp and grandeur, Cardinal Herbert Vaughan solemnly blessed the foundation stone of his new cathedral. This action signaled the beginning of the long-awaited construction of the new Roman Catholic cathedral in central London. At a celebration following the impressive ceremony, Vaughan sketched his plans for the future of his metropolitan church. This was to be no ordinary place of worship. Vaughan pointed out 'that the Catholic body must have a Cathedral in which the sacred liturgy of the church should be carried out in all its fulness day by day, and many times a day, as it was of old in Westminster and in Canterbury.'[31] The ecclesiastical and lay dignitaries present greeted this vision with applause.

If Vaughan wanted to bring back the glories of the pre-Reformation Catholic Church to Britain, then he could not ignore the English Benedictine Congregation. As in the days before the destruction of the Henrician reforms, monks must breathe life into this new Westminster. And English monks were eager to accommodate the Archbishop's wish. Vaughan revealed that his 'anxiety with regard to the Cathedral was allayed by the readiness with which he found the English Benedictine Fathers, full of life and energy and numbers, ready to come back to Westminster.'[32] The monks of St. Gregory's, Downside, whom the Cardinal knew and admired, would supply the manpower. The suburb of Ealing in West London, would be a suitable location for these Benedictines, who would take charge of the liturgy in Vaughan's cathedral.

Cardinal Vaughan's plan was simple: '...while safeguarding the position and rights of the Chapter, to hand over the whole working and management of the Cathedral to the monks.'[33] As in the Middle Ages the cathedral would be staffed by the Black Monks. A Prior would be the immediate superior, and Vaughan would enjoy the privileges and jurisdiction of an Abbot. According to his biographer, this vision '...at one time certainly represented what the Cardinal meant when he spoke of the Benedictines coming back to Westminster.' Moreover, Vaughan wanted to hand over 'to the Benedictines the two missions in Westminster, which would ultimately be incorporated in the Cathedral parish, so that they might become familiar with the district they would have to work in when the Cathedral was opened.'[34] Cardinal Vaughan maintained that 'there could be no higher or holier work any body of men could be called upon to undertake, and he still unhesitatingly counted on the co-operation of the monks.'[35]

To bring the Benedictine monks to London was the first step. Their community had settled at Downside near Bath in 1814, and by the 1890's the community had grown to a mature membership. The monks were committed to missionary work and the conversion of England to Roman Catholicism.[36] In May 1896 Cardinal Vaughan informed the superior of Downside Abbey, Prior Edmund Ford, that he was 'disposed to give' a mission in Ealing to the Benedictines of that monastery.[37] He also told Ford that a proper site for this new foundation could easily be purchased there.[38] Ford's answer was short: 'as soon as I can I will go and see Ealing.' The Downside superior also indicated that he entertained his own vision for the future of the Benedictines in London: 'Your Eminence would I presume wish us to try and do more than merely take charge of the mission?'[39] If Benedictines from Downside settled in London, they must be involved in active parish work in addition to their ceremonial duties at the cathedral. Rendering the liturgy of Westminster Cathedral exclusively was inappropriate.[40]

Hugh Ford was born on 23 March 1851 at Clifton Park. When he was ten, his parents sent him to Downside School, which at that time had an enrollment of over fifty students. Staffed by the monks, Downside could proudly boast of several famous men who were educated at the Benedictine school, such as the future Bishop of Birmingham, William Ullathorne, and Roger Vaughan, the future Bishop of Sydney. Herbert Vaughan, who wanted the Downside monks to come to Westminster, had also attended the school. His biographer quotes a contemporary who described young Ford as 'a pale delicate-looking boy, prim and precise in manner and dress, not like other boys, more thoughtful and quick.'[41] Believing that he had a Benedictine vocation, he entered the novitiate at Belmont in November 1868, and took Edmund for his religious name. Three years later, Edmund Ford made his solemn profession as a monk. Illness, however, forced him to interrupt his studies at Belmont, and he returned to Downside in 1871.

Because of his questionable health, Minor Orders were postponed, but he made his solemn profession on 24 January 1873. During the same year, his superiors decided that a sea voyage and long holiday might provide a cure for the sickly young monk, and in November he left for Australia. After he returned to Downside in 1876, Dom Edmund was appointed Sub-Prefect, a position which carried with it the responsibility for discipline throughout the school. Ford's health seemed to improve, and he was ordained deacon in 1877, and priest the following year. It appeared that his career would be in education. Appointed Prefect of Studies in 1878, he began to introduce lay masters into the school and also instituted a board with lay membership which discussed school policy. In 1884, Dom Edmund was sent to Rome with two confreres to start a house of studies for his congregation; his stay in Italy lasted only one year.

Ordered back by the President of the English Benedictine Congregation, Dom Edmund served a brief term as Prior of Downside (1885-1888). According to his biographer, these were years of growth and development for Downside. Improvement in the physical plant, expansion of the school, and the opening of the Lady Chapel were supervised by Prior Ford. In 1889, the ex-prior took up residence at the Benedictine mission at Beccles. But he was soon back at Downside; in July 1894 he was again chosen as Prior. During the foundation stone ceremony at Westminster Cathedral, Prior Ford heard and approved of Cardinal Vaughan's dreams about monks conducting the services at his new cathedral. Both churchmen, therefore, relished the thought of a Benedictine presence at Westminster Cathedral, but Ford had strong views about the nature of the work and the extent of the involvement of his monks in London.

The Prior maintained that a Benedictine presence in the capital was imperative, but any rash or unplanned action would be harmful. A man of prudence, Ford was not mesmerized by the imagination and idealism of Cardinal Vaughan. 'I cannot but express to your Eminence our grateful acknowledgment for offering us the work that you suggest at Ealing,' he wrote to the Cardinal, 'and our appreciation of the confidence placed in us by entrusting it to us...'[42] Work for the monks, however, must be found: 'Your Eminence will recognize the dangers in establishing a religious community without sufficient occupation for its members and the consequent difficulty in maintaining a religious spirit...Hence I feel,' he continued, 'a scruple in sending a religious anywhere without assigning a definite work that he could and would do.'

In the future, Ford suggested, a school might be a possibility, but parish work must definitely supplement the choral duties of Westminster Cathedral. Consequently, 'we may have a flourishing community at

Ealing' in a few years. Ford concluded his letter to Vaughan by pointing out that pastoral work in Ealing would not detract from liturgical duties in London. 'I would add that the establishment of a house at Ealing would not render it more difficult to find men for the Cathedral, on the contrary it would I think render it easier by providing another community from which to draw when the time comes.'[43] Ford's position was, therefore, clear. He would gladly assign monks for Westminster Cathedral, but only if pastoral duties formed part of the agreement.

Within a fortnight, Cardinal Vaughan responded favourably to Prior Ford's conditions. Vaughan would welcome the monks in Ealing if certain conditions were met: 'Provided the consent of the Holy See be obtained,'[44] Ford was authorized to lay a foundation at Ealing provided that the new monastery 'is not to include the opening of any school other than a Public Elementary School'; the monks would provide for the spiritual needs of the area and live a conventual life; if the foundation did not succeed in five years, the Archbishop would repay the Benedictines the amount spent on housing and the property; and finally, the monks must agree to sing the Divine Office at Westminster Cathedral. The Cardinal was explicit and forceful on this point. 'One of the principal reasons inducing the Cardinal Archbishop to invite the Benedictines to open a house at Ealing,' he concluded in his letter to Ford, 'is that they may be sufficiently near to Westminster to contribute to the choral service of the Cathedral.'[45] If these guidelines were acceptable to the Downside Benedictines, Cardinal Vaughan would welcome the monks into his archdiocese. Edmund Ford, however, had won a major concession: his monks would sing their breviary in the stalls of Westminster; but they would also work at a nearby parish in Ealing. Ford's next step was to secure the permission of the Abbot President of the English Benedictine Congregation and his council.

With Vaughan's offer of 7 June 1896, Prior Edmund Ford wrote to Dom Anselm O'Gorman, the President, and his advisers, presenting strong arguments in favour of sending Benedictine monks to London.[46] Monks could live a community life at Ealing, conduct an urban parish, and be near to their liturgical obligations at Westminster Cathedral. 'It is said to be one of the best districts near London still unoccupied as a parish,' Ford argued, and 'the district is rapidly developing and will have the character of a high class suburb.'[47] Moreover, monks could take the fifteen minute trip on the Great Western Railway to central London and their work at the cathedral. Within a month, the President of the English Benedictine Congregation had informed Ford that the Council had 'decided unanimously to accept the foundation which was offered, as well as the monastery to be built successively, and eventually the mission of the place called Ealing...'[48] Ford immediately petitioned Pope Leo XIII: 'Having obtained the permission from the Superiors of our Congregation, as well as the assent of...the Cardinal Archbishop of Westminster, we humbly implore from the Holy See the faculty to found in Ealing a new residence, as well as to build later a monastery, and eventually to accept from the same Cardinal the mission of the same place Ealing.'[49] On 28 October 1896, Cardinal Vaughan informed Edmund Ford that he had 'received the necessary permission from the Holy See for you to take Ealing: the conditions being those we agreed upon.'[50]

It appeared that Cardinal Vaughan's dream to have Benedictine monks associated with his new cathedral, as they had been with the old, would come to fruition. Downside had given its approval to the project, and began to appoint members of the community to the new Ealing mission. In 1896, Prior Ford purchased two acres of land and a stately dwelling, Castle Hill House, for the new Ealing Benedictine community. On 13 March 1897, Dom Bernard Bulbeck arrived, and began to minister to the Roman Catholics of the area. Both the Archbishop and the Prior treasured their plans for the new Benedictine monastery, but problems and conflicts soon developed.

Vaughan's biographer argues that the Archbishop almost immediately recognized difficulties in the arrangements he had made with the Downside Benedictines. Westminster Cathedral was to be no ordinary church, but 'a Cathedral in the heart of the Empire, making its appeal to a vast multitude and destined for the service of a whole people.'[51] Consequently, 'it seemed incongruous that such a national centre of spiritual and far-reaching activities as he hoped the Cathedral would become, should be under the control of any single Religious Order, however ancient and however distinguished.'[52] Most importantly, the secular clergy resented the invasion of these monks.

Cardinal Vaughan had tried to be especially sensitive to the feelings of his Cathedral Chapter. In 1894, for example, the Chapter had been informed that 'the Cardinal was arranging conditions to safeguard the rights of the Chapter in the new Cathedral, in view of the appointment of the Benedictines to carry on the services.'[53] The Chapter, however, was uneasy. At one of their regular monthly meetings, on 8 January 1895, attention was directed to the question of the Benedictines, and the secretary 'was requested to seek for and bring any notes of a meeting held at Archbishop's House when the plan was first proposed by His Eminence in 1894.'[54] The Chapter again discussed the question of the monks at the following month's meeting. It was at this time that the secretary admitted that he could not find those minutes which outlined the conditions proposed by the Cardinal to safeguard the rights of the Chapter. Vaughan continued to inform this body of the progress concerning the monks. In October 1896 the Chapter was given a copy of the Cardinal's offer to Prior Ford[55] to settle in Ealing,[56] and during the next meeting he informed the Chapter that he had received the rescript from Rome which sanctioned the foundation of the Benedictines in the archdiocese.[57] Cardinal Vaughan clearly remained committed to Benedictines conducting the Divine Office at Westminster Cathedral. That would be the extent of their responsibilities; the secular clergy would manage the other affairs of the cathedral.[58] Edmund Ford also had certain definite plans for his monks at Westminster Cathedral.

On 7 December 1898, Ford wrote to Cardinal Vaughan enclosing a series of proposals, asking him, 'to write to me any remarks thereon which may enable me to revise them in a form which would meet with your Eminence's approval and which with your consent I could lay before our fathers.'[59] Ford maintained that he framed these suggestions 'with the hope that they may prevent friction and quarrels in the future.' He offered Vaughan an escape from the association of the monks with the daily affairs of the cathedral: 'With this view, I would leave each Archbishop free from any obligation to employ the monks in any way unless he chose to do so, so that at the death of each Archbishop the right of the monks to carry on any work in or connected with the Cathedral would cease.' In Ford's mind, however, this would not diminish the importance or significance of the Benedictine presence. 'On the other hand I suggest that the monastery at Westminster should be founded by your Eminence, i.e., that you should secure us in our residence there with certain endowments and the use of one of the Chapels in the Cathedral...and that of this minimum no Archbishop should be able to deprive us.'

Ford argued for the right of the Benedictines to engage in pastoral work at the cathedral, but the duties entailed (for example, the number of daily masses, confessions, homilies and, of course, the portions of the Divine Office to be sung) should be carefully defined and agreed upon by both the monks and the ordinary. Moreover, 'the monks would have no claim to do the above works; each Archbishop would be free to exact these duties or not as he pleased. Anything beyond these specific duties would be matter of mutual agreement between the monks and each Archbishop.'[60] Ford believed that the new London foundation should have between a dozen and twenty members, and that each should be paid a yearly salary of £120, which 'is not excessive, considering the position and the necessary expenses of the position, beyond the personal expense of the men.'[61] The Archbishop should take the responsibility for all the revenues and the maintenance of the cathedral, but 'some portion of the revenue should be paid by him to the monks varying according to the work which they may be doing.'[62] Ford concluded his letter to the Archbishop, maintaining that two principles were important: 'the Archbishop ought to feel that the whole revenue of the church belongs to his administration and the monks ought to be given some direct pecuniary interest in the receipts of the Cathedral.'[63]

Cardinal Vaughan initially agreed to this proposal, but difficulties quickly appeared. According to Snead-Cox, 'the more the Cardinal considered the problems incidental to the activities of a double set of clergy, serving under separate superiors, and yet engaged upon a common work in the same place, the more insoluble they seemed.'[64] More importantly, there was the danger that jealousy and competition might develop between the secular clergy and the recently arrived monks. Another problem, specifically Benedictine, also clouded the horizon. All English Benedictine monks took a 'missionary oath,' which bound them to work for the conversion of England to Roman Catholicism. The General Chapter of the Congregation, and not the superiors of individual houses, was the governing body of the English Benedictine Congregation. The Chapter could, for example, transfer a monk from one house to another, or re-assign a monk from parish to parish. 'The monasteries were looked upon as little more than Seminaries in which the monks spent a few years of their life preparing themselves for their *real* work, the apostolic mission.'[65]

The Chapter could, and did, appoint monks throughout the English mission territory at will. Since all English Benedictines were pledged to the missions, 'it was hardly expected that they would acquiesce in any arrangement which might permanently exclude them from missionary work altogether.'[66] To extinguish any rivalry between the secular clergy and the Benedictine monks and to side-step the obstacle of the missionary oath, while retaining the presence of monks, Cardinal Vaughan proposed a solution which caused great consternation among all elements of English Roman Catholicism.

If English Benedictines posed difficulties, why not another congregation of monks? A solution to Vaughan's 'difficulties seemed to have been found when he thought of another Benedictine Congregation which, unlike the English Benedictines, had no missionary character, and so was prepared to devote itself exclusively to a life of prayer and the work of singing the Divine Office.'[67] Long renowned for their liturgical expertise in the rendering of plainchant, the monks of Solesmes appeared to be the perfect candidates, and so Cardinal Vaughan began to negotiate with these French monks.

3. The Saga of the French Monks

If Cardinal Vaughan wanted to grace Westminster Cathedral with beautiful liturgy and music, the accomplishments of Solesmes Abbey in France could not be ignored. Since the middle of the nineteenth century, the Abbaye Saint-Pierre near the village of Solesmes had been recognized as the pioneer in liturgical studies, especially plainchant. Founded as a priory in the eleventh century, Solesmes was destroyed by the English during the Hundred Years' War, only to be rebuilt during the Renaissance. Fueled by the attacks of the Enlightenment against organized religion, the anti-clericalism and secularism generated by the French Revolution naturally attacked the alleged corruption and parasitical lifestyle of the monastic houses. As a consequence of this Solesmes was dissolved, and its monks dispersed throughout the country. In 1833, the local curate, Prosper Guéranger (1805-1875), purchased the monastic property at Solesmes, eventually restored the Benedictine horarium, and was appointed in 1837 its first Abbot by Pope Gregory XVI. Soon afterwards, Rome honoured Solesmes and designated it as the head of a new French congregation of Benedictine monks.

In addition to being a founding father of nineteenth century French monasticism, Guéranger created at Solesmes 'a community whose spiritual life was above all centred in experienced contact with the prayer of the Church.'[68] Moreover, Guéranger rejected some of the French or Gallic forms of worship, and favoured instead the Roman liturgy. Consequently, this signaled a renaissance for plainchant insofar as he was 'interested in restoring at Solesmes pure Benedictine practice, including the authentic Gregorian chant.'[69] The proper rendition of chant, therefore, became Guéranger's chief concern.

His methodology and the quality of liturgical music sung at Solesmes soon attracted a following throughout Europe. Guéranger was a 'pioneer in drawing general attention to the beauty of the forms and texts that had been preserved in the Roman liturgy....'[70] His numerous publications, his scholarly research into the history of plainchant and his maxim that one must go back to the original sources, earned both Solesmes and its Abbot an international reputation. Guéranger, therefore, was cast as a liturgical expert of the highest calibre. Vaughan's firsthand experience of the Solesmes liturgy during his European trips had impressed him greatly. Further, Guéranger's exaltation of the Roman liturgy stereotyped him as an Ultramontane, and this also appealed to Vaughan's sensitivities.

The fame of the Solesmes school of liturgical interpretation continued after Guéranger's death. Another monk, Joseph Pothier (1835-1923) continued musical research and published *Les Mélodies grégoriennes d'après la tradition* in 1880. Here, 'the laws of oratorical rhythm were better defined and more solidly established, and the role and the nature of the Latin accent brought to light.'[71] His other works, based on ancient manuscripts, resurrected the style and form of the original chant. Throughout the century, therefore, the liturgical method of Solesmes and its interpretation gradually gained an acceptance by the ecclesiastical authorities. But the changing political climate in France did not smile on Solesmes; the government closed the monastery in 1880 and again from 1882 to 1896. For a short period of time. Abbot Paul Delatte (he was Abbot from 1890 to 1920) successfully struggled to restore a monastic routine in the face of French secularism. By bringing a choir of Solesmes monks to England, Vaughan would earn praise as a saviour—as well as a promoter—of their great tradition.

In addition to the sympathy felt towards their co-religious on the continent, the approval and use of the Solesmes liturgy at Rome also impressed the English Catholics. In 1901, for example, *The Tablet* reported that 'the Holy Father sent a brief of commendation to the Benedictines of Solesmes in recognition of Plain Chant in accordance with ancient tradition.'[72] In commenting on this papal brief of Leo XIII, the paper noted that 'one thing is certain, that if uniformity is to be secured in the chant of the Church, it will not be realized in the universal adoption of the Ratisbon edition.'[73] The article continued, 'in Rome itself the Solesmes edition is used in the Vatican Seminary, in the French, Capranican, and the South American Colleges, and in the Benedictine College of St. Anselm's.' In Cardinal Vaughan's mind the services of the Solesmes monks guaranteed excellent liturgical services at Westminster Cathedral, and he urged Abbot Delatte to respond to his offer.

The exact date is not known, but by the early summer of 1899 a preliminary understanding had been reached between Cardinal Vaughan and Abbot Paul Delatte. Vaughan's invitation to Delatte has not survived, so some mystery surrounds its exact contents. It does appear, however, that the English Cardinal only wanted the Solesmes monks on a temporary basis. Delatte's notes support this:

> It seems to me that it is difficult, at the moment when the Cardinal is making such an honourable offer, to foresee the future and even predict the moment when the Abbey of Westminster [Westminster Cathedral!] having been provided with English personnel...the French element shall be expected to withdraw on its own initiative.[74]

Delatte wanted to avoid any secrecy in his dealings with Vaughan, and he also understood the Cardinal's desire for an experimental French foundation in London. 'It will be the natural thing to give back to the English Benedictine Congregation a house which rightly belongs to it,' his notes further record, 'and perhaps it would be preferable to say this openly, and to write it into the Charter of the Foundation, so that we do not appear in any way as interlopers or usurpers.'[75] Delatte's papers reveal that he gave more than cursory attention to the proposed London scheme: there are references to a year's trial period (September 1900 to September 1901); the actual construction of a monastery; the number of monks needed; the endowment required; and regulations for the monastic life of the French monks. Before replying to Cardinal Vaughan's offer, Abbot Delatte confided with and sought the advice of his friend, Bishop Abel Gilbert.[76]

Delatte had informed Bishop Gilbert of his intended response to Cardinal Vaughan's proposal. Gilbert replied in a lengthy letter congratulating the Abbot on his reply to Vaughan. This Bishop, however, was not reserved, still less an anglophile, and he challenged Delatte to seize this valuable opportunity:

> The project itself appears to me one of the most eminent things a religious family could become interested in. In my eyes it is a new invasion of England, tottering in its Protestantism, by the monks, who re-establish there assuredly and with a rapidly-spreading influence, liturgical worship in its most exact and most beautiful form...and scholarly orthodoxy, in a local and special form, adjusting slightly, thanks to very suitable specialists, to the needs and the deficiencies of Anglican theology...[77]

The spirit and character of the Solesmes Congregation must be safeguarded, and this could be guaranteed by a firm commitment to a scholarly apostolate.

Bishop Gilbert gently chided Delatte on the Abbot's acceptance of Cardinal Vaughan's suggestion that the French foundation should only be temporary. 'What is needed is not a trial,' he urged, 'but a triumph'; continuing,

> What is necessary is not preliminary steps leading to a progressive ascent, there is needed something substan-

tial from the beginning, which compels recognition and inspires respect, capable even of being lessened later without diminishing the results accomplished at a first stroke. In fact you have, dear friend, to assert yourself in the public opinion from the moment of the first contact; to furnish the Cardinal with a triumph from the very beginning; not to leave any objection that he has to answer; not to leave him with a hostile statement that he can shrug off with a smile.

The French must, moreover, be independent, and avoid any co-operation with the English Benedictines! It was not the presence of a few Britons in the new monastery that would be objectionable but 'it is the idea that you need them, that they know it, or would think so.' 'Guests of yours, that is possible,' Bishop Gilbert mused, but 'co-founders with you, to me that seems full of dangers.'[78]

Abbot Delatte's response to Vaughan's invitation, however, reflected the cautious and prudent approach of his notes, and rejected the ecclesiastical jingoism of Bishop Gilbert. In general, his lengthy letter was enthusiastic about the prospect of French monks from his monastery being associated with Westminster Cathedral. The Abbot's answer was intended 'to fix the conditions which appear...to render possible the foundation of the Abbey of Westminster, and to determine the part to be undertaken by the congregation of Solesmes.'[79] Delatte explained the reasons behind the French eagerness. He did so by appealing to the universal and catholic character of the Roman Church. Abbot Delatte believed that the proposal of the Archbishop 'proves to us that Catholics are united by a tie stronger than that of nationality.'[80] The future of Westminster, however, 'will not be definitely assured until the services of the Archiepiscopal Church have been entrusted to monks taken from British soil.' Delatte strongly rejected in fact Bishop Gilbert's approach; no action or plans could exclude the English Benedictines. 'It is, therefore our duty to tend towards this end and to act, at the moment, in such a way as to ensure for the future what we have foreseen and desired.'[81]

By the turn of the century, Dom Aidan Gasquet (1846-1929) had already been recognized as an eminent historian and a leading authority in questions dealing with English Roman Catholicism.[82] He also enjoyed a reputation throughout European monastic circles as an influential member of the English Benedictines. For these reasons, Abbot Delatte contacted him about the possibility of the Solesmes monks establishing a foundation in London. While a student, young Gasquet believed that he might have a monastic vocation, and in 1866 he entered the Benedictine novitiate at Belmont. A year later, Dom Aidan returned to Downside to teach. He was ordained a priest in 1874 and soon took charge of the studies at the school where a contemporary described him as 'reveling in work' and 'eaten up with activity.'[83] In 1878, he became Prior at Downside, a post he held for nearly seven years. During his term of office, the abbey church was enlarged and the school modernized, and his friendship with the medieval-ist and liturgist, Edmund Bishop, helped shape the young Prior's future vocation as an historian. Overwork and exhaustion contributed to heart problems, and this eventually forced Gasquet to resign the office of Prior, in the summer of 1885.

From Downside, he went to London for a period of recuperation, but at the same time he also started to study British history, and began to research at the British Museum. The times were encouraging for ecclesiastical historians: Leo XIII had recently opened the Vatican archives to serious scholars, and encouraged clergymen to devote themselves to a career in church history. Supported in his new academic vocation by Cardinal Manning, Gasquet was allowed to stay in London and continue his work. The British Museum and the Public Record Office supplied the material for Gasquet's two-volume work, *Henry VIII and the English Monasteries,* published in 1888 and 1889 respectively. These books, which seriously questioned the traditional Protestant view of the Reformation, were well-received, and Gasquet soon found himself fêted as an accomplished historian, although David Knowles has expressed serious reservations about Gasquet's originality as a thinker.'[84] Knowles also pointed out Gasquet's frequent inaccuracies and remarked that 'one or two of his later compositions gave one the mental impression of being lost in a maze or engulfed in a nightmare.'[85] More importantly, Professor Knowles believed that 'there was a root of something in Gasquet which led him to ignore even the most cogent evidence against anything he had written.' Despite these shortcomings, Aidan Gasquet's works, especially those dealing with the history of *The Book of Common Prayer,* caught the eye of Rome. The question of the validity of Anglican Orders had again surfaced.

With his historian's credentials and his knowledge of the Tudor era, Gasquet seemed a natural choice to join his fellow Englishmen, Mgr J Moyes and Fr D Fleming, as a member of Leo XIII's international commission of 1896 to reconsider the Anglican claims. The work of the commission and the condemnation of Anglican Orders in the *Apostolicae Curae* (1896) brought him international status, but the trip to Rome also introduced him to Merry Del Val, the future Secretary of State, and Pope Leo XIII. In 1899, Leo XIII commissioned Gasquet with the task of carrying out the reform of the English Benedictine Congregation.[86] This was the churchman—later to be President of the English Benedictine Congregation in 1900, a possible successor to Cardinal Vaughan in 1903, commissioned to revise the *Vulgate* in 1907, and created a Cardinal in 1914—whom Abbot Delatte approached in 1899.

Abbot Delatte argued that he must meet with Aidan Gasquet,[87] and acquaint him 'with the terms upon which the French Colony of Monks are to take up their position.'[88] 'They are brothers in religion,' he asserted, 'and such a course of action would be both right and equitable.'[89] In spite of their missionary character, the duties associated with Westminster Cathedral must eventually be transferred to the English monks, yet the French monks 'would be allowed to put forward their claim for definitely remaining in England.'[90]

Delatte had originally contemplated a trial period of one year for his monks in London, but Bishop Gilbert's insistence on a longer time-span triumphed. Vaughan's proposed year, September 1900 to September 1901, was insufficient, and Delatte urged a three-year period with 'the understanding that they [the French monks] will be there to render service.'[91] If the time came when his monks were no longer needed by the Archbishop, Delatte agreed to withdraw them from Westminster: 'I am certainly of opinion that the only grounds upon which we can lay a solid foundation for establishing our Religious in Westminster are those of perfect freedom for both parties.'[92]

Abbot Delatte worked for a spirit of compromise, but had no doubt that the French monks would not only remain, but prosper in central London. He even approached Vaughan about the specifications of the future monastic buildings. In the summer of 1899, he informed the Cardinal, '...the plan of the monastery which is to be founded and built...[should] be prepared by a monk.'[93] The monastery would contain rooms for thirty French monks, a refectory, cloister, and Chapter House. Individuals wanting to make a retreat would also be received. Delatte argued that the Solesmes Congregation must still retain control over St. Michael's Abbey at Farnborough,[94] 'for the health of the monks would certainly suffer from being constantly detained without any relaxation in the centre of a large city like London.'[95]

The Abbey of Solesmes, however, could not promise a full contingent of French monks: 'I can only place at Your Eminence's disposal the Fathers of the community of St. Michael to which I will add three or four monks taken from Solesmes.'[96] The English Benedictines must augment the French. 'If the Anglo-Benedictine Congregation will consent to supply four or five subjects,' Delatte believed, 'this will bring the figures up to about twenty for the first or trial year, 1900-1901.'[97] Payment, immediate housing, and pastoral duties could be discussed at a future date. Chanting the Divine Office would be the important responsibility of the Solesmes monks. Abbot Delatte briefly mentioned plans for a monastic library, and drew attention to Vaughan's desire to build one, which was 'to be entrusted to the care of one of the monks.'[98] In conclusion, the Abbot forecast the sensitive and emotional difficulties facing French monks at Westminster. 'However, the most difficult problem of all will be that of arranging a *modus vivendi* between the regular secular clergy in the Cathedral where the Monks, the Chapter and the parish priests will be thrown together.'[99]

Cardinal Vaughan immediately sought the counsel and advice of Mgr Moyes, Canon of the cathedral, who in turn prepared for the Cardinal two documents: a précis of Abbot Delatte's letter of 11 June 1899, and a list of stipulations based on the Delatte letter modified with the necessary explanation for any change. In a covering letter, Mgr Moyes stated that other questions needed to be addressed, for example, the horarium, charges for maintenance, use of the sanctuary, but these could wait. In Moyes' point of view,

> the coming of the monks is doubly important, not only
> to furnish the basis of the plain-chant and secure the
> ideal of the Liturgical Office (which ought to be inde-
> pendent of any consideration of the attendance of the
> people) but as planting in our midst a permanent body
> of spiritual and learned men who will think, and study
> and write in all those departments of research which
> affect intellectually the conversion of England.[100]

Moyes argued that their 'spiritual life would be to us a constant guarantee of their humility, orthodoxy, and loyalty of spirit, such as we cannot easily have with mere student units.'[101]

Moyes' abstract of Delatte's letter emphasized the vague wording of the Abbot's proposals. He drew attention to the fact that 'the agreement between the Cardinal and the Abbot is based on the condition that the position of the monks at the Cathedral shall rest upon a title which is purely precarious...'[102] Moyes contended that in any agreement 'it ought to be stated that the authority to be satisfied on this important point is the Archbishop.'[103] In respect of the three-year trial period, he believed that this was desirable and that 'nothing of the nature of a contract or binding agreement of any kind be contemplated: better still if 'the period of experiment becomes continual and the monks remain while the Archbishop is satisfied with the working.'[104] Delatte favoured a monastery to house his monks immediately, but Moyes believed this would 'seem to commit the See to a permanent Monastic connection before the period had elapsed.'[105] Consequently, he advised Vaughan to avoid setting a date for the construction of a monastery and that special care 'should be taken that nothing on the part of the monks of Solesmes be allowed by which a vested interest be created in favour of the monks on the soil of Westminster Cathedral.'[106]

Moyes also detailed his thoughts on the possible liturgical duties of the Solesmes monks. He revealed a fear that they might become permanently entrenched at Westminster Cathedral. In respect of the Divine Office, Mgr Moyes suggested that the monks 'ought not to have the right to the choir, [as Delatte had suggested] but to the use of the choir during the hours of liturgical service.'[107] In other words, the stalls would be reserved for the monks but should not be considered as their exclusive and private property. The schedule of services should be the subject of future discussions between the monastic and parochial superiors and subject to the approval of the Archbishop. In no way, however, should the Divine Office take precedence over any parish or congregational function. In his letter to Vaughan, the Abbot of Solesmes had insisted that his monks, in addition to singing, be entrusted with the maintenance of order in the church, its cleaning, and 'the heating of the Cathedral.' Again Moyes sought to limit the power and authority of these French monks. 'The first alone of these—the singing of plain-chant,' he suggested, 'properly belongs to the monks.' 'The remaining three...ought to be done under the authority and direction of the Cathedral Administration or a Committee appointed by the Archbishop...'[108] Moyes suggested that marriages, baptisms, burials and their respective fees remain a 'matter for arrangement between the Archbishop and his parochial Administrator.'[109] Even the proposed library must not be handed over to the monks; it must be archiepiscopal, not monastic. A librarian, who was not a Benedictine, would supervise its operation.

Incorporating the above suggestions and amendments, Monsignor Moyes composed a new agreement.[110] This document, *Preliminary Articles of Agreement,* was sent to Cardinal Vaughan to serve as the basis for continued talks with the French. According to this proposal, the monks of Solesmes would be a valuable addition to the fabric of the cathedral, but under no circumstance should they be extended a *carte blanche*. Moyes also informed the Cardinal that trouble might plague his plan to import the French. He warned that 'in a Cathedral in which the Ordinary, the Chapter, and the monks and the Parish priest or parochial Administrator tread on the same ground there will be a certain measure of complex working.'[111] Mgr Moyes suggested the creation of a permanent committee consisting of all concerned parties to work out any future difficulties. He prized the contribution the Solesmes monks would make to Westminster Cathedral, but he emphasized that control must not pass from the Archbishop. Moyes concluded his letter to Cardinal Vaughan with the following advice: 'I hope for the good of the Church in England, Your Eminence will press forward with a strong hand.'[112]

By the summer of 1899, therefore, Cardinal Vaughan had already won pledges of support and commitment from two Benedictine Congregations. But the flow of financial contributions for the construction of his dream cathedral dried to a trickle. Vaughan was forced to remind the faithful of their responsibilities, and the pages of *The Tablet* became his platform. One article, 'Our Catholic Opportunity,' pointed out to its readers that a revival in English Roman Catholicism was flourishing, and on the other hand, a growing reaction against Anglican practices was evident. 'To all who keep watchful eyes upon the religious signs of the times,' *The Tablet* recorded, 'nothing can be more certain that a large, an influential, and a daily increasing section of the English people is undergoing a reaction from the beliefs, the methods, and the spirit of the Protestant Reformation.'[113] The Reformers 'introduced doctrinal poverty and called it Evangelical purity. They imposed liturgical baldness and called it Evangelical simplicity.' The English mind and spirit, however, could not tolerate such aberrations: 'The religious life of a great and generous people could not be forever cramped within such starved and pitiable ideals.'[114] Part of the mission of the new cathedral would be to bring these questioning Anglicans into the fold of Peter:

> Then just as the English People are moving away in
> disillusionment from the ideals of the Reformation, and
> are becoming more and more earnest in their cry for that
> which is beautiful and stately in worship, so there exists
> for the Catholic Church in this country a duty to meet it,
> and to prove that she alone possesses, and that she alone
> can give, in all its truth and fullness, that for which the
> souls of this land are seeking, and for which so many
> have happily learned to hunger.[115]

Vaughan claimed that an ornate building complete with 'the beauty and completeness of the Catholic Liturgy in all its wondrous power...' would quickly draw converts. Consequently, it was imperative that English

Roman Catholics continue to contribute: 'Its success in this high mission will be what the Catholics of this land make it.'[116]

During the spring, Cardinal Vaughan used the columns of *The Tablet* to keep English Roman Catholics informed of the construction of their cathedral. In one account, the writer described in detail the construction of the building, and even implied that the new church might rival St. Paul's. Still money was urgently needed. Cash donations since June 1894 had amounted to over £100,000, but the article warned: 'still it is necessary to point out that if the Cathedral is to be solemnly opened in September, 1900, more money is wanted and wanted quickly.'[117] In the June edition it was noted that some progress had been made. Work on the choir-stalls for the monks, for example, had been completed. However, Catholics were urged to continue their generosity: 'Surely the devotion of the English people to the Holy See should of itself enable funds to be raised sufficient to complete the carcase of St. Peter's Chapel.'[118]

Cardinal Vaughan believed that Westminster Cathedral would shine as an example of the piety of English Catholics, and would draw some Anglicans out of their liturgical malaise, leading them to the splendours of Roman Catholicism. He touched on another emotion: an appeal to patriotism—illogical in light of the Cardinal's negotiations with the French monks!—was the theme of a pastoral letter from Archbishop's House. The pages of *The Tablet, The Times,* and *The Weekly Register* printed Vaughan's challenge to the laity for contributions to their new church, which 'will be not only the Mother Church of the principal English diocese, but the Metropolitan Church of the Province of Westminster.'[119] The pastoral emphasized the themes of patriotism and chauvinism. 'The truth is,' the Cardinal pleaded, 'that the Westminster Cathedral must be...much more than the chief church of a diocese...London is the capital of the British Empire, and the highest city of the world.' London represented the 'centre of British power, British policy, and British wealth.' Westminster Cathedral, therefore, embodied the greatness of London and Great Britain. Vaughan believed that 'every member of every flock in this country has an interest in this House of the Lord which zealous and brave hearts are endeavouring to set up in Westminster, near the ancient shrine of the old religion of the land.'[120] Westminster Cathedral, therefore, captured the magic of England's past, represented the spirit of the present generation, and pointed toward the future greatness of the country's Roman Catholics. In light of this, Cardinal Vaughan's invitation to the Solesmes monks seemed incongruous to many English.

4. The Monks Versus the Secular Clergy

The year 1899 witnessed a revolution in the philosophy and character of the English Benedictine Congregation. An editorial in *The Weekly Register* reported that the priories of Ampleforth, Douai, and Downside had been raised to the dignity of abbeys through the action of the Holy See. The article declared that the history of the English Benedictine Congregation was 'intimately bound up with the Catholic Church in England in a way which is peculiar to itself;'[121] that 'No Religious Order is so thoroughly English as the Benedictine; it appeals to the English taste and the English character as no other ever has.' It must be 'the fact that the English Benedictines are representatives of the ancient Abbey of Westminster,' and the article concluded, 'that such perceptions led Cardinal Vaughan to form the intention—which he had publicly announced on more than one occasion—of attaching them to the new cathedral.'[122] *The Catholic Times and Catholic Opinion* also rejoiced in the new honours bestowed on the English Benedictines. 'What Catholic can forget all that the Fathers of St. Benedict did for religion in the dark days of persecution? What Catholic forgets the noble and self-sacrificing labours of St Benedict's cowled sons up and down the length and breadth of England to-day?'[123] The present, according to many English Catholics, would be the fitting time to install these English monks in the new Westminster Cathedral.

The change referred to in the press constituted a substantial revolution in the governance and direction[124] of the English Benedictines: the missionary character was altered in favour of a more traditional Benedictine and monastic flavour. Edmund Ford, the Prior of Downside, claimed that 'with the growth in the number of the secular clergy, the assistance of the monks on the parishes was not of such paramount importance and that the monastic life should again become the predominant factor in English Benedictine polity.'[125] Ford argued that the 'English Benedictines had for many decades lived under a *lex particularis,* especially formed to meet abnormal circumstances which had long ceased to operate, and the continuance of such a system was unreasonable and illogical.'[126] This emphasis on the monastic as opposed to a parochial character was opposed by a majority of the English Benedictine Congregation, and it took the personal intervention of Pope Leo XIII in 1899 to settle the so-called 'constitutional crisis.'

The Pope issued a bull, *Diu Quidem,* which effectively transformed the constitutions of the English Benedictine Congregation. In the first place, *Diu Quidem* raised the Benedictine priories to abbeys. Recognizing that 'there is a danger lest such divergence of opinion...should occasion a loss of mutual charity,' *Diu Quidem* stated the following:

> Judging then that these evils should be prevented, we
> have taken the whole matter again into our own hands:
> and we will and prescribe that in compiling the Consti-
> tutions of the English Benedictine Congregation the
> following enactments be inserted, to be always and
> inviolably observed.[127]

The first 'enactment' was the establishment of independent abbeys which enjoyed all the traditional privileges and authority and autonomy.[128] *Diu Quidem* also commanded the English Benedictines to observe a series of earlier legislative principles embodied in the bull *Religiosus Ordo* (1890).

Cardinal Vaughan contacted the Solesmes monks because of the loose administration of the English Congregation and their devotion to missionary travels. *Diu Quidem* rectified this. Vaughan also worried about the possible instability of the English monks if stationed at Westminster because of their missionary oath. The bull *Religiosus Ordo* addressed this concern. This document reasserted and emphasized the monastic character of life for the English Benedictines. The bull succinctly addressed the problems:

> At the present moment matters have come to such a
> pass, that the very peace of the body is in danger: for
> there are some who call in question whether the English
> Benedictine Congregation is in its essence and nature
> monastic or missionary: and again whether the supreme
> authority belongs to the monasteries, and the missions
> ought therefore to be subject to the monasteries; or
> whether the missions are free to carry on their work by
> their own laws, and are exempt from all obedience to the
> monasteries.[129]

'Now it is perfectly clear,' it continued, 'that the English Benedictine Congregation is by its very nature monastic.'[130] A sense of permanence, structure, and stability was introduced into the English Benedictine Congregation. What Cardinal Vaughan feared most had been rectified by the actions of the Vatican. But he had already approached the French! He was now in the unenviable position of having offered the same position to two different groups of monks. Moreover, Cardinal Vaughan did not expect opposition from members of his flock to the Solesmes scheme. The revelation that French monks might replace the English Benedictines was greeted with patriotic shock.

The 15 July 1899 edition of *The Weekly Register* reported that it was 'surprised that we do not hear from England any comment upon another arrangement, *viz.* that the Cardinal Archbishop has arranged to put his new Cathedral at Westminster into the hands, not of the English Benedictines...but of the Benedictines of Solesmes.'[131] The paper stated that 'this was a step of very doubtful expediency, and not likely to conduce to harmony in England.'[132] A week later, the same paper told its readers that there was strong opposition to this plan from the Cathedral Chapter of Westminster, and consequently this might jeopardize Cardinal Vaughan's plan to introduce the French monks into London: 'At any rate, it relieves us, for the present, from the necessity of commenting on the proposed introduction of foreigners into the English Cathedral.'[133] The report pointed out that a financial drive for the Cathedral had recently been launched, and 'that appeal would be greatly assisted by an assurance that the Cathedral will be national and English in fact as well as in name.[134] But the paper was soon forced to admit that its confidence that the French scheme would be abandoned was premature.

The title of the next editorial, 'A New Alien Priory,' captured the indignation of the paper. The Cathedral Chapter, according to this report, opposed the Cardinal's wishes, and therefore

> it would be an act of cowardice on our part if we failed to assure the members of the Chapter that they will have the support of the great majority of the Catholic clergy and laity of England in resisting an arrangement which would be one of the greatest blunders that has yet been committed in the administration of the English Church.[135]

The editorial claimed that 'the rank and file of Catholics have a right to be heard.' That 'clergy and laity are not dumb driven cattle, and when they see that there is imminent danger of a false step being taken which will injure the Church and put back her advance, they will be wanting in their duty if they did not at least remonstrate.'

With a touch of irony, the paper commented that when it first heard the rumours of the invitation of the French monks to Westminster Cathedral, 'we regarded the story as the invention of an enemy.' It continued, 'The report seemed so wildly improbable that we hesitated to credit it.' So appeals to patriotism strengthened the case against the French: 'It is bad enough to have any foreigner forced upon us,' the paper quipped, 'we have only to imagine the effect on the English mind of a national English

189

cathedral with forty Frenchmen piping the office in an apse behind the high altar.' Any non-English element detracted from the dignity of Westminster, but 'France, of all the countries in the world just at the present time, is chosen as the country from which they are to be imported.'[136]

Not all English Roman Catholics sympathized with the objections raised by the editorials in *The Weekly Register*. One of its readers did hope that the article 'had its desired effect, and put an end to the project of having the Cathedral of Westminster served by foreigners.'[137] Economics and the extent of French power were the questions raised by this weak protest. But many Catholics supported Cardinal Vaughan. *The Catholic Times and Catholic Opinion* told its readers that 'the Cardinal may be trusted to have acted for the best' by negotiating to bring the Solesmes monks to Westminster.[138] No doubt, the article continued, 'only the most weighty reasons have impelled him to select the Benedictine Fathers of Solesmes for the performance of the sacred functions to which their lives will be devoted.' It noted that 'the Church in this country will be enriched by the presence of one more of the religious Orders which adorn while they serve the Kingdom of God on earth.' The paper urged people of all classes to give the French a traditional warm English welcome. As for the English monks, the article concluded:

> It would have been a thousand pities to take away any of the English Benedictines from the work which in missions and colleges they have for so long and with such steadiness and ability performed for the church in this land.'[139]

Those who supported the Cardinal, however, did not avoid the questions of the English Benedictines or patriotism. 'If he elects to secure the services of the English Benedictines we shall all rejoice,' but '...we should lament the loss of their invaluable services from mission and school.'[140] In response to such cries as 'foreigners' and 'the invasion of foreign monks,' the paper retorted, 'We have no more dread of an invasion of foreign monks than we have of an invasion of Chinese Black Flags.' If the Solesmes monks chant the Divine Office, 'we shall still sleep quite calmly, as little terrified at the prospect [as] of the invasion of Polar bears.' Gone are the days when outsiders can harm the British character; 'the English people can afford to be large minded in these matters.'[141] The edition for 25 August pleaded that 'more than one Benedictine monastery might conceivably exist in the city of Westminster.'[142] The author also posed an interesting solution to the problem: permit the Solesmes monks to serve the new Westminster Cathedral; but 'so long as the Ampleforth Community continues there will be no other legitimate representative of St. Peter's Abbey, Westminster.'[143]

Even readers of *The Weekly Register* attacked the paper's harsh treatment of the French monks. One correspondent, for example, accused the paper of manufacturing an argument which seemed 'as if it had come straight out of any Protestant History of England.'[144] This writer scorned its attitude and reminded the editor that 'we do not wish to adopt the early anticipations of Protestantism which produced the Statutes of Praemunire and Provisors. 'Theodore, Lanfranc, Anselm, are names of foreigners,' the article continued, and 'a foreigner received John Henry Newman into the Church.' The main argument in favour of Cardinal Vaughan's plan, however, was the catholicity of the Roman Church. 'The Church is Catholic, and when once the principle of nationality is admitted you historically approach schism, you come to Orthodox Russia and Protestant England.'[145]

If the laity and Catholic press approached the question of the French monks from different viewpoints, the mind of the secular clergy was also far from unified. From the beginning of the controversy, the focus was on what action the Cathedral Chapter would take.[146] The viewpoint of the Chapter remained clouded, but it appears that they expressed 'strenuous opposition' to the presence of the Solesmes monks at Westminster.[147] *The Weekly Register* reported that the Chapter viewed Vaughan's proposal with disfavour, which was 'practically unanimous,' but by the end of July 1899 it had 'not yet arrived at a formal decision.'[148] At the July Chapter meeting, presided over by Vaughan, the Cardinal placed before it 'his plan concerning the ritual and choral arrangements for the new Cathedral' and read the letter from Abbot Delatte which outlined the French conditions.[149] Vaughan then tried to calm any fears. He insisted that 'no binding agreement should be made between the parties' until four years had elapsed. Moreover, the Solesmes Benedictines would not usurp the duties of the secular clergy. According to Vaughan, 'the monks would be responsible merely for the conduct of the daily Cathedral Service — High Mass and Vespers.' 'They would neither preach nor hear confessions. Being strictly cenobites, they would confine themselves to prayer and study.' The official record expressed a benign consensus and 'after further conversation, the subject was closed.'[150] *The Weekly Register* continued to assure the Canons, however, that they could count on the support of loyal Roman Catholics in resisting the presence of the French monks in London. While the press argued the merits of the Solesmes scheme, and while the Chapter debated what course of action it would take, a pamphlet appeared which proposed that the secular clergy exclusively should run and administer Westminster Cathedral.

Written by Ethelred L Taunton,[151] *A Letter to His Eminence Herbert Cardinal Vaughan Archbishop of Westminster on the Work of the Clergy at the Westminster Cathedral* championed the rights and privileges of the secular clergy at the new Cathedral. The author praised Vaughan for his dedicated work 'of raising the clergy to their rightful place in the English Church.'[152] The English clergy, Fr Taunton maintained, '...want opportunities; they want to be called upon to *do* something.' As for members of religious orders, 'the monastic Order is not opposed to the Clerical Order...It runs along side of it, keeps it, and sustains it in the divinely appointed work.'[153] His objective was not to compare, to praise, or to criticize, but to argue for the rightful place of the secular clergy at Westminster Cathedral. 'The clergy can do the work of the cathedral: they can be made to do the work as efficiently as anyone else.' 'The new Cathedral,' he maintained, 'will be an object lesson to the whole of England.' His position was strong and forceful:

> Who, then, so fit to do the Church's work as the Sons of the Diocese? Who so capable as those who, by divine institutions are servants of the Sanctuary? Let your Clergy have this opportunity, let them be called upon to do the liturgical work; and I will warrant your Eminence will have reason, and good reason, to be proud of your own sons.[154]

Benedictines in charge of the Cathedral's liturgy, whether French or English, insulted the secular clergy. 'But we shall never get any real Liturgical progress amongst us,' he pleaded with Cardinal Vaughan, until 'the Clergy *do* the Liturgy themselves and inspire a love for it in others.'[155] Public worship at Westminster must be an example to all English Catholics, and it must reflect the spirit and personality of the nation: 'Ostentatious pageantry, tickling of ears, attracting crowds to hear some singers are not your Eminence's objects.' Taunton suggested the following: 'a small College of six Priests, with a Canon in residence, to represent the Chapter,'[156] and a choir-school would supply trained voices for the future.

Fr Taunton not only opposed the invitation to the Benedictines, but also mocked the style of music perfected by the Solesmes monks. Plainchant, he maintained, 'ought to be the foundation of every Ecclesiastical Choir School,' but not the tradition of the Solesmes monks. The style found 'in the manuscript by the Solesmes editors is not in any way representative of the pure Roman Type.' He also appealed to the nationalism of the English Catholics in rejecting this French interpretation: 'I have more than a suspicion that future research...will show that the true source of the Solesmes Chant is Gallican, not Roman.'[157] In conclusion, Fr Taunton believed that 'there is a most happy opportunity of carrying on your Eminence's desire to help the clergy to their rightful position by making them do a work which is theirs by every claim.'[158]

Despite some isolated protests and objections against the settlement of French monks at Westminster Cathedral, Cardinal Vaughan could still count on the support of some English Roman Catholics. Letters to the Catholic press and editorials expressed unquestioned loyalty to the will of the Cardinal Archbishop. The threat of open rebellion on the part of the Cathedral Chapter failed to materialize; throughout the summer this body vacillated and failed to reach a consensus. Consequently, Cardinal Vaughan continued to hope for a successful outcome of his desire to install a choir of French monks in London. In June 1899, he even visited the Abbey of Solesmes to meet with Abbot Delatte about his project,'[159] but no evidence survives which sheds light on this meeting. Nonetheless, this visit must have raised the expectations of the French. Fr Ferdinand Cabrol, the French superior of Farnborough Abbey, emerged as an instrumental person in these discussions.

In July 1899, Cabrol expressed both caution and a contempt for the English monks. 'You have heard the news about the [English] Benedictine Congregation,' he wrote Delatte, 'they have abbots now...I doubt whether they will save them.'[160] He correctly believed that resistance on the part of the English Benedictines to the arrival of the French in London had halted the negotiations. Cabrol warned the Abbot not to trust or co-operate with the English: 'Had we put the Cathedral on a good footing, they would come to take it over.' He used examples from contemporary Anglo-French foreign policy disagreements to illustrate his point.

> Let us not be too generous with them. It's always the
> same old story. We shriek like badgers because they
> occupy Egypt, and we are the ones who gave it to them!
> Let us not make another Egypt for their advantage. It
> seems to me that this is the lesson for now.[161]

But in spite of this prejudice, Cabrol continued to function as an intermediary between Vaughan and Delatte.

In early August, he told Cardinal Vaughan that Abbot Delatte was still keen about the possibility of a London foundation. Aware of some criticism in England, Delatte was 'not worried about it,' and Cabrol confessed that this 'little press rumour leaves us unconcerned.'[162] What did concern the Solesmes officials was the threatened opposition of the Chapter, who allegedly wanted to 'prevent this foundation or reduce the role of the monks to insignificance.' Cabrol confessed to Vaughan that he had information that the Cathedral Chapter 'will never accept that this monastery becomes an abbey with a Benedictine Abbot who would be endowed with all the rights of his title.' Consequently, 'I do not see how we could accept this monastery if the right to make it an abbey were refused.' Fr Cabrol expressed a wish to continue communications with Cardinal Vaughan, and concluded with an example of historical irony:

> This opposition of a few English Catholics reminds me of Charlemagne, the Great Charlemagne, who, in order to raise the standards of the Gauls, went to seek teachers like Alcuin and other great Englishmen in England, to put them at the head of our schools. France felt honoured and had applauded these men. What does *The Weekly Register* think about that?[163]

Vaughan replied by addressing the attack in *The Weekly Register* and expressing the hope that neither he nor the Abbot 'will be troubled by it, or by anything else that may be said.'[164] He promised to 'speak when the time comes in a way that will more than vindicate the honour of Solesmes.' The French must be patient: 'A reaction will certainly come about—and we can all afford to wait a little.'[165]

Cabrol assured Delatte that Vaughan was 'truly good, and whatever happens, he will have shown himself a friend toward us.'[167]Cabrol admitted the existence of a press campaign against Solesmes, but maintained that it was 'a staged disturbance.' Vaughan's advisors were questioning his policy and for this reason, Cabrol urged Delatte 'to take a very clear position, and show him that we are ready to do anything to oblige him.'[167] At the end of August, Fr Cabrol informed the Abbot that Cardinal Vaughan still wanted monks from Solesmes, but that the opposition in England still remained intransigent: '...the Cardinal is desirous of having us, but is [he] strong enough to impose his will on his Chapter, and to give us the appropriate conditions and guarantees?' He again urged caution, and suggested that in 'these circumstances there is nothing to do but wait...'[168]

Cardinal Vaughan faced a more serious problem. What about the monks of the English Congregation whom he had originally invited to settle in London and to conduct the liturgy at his new cathedral? Moreover, the early correspondence and negotiations with the Solesmes monks was carried out without the knowledge of the English Benedictines. The 'Constitutional Crisis' had removed one of Vaughan's original reservations about the Downside monks. A group of English Benedictines had arrived in the London area; land had been purchased in the suburb of Ealing, and construction of a church had begun. During the summer of 1900, Cardinal Vaughan had to inform officials of the English Congregation that he had approached and asked the French to assume those responsibilities already promised to them. The Cardinal not only acted out of politeness; he was forced to admit his action, for the Abbot of Solesmes had made it clear to Vaughan that his monks would come to London only if the co-operation of the English Benedictines was assured. So Cardinal Vaughan sheepishly inquired whether the English monks would relinquish their promised position at Westminster Cathedral and assist the French in conducting the liturgical services.

5. Cardinal Vaughan, the Benedictines and the French Monks

Cardinal Vaughan wrote to the President of the English Benedictine Congregation in November 1900—over a year after he began talks which settled the preliminaries with the French monks. Lack of concern or interest on the part of the English Benedictines is difficult to explain, although one factor might have been that the recent canonical and administrative changes imposed by the Vatican consumed the time and energy of the English superiors.'[169] Nevertheless, on 27 November 1900, Cardinal Vaughan wrote to Abbot Gasquet, recently elected President of the English Congregation, inviting him to come to London for 'a good quiet talk with me. '[170] The Cardinal suggested that they dine alone, and devote two or three hours to serious conversation in the afternoon. On 28 November, Abbot Gasquet paid the Cardinal a visit, which lasted several hours. According to Gasquet's notes, 'the most important matter discussed, however, was concerning the Cathedral.'[171] Both parties agreed to speak openly and frankly; Gasquet's interpretation was that 'the whole thing may be put in the proverbial nut-shell.'

> He wants office said in the W[estminster] Cathedral;
> but 'the Canons' (he said) and many of the clergy desire
> that the monks be absolutely confined to the singing of
> the office and have nothing to do in the church.

By this innocent remark Vaughan broached the sensitive issue: the establishment of the Solesmes Benedictines at Westminster. Vaughan struggled to explain why he now desired the French instead of the English Congregation. 'He could not ask us, or indeed any English to undertake to be mere hired choir men,' Gasquet noted, 'and looked around and found the Solesmes monks willing to take the position.' Vaughan tried to calm Gasquet's visible irritation by indicating that he would make no agreement with the French monks independent of the English. According to Abbot Gasquet, 'he was unwilling to come to terms with them (wh[ich] he had not done as yet) without telling us and asking us to approve their coming.'[172]

In addition to this surprise, Gasquet was indignant at the Cardinal's flippant request. What about the previous agreement with the English Congregation? What about the money expended, and the people already committed to the Ealing mission? In addition to these queries, the suggestion that a French congregation replace his own upset the Abbot President. He recorded that 'I pointed out the grave difficulty and the reflection...upon us in the public mind.'[173] A 'public insult' was Gasquet's precise choice of words. Moreover, he could 'not conceive how the French O.S.B. could have for a moment entertained the scheme of coming into our province — it was in direct contradiction of our privileges.' The English Abbot asked to see a copy of Abbot Delatte's letter which contained his proposals and conditions for sending French monks to Westminster.[174] He informed the Cardinal that the English Congregation would hold a chapter in February 1901. Gasquet suggested that Vaughan compose a letter which dealt with the Westminster question, promising that he would present the entire matter before the monks at that meeting. Abbot Gasquet ended his recollection of this interview with two questions: 'Why does the Card[inal] want us to say we will agree to the French coming; and he does not generally consider the feelings of other people...there must be some reason, but what?'[175]

On 20 December, the Duke of Norfolk invited Aidan Gasquet to breakfast at Norfolk House. Afterwards, the Duke asked him what he thought about the possibility of the French Benedictines coming to Westminster Cathedral to take charge of the liturgy. The Abbot promised to be candid and informed the Duke 'that it was most objectionable in itself...and must inextricably be construed into a distinct insult to us English O.S.B.' Norfolk thanked Abbot Gasquet for his remarks, and confided that Cardinal Vaughan had already spoken to him about the matter. The Duke informed Gasquet that he told Vaughan 'he would have no part in bringing a body of French O.S.B. into London unless it was clearly understood that their English Brethren were quite satisfied.' 'We Catholics,' he concluded, 'have had enough of these misunderstandings....' His meeting with the Duke of Norfolk made it clear to Gasquet that Cardinal Vaughan was serious about bringing the Solesmes Benedictines to London.

Vaughan had himself tried to enlist the support and backing of influential Roman Catholics, like the Duke of Norfolk, for his plan. It appeared, however, that it depended on the support of the English Benedictines. Without it, the Cardinal could not count on the backing of English Catholics. 'This explains,' Gasquet remarked,' why the Cardinal wants us to say we will agree.'[176] Clearly, Cardinal Vaughan had given up on the idea of the English Congregation being associated with the liturgy at Westminster Cathedral. But on the other hand, he urged members of the English Catholic Church to welcome the French monks of Solesmes instead. If the English Benedictines raised a storm of protest, or if they refused to co-operate with the French, Vaughan's dream would never materialize. Since it appeared that the liturgical duties would not be offered to his congregation of monks as agreed earlier, Abbot Gasquet worked to ensure that the French would never enjoy the prestige of conducting the services in Westminster Cathedral. He faced strong opposition to this plan of scuttling French hopes.

The Tablet continued to print laudatory articles concerning France, its special relationship with Catholic England, and the common bond which united the faithful of the two nations. In an essay entitled 'France and the Conversion of England,' one author described the goals of the priests of the French order of St Sulpice as: 'To organize, promote, and foster throughout the whole Christian world a Crusade of Prayer for the return of England to the one True Fold.'[177] Unity of purpose and spirit, therefore, transcended the English Channel. The author also described the relationship between French and English Roman Catholics as a '...Holy Alliance held out to us, the spiritual partnership offered to us...' Moreover, the English must cooperate and not compete with their French co-religious: 'We can at least be something more than an approving spectator and a sleeping partner.' The article concluded with a quote from Cardinal Vaughan which emphasized the 'services of charity rendered by the glorious Church of France to the Church of England' begun in 429 AD when Pope Celestinus sent St. Germain of Auxerre to England to extinguish the Pelagian heresy.[178]

In November 1900 *The Tablet* printed a report from the Anglican paper *The Church Times,* which described a visit to the Abbey of Solesmes. *The Tablet,* usually scornful of Anglo-Catholic principles and liturgy, published this Anglican essay in praise of the French community. The connection of the French monastery with plainchant was emphasized. 'Solesmes, in fact, is the starting point, the centre of a remarkable liturgical and musical revival in the Latin Church, which is making itself distinctly felt in all quarters of the globe.'[179] In virtual challenge to English Roman Catholics, the author noted that 'we of the Church of England owe a debt of gratitude to Solesmes for having given us a fresh impulse in the correct revival of plainchant.' The article praised every aspect of the French abbey from the architecture to the smallest detail of the daily worship of the monks. The liturgy, naturally, was singled out for admiration:

> You cannot leave Solesmes without a feeling of regret, but there is, at the same time, thankfulness that once in your life, you have been privileged to hear and see the inspired worship of Benedictine monks and nuns, who have restored to the Church that precious heritage of the ages, the plainchant.'[180]

Newspaper reports and essays in the Roman Catholic press however, were not enough to frustrate the opposition of Aidan Gasquet to a Solesmes foundation at Westminster Cathedral.

By the end of 1900 Abbot Gasquet still did not know the details or the extent of the arrangements between Cardinal Vaughan and Abbot Delatte. Gasquet's understanding of the situation was admittedly sketchy: the English monks were to be supplanted at Westminster by the monks of Solesmes; for reasons of diplomacy, public approval of this arrangement by the English Congregation was necessary; but the precise nature of the agreements eluded him. A letter from Cardinal Vaughan soon cleared up the mystery. On 24 December 1900, Vaughan sent Gasquet a packet of documents. The Cardinal explained in a covering letter that he was forwarding 'a formal and official letter on the Cathedral as agreed, together with the original and translation of the Abbot of Solesmes' letter.'[181] Cardinal Vaughan asked Gasquet to return Delatte's letters, but for the time being to 'use them with due reserve and discretion.' He pleaded with the Abbot to try and convince his fellow Benedictines 'that the course contemplated is the only practical one.' 'A generous approval of the English Benedictines,' Cardinal Vaughan concluded, 'would produce, I think, a most favourable impression upon the Church in England as showing a breadth and large mindedness, not always found in Ecclesiastics or in corporations.'[182] Vaughan did not comprehend the intricacies of ecclesiastical politics, and failed to understand the competition and rivalry between religious congregations of the same church. 'He was not a scholar, nor indeed an intellectual; as a member of one of the old Catholic families, he was brought up to accept without questioning the teaching and policy of the Church.'[183]

Cardinal Vaughan's 'formal and official letter' to the General Chapter of the English Benedictine Congregation traced the history of the construction of Westminster Cathedral, his desire to make the Divine Office an essential part of its life, and emphasized that he had naturally turned to the English Congregation first. The long connection of Benedictine monks with the memory and name of Westminster, and his personal and affectionate dealings with Downside since the 1840s, motivated this decision. Consequently, the Cardinal confessed that he owed 'an explanation of the position in which I now find myself.'[184] He pointed out that difficulties, which 'seemed almost insurmountable,' immediately jeopardized his plan for a monastic foundation at Westminster Cathedral. He reduced the problem to one essential:

> *viz.* the difficulty of so adjusting the rights, the life and the action of two independent Bodies — such as a Body of Regulars who by their Constitution are also Missioners, and a body of Secular Missionary Priests within the same Cathedral — as to preserve intact the rights of each and yet maintain that perfect peace and harmony which is the first condition in a work of co-operation.[185]

Westminster, being the metropolitan cathedral and the centre of the English hierarchy, care of the parish and the public devotions in the church should properly be under the control of the secular clergy. Consequently, this 'would at once confine the action of any religious Body attached to the Cathedral to the daily choral rendering of the Liturgy.'

The Cardinal's logic led to the following conclusion: the character of the English Benedictine Congregation necessarily excluded it from performing the Divine Office. Although three years earlier Vaughan was ecstatic about the possibility of Downside Benedictines occupying the stalls of Westminster, he now illustrated for Gasquet one hindrance: '...it has been pointed out to me, and I admit with undeniable reason, that I could not expect a Religious Congregation like yours to sacrifice the missionary character of their Constitution by confining its members to the choral service of the Cathedral to its exclusion from all active work in the ministry.' Vaughan for some reason chose to ignore the recent changes in the English Benedictine Constitution, which downplayed the missionary and emphasized the monastic character of the Order. He also argued that two separate and independent bodies of religious men, with their respective superiors and entrusted with similar tasks in the same church, 'would involve too great a risk for either of us to consider it prudent or wise to make the attempt.'[186]

Yet Cardinal Vaughan saw no problems or incongruities in approaching the French monks. The absence of a missionary or active apostolic life attracted him to the Solesmes Congregation: '...their Constitutions confine their vocation to the solemn rendering of the Office, and forbid them to take part in the work of the ministry and other external work, such as the foundation of Colleges etc....' 'Here,' the Cardinal put to Gasquet, 'seems to be a solution of the difficulty that has arisen.' Points of possible friction and conflict would also be reduced to a minimum if the French, rather than English monks, conducted the worship in Westminster Cathedral. The contemplative and academic character of the Solesmes Congregation would not clash with pastoral duties, which would be the prerogative of the secular clergy. Vaughan admitted that nothing definite had been decided. Out of courtesy, he approached the English monks, '...the Body with which I have already been in communication,' to inform them of his present plan. The Abbot of Solesmes, he confessed, was eager to settle in London. Consequently, 'I have received from him a reply full of generous sentiments, and of respect for his Anglo-Benedictine Brethren, with the sketch of a plan that is perfectly satisfactory to myself as a basis for a tentative agreement.'[187] Vaughan had also enclosed Delatte's letter of June 1899 which spelled out the latter's proposals.

But the transfer of liturgical duties to these monks was not all Vaughan envisioned. The Solesmes settlement 'would in due time become independent and not continue as a dependency on the Mother House abroad.' This suggestion must have shocked and disturbed Abbot Gasquet. Not only was he asked to relinquish the honour of chanting the Latin office in Westminster Cathedral to a group of French monks, but he was also requested to give his approval to the existence of a permanent French monastery attached to the Cathedral. The Cardinal ended his letter in a manner which appeared insensitive, and even insulting, to the proud English Congregation:

> I am, therefore, anxious to lay this matter before you as
> Abbot President of the English Benedictines, and to act
> in such manner with you as should render it impossible

for anyone to feel that an affront has been offered to the Anglo-Benedictine Congregation, or that they have been treated by me without consideration and courtesy. I have, therefore, ventured to send you this letter, and to say that, if you see any other practical arrangement that would be more satisfactory to you, I shall be pleased to examine it with you.[188]

Cardinal Vaughan had seriously underestimated the pride of the English Benedictine Congregation. Like Wiseman fifty years earlier, he miscalculated the homage, reverence, and tradition attached to the memory of Westminster. It must be served by English monks; to invite a foreign order would be virtually sacrilegious. Vaughan simply misread the sensitivity of the English Benedictines. 'What had seemed to the Cardinal just an act of fellowship between men working for a common cause, to the English Benedictines presented itself, and not unnaturally, in a very different light...they thought it an impossible proposal...'[189]

Before the opening of the Chapter of the English Benedictine Congregation, scheduled for February, Abbot Gasquet had determined that Vaughan's proposal, idealistic but unworkable, must be defeated. He began to formulate his opposition which would be presented to the Chapter. He believed that the Cardinal's dream to build a new Westminster was foolish. The Abbey of Westminster was dead, and to attempt a resurrection, 'ridiculous.'[190] Before considering co-operation with the foreign monks, Gasquet had to demand from the Cardinal a detailed schedule of duties the English would perform. 'What then is the work,' he queried, 'the members of the venerable Eng[lish] Cong[regation] are...to take part in?' He maintained that it was 'difficult to believe that such a scheme should be calmly put forth by the Sol[esmes] O.S.B.'[191] 'Still more difficult,' he explained,

> to conceive a state of mind which would permit them to believe that we—members of a body which has come down...unbroken...from the days of St Augustine... should not only calmly permit without protest such a scheme to be initiated, but were to be invited to assist in our own public degradation.[192]

Consequently, the Abbot President of the English Congregation determined to defeat Cardinal Vaughan's plan to bring the French monks into central London. If the English Benedictines refused to assist the French, or if the English conveyed a feeling of outrage or embarrassment, then this silly idea would certainly fail.

Despite Cardinal Vaughan's negotiation with the French and his communications with Abbot Gasquet, some of his public statements and actions demonstrated his indecision. A homily he preached at the Downside foundation at Ealing, for example, gave the impression that he still hoped that the Ealing monks would help at Westminster Cathedral. In his remarks, Vaughan thanked the Benedictine Fathers and rejoiced in the fact that 'the great and ancient Order of St Benedict should have full representation in the Diocese of Westminster.'[193] Vaughan expressed the gratitude of his archdiocese at the success of the monks, and urged the parishioners to support their new monastic foundation. The Tablet, in conclusion, drew attention to the role of the Benedictines in London: 'in no unseemly haste they have satisfied the wants of the day, but they have laid their lines for the future...[the new Ealing Church] is intended to serve for monastic, collegiate, and parochial purposes.'[194]

While conversation progressed in England, the French Congregation was puzzled at the silence and the inaction of Cardinal Vaughan in failing to issue the formal invitation to come to Britain. Abbot Delatte continued to be positive about a Solesmes foundation in London, and he related this optimism to his friend, Bishop Gilbert. The Bishop's response was typical of his earlier letters: 'I rejoice deeply with you at the vitality and expansion of this dear family.'[195] The delay on the part of Cardinal Vaughan constituted another matter, and the Bishop believed an explanation could be found in the area of international affairs:

> As to Westminster, I had seen, since the beginning of the Transvaal Affair, that if this noble creation would not become impossible, it would be temporarily or indefinitely postponed. One can see that there is a ferocious wave of 'Gallo-phobia,' and there may, or rather there must, arise from this incident, international strife, despite our cowardly action, strife which delays, very obviously, the taking possession [which is] so much the target of a French monastic element.[196]

Westminster Cathedral does not appear in the correspondence of the French officials until October 1900, and here Abbot Delatte finally expressed his frustration over the delay on the part of Cardinal Vaughan.

Delatte' s uneasiness about Vaughan's hesitation became clear early in this letter. 'It is true that I accepted Westminster in principle, but nevertheless under conditions which, after a year and a half, have not yet been formally accepted, since no notification has come to me.'[197] As in the case of Bishop Gilbert, Delatte recognized the importance of nationalism and foreign affairs in the negotiations. Delatte informed Cabrol that the Cardinal's 'caprices over the Boer War and over the Dreyfus Case were deeply displeasing to me...It does not attract me very much to enter into very close relations with a man who is capable of swerving to that extent.' But Delatte understood the reason for this attitude: 'He will have his Englishman's soul forever, until the hour when he renders it to God.' The important section of the letter, however, contained the Abbot's decision to modify seriously his earlier arrangements with Cardinal Vaughan. One reason for a reconsideration was the rumour that Gasquet would be the next Archbishop of Westminster:'....what will our position be? Will we even have time to establish ourselves?' But the crucial reason which forced Delatte to back out was Cardinal Vaughan's lack of direction.

Abbot Delatte told Cabrol of Farnborough that at the present he could only contribute a reduced contingent of Solesmes monks to the proposed London foundation. 'The effort which I could have agreed to last year in order to form with you the Westminster community, I could no longer undertake today with a reduced house.' He related that he felt '...free as far as England was concerned' and had already sent monks to another foundation, St. Paul's, Wisques,[198] and had promised to send more. So the Abbot then asked Cabrol if the Farnborough community might be willing to transfer to Westminster: 'Would you be numerous enough with the few men the English congregation might furnish you with? It is up to you to see.' The Abbot concluded that he was 'forced to dissociate' himself for one reason: '...the Cardinal can blame no one but himself; his silence of a year seemed to me to be equivalent to an abandonment.'[199] Bishop Gilbert offered some predictable advice. He realized that any immediate solution was out of the question, but cautioned against Delatte's abrupt change of policy: 'I am more disheartened and overwhelmed by the present ignominy than I am dumb-founded and discouraged by the announcement of a decisive ruinous solution which to me is *impossible*.'[200] In the next month, Gilbert again begged Delatte to reconsider: 'in such a far-reaching undertaking a few years spent in preambles and in cautiously feeling one's way along are not much, when one thinks of this seizure of the lofty orthodox and doctrinal apostolate of England, which is what I perceive under all this music you are asked for.'[201] As Bishop Gilbert was warning Delatte against any rash action, the General Chapter of the English Congregation met at Downside Abbey.

6. The Abbot Versus the Archbishop

The General Chapter of the English Congregation convened at Down-side Abbey in February 1901. Speculation and mystery surround the debates and discussions concerning Westminster Cathedral, but it appears that Gasquet's violent opposition to Cardinal Vaughan's Solesmes proposal captured the consensus of the membership, which probably had serious reservations itself about the plan. Written on behalf of the Congregation on 13 February, Gasquet's report thanked Cardinal Vaughan for the 'kind communication of December 24th...[but] the authorities of our Congregation have as yet never received from you any definite offer to serve your Cathedral.'[202] According to Gasquet, the Chapter noted the anxiety of the Cardinal not to insult or affront the English Benedictines. Moreover, the Abbot President stated that the Chapter had never rejected or abandoned its traditional claim to Westminster, which Vaughan had suggested in the past. 'We would willingly entertain and consider any scheme for our serving... Westminster,' Gasquet reported, 'which your Eminence, conjointly with your Canons, would formulate, provided it was not inconsistent with the vocation of the English Benedictines as recently determined by the Holy See.'

Castigating the Cardinal Archbishop for his failure to make a firm and detailed commitment to the English monks, even after promising the native congregation the honour of serving at the new Westminster Cathedral, Abbot Gasquet informed Vaughan of the mind of the Chapter. The English Benedictines 'cannot be expected to give either assistance or countenance to the establishment of any community of foreign Benedictines in our English Metropolitan Cathedral.'[203] This action alone demolished the original agreement between Vaughan and Abbot Delatte. Moreover, hurt pride and a broken promise contributed to the Chapter's hostile mood: 'Such a foundation cannot fail to be regarded as a serious reflection on our venerable Congregation, more especially in view of your Eminence's public declarations that you intended to establish English Benedictines at Westminster.' As far as the Chapter was concerned it would not condone any French presence in London. If monks were to be at Westminster, they must be English. The blame must rest with the Cardinal if no Benedictines graced the choir of his cathedral. 'The Abbot-President and his Assistants,' he reminded Vaughan, are ready at any time to consider any scheme which may be proposed by Your Eminence and your Chapter.'[204]

Along with this official notification of the General Chapter's decision, Abbot Gasquet enclosed his personal criticism of Cardinal Vaughan's scheme. 'You asked me to be quite frank,' he wrote in a letter of introduction, and 'I hope that you will not think that I am outspoken in criticizing the French scheme.'[205] He told Vaughan that he could not believe that the Cardinal had 'really studied the French Abbot's letter, for the proposals made are so very different to any that you told me you had received from Solesmes.' As an introduction to his long, detailed and fatal critique of the so-called French scheme, the Abbot pinpointed the chief motive for his opposition to Vaughan's plan: 'at any rate you will see from my criticism that we could not, consistently with our oaths to maintain our rights and privileges, do anything but oppose the proposal of the Solesmes Fathers to come over here to set up a rival Congregation.'

Abbot Gasquet's lengthy diatribe demonstrated his scholarship, his knowledge of English religious history, and his fierce determination to prevent the French monks from establishing themselves at Westminster Cathedral. Gasquet sketched the history of the negotiations between the Cardinal and the English Congregation concerning the possibility of the latter staffing the London Cathedral. Gasquet reminded him that the initiative came from the Cardinal: 'You asked me to be the intermediary between yourself and the Superiors of the English Benedictine congregation to obtain a body of monks for the purpose.' Your Eminence came to us; and I am confident that we should never of ourselves have thought of what you proposed.' Gasquet admitted that he had realized the difficulties involved, the jealousies the plan would stir up, and how 'it would hamper us in any future undertakings.' 'And only on the supposition that we were serving the broader interests of the Church in England could we have been justified,' Gasquet stated, 'would the Benedictines of Downside have ever abandoned some of their present commitments.'[206]

Gasquet reminded Vaughan that he told him immediately 'that the only way in which a scheme such as yours could possibly work would be to entrust the entire management of the Cathedral to the body of monks.' Due care had also to be taken to preserve the position and rights of the Cathedral Chapter. Abbot Gasquet continued to point the accusing finger. It was Vaughan who suggested that the monks take over two missions which would ultimately be incorporated into the Cathedral parish 'in order that we might get to know the district in which we have to work...' It was Vaughan who publicly announced on many occasions that he had requested the English Benedictines to take up this work. 'If then there has been any error as to what your Eminence wanted of us,' Abbot Gasquet reasoned, 'the mistake did not originate with us.'

Abbot Gasquet accused the Cardinal of deception in negotiating with the Solesmes monks. He acknowledged that he had heard rumours that the Cardinal was 'in treaty with foreigners who had agreed to come merely to act as a paid choir to sing the offices.'[207] But he maintained that he' treated the matter as merely one of the many unfounded stories constantly being spread about one in your exalted position.' Another reason why the Abbot dismissed these stories as unfounded gossip was Cardinal Vaughan's public and private statements of support for the English Congregation, and his desire to have at Westminster Cathedral 'the one body which had come down in unbroken succession from the days of St Augustine....' His accusation of ecclesiastical duplicity emphasized the illogical point in Vaughan's plan: 'You now, however, ask me not only to put before our Fathers a scheme proposed by the Abbot of Solesmes for serving your Cathedral, but to induce them to facilitate its working by giving their approval to the French fathers coming to London and even by actively co-operating in *their* work at your Cathedral.'

Patriotism and national pride played its part in the bruised feelings of the English Benedictines:

> It would of course be useless to disguise the fact that we English Benedictines, who have been connected with this country for so many centuries and who have borne the burden and heat of the day during the years of persecution, cannot see with pleasure a position, which must be regarded as the most prominent occupied by the Order in England, assigned to foreigners.[208]

He admitted that he did not expect Vaughan to appreciate the *convenances des choses* between different congregations of Benedictine monks, but he could not 'comprehend how ordinary feelings of delicacy did not force the French fathers to at once decline your offer to intrude themselves into the province of another well established congregation in another country.' Vaughan might have been naive, but according to Gasquet the Solesmes Congregation had broken ecclesiastical protocol. Had he been asked to establish an English abbey on French soil, Gasquet told the Cardinal that 'we should never dream of setting up a rival to a Benedictine congregation already existing in France.'[209] The English Abbot attacked the French for even considering the Cardinal's proposals, but finally excused Vaughan because he 'could not be expected to understand this and not unnaturally desired to secure what appeared to suit your purpose best.'

The Cardinal must shoulder the blame for a large part of the *débâcle*. Gasquet noted that the original letter from Abbot Delatte differed in essential points from the English translation, which had been sent to

Downside Abbey from Archbishop's House. Gasquet also called attention
to his meeting at Mill Hill with Cardinal Vaughan. Here, according to
Abbot Gasquet, the Cardinal stated that the French 'were willing to come
to Westminster to do nothing beyond the singing of the office, to take no
part in the management of the Cathedral and not to look for any influence
of work beyond the monastery walls.'[210] Delatte's letter suggested more
than this. Gasquet, therefore, listed the aspects which proved that the
French had more in mind than the singing of the Divine Office: they
refused to be bound by any written agreement; they wanted a monastery
built for them in Ashley Gardens (adjacent to the Cathedral); and Abbot
Delatte had even admitted that the monks he would send to London
possessed either weak or horrible voices! Abbot Gasquet argued that the
Solesmes monks could not contribute much to the liturgy, pointing out that
Delatte admitted that 'hired and trained singers, the choir school and choir
master...'[211] must assume the duty for the Cathedral's worship. Why, then,
did the Solesmes monks want to settle in London?

> It will be seen by the above that the French Fathers
> contemplate very much more than the mere singing of
> their office and practically require to have the manage-
> ment of the Cathedral with the small exception of
> matters strictly parochial, all of which are moreover to
> be confined to a side chapel...They have visions of
> people resorting to them for advice and direction...they
> still hope to find in the neighbourhood of your Cathedral
> a well kept hotel 'where priests, religious and others'
> who could not be accommodated within the monastery,
> might lodge.[212]

The Abbot of Solesmes, he believed, desired nothing less than the
establishment of a colony of French monks in London. Gasquet even
accused Abbot Delatte of ingratitude. 'It is difficult to believe,' the Abbot
told Vaughan, 'that it could have been put forth seriously by Benedictine
brethren who have received nothing but kindness from us and who owe
their very presence at Farnborough to my own suggestion to the late
Bishop of Portsmouth.'[213] Frenchmen cannot comprehend the English
Catholic mind, and their presence at Westminster would insult the pride of
the English monks and the nation. Therefore, Abbot Gasquet concluded,
it would be impossible that the 'Monks of a congregation already existing
in England should calmly permit without protest the initiation of such an
infringement of our rights and privileges, but accept their invitation to co-

operate in their scheme and thus assist in the dismemberment of our own body and in our own public degradation.'[214] Gasquet closed this long letter by excusing the Cardinal from any malicious intent: 'it is obvious to every one of us that you could not have understood the proposals made in the Abbot of Solesmes letter.'[215]

The refusal of the English Benedictine monks to cooperate with the French, and their strong protests over the wisdom and prudence of Cardinal Vaughan's proposal, effectively destroyed the Cardinal's hope to have Benedictines associated with Westminster Cathedral. Yet, according to Snead-Cox, 'those who were much with Cardinal Vaughan in those days knew that he received the reply of the English Benedictines without disappointment.'[216] Vaughan still believed that the French were straightforward and honest, even generous, in their dealings with him.

Vaughan replied to Abbot Gasquet's critique and tried to assure him that the French monks had not attacked or maligned their English counterparts: 'I should assure you that they have spoken and acted with great kindness and consideration for the English Benedictine Congregation.'[217] Cardinal Vaughan refused to accept Gasquet's 'interpretation of the Abbot's [Delatte's] designs,' and explained how the Solesmes Abbot desired to act in a 'friendly way and in co-operation with them.' The Cardinal apologized for the shoddy translation of Delatte's letter, informing Gasquet that some of his objections to the content of the letter were meaningless since these had already been renegotiated.

Gasquet's reply to Cardinal Vaughan's attempted apology and explanation of his Solesmes plan revealed that the English Abbot would still not yield in his criticisms. Four points were clear and obvious: In the first place, Gasquet still maintained that the 'Abbot of Solesmes's meaning seemed perfect [sic] clear and definite.'[218] No amount of rationalization could erase the fact that the French Benedictines intended to establish a permanent monastic foundation on English soil. Gasquet then singled out the main problem which troubled the negotiations of the past five years: the 'whole matter of West[minster] involved...great diff[iculties].' The history and heritage attached to the name of Westminster recalled the greatness of Britain's past; a French association with this hallowed tradition would produce vindictiveness and hatred on the part of the English. His third point addressed the question of rivalry. Gasquet claimed that there existed a 'strong feeling...among secular priests against religious,' and consequently if any Benedictine, native or foreign, were to conduct the liturgy at Westminster Cathedral, conflict and bitterness would explode within English Catholicism. In light of this observation, Abbot Gasquet's fourth point offered a solution, which the Cardinal eventually adopted. To put an end to the tension between the French and English Benedictines, and also to eliminate any animosity between the religious and secular clergy of England, he suggested that secular priests perform the ceremonies. In addition to this, a choral school might be established to supply the trained singers to perform vespers and the High Mass. Gasquet's proposals were welcome news to Vaughan, who saw a quiet way out of the Westminster Cathedral problem. Until the spring of 1901, the Cardinal had no idea of the difficulties arising from the questions of jurisdiction, problems of nationality, and the reverence for the memory of Westminster. Vaughan's biographer recorded that 'he learned of the breaking off of his negotiations with the French and English monks with equanimity, but perhaps a truer word would be "relief."'[219]

Since the English Benedictines refused to sanction his plan, Cardinal Vaughan informed the French monks that it would be impossible for them to come to London. He still had no idea that the French had already changed their minds. Vaughan, therefore, wrote to Fr Cabrol, their superior, telling him the news that the English monks had refused to co-operate with the French. Cabrol replied by relating that he had been keen on forming a 'schola at Westminster capable of singing Gregorian Chant....'[220] Saddened but not shocked by the actions of the English Benedictines, he informed Vaughan that he possessed little knowledge of 'the details of the decision taken by the General Chapter of which Your Eminence writes.' He admitted that he was 'not surprised because...[he] knew of the very determined opposition of the English Benedictines to the project of Your Eminence.' The Cardinal eventually informed Abbot Delatte of the altered situation, and sent him a copy of Gasquet's letter which announced the decision of the General Chapter of the English Benedictines.

Cardinal Vaughan, however, still needed clerics to take charge of the services at Westminster. Even at this point, Cardinal Vaughan hoped that the English Benedictines might help. 'We are now in this impasse,' he told Gasquet, 'I said I am willing to consider a proposal from you: and you reply that you are willing to consider one from me.' It was no secret that the Cathedral Chapter had expressed serious reservations about Benedictine monks of any nationality working in the new cathedral. Gasquet's solution to the impasse was acceptable: Why not relinquish to this body the duties which were previously to be entrusted to monks? Vaughan determined, therefore, 'to fall back upon a simpler and bolder solution and, to the huge delight of the whole archdiocese, decided to entrust the rendering of the liturgy of the Cathedral to the Secular clergy.'[221] The Bishop-Auxiliary of the Archdiocese of Westminster, Bishop Brindle, conveyed Cardinal Vaughan's decision to a receptive Chapter.[222] At the 23 April meeting of

1901 Brindle announced that Vaughan 'had given up his intention of establishing Benedictine monks in the Westminster Cathedral for the singing of Divine Office.'[223] Part of the failure to procure Benedictines for the new Westminster Cathedral could be traced to the words and deeds of the monks of Downside. 'The Benedictine monks in England had expressed their inability to undertake the task,' the Provost, Mgr Michael Barry, stated, 'and had declared their resolve of protesting before the Holy See, if Benedictine monks were introduced for the purpose mentioned from France.' Consequently, secular priests of Westminster Archdiocese, 'whose selection would be determined by their fitness for the work,' would now supervise and perform the liturgical services at the Westminster.

Cardinal Vaughan personally revealed this new plan for his clergy during the annual meeting of the Westminster Diocesan Synod in 1901. The Cardinal explained that an essential function of the new cathedral would be the performance of the Divine Office and celebration of High Mass. 'A high standard of church music and religious ceremonial must accompany the liturgy,' he told the priests, and 'its religious services should leave nothing to be desired as to solemnity and devotion.'[224] Vaughan concluded that originally he 'had thought of the great Benedictine Order, and had both publicly and privately expressed the hope that the Liturgical services of the Cathedral might be confided to their care.' However, 'difficulties had arisen that appeared insuperable.' The Cardinal assumed, therefore, that the secular clergy would gladly undertake this task, and he informed the Synod that the plans were already being considered by the Chapter. He declared that he saw many advantages in this, and 'one thing only was more important, and that was the establishment in the Cathedral of a really high standard of Liturgical service, both as to music and ceremonial.' The Archbishop ended his report by expressing his confidence in the ability of the clergy to undertake this new and important charge. But he also issued a warning to the Synod: 'If they failed, it would become necessary to call in some body of men who make the Liturgy their one and only work.' This threat demonstrated that Benedictine monks might still be recruited if needed.

The Roman Catholic press had prepared the public for this change. A few years earlier, *The Tablet* had reported Cardinal Vaughan's earnest wish to bring Benedictine monks into the precincts of his new cathedral. Its columns now announced that the monks would not be invited; the honour of conducting the cathedral's liturgy would be the work of the secular clergy instead. The article stated that 'much public interest has for some time past centred on the question how and by whom the solemn Liturgical Offices of the Church are to be rendered in the new Cathedral.'[225] *The Tablet* noted the 'unforeseen difficulties which had arisen when it had been proposed to call in the services of a Religious Order for the daily religious chant of the Liturgy....' Consequently, 'the Cardinal Archbishop announced that he gladly availed himself of the readiness of the Secular clergy to take up the work.' The clergy, the report stated, were overjoyed and eager. Nonetheless, a touch of nostalgia and sadness crept into the columns of *The Tablet:* 'We confess we would have been glad...to see the cowls of the Benedictines back in Westminster....'

Some historical link or bond existed between the two Westminsters, and it might have been fitting for monks to be associated with the new cathedral. But 'apart from the old associations which cluster around the site of Westminster, is it not after all better, and more in accordance with the fitness of things, that the Secular clergy should themselves render the Liturgy in the new Cathedral?'[226] Moreover, it would have been anomalous to entrust the services of the cathedral, which represented all England, to a single religious order, the Benedictines. For this purpose, Vaughan 'obtained permission from Rome to increase the number of Canons of the Metropolitan Chapter from twelve to eighteen, and make provisions for a body of eighteen Cathedral Chaplains.'[227]

In the spring of 1901, the Chapter of Westminster Cathedral 'uniformly declared its entire concurrence with the proposal made by his Eminence with respect to the Choir Service of the Cathedral.'[228] And in May 1902, the Divine Office was sung for the first time in Westminster Cathedral. Cardinal Vaughan, therefore, achieved the singing of plainchant, the loyalty and gratitude of the Cathedral Chapter and peace between religious and secular clergy, but not the services of Benedictine monks— French or English.

The failure of Cardinal Vaughan to grace his new and magnificent cathedral with the melodies of the Benedictines chanting the Divine Office demonstrated that English Catholicism was not as unified as some tend to believe. The Catholic press of the period constantly ridiculed the divisions, squabbles, and conflicts within the Established Church, and painted Roman Catholicism as the one, unified, catholic church. According to this argument, the division of High and Low Church did not plague Roman Catholicism; evangelical and Anglo-Catholic parties, some boasted, did not trouble the Catholic community. The conflict concerning the performance of the liturgical duties at Westminster Cathedral, however, revealed that jealousy and rivalry also beset the Roman Catholics.

Within English Catholicism, competition between the religious and secular clergy could be traced back to the Middle Ages. Cardinal Vaughan's initial impulse to entrust the liturgy at Westminster to the English

Benedictines fanned and renewed the fires of distrust. Although not as violent as in the past, the secular clergy resented Vaughan's proposal and successfully resisted his desire to hand over Westminster Cathedral to the monks of Downside Abbey. The monks at Ealing were aware of this tension and animosity. One of them, Dom Gilbert Dolan OSB, wrote to Downside and noted 'a certain antagonism to us lately in the curia at Archbishop's House...as though the anti-French manifesto with regard to the serving the new Cathedral must be visited on our heads.'[229] Dolan concluded succinctly, *'that* scheme I hear is "off," and we must suffer for the rebuff its proposer has received from the Chapter of Westminster.'

Sadly, there was not unity of purpose within the Benedictine Order itself; altruism and service to the Church were sacrificed to national pride, patriotism, and inter-congregational feuds. If the services of the French monks were to be obtained instead of the English monks, two conditions were necessary: the English Benedictines must give their public approval; and the same congregation must supply some monks to assist the French, who would receive the honour and glory. Abbot Aidan Gasquet vigorously opposed both, and thus he ensured that the French monks, who already had had second thoughts, would reject Vaughan's invitation, If Westminster was not in English Benedictine hands, French Benedictines would certainly not occupy its stalls.

The troubles over Westminster Cathedral also revealed some insights into the personality of Cardinal Vaughan, the spokesman of English Roman Catholicism. By nature a romantic, he planned the construction of his new cathedral complete with a contingent of Benedictines. For the Cardinal and some pious Catholics, it would become a new Westminster arising from the destruction of the Reformation. Vaughan eventually emerged from the problems he created successfully, but one can see his ecclesiastical naivety and unreasonable idealism in that he actually believed that the secular clergy would relinquish their claim to officiate in the new cathedral to the Benedictine monks. Gasquet believed that Cardinal Vaughan showed his true colours in the problems he created with regard to the Benedictines and Westminster Cathedral. According to him, 'it is very sad how completely out of all touch he appears to be with everyone.'[230] But there were wider implications: 'Altogether the general outlook in England is very depressing and one has to say one's prayers and mind one's own business as best one may.' More importantly, 'the position of Catholics made by Cardinal Manning has been very much lowered.'

The Cardinal conceived the Roman Church to be a universal organization which transcended national boundaries. He quickly discovered, however, that nationalism was not confined to politics and foreign policy; it also infected religious groups. The fierce and dogged opposition of the English monks to the French shattered Vaughan's illusion. In the end, the secular clergy won the privilege to conduct the services at Westminster, and the troubles quickly faded away. In 1947, Dom Bruno Hicks OSB, the former Abbot of Downside, correctly commented on Cardinal Vaughan's solution to the Westminster controversy:

> Whatever sentimental regret may be felt on historical grounds that the Benedictine monks are not again at Westminster, no one can deny that the Divine Office and the Liturgical services are carried out in the Cathedral to-day in a manner comparable to that which obtained in the great abbeys of England before the Reformation.[231]

7. Cathedral Resplendent: The Fruition of a Dream

Thus the year 1902 marked the opening of Westminster Cathedral. 'You will be pleased to hear,' Cardinal Vaughan wrote to his friend Lady Herbert of Lea, 'that we had the whole of the Divine Office and High Mass for the first time on Ascension Day, in the Chapter Hall.'[232] He could not disguise his pride: 'the Hall has been arranged like the Sistine Chapel and looks beautiful.' Worship and liturgy continued to occupy an important part in the Cardinal's plans for his new cathedral. In addition to entrusting the liturgy to his secular clergy, Vaughan founded a choir school, and the spirit of Benedictinism lingered here: the first director of music and choir master, R R Terry, came from Downside School. Soon afterwards Cardinal Vaughan formed a College of Cathedral Chaplains.

During that same year, J F Bentley, architect of the cathedral, died. The Cardinal paid tribute to him and remarked that 'he put the whole of his life and soul into the Cathedral and it killed him, not the designing but the carrying it out.'[233] It was fitting that on 26 June 1903 Cardinal Vaughan's own requiem was the first large religious service to be conducted in the cathedral he laboured to construct. Vaughan's successors at Westminster— Francis Bourne (1861-1935), Arthur Hinsley (1865-1943), Bernard Griffin (1899-1956), William Godfrey (1889-1963), John Heenan (1905-1975), and Basil Hume (1923-)—all continued to enrich the cathedral, making it a proud symbol of Roman Catholicism and a fitting place of worship.

The connection between London and the Benedictine monks which Cardinal Vaughan had originally proposed also became a reality. The Downside mission in Ealing prospered. The parish grew rapidly, and the church had to be enlarged during the century to meet the increase in parishioners. In 1902, Dom Sebastian Cave OSB, opened a school in Ealing to educate young boys with traditional Benedictine ideals. The current enrollment is approximately eight hundred. Alongside parish and school, the monastic community quickly showed signs of permanence. In 1916 Ealing became a priory, but still remained dependent on Downside. It was recognized as an independent priory in 1947, and was raised to the rank of abbey in 1955. In addition to parochial and educational responsibilities, Ealing Abbey also sponsors prayer and retreat centres.

The fortunes of the French Benedictines did not fare as well; the Solesmes monks did come to England, but under difficult circumstances. In 1901, the French government's anti-clerical policies forced them to flee France and journey to England, where they took refuge on the Isle of Wight. It was not until 1922 that these Benedictines returned to Solesmes. The French foundation at Farnborough grew steadily. In 1903, it was created an abbey, and Dom Ferdinand Cabrol was elected its first Abbot, an office he held until his death in 1937. The monastery is currently affiliated with the Subiaco Congregation. In addition to teaching and pastoral duties, the abbey also operates a press.

The relationship between Westminster Cathedral and the Benedictines became more intimate in 1976 when Abbot Basil Hume OSB, of Ampleforth, was appointed Archbishop of Westminster by Pope Paul VI. An ecumenical service and Latin vespers at nearby Westminster Abbey concluded the celebrations surrounding his installation on 25 March 1976. The Catholic press quickly pointed out the symbolism of this ceremony: 'the visit is at the invitation of the Dean of Westminster and will be the first time for more than 400 years that this service has been sung in the Abbey in the traditional Latin plainsong.'[234] *The Universe* noted that Latin vespers had a double significance for the new Archbishop of Westminster. In the first place, it emphasized the importance Hume placed on prayer and, secondly, it demonstrated 'his conviction that Christian unity is best achieved by "praying churches."' The article ended happily with a reference to the 'Benedictine heritage of the new Archbishop.'

To commemorate the 1500th anniversary of St Benedict's birth, a special mass was celebrated in Westminster Cathedral in July 1980. The cathedral choir and Benedictines from England and abroad provided the music: 'Trumpets and tympani greeted a procession of 300 monks as they entered Westminster Cathedral last Friday,' *The Universe* reported.[235]

'With 130 Benedictines nuns they represented the 44 monasteries and priories of Benedictines and Cistercians...in England.' After this service, the monks and nuns walked to Westminster Abbey to sing Latin Vespers. The press did not fail to grasp the significance of this. 'The history behind the Abbey setting, the united prayer, the presence of the Anglican Benedictines, opened vistas of a long-term ecumenism rooted in the pursuit of a spiritual ideal tested by time.' During that summer of 1980, therefore, Cardinal Vaughan's dream to unite Benedictinism with the hallowed name of Westminster was finally realized.

Notes

[1] O. Chadwick, *The Reformation* (Middlesex: Penguin Books, 1972), p. 31.

[2] Ibid., p. 33.

[3] Ibid., p. 39.

[4] Ibid., p. 109.

[5] M. Powicke, *The Reformation in England* (London: Oxford University Press, 1973), p. 28.

[6] O. Chadwick, ibid. p. 105.

[7] G. Cragg, *The Church and the Age of Reason 1648-1789* (Middlesex: Penguin Books, 1972), p. 139.

[8] J. Bossy, *The English Catholic Community 1570-1850* (London: Darton, Longman, Todd, 1976), p. 296.

[9] Ibid., p. 297.

[10] O. Chadwick, *The Victorian Church,* Part I. p. 278.

[11] J. D. Holmes, *More Roman than Rome: English Catholicism in the Nineteenth Century* (London: Burns and Oates, 1978), p. 74.

[12] O. Chadwick, *The Victorian Church,* Part II (London: Adam and Charles Black, 1972), p. 242.

[13] E.S. Purcell, *Life of Cardinal Church Archbishop of Westminster* (London: MacMillan Co., 1896), p. 353.

[14] Quoted in S. L. Leslie, *Henry Edward Manning: His Life and Labour* (London: Burns and Oates, 1921), p. 171.

[15] Ibid., pp. 171-172.

[16] E.S. Purcell, ibid. p. 354.

[17] S. Leslie, ibid. p. 171.

[18] A. McCormack, *Cardinal Vaughan* (London: Burns and Oates, 1966), p. 289.

[19] J.G. Snead-Cox, *The Life of Cardinal Vaughan* vol. 2 (London: Burns and Oates, 1910), p. 317.

[20] E. Norman, *The English Catholic Church in the Nineteenth Century* (Oxford: Clarendon Press, 1984), p. 345.

[21] Ibid.

[22] J.D. Holmes, *More Roman than Rome: English Catholicism in the Nineteenth Century,* p. 199.

[23] E. Norman, *Roman Catholicism in England from the Elizabethan Settlement to the Second Vatican Council* (Oxford: Oxford University Press, 1985), p. 95.

[24] Ibid.

[25] For biographies on Cardinal Vaughan see: A Mill Father, *Remembered In Blessing: The Courtfield Story* (London: Sands Co., 1969); and J. G. Snead-Cox, *The Life of Cardinal Vaughan* 2 vols. (London: Herbert and David, 1910).

[26] J.D. Holmes, Ibid., p. 201.

[27] Ibid.

[28] J.G. Snead-Cox, ibid. vol. 2, pp. 319-320.

[29] A. McCormack, ibid. p. 288.

[30] Ibid. p.291.

[31] *The Tablet* (London), 6 July 1895.

[32] Ibid.

[33] J.G. Snead-Cox, ibid., vol. 2, p. 347.

[34] Ibid.

[35] Ibid., p. 348.

[36] For a history of the English Benedictines in the nineteenth century see British Museum, *The Benedictines in Britain* (London: The British Library, 1980); E. Cruise, "Development of the Religious Orders," in *The English Catholics 1850-1950* (London: Burns and Oates, 1950); and B. Green, *The English Benedictine Congregation* (London: Catholic Truth Society, 1980). The following biographies are also useful: B. Hicks, *Hugh Edmund Ford* (London: Sands Co., 1947); and S. Leslie, *Cardinal Gasquet: A Memoir* (New York: P.J. Kenedy, 1953).

[37] B. Hicks, ibid.

[38] Vaughan to Ford, 5 May 1896, Ford Papers, Ealing Abbey Archives, London.

[39] Ford to Vaughan, 6 May 1896, Ford Papers.

[40] B. Hicks, ibid., p. 73.

[41] B. Hicks, ibid., p. 14.

[42] Ford to Vaughan, 5 June 1896, Ford Papers.

[43] Ibid.

[44] Vaughan to Ford, 17 June 1896, Vaughan Papers, Archives of Westminster Archdiocese, Archbishop's House, London.

[45] Ibid.

[46] For a description of the governance of the English Benedictine Congregation, see Hicks, ibid., pp. 100-137. Hicks also presents an excellent discussion of the changes forced upon the English Congregation by Rome during this period, the so-called 'Constitutional Crisis.' B. Green, *The English Benedictine Congregation,* pp. 82-87, also has a good discussion.

[47] Ford to Fathers, 18 August 1896, Ford Papers.

[48] O'Gorman to Ford, 29 September 1896, Ford Papers.

[49] Petition, 10 October 1896, Ealing Abbey Archives.

[50] Vaughan to Ford, 28 October 1896, Ford Papers. The Ealing Archives has a copy of the Roman rescript.

[51] J.G. Snead-Cox, ibid., vol. 2, p. 347.

[52] Ibid., pp. 347-348.

[53] *Minutes of the Cathedral Chapter of Westminster, 31 January 1878 to 7 November 1899,* vol. 4, 4 December 1894, St. Mary's Presbytery, East Finchley, London.

[54] Ibid., 8 January 1895.

[55] See pp. 171f.

[56] *Minutes of the Cathedral Chapter of Westminster, 31 January 1878 to 7 November 1899,* 6 October 1896.

[57] Ibid., 3 November 1896.

[58] J.G. Snead-Cox, ibid., vol. 2, pp. 347-348.

[59] Ford to Vaughan, 7 December 1898, Vaughan Papers, Archbishop's House.

[60] Ibid.

[61] Ibid.

[62] Ibid.

[63] Ibid.

[64] J.G. Snead-Cox, ibid., vol. 2, p. 349.

[65] E. Cruise, *Development of the Religious Orders,* p. 457. The author also notes that 'such Constitutions had been formed to allow the English Benedictines to concentrate all their energies upon missionary work at a time when the number of secular priests were woefully inadequate' p. 457. See pp. 30-31 for the radical changes imposed on the English Benedictine Constitutions by the Vatican. The British Library, *The Benedictines in Britain,* pp. 97-99, presents a good discussion of the missionary character of the English Benedictines.

[66] J.G. Snead-Cox, ibid., vol. 2, p. 349. Prior Ford, however, was in favour of a more monastic as opposed to missionary spirit for the English monks. Yet he faced strong opposition from the General Chapter.

[67] Ibid.

[68] E.B. Koenker, *The Liturgical Renaissance in the Roman Catholic Church* (Chicago: University of Chicago Press, 1954), p. 10.

[69] Ibid.

[70] J.A. Jungmann, *Public Worship* (London: Challoner Publication, 1957), p. 30.

[71] *New Catholic Encyclopedia,* s.v. 'Music of Solesmes.'

[72] *The Tablet,* 1 June 1901.

[73] The Ratisbon edition represented the liturgy and interpretation of a rival school.

[74] 'Note of Dom Delatte,' Summer 1899, Delatte Papers, Solesmes Abbey Archives, France.

[75] Ibid.

[76] Bishop Abel Gilbert was the Bishop of Le Mans, the diocese in which the Abbey of Solesmes is situated, from 1894 to 1898. At the time of his correspondence with Delatte about the possibility of an English foundation, he was the titular Bishop of Arsinoe. He died in 1914.

[77] Gilbert to Delatte, 10 June 1899, Delatte Papers.

[78] Ibid.

[79] Delatte to Vaughan, 11 June 1899, Vaughan Papers, Archbishop's House, p. 1.

[80] Ibid.

[81] Ibid.

[82] M.D. Knowles, *Cardinal Gasquet as an Historian* (London: The Athlone Press, 1957), p. 3.

[83] Ibid., pp. 15-17.

[84] Ibid., p. 18.

[85] Ibid., p. 19.

[86] Ibid.

[87] See the following for the life of Cardinal Aidan Gasquet: D. Knowles, ibid., and S. Leslie, *Cardinal Gasquet: A Memoir* (New York: P.J. Kenedy, 1953).

[88] Delatte to Vaughan, 11 June 1899, Vaughan Papers, Archbishop's House p. 2.

[89] Ibid.

[90] Ibid.

[91] Ibid., p. 3.

[92] Ibid., p. 4.

[93] Ibid., p. 5.

[94] In 1887 the Empress Eugenie established a monastery at Farnborough for Canons of the Premonstratensian Order. In 1895, monks from Solesmes replaced the Canons. There was also another French foundation on English soil. Because of anti-clericalism in France, monks from La Pierre-qui-Vire established a foundation at Buckfast in 1882. It became independent in 1899 and an abbey in 1903.

[95] Delatte to Vaughan, 11 June 1899, Vaughan Papers, Archbishop's House, p. 6.

[96] Ibid.

[97] Ibid., p. 7.

[98] Ibid., p. 8.

[99] Ibid.

[100] Moyes to Vaughan, 17 July 1899, Vaughan Papers, Archbishop's House. At the end of June, Cardinal Vaughan visited Abbot Delatte at Solesmes. There is no information available on the length or nature of the visit.

[101] Ibid.

[102] Moyes, 'Westminster Cathedral and the Monks of Solesmes: Memorandum,' July 1899, Vaughan Papers, Archbishop's House.

[103] Ibid., p. 2.

[104] Ibid., p. 3.

[105] Ibid., p. 4.

[106] Ibid.

[107] Ibid., p. 6.

[108] Ibid., p. 7.

[109] Ibid., p. 8.

[110] Moyes, 'The Westminster Cathedral and the Monks of Solesmes: Preliminary Articles of Agreement, July 1899, Vaughan Papers, Archbishop's House.

[111] Moyes to Vaughan, 17 July 1899, Vaughan Papers, Archbishop's House.

[112] Ibid.

[113] *The Tablet,* 18 February 1899.

[114] Ibid.

[115] Ibid.

[116] Ibid.

[117] *The Tablet*, 13 May 1899.

[118] Ibid.

[119] *The Tablet*, 1 July 1899; *The Times*, 30 June 1899; and *The Weekly Register*, 1 July 1899.

[120] Ibid.

[121] *The Weekly Register*, 15 July 1899.

[122] Ibid.

[123] *The Catholic Times and Catholic Opinion* (London), 21 July 1899.

[124] See pp. 186f.

[125] E. Cruise, *The Development of Religious Orders*, p. 458.

[126] B. Hicks, *Hugh Edmund Ford*, p. 134.

[127] *Diu Quidem*.

[128] On 26 September, 1900, Edmund Ford was elected the first Abbot of Downside Abbey.

[129] *Religiosus Ordo*.

[130] Ibid.

[131] *The Weekly Register*, 15 July 1899.

[132] Ibid.

[133] *The Weekly Register*, 22 July 1899.

[134] Ibid.

[135] *The Weekly Register*, 29 July 1899.

[136] Ibid.

[137] *The Weekly Register*, 5 August 1899.

[138] *The Catholic Times and Catholic Opinion*, 21 July 1899.

[139] Ibid.

[140] Ibid., 4 August 1899.

[141] Ibid.

[142] Ibid., 25 August *1899*.

[143] Ibid.

[144] *The Weekly Register*, 5 August 1899.

[145] Ibid.

[146] See pp. 209-10.

[147] *The Weekly Register*, 22 July *1899*.

[148] Ibid., 29 July 1899.

[149] *Minutes of the Cathedral Chapter of Westminster 31 January 1878 to 7 November 1899*, 4 July 1899.

[150] Ibid.

[151] Taunton, according to the *Catholic Directory*, 1899, was on sick leave when he wrote this pamphlet. He died in 1907. See *The Tablet*, 18 May 1907, for his obituary.

[152] E.L. Taunton, *A Letter to His Eminence Herbert Cardinal Vaughan Archbishop of Westminster on the Work of the Clergy at the Westminster Cathedral* (Exeter: Western Times Office, 1899), p. 5.

[153] Ibid., p. 6.

[154] Ibid.

[155] Ibid., p. 7.

[156] Ibid., p. 8.

[157] Ibid., p. 10.

[158] Ibid.

[159] Vaughan to Delatte, June 1899, Delatte Papers.

[160] Cabrol to Delatte, 25 July 1899, Delatte Papers

[161] Ibid

[162] Cabrol to Vaughan, 4 August 1899, Vaughan Papers, Archbishop's House.

[163] Ibid.

[164] Vaughan to Cabrol, 3 August 1899, Delatte Papers.

[165] Ibid.

[166] Cabrol to Delatte, 5 August 1899, Delatte Papers.

[167] Ibid.

[168] Cabrol to Delatte, 28 August 1899, Delatte Papers.

[169] See pp. 186f.

[170] Vaughan to Gasquet, 27 November 1900, Gasquet Papers, Downside Abbey Archives, Downside Abbey, Somerset.

[171] 'Memorandum As To The Question of Serving Westminster Cathedral,' Gasquet Papers, p. 1.

[172] Ibid., p. 2.

[173] Ibid.

[174] Delatte to Vaughan, 11 June 1899, Vaughan Papers, Archbishop's House.

[175] A. Gasquet, 'Memorandum,' Gasquet Papers, p. 2.

[176] Ibid.

[177] *The Tablet,* 6 October 1900.

[178] Ibid.

[179] *The Tablet,* 10 November 1900.

[180] Ibid.

[181] Vaughan to Gasquet, 24 December 1900, Gasquet Papers.

[182] Ibid.

[183] E.E. Reynolds, *The Roman Catholic Church in England and Wales* (Wheathampstead: Anthony Clarke, 1973), p. 353.

[184] Vaughan to Gasquet, 24 December 1900, Vaughan Papers, Archbishop's House.

[185] Ibid., p. 2.

[186] Ibid., p. 3.

[187] Ibid., p. 4.

[188] Ibid.

[189] J.G. Snead-Cox, *The Life of Cardinal Vaughan* vol. 2, p. 356.

[190] A. Gasquet, 'Notes,' December 1900, Gasquet Papers.

[191] Ibid., p. 2.

[192] Ibid.

[193] *The Tablet,* 2 December 1899.

[194] Ibid.

[195] Gilbert to Delatte, 21 January 1900, Delatte Papers.

[196] Ibid.

[197] Delatte to Cabrol, 29 October 1900, Delatte Papers.

[198] St. Paul's, Wisques, was founded from Solesmes in 1889 and became a conventual priory in 1895.

[199] Delatte to Cabrol, 29 October 1900, Delatte Papers.

[200] Gilbert to Delatte, 23 January 1901, Delatte Papers.

[201] Gilbert to Delatte, 24 February 1901, Delatte Papers.

[202] Gasquet to Vaughan, 13 February 1900, Gasquet Papers.

[203] Ibid., p. 2.

[204] Ibid.

[205] Gasquet to Vaughan, 17 February 1901, Vaughan Papers, Archbishop's House.

[206] Ibid., p. 2.

[207] Ibid., p. 3.

[208] Ibid., p. 4.

[209] Ibid., p. 5.

[210] Ibid., p. 6.

[211] Ibid., p. 9.

[212] Ibid., p. 10-11.

[213] Ibid., p. 14.

[214] Ibid., p. 15.

[215] Ibid.

[216] J.G. Snead-Cox, *The Life of Cardinal Vaughan* vol. 2, p. 357.

[217] Vaughan to Gasquet, 3 March 1901, Vaughan Papers, Archbishop's House.

[218] A. Gasquet, 'Notes of Reply to Card. Vaughan of March 3,' Gasquet Papers.

[219] J.G. Snead-Cox, ibid., vol. 2, p. 357.

[220] Cabrol to Vaughan, 17 March 1901, Vaughan Papers, Archbishop's House.

[221] J.G. Snead-Cox, ibid., vol. 2, p. 357.

[222] The Metropolitan Chapter was erected on 19 June 1852. In 1901 the following were members: Provost, Right Rev Mgr Michael Barry, V.G. Canons: Right Rev Mgr W.A. Johnson, D.D. (Penitentiary); Very Rev Cornelius J. Keens; Right Revv Mgr James Moyes, D.D. (Theologian), Mgr Patrick Fenton; Very Revv Leopold Pycke, Reginald Tuke, William L. Gildea, D.D., Edmund Surmont, D.D., Alfred White.

[223] *Minutes Of the Cathedral Chapter 1899 to 1946,* vol. 5, 23 April 1901.

[224] *Synod of Westminster,* XXXII-XLI, 1893-1902, Archbishop's House, p. 101.

[225] *The Tablet,* 15 June 1901.

[226] J.G. Snead-Cox, ibid., vol. 2, p. 360.

[227] G. Wheeler, 'The Archdiocese of Westminster,' in G.A. Beck, ed., *The English Catholics 1850-1950,* p. 170.

[228] *Minutes of the Cathedral Chapter of Westminster 1899 to 1946,* 23 April 1901.

[229] Dolan to Ford, 12 October 1899, Dolan Papers, Ealing Abbey Archives.

[230] Quoted in S. Leslie, *Cardinal Gasquet: A Memoir,* p. 198.

[231] B. Hicks, *Hugh Edmund Ford,* pp. 73-74. The Benedictines from Downside Abbey, however, did not leave London, but remained in Ealing. The parish grew, and in 1902, a school was started. In 1916, the foundation became a dependent priory, in 1947 an independent priory, and in 1955 it was raised to the rank and dignity of an abbey.

[232] Quoted in A. McCormack, *Cardinal Vaughan,* p. 296.

[233] Ibid.

[234] *The Universe,* 19 March 1976.

[235] *The Universe,* 18 July 1980.

CHAPTER XI

THE RETURN OF THE
BENEDICTINES TO LONDON

T he year 1895 marked a high point for English Roman Catholics. A visible sign of their stability, accomplishments, and even respectability, neared completion: a new majestic cathedral would soon grace central London. The proud Cardinal Archbishop of Westminster, Herbert Vaughan, blessed the foundation-stone in June 1895, and at a banquet following this impressive ceremony, revealed his plans for the future of Westminster Cathedral. He believed that "the Catholic body must have a Cathedral in which the sacred liturgy of the church should be carried out in all its fulness day by day, and many times a day, as it was of old in Westminster and Canterbury."[1] But who would staff this new church and put into practice the Cardinal's dreams? If Vaughan wished to recreate the atmosphere of pre-Reformation England, then clearly Benedictine monks must come to London and occupy this new Westminster as they had the old.

The Benedictines had once flourished in the capital, only to be dissolved by the reforming zeal of Henry VIII. Mary the Catholic welcomed them back into the precincts of the Abbey, but her sister soon reversed this policy. Consequently, English monastic life found refuge on the Continent, until the aims of another revolution drove the inheritors back to England at the end of the eighteenth century to begin the reestablishment of the English Benedictine Congregation on native soil. And the successors of these monks willingly responded to Cardinal Vaughan's call in 1895. *The Tablet* reported that the Cardinal's "anxiety with regard to the Cathedral was allayed by the readiness with which he found the English Benedictine Fathers, full of life and energy and numbers, ready to come back to Westminster."[2] The monks of St. Gregory's, Downside, with whom he was well acquainted, agreed to supply the liturgical manpower. Ealing, close to central London and Westminster Cathedral, seemed a suitable location for this new Benedictine foundation in London.[3]

Benedictine monks had previously ministered at Ealing, a growing and prosperous suburb west of the capital, sometime before the Cardinal's plan to establish them there. According to Dom Gilbert Dolan, OSB, an historian of the Benedictine Order in England and later superior at the Ealing mission (1899-1907), "Ealing was under the spiritual care of the Benedictines from AD 1825 to AD 1850."[4] "The register of baptisms of the Acton Mission during that period," he wrote, "contains several entries relating to Ealing." Dom Gilbert's research revealed that the "first entry is of date July 16, 1825, about which time the Benedictine Fathers seem to have come to Ealing." He also identified Dom William Scott, OSB, as the first monk to reside at Acton. "The Acton Mission covered a wide area; beside Acton itself, the following places...were served by it: Ealing, Turnham Green, Hanwell, Brentford, and Shepherd's Bush." Dom Gilbert discovered approximately a dozen Ealing residents who were baptized by the Benedictines from Acton. Moreover, the 1850 census of that mission contained the names of fourteen parishioners who lived in the borough of Ealing.[5]

In May 1896, Cardinal Vaughan approached the superior of the Downside Benedictines, Prior Edmund Ford,[6] and suggested that a certain piece of real estate in Ealing "would make an excellent gift for you...and I sh[ould] be disposed to give you the Ealing mission."[7] From here, the monks could journey into London to conduct the liturgical services at the new cathedral. The Cardinal continued to tempt Ford and remarked that the Visitation Sisters owned the estate, but had assured him that it could be purchased for "something under 4000 pounds." Prior Ford responded and told the Cardinal that he planned to be in London soon, and "could look at the property then."[8] But, shrewd and far-sighted, Ford also indicated that he entertained certain other plans for a monastic foundation in London: "Your Eminence would I presume wish us to try and do more than merely take charge of the mission, but when I have seen the property I will call," On the same day that Ford responded to Cardinal Vaughan's letter, he also informed Abbot Benedict Snow,[9] who was living in Dulwich, of the invitation to consider a mission in London. Ford sent him Vaughan's correspondence and asked if he could "go and look at Ealing with a view to the enclosed...if you have an opportunity, you might call at Archbishop's House and learn...all the details of the mission. We could then decide on the answer to the Cardinal."[10]

Abbot Snow visited Ealing within the week, and his report back to Downside bubbled with enthusiasm and excitement. "I went to Ealing today," he told Ford, and found it "a very pleasant place, beautifully wooded, and thoroughly suburban."[11] Snow emphasized the strictly residential character of the neighbourhood and drew Ford's attention to the presence of two railway stations. He described the prospective site of the new foundation, Castle Hill House, as "beautiful" and "a good substantial house." A group of nuns currently occupied the dwelling, but according to Snow "find the place too small for them and too near the road...so they are only there temporarily and looking for a larger place." The titular abbot apologized that he could not offer much information on the local Roman Catholic population, which averaged over one hundred families, or its priest, Rev Richard O'Halloran.[12] "I thought it best not to call on him as I gather from the Cardinal's letter that he might not know anything about the offer." Snow concluded his report with guarded optimism: "I think it is a promising place in a rising neighbourhood but the difficulty is to get a return for the 4000 pounds purchase money — a debt and no church." Like Ford, Snow's dream went beyond responsibilities at Westminster Cathedral. He encouraged Ford, but also pointed out problems connected with Ealing's future growth: "uncertain prospects of [a] school, uncertainty of means of support, burdens of interest, and the erection of a church."[13]

Vaughan's idealism and imagination failed to mesmerize the more pragmatic Ford. Singing the Divine Office in the archiepiscopal choir stalls could not justify the expense involved in a new foundation. He believed that a Benedictine presence in the country's capital was imperative, but his reply to the Cardinal reflected the cautious realism suggested by Abbot Snow. Thus: "I cannot but express to your Eminence our grateful acknowledgment for offering us the work that you suggest at Ealing, and our appreciation of the confidence placed in us by entrusting it to us."[14] However, Ford insisted that suitable and profitable employment must be found for his monks. "Your Eminence will recognize the dangers of establishing a religious community without sufficient occupation for its members and the consequent difficulty in maintaining a religious spirit. Hence I feel a scruple in sending a religious anywhere without assigning a definite work that he could and would do." Sometime in the future, he suggested, a school could provide that needed income and security for his monks. But "the prospects of a school can only be tested by further acquaintance with the existing neighbourhood, and some data to forecast its future development."

In addition to an educational apostolate, Ford believed that parochial work in Ealing itself must definitely supplement the liturgical responsibilities at Westminster Cathedral. He suggested that the Cardinal grant him permission to send a monk to Ealing "at once to get things together and attend to the spiritual wants of the people." "Shortly after," he continued, "I have little doubt that I could give him a companion to attend to the convent" near the mission. Ford emphasized that the pastoral work of his monks would not detract from or limit their liturgical responsibilities at Westminster Cathedral. "I would add that the establishment of a house at Ealing would not render it more difficult to find men for the Cathedral, on the contrary it would I think render it easier by providing another community from which to draw when the time comes." Ford's position, therefore, was clear. He would gladly supply monks to meet the Cardinal's needs, but parochial duties and the possibility of a school should form part of the bargain. "If this meets with your Eminence's approval," he concluded, "I should be willing to take the risk of purchasing the property, which will be a substantial earnest of our intention to carry out your wishes."

Ford also enclosed a more personal note with his formal response to Vaughan's invitation. He noted that questions concerning the future relationship between the monks working at the cathedral and the foundation at Ealing on the one hand, and those at Downside on the other, had surfaced in community discussions, but he remarked that it "would be better to let these work themselves out as time goes on."[15] The Prior hinted that the interests of Downside might be compromised if definite and ironclad arrangements were made at such an early date. Ealing, for example, might become an independent priory within a decade. He also admitted that he was a novice at establishing new foundations, and consequently had sought more experienced counsel. He suggested an interview with the Cardinal to explore and discuss the future of a Benedictine foundation in London.

Within a week, Vaughan responded and told Ford that he also wanted a meeting, and suggested 11 June as a possible date. But he pointed out a flaw in Ford's plans for Ealing. A Benedictine school in the suburb would create problems. Without giving any specific reason, Vaughan noted "that certain difficulties have arisen as to a College at Ealing."[16] "Not [that] there is no need of one and the need will become greater each year in the neighbourhood," the Cardinal wrote, but "Wanstead presents many advantages and would be a better place than Ealing in several respects." On the other hand, he did not comment on the question of parochial duties for the monks. Discussion and compromise could clarify other issues.

The desired interview took place on 11 June at Archbishop's House; no minutes or notes of the meeting survive. After much discussion, Vaughan and Ford reached a series of agreements, which the Cardinal later enumerated in a letter to the Prior. Vaughan's language exhibited a forcefulness of thought and clarity of purpose: "in reference to our conversations on the proposal that you should open a house at Ealing and take charge of the mission I make the following conditions."[17] "Provided the consent of the Holy See be obtained," Vaughan promised to authorize Ford to "make a Foundation at Ealing." In respect to the possibility of a school run by the monks, he stipulated that the Benedictine mission "is not to include the opening of any school other than a Public Elementary School." Moreover, "special permission" from the ordinary of the archdiocese must be obtained before there could be any departure from this condition. Two elements, he told Ford, must highlight the life and spirit of the urban monks: "the serving of the mission in the usual way"; and the "establishment of a Religious Community of your Order and the observance of Common Life according to your rule, within five years from the date of your going to Ealing." If a community of six monks failed to materialize during this trial period, Vaughan claimed the right to take possession of the property and promised to repay the Benedictines for any money expended. The final point stated the primary purpose behind the Cardinal's negotiations with the Downside monks: "One of the principal reasons inducing the Cardinal Archbishop to invite the Benedictines to open a house at Ealing is that they might be sufficiently near to Westminster to contribute to the Choral service of the Cathedral."

Vaughan had presented his five terms or conditions succinctly enough. To the Prior's mind, however, they seemed too narrow, too restrictive; a compromise needed to be reached with Archbishop's House before he could commit his monks to this new venture. Ford's notes, for example, emphasized that the application to Rome would be for permission to establish "a *domus* at Ealing with the care of a mission attached."[18] He wanted it understood that the foundation would eventually seek "the full ecclesiastical position, rights and privileges of a Benedictine monastery" when a sufficient number of monks resided at Ealing. Ealing must not be regarded as a transient or temporary experiment. Ford also believed that the Cardinal's stipulation regarding a school connected to the foundation "would not prevent us...from having private pupils, as is permitted to any mission..." According to his biographer, the ban on a secondary school did not trouble Ford. "He anticipated that when the parish at Ealing began to grow there would be many parents desirous of having a Catholic day school for their boys, which would secure their not having to attend non-Catholic establishments."[19] Moreover, Ford maintained that Vaughan's conservatism and caution might frustrate any future expansion in Ealing, and he argued that the monks "ought to be free to deal with the land we buy for ourselves in the way most advantageous."

Consequently, Ford arranged to meet with Vaughan on 29 June 1896 at Belmont Priory to discuss some modifications in the Cardinal's proposal. Ford's notes reveal that his suggested changes or amendments "were read to the Cardinal...and approved by him."[20] Ford successfully negotiated an alteration in Vaughan's original proposal which dealt with the arrangement giving the Cardinal the power to purchase the property if the community did not number six monks within five years. The revision read:

> The Archbishop shall have the power to purchase from you [the Benedictine Order] at cost price the land now bought for the mission and to repay you any money which your Order may have expended upon the land, for the benefit of the mission or upon buildings which the Archbishop shall not have considered unnecessary for the mission, and the Benedictines shall retire from Ealing.

The stipulation dealing with the membership of the community and a timetable, therefore, was dropped. The Cardinal also accepted Ford's arguments about pastoral work and the necessity of viewing Ealing as a foundation which might evolve into a permanent monastic community. But Vaughan would accept no modification in his prohibition against a secondary school associated with the mission.

After this meeting, Prior Ford again approached Abbot Snow and sought his advice on the wisdom and feasibility of these modifications. From the beginning, Snow had cultivated a keen interest in the Ealing project. In June, for example, he visited a solicitor's office and inquired about the condition of the property, the price, and terms of sale.[21] Ford told his friend that the Cardinal had accepted some changes, but he "would not modify the wording of his proposal" about a Benedictine school in Ealing.[22] According to the Prior, Vaughan expressed a fear that even a dozen students "would take the cream of the neighbourhood and leave S. Charles the rest..." Vaughan obviously wanted to protect the interests of the nearby Bayswater school, but on the other hand, he would permit the monks to educate one or two students for financial help. Ford also revealed that he hesitated to make any firm or binding commitment about the responsibilities of his monks at Westminster Cathedral. This letter to Abbot Snow contained a sense of urgency: Ford wanted to purchase the Ealing property immediately. "The nuns will be getting impatient," he maintained, and "...we shall have to be ready with a proposal for getting the money." Moreover, the Prior's own plans for the monks dictated quick action. He passionately argued that the establishment of a foundation with

"… the full ecclesiastical position, rights and privileges of a Benedictine monastery," and not liturgical rights at the Cardinal's cathedral, remained his primary goal. Consequently, "we had better get this while we can; the time when it would take effect would depend on ourselves. Another Archbishop might oppose us in this."

Snow's response revealed his optimism. "As far as I can judge I think Ealing a very desirable locality for a settlement," he wrote to Ford, and "it is a growing place within easy distance of London and as good a situation as we are likely to get in the Suburbs in the Westminster Diocese."[23] He urged Ford not to worry about finances. In the first place, "a priest ought to be able to get a living of the Catholics that are now there." Moreover, the nearby convent might employ another monk as a chaplain. Finally, the price asked for the house and grounds, 4000 pounds, did not represent an excessive amount, and he told Ford that "as far as one can judge, the value of the land will increase should we — after a trial — be inclined to give it up."

Snow could not restrain from commenting on the Cardinal's only firm prohibition concerning the establishment of a Benedictine colony in Ealing. A school would ensure the success of the enterprise, and consequently he saw the Cardinal's rigid stipulation as unrealistic and unworkable. According to the Abbot:

> the neighbourhood seems to be such that a school somewhat higher than an elementary one will become a necessity to prevent children going to private Protestant schools, and as soon as this evil can be demonstrated it will be very difficult for the ecclesiastical authorities to refuse a higher grade school for boys to rescue them from Protestant hands.

Like Ford, Abbot Snow was not smitten by Vaughan's romantic musings about monks, plainchant, and the metropolitan cathedral; the success and stability of the monastic establishment took precedence. "The Choral Service at the Cathedral might be a blunder," Snow informed his friend, "but this [Vaughan's conditions] is so worded that it can scarcely be held to be as a condition *sine qua non.*"

Ford also sought the opinion and advice of other English Benedictines. Should Downside accept Vaughan's proposals and settle in Ealing? Dom Benedict Tidmarsh[24] told Ford that "the Cardinal's offer should be favourably considered, and if possible accepted, with perhaps some modification."[25] Like Abbot Snow, he pointed out that "the restriction as to a school seems rather unreasonable, as not likely to interfere with any existing schools in the Diocese." Some question also existed concerning the responsibilities and duties of the monks at Westminster Cathedral: "1 suppose it only means assisting on great occasions or great Festivals, but even thus it w[ould] be depriving the Ealing House of its regular Choir duties." Singing the Divine Office in central London must not eclipse the primacy of the monastic routine at Ealing. Dom Benedict told Ford that "regular daily attendance at Westminster would be out of the question." And then, he continued, "travelling to and fro frequently would be prohibitive." Even with these doubts, he urged Prior Ford to accept the Cardinal's offer.

Another Benedictine, Dom Wulstan Richards, also gave his encouragement: "I cordially approve of the purchase of the site at Ealing and also of accepting the terms of the Cardinal." He pointed out that the monks could no longer "get into London with a free hand, and we must accept such a qualified gift..."[26] Moreover, there was no reason why the "London house of studies [Great Ormond St.] could not be transferred to Ealing, a more healthy and fitting home than where it is at present."[27] He told Ford that the amount of money asked for the Ealing property could not be considered unreasonable; such a fine dwelling could not be built for less. Consequently, the Cardinal's conditions or stipulations should be accepted. London represented a precious prize and "a foothold at last" secured for the Benedictines.[28] Dom Wulstan ended his letter by telling Ford that he would receive the "congratulations of every Gregorian" if he could "bring this negotiation to a successful issue."

By the end of June 1896, the occupants of Castle Hill House, the Visitation Sisters, had also become anxious about the future of the estate, and their Mother Superior contacted Prior Ford. She explained that her community was "on the point of leaving for Harrow and...should be very grateful to know from you whether you are still entertaining thoughts of taking this place. We should of course be very pleased if we are succeeded here by a religious community, and we are anxious to have a line from you as several other persons have been enquiring about the house."[29] Throughout the summer, the nuns continued to woo the Benedictines. Thus: "It was very good to get y[our] letter and to hear it was almost settled about Ealing,...it will be very nice having your Fathers so near."[30] Ford's interest in Castle Hill House never wavered: he told the nuns that he remained optimistic the Cardinal would approve the Ealing foundation; and he emphasized that the Abbot President of the English Benedictine Congregation and his council would be swayed by the reasonable price.[31] The next step, therefore, was to secure the permission of Abbot President O'Gorman and his advisors.

Encouraged thus by Abbot Snow and other monks, Ford wrote to Dom Anselm O'Gorman, the President of the English Benedictine Congregation, and to the members of the Regimen, his council, presenting strong arguments in favour of sending monks from Downside to London.[32] On 17 August, Ford informed the President that "the Cardinal has asked us to open a house at Ealing and offered us the Mission."[33] He told Dom Anselm that Vaughan extended "the offer with the hope that we may later on have a community there." Consequently, Ford suggested that the President begin exploring the possibility of approaching Rome for permission to make a foundation at Ealing. On the following day, he sent the President and the Regimen copies of Vaughan's revised conditions and a summary of Abbot Snow's glowing appraisal. In addition to these documents, he added his personal reasons for accepting the Cardinal's invitation. He believed that the monks could both live a monastic life and conduct an urban mission. "It is said to be one of the best districts near London still unoccupied as a parish,...[and] the district is rapidly developing and will have the character of a high class suburb."[34] Moreover, the Ealing monks could make the fifteen minute trip on the Great Western Railway to central London and their work at the cathedral. The fate and future of Benedictinism in Ealing rested with the President and his advisers.

President O'Gorman replied thanking Ford for the information concerning the London project and asking if he would consider presenting the details to the Regimen in person. But the Prior hesitated; claiming he had already sent all the necessary information.[35] If requested, however, he would meet with O'Gorman and clarify any problems or difficulties. The President did not pressure Ford, and immediately began to poll the members of the Regimen. One member's reaction concerned finances: how "means for their support [could] be provided by the people at Ealing, where everything—congregation included—has to be created."[36] But he also told O'Gorman that he would not campaign against the proposal.

In his letter to another member, the President revealed his own misgivings. He could not share the enthusiasm generated by Ford and Snow, and raised the possibility of the "establishment at Ealing being of some difficulty for Downside."[37] Poverty of manpower presented the chief obstacle, but he also noted that "all the Gregorian family wants it." This letter ended with O'Gorman's candid comments on the question:

> As for myself, I feel inclined to grant the permission.
> The money question seems safe and if they cannot carry
> Ealing on, they will have to drop it, or some of the other
> establishments in London. It will be extremely advan-

tageous to have one or more sites near London for
recruiting purposes and for a proper display of our life
and liturgy.

The response to O'Gorman's statement was short: "I do not make any
objections to the project."[38] The third member of the Regimen had some
doubts, but nonetheless also gave his support to the foundation. "In view
of the opinion of so shrewd a man as Abbot Snow and the Unanimity of the
Gregorian *Familia,*" he informed the Abbot President, "by all means let
them take Ealing."[39]

With this support and encouragement, O'Gorman wrote to Ford: "In
a few words the whole Regimen consents to accept the new establishment
at Ealing."[40] Consequently, he gave Ford permission to petition the Holy
See as soon as possible, but his advice also went beyond the narrow limits
set by Cardinal Vaughan. He told Ford to ask for approval "...to erect a
college and monastery in addition to serving the mission...We must take
every precaution for future development." He also warned him of the
possibility of trouble from an unexpected quarter. The current priest at
Ealing, Fr. Richard O'Halloran, had already sent him [O'Gorman] a
threatening letter protesting at the invasion of monks into his mission
territory. "The poor fellow is very sore about the matter," he concluded. In
another letter, O'Gorman gave Ford virtually a free hand in his dealings
with the Cardinal, and told him that "whatever modifications the Cardinal
and yourself may make, I suppose they will at least be the *framework* for
any future documents."[41]

When informed about the decision of the President and the Regimen,
a joyful Abbot Snow told Ford that he was "glad there is no trouble on the
part of the President."[42] He expressed some anxiety, however, about
O'Gorman's language, which he thought emphasized the establishment of
a parochial mission and minimized the future of a stable monastic life as
"quite subsidiary." Consequently, he urged Ford to be forceful in his
petition to Rome and to stress his desire to eventually establish a full
Benedictine monastery in Ealing. Throughout September 1896, Snow
busied himself in the Ealing project. He informed Ford that negotiations
with the nuns for Castle Hill House were progressing smoothly; if both
parties could agree on the price, a contract could be drawn up immediately.[43] In addition to Castle Hill House, he explored other nearby sites
along Montpelier Road. Snow's vision for Ealing continued to expand, and
he began to dream of a grand majestic church staffed by the monks: "a
Church when placed on our site will be in a commanding position at the top
of the new road and easy of access to the bulk of the people."

At the end of September, Ford received the official approval from the Abbot President. It stated:

> According to our Constitution I have reported the question to the three Reverend *Definitori* of the Regimen. After mature consideration, we decided unanimously to accept the foundation which was offered as well as the Monastery to be built successively, and eventually the mission of the place called Ealing, subject to the conditions requested by the Bull *Romanos Pontifices* concerning the permission of the Ordinary and the Holy See.[44]

The time was now ripe to enter into serious negotiations with the Visitation Sisters for the purchase of Castle Hill House. Ford believed that he had to push on even if the Holy See questioned the wisdom of the plan. "Even if Rome makes a difficulty we should not give up," he wrote to Snow, "but fight it out, and we cannot expect the nuns to wait."[45] Before Ford sent the petition to Rome, therefore, Snow concluded the negotiations and signed a contract which transferred ownership of Castle Hill House to the Benedictines.[46] With house and property secured, Prior Ford turned his attention to Cardinal Vaughan and Rome.

On 1 October 1896, the day the sale of Castle Hill House was finalized, Ford informed the Cardinal that the monks of Downside were ready to take possession of Ealing. Ford enclosed a packet of documents which included a formal petition from the Regimen to the Roman authorities, the permission of Abbot President O'Gorman to Ford, and the five conditions earlier agreed upon by himself and Cardinal Vaughan. No change was suggested concerning the Cardinal's stipulations on a school. The Prior also pressed Vaughan to expedite matters as quickly as possible. "If Your Eminence would forward the papers to your agent in Rome for presentation and would accompany them with a letter expressing your wish to see the petition granted," he suggested, "the business would be attended to at once."[47] Ford pointed out that he had enclosed several copies of the terms under which Vaughan invited the monks to settle in Ealing. He suggested that the Cardinal sign and date one copy, and return this to him at Downside. Ford also reminded Vaughan of the modifications or amendments which they had agreed upon earlier at Belmont. Within a week, Vaughan had signed the agreement and returned a copy to Ford. Approval by Rome constituted the next hurdle.

Ford sought the advice and expertise of the Abbot President, requesting that he draw up the actual petition to Rome.[48] This O'Gorman did. Ford expressed his thanks and announced that he would now ask Vaughan to forward it on to Rome. "This will make the petition his business and will secure it attention and at the same time keep me straight with his Eminence."[49] O'Gorman's document read as follows:

> After obtaining the permission of the Superior of our Congregation, as well as the assent of the Cardinal Archbishop, [the petitioner] humbly implores of the Holy See the faculty of founding a new residence in Ealing as well as of building a monastery later on and eventually of accepting from the same Cardinal the mission of the same place, Ealing, under the following conditions stated by his Eminence the Cardinal Archbishop of Westminster.[50]

The five conditions or stipulations were then appended without comment. On 20 October 1896, Propaganda Fide granted the request.[51] A week later, Vaughan informed Prior Ford that he had received "the necessary permission from the Holy See for you to take Ealing...the conditions being those we agreed upon."[52] Matters then moved quickly. The Chapter of Westminster Cathedral was informed of Rome's action in early November.[53] And Archbishop's House asked Prior Ford for the names of the monks who would soon be assigned to Ealing for inclusion in the new archdiocesan *Directory*. [54] There was one ominous development, however. In response to Prior Ford's request for a copy of the Roman rescript, the Cardinal's secretary informed him that "there is likely to be some delay in the execution of the Rescript" because of "the opposition of the priest now at Ealing," Rev. Richard O'Halloran.[55]

Armed with the Roman document and Vaughan's permission, the Benedictines moved to take possession of their recently purchased property in Ealing. Ford quickly assigned two monks to take up residence at Castle Hill House. In December 1896, the *Downside Review* told its readers "that Dom Bernard Bulbeck and Dom Aidan Howlett have been selected to start our new mission at Ealing, which promises to become an important railway centre in the near future."[56] At the age of 71, and plagued throughout his life by poor health, Dom Bernard seemed an unlikely candidate to don the mantle of a pioneer and take charge of the new London foundation. But "his quiet and genial disposition seemed to render him the most fitting to be the first to take possession of the mission...at Ealing."[57] Thirty years his junior, Dom Aidan's primary responsibility was ministering to the spiritual needs of a nearby convent.

In the spring, Archbishop's House granted ecclesiastical faculties to Dom Bernard and to any priest sent to assist him.[58]

Despite his age and questionable health, Dom Bernard exhibited a spirit of dogged determination in his new assignment. In April, for example, he reported that already twenty parishioners attended his Sunday morning mass. In the autumn, he boasted to Ford that he had counted over one hundred worshippers on a recent Sunday. But the strain began to take its toll. Two Sunday masses were urgently needed, but he confessed that he could not handle the additional work: "I doubt if I shall be able to manage it [the extra mass]...it win be a sad affair if I fall and collapse."[59] He asked Ford for the assistance of an "active priest" to do the work he could not manage. Without additional help, Dom Bernard feared that he would get "a bad name, which will be a pity after all this fuss." But his campaign to obtain the services of an additional "active priest" did not succeed.

Dom Bernard's state of health and age, however, did not go unnoticed. In the minds of some, Ealing needed youth, vigour, and enthusiasm. Dom Aidan Gasquet, for example, realized that fresh blood had to flow into the new mission. "What we want...at Ealing is the man," Gasquet told Prior Ford during the summer of 1898.[60] "The more I think of it," Gasquet continued, "the more I fancy Fr. Gilbert [Dolan] to look after things." Cardinal Vaughan also expressed some anxiety about Ealing. In December 1898, he wrote to Ford and informed him that he was "much concerned about the condition of Ealing."[61] The Cardinal's worry naturally revolved around Dom Bernard. "Father Bulbeck is a holy and venerable man," Ford was told, "but he has not the physical and mental vigour to contend successfully against the difficulties of his position." Someone must replace Dom Bernard, and Vaughan did not mince words. He told Ford that he "must insist upon...placing there, with as little delay as possible, a Father who will be fit for the position of superior." Ford also realized a change was needed and sent a copy of Vaughan's evaluation of Dom Bernard to Abbot President O'Gorman and remarked "that the delay in Fr. Dolan's being at Ealing is seriously harmful to us."[62] With pressure mounting, the Benedictine authorities finally took action. In March 1899, the *Downside Review* reported that "Dom Gilbert Dolan has been appointed to take charge of the Mission at Ealing."[63]

When Dom Gilbert Dolan arrived at Ealing on 5 January 1899, he brought with him a varied background and a tenacity of will which coloured his tenure as the superior of the London monks.[64] A native of Kentish Town, Dom Gilbert was born on 2 February 1853, and later received his education at Downside.[65] He entered the novitiate in 1870, and was ordained a priest in 1878. At Downside, he exhibited a keen interest in architecture and history, and as the community's librarian and archivist, "he collected and bound up a large number of pamphlets...relating to English Catholicism since the Reformation." A gifted preacher, he enjoyed the reputation of "originality of mind [which] gave to his sermons an interest peculiarly their own..." A Downside monk later reminisced that the secret of Dom Gilbert's success and influence extended beyond his rhetorical skills: "...beneath the gentle, cheery temper was a depth of spirituality and a love of prayer which, overlooked by many in the days of his activity, came out in the last years of his life that none could fail to see."

Prior Ford placed the highest confidence in Dolan's ability. "No one except perhaps myself realizes the heavy work you have in front of you at Ealing," Ford told him.[66] "It is comparatively an easy thing to start a mission, but at Ealing you are beginning a monastery," he continued, and "within a few years we want to see a monastic church there and a Community attached to it." Ford's commission to Dom Gilbert seemed Herculean. "If we are to have a monastery at Ealing we must have room enough for a school, sufficient ground to enable the community to be out of doors without being obliged to go out into the streets, [and] land for monastic buildings." And this represented only the beginning. "As we shall be securing the mission," Ford went on, "we shall want more room for public building for the use of the people, reading rooms, boys' recreation rooms, guild rooms, besides the Church and its special building."

Dom Gilbert's successes during the next few years guaranteed the stability and life of the foundation, and his determined leadership also radically altered the nature of the agreement between the monks and Cardinal Vaughan. While keeping to strict economies, he worked to buy adjacent properties for future growth and expansion. The congregation continued to increase, and he personally directed the initial phases of the construction of a church. In 1899, two bays of the current abbey church were completed. At the solemn opening, Cardinal Vaughan preached the sermon. He emphasized that "it was altogether fitting, and for the advantage of the Church at large that the great and ancient Order of St. Benedict should have full representation in the diocese of Westminster."[67] "In this new foundation," Vaughan continued, "the Benedictines have followed their own traditions." This church, he concluded, "is intended to serve for monastic, collegiate, and parochial purposes."

Dom Gilbert also orchestrated other aspects of Ealing's development. Although the Cardinal had serious reservations about the educational work of the Ealing monks, the Benedictines always realized that a school was essential. A month after his arrival, Dolan urged Downside to take action on the future of a school. In 1902, he again argued that a school would make the foundation a centre of importance. The officials at Downside gave their consent, approached Cardinal Vaughan, and the latter rescinded his earlier prohibition. Soon afterwards, the monks opened a school.[68] Dolan was more cautiously inactive in his approach to another problem; the refusal of Rev. Richard O'Halloran to leave Ealing. Ignoring Vaughan's demand that he surrender his mission to the Benedictines, O'Halloran vilified the Cardinal and the monks from his pulpit and in the columns of the local press. Ecclesiastical suspension in 1897 did not silence him, but the Catholics of Ealing slowly transferred their allegiance to the monks. His flock continued to dwindle, whilst that of the Benedictines grew.[69] When Rome excommunicated Fr. O'Halloran in 1914, only a handful attended his services.[70] More significantly, however, Vaughan's initial plan that the Ealing monks be responsible for some of the liturgical services at Westminster Cathedral also failed to materialize.

The Cardinal's biographer wrote that "it may be doubted whether, under any circumstances, Cardinal Vaughan would have consented so far to bind the hands of his successors in the See as to hand over to a Religious Order the possession of a chapel in the Cathedral in perpetuity."[71] Moreover, a recrudescence of the old rivalry between the secular and religious clergy might erupt if both had duties connected with the new Westminster. In order to escape this impasse, Vaughan even proposed that an outside party, the French Benedictines of Solesmes, be invited to London. Not surprisingly, this scheme was resisted by all parties: the English Benedictines, the secular priests, and interested members of the laity who voiced their horror in the pages of the Roman Catholic press. Consequently, Vaughan put aside his chief reason for inviting the Benedictines to Ealing and opted for the obvious solution: the secular clergy would render the liturgy at his cathedral. In *The Tablet,* he confessed that "the best arrangements sometimes leave room for regrets, and we confess we would have been glad if it had been possible to see the cowls of the Benedictines back in Westminster, and to know that there were opportunities for joining in their religious chant."[72] With much sorrow, Vaughan concluded: "and yet, apart from the old associations which cluster around the site of Westminster, is it not after all better, and more in accordance with the fitness of things, that the Secular clergy should themselves render the Liturgy in the new Cathedral?"

Secular priests, therefore, would be entrusted with the responsibilities which Vaughan had hoped would become the work of the English Benedictines of Ealing. Yet the future at Ealing seemed secure: the membership of the mission continued to grow; and the school was educating the Roman Catholic youth of the area. Consequently, the monks quickly and firmly implanted themselves and took root in the life of this part of London.

Notes

[1] *The Tablet,* 6 July 1895.

[2] Ibid.

[3] The Benedictines had opened a house in Dulwich during the early 1890s. Another house was established at Great Ormond St. to serve as a house of studies. Neither developed into an autonomous community.

[4] "Memorandum" in *Liber Baptizatorum, 1897*-1919, Ealing Abbey Archives, Ealing Abbey, Charlbury Grove, London.

[5] Ibid.

[6] For a biography of Ford and his influence on the development of the English Benedictine Congregation, see B. Hicks, *Hugh Edmund Ford* (London: Sands Co., 1947).

[7] Vaughan to Ford, 5. May 1896, Ford Papers. With the exception of footnote 35, all the Ford Papers are housed at Ealing Abbey.

[8] Ford to Vaughan, 6 May 1896, Ford Papers.

[9] Abbot Benedict Snow was the titular Abbot of Glastonbury.

[10] Ford to Snow, 6 May 1896, Ford Papers.

[11] Snow to Ford, 12 May 1896, Ford Papers.

[12] *Cardinal Vaughan and Father O'Halloran: The Rights of the Secular Priests Vindicated,* 1901, contains a biography of O'Halloran, his long feud with Cardinal Vaughan, and the stormy controversy which erupted when O'Halloran refused to hand over his mission and leave Ealing. The pamphlet was privately printed by Fr. O'Halloran. The *Middlesex County Times* also sheds valuable light on the career of O'Halloran and his role in the Benedictine foundation at Ealing.

[13] Snow to Ford, 3 June 1896, Ford Papers.

[14] Ford to Vaughan, 5 June 1896, Ford Papers.

[15] Ford to Vaughan, 5 June 1896, Ford Papers.

[16] Vaughan to Ford, 10 June 1896, Ford Papers.

[17] Vaughan to Ford, 17 June 1896, Ford Papers.

[18] "Notes: Ealing," 28 June 1896, Ford Papers.

[19] B. Hicks, *Hugh Edmund Ford,* pp. 76-77.

[20] Handwritten note on Vaughan's original 5 June 1896 proposal, Ford Papers.

[21] Snow to Ford, 11 June 1896, Ford Papers.

[22] Ford to Snow, 6 July 1896, Ford Papers.

[23] Snow to Ford, 7 July 1896, Ford Papers.

[24] Dom Benedict Tidmarsh was the Procurator of the Southern Province of the English Benedictine Congregation.

[25] Tidmarsh to Ford, 23 July 1896, Ford Papers.

[26] Richards to Ford, July 1896, Ford Papers.

[27] At that time, located at Great Ormond St.

[28] Richards to Ford, July 1896, Ford Papers.

[29] Sister Mary to Ford, 21 June 1896, Ford Papers.

[30] Sister Mary to Ford, 8 July 1896, Ford Papers.

[31] Ford to Sister Mary, 13 July 1896, Ford Papers.

[32] For a description of the governance of the English Benedictine Congregation at this time, see B. Hicks, *Hugh Edmund Ford,* pp. 100-137.

[33] Ford to O'Gorman, 17 August 1896, Ford Papers.

[34] Ford to Fathers, 18 August 1896, Ford Papers.

[35] Ford to O'Gorman, 21 August 1896, Ford Papers, Downside Abbey Archives, Bath.

[36] Morrall to O'Gorman, 23 August 1896, Ford Papers.

[37] O'Gorman to Wood, 26 August 1896, Ford Papers.

[38] Wood to O'Gorman, 28 August 1896, Ford Papers.

[39] Doyle to O'Gorman, 28 August 1896, Ford Papers. The Downside community had earlier given its approval to the Ealing foundation.

[40] O'Gorman to Ford, 3 September 1896, Ford Papers.

[41] O'Gorman to Ford, 9 September 1896, Ford Papers.

[42] Snow to Ford, 15 September 1896, Ford Papers.

[43] Snow to Ford, 23 September 1896, Ford Papers.

[44] O'Gorman to Ford, 29 September 1896, Ford Papers.

[45] Ford to Snow, 30 September 1896, Ford Papers.

[46] Almost immediately, Prior Ford began to search for tenants to lease space to on a short term basis.

[47] Ford to Vaughan, 1 October 1896, Ford Papers.

[48] Ford to O'Gorman, 12 September 1896, Ford Papers.

[49] Ford to O'Gorman, 25 September 1896, Ford Papers.

[50] Petition of Prior Ford to the Holy See, Ford Papers.

[51] A copy of the rescript can be found among the Ford Papers at Ealing Abbey.

[52] Vaughan to Ford, 28 October 1896, Ford Papers.

[53] Notes Extracted from the Agenda of the Chapter of Westminster, 6 October 1896, Ford Papers.

[54] Johnson to Ford, 2 November 1896, Ford Papers.

[55] Johnson to Ford, 7 December 1896, Ford Papers.

[56] "Odds and Ends," *Downside Review,* December 1890, p. 314.

[57] "Obituary of Reverend Dom Bernard Bulbeck," *Downside Review,* December 1901, p. 343.

[58] Johnson to Bulbeck, 10 April 1897, Ford Papers.

[59] Bulbeck to Ford, 11 October 1897, Ford Papers.

[60] Gasquet to Ford, 28 June 1898, Ford Papers.

[61] Johnson to Ford, 19 December 1898, Ford Papers.

[62] Ford to O'Gorman, 21 December 1898, Ford Papers.

[63] "Odds and Ends," *Downside Review,* March 1899, p. 111.

[64] Dom Gilbert remained at Ealing until 1907.

[65] "In Memoriam: Dom Gilbert Dolan," *Downside Review,* 1914, pp. 252-254.

[66] Ford to Dolan, 28 February 1899, Ford Papers.

[67] *The Tablet,* 2 December 1899.

[68] Approximately eight hundred students currently attend the school conducted by the monks at Ealing.

[69] In 1903, for example, Dom Gilbert estimated that over five hundred people attended his Sunday services. For the same period, only sixty-five attended O'Halloran's church.

[70] Unreconciled to the Roman Catholic Church, Fr. O'Halloran died on 13 October 1925. Laymen conducted a prayer service at his mission where he had lived in retirement. The same individuals also presided at a graveside ceremony at nearby Hanwell.

[71] J.G. Snead-Cox, *The Life of Cardinal Vaughan,* vol. 2 (London: Burns and Oates, 1910), p. 349.

[72] *The Tablet,* 1 June 1901.

CHAPTER XII

BISHOPS AND BENEDICTINES: THE CASE OF FATHER RICHARD O'HALLORAN

Eclesiastical rogues, misfits and outcasts often possess some magnetic or magical quality. The lives and activities of these men and women may provide comic relief for scholars bored by research into spirituality, administrative reform or questions involving the relationship of Church and State. On the other hand, they may exemplify some novelty or pioneering effort; as a consequence, their insights might have been blackened by more cautious contemporaries who resorted to mockery or accusations of heresy. Some of these people may be prophets who had the courage to point the bony finger at scandal or abuse, and whom officialdom was quick to brand as deviants. Finally, they may be people caught in the ecclesiastical maelstrom of change. Unable to adapt, they lash out against the structure. These streams converge in the life of the Revd Richard O'Halloran (1856-1925). During his stormy career, he publicly attacked the alleged misuse of power by archbishops and bishops. Always proclaiming his loyalty to Rome, O'Halloran threatened schism several times. He also believed that the religious orders throughout England were involved in a grand conspiracy to destroy the rights of the secular clergy. Fr O'Halloran's experiences with the Benedictine monks in the London suburb of Ealing confirmed his suspicions.

Questions concerning the extent of episcopal power and the rights of the clergy had always sparked disputes within English Roman Catholicism. In 1688, England and Wales were divided into four districts administered by vicars-apostolic in episcopal orders, and the country was placed under the jurisdiction of Propaganda Fide. Because of the substantial increase of Roman Catholics, the number of districts and bishops was doubled in 1840. But this system of governance satisfied no one. Both the clergy and the vicars-apostolic wanted the restoration of a proper hierarchy, but for different reasons. 'While the vicars-apostolic wanted a hierarchy because they wanted more freedom from Rome, their clergy wanted more freedom from vicars-apostolic.'[1] The clergy had many grievances: a priest could be moved at the whim of the vicar-apostolic; there was no consultation on the choice of vicar-apostolic; and the fear that a bishop might be chosen from one of the religious orders haunted many clerics. Moreover, the ultramontane spirit of the bishops angered members of the secular clergy. 'Therefore the priests of England wanted missionary status ended, canon law introduced, chapters to advise at the selection of a bishop, and no removal without due process.'[2]

The Restoration of the Hierarchy in 1850, however, increased the authority of the bishops over their priests. 'At the same time all rights and powers hitherto belonging to the vicars-apostolic were expressly trans-ferred to the new bishops, who thus acquired all the advantages of a traditional episcopate while retaining the freedom of action characteristic of the missionary regime.'[3] The Boyle affair in Westminster illustrated that tensions between a priest and his bishop still existed. Archbishop Nicholas Wiseman wanted a change of personnel at an Islington mission, but Fr Richard Boyle declared that Wiseman had no right to dismiss him because he had spent his own money on the mission. Boyle finally agreed to leave after the archbishop promised financial compensation, but the controversy had only started. Fr Boyle had supplied information for a series of articles in a French journal which criticized the English hierarchy. *The Tablet* printed an article by Wiseman which claimed that Boyle had been expelled from the Jesuits, and this became the basis for a well-publicised libel case in 1854, which eventually ended in a compromise. The policies of Archbishop Wiseman's successor, Henry Edward Man-ning, ensured wide support from the secular clergy, but the situation soon changed with Cardinal Herbert Vaughan. Disliked by a number of his priests, Vaughan's personality and programmes brought distrust and discord into the archdiocese. Cardinal Vaughan's apparent fondness for the Benedictine order also touched a sensitive nerve in the secular clergy.

The suspicion between religious orders and the secular clergy had threatened the unity of Roman Catholicism in medieval England. Instead of closing ranks, the Roman Catholic priesthood continued to suffer internal dissension during the Reformation. The Appellant controversy during the early seventeenth century saw a fragile Roman Catholicism almost destroyed because of the rivalry between the Jesuits and the secular clergy, who opposed the appointment of George Blackwell as archpriest because of his pro-Jesuit leanings. This tension continued during the period of the Penal Laws, and, at the beginning of the nineteenth century, it had become a feature of England's Catholic life. As the religious orders increased in numbers and influence, they 'encouraged the idea that they should be entrusted with a greater share of the English mission and it was even suggested that future bishops should always be chosen from the ranks of religious....'[4] The secular clergy, not surprisingly, wanted to be governed by secular bishops and, in 1840, sent a petition to Rome which outlined their opposition to the appointment of religious as bishops.

The vicars-apostolic also exhibited a feeling of mistrust and suspicion of the regular clergy. Bishop Peter Augustine Baines, a Benedictine, quarrelled with the monks of Downside during the 1820s and remarked upon 'the dissatisfaction and disputes which have constantly subsisted between the bishops and the Religious Orders, which until the middle of the century, proved the greatest impediment to the normal conduct of ecclesiastical administration.'[5] Some churchmen believed that the religious orders fostered an anti-episcopal spirit, worked to undermine the authority of the vicars-apostolic and, to the secular clergy, appeared as rivals for patronage and ecclesiastical preferment in the English missions. It was the Society of Jesus, restored in 1814, which presented the real threat to the integrity of the bishops and the secular clergy. Their suspicion was 'derived partly from international jealousies about the Society's influence, concentrated in Rome itself and carried to different countries, and partly from the English demonology of anti-Catholicism, in which the Jesuits were depicted in the most disagreeable fashion.'[6]

Various bishops tried to circumvent the power of the Jesuits. Bishop Thomas Griffiths, appointed vicar-apostolic for the London District in 1836, feared the encroachment of the Jesuits on his authority. He tried to keep them out of Farm Street, arguing that the Jesuits 'wanted a superfluous West-End mission and were not prepared to go to the less attractive parts of the city where they were needed.'[7] Cardinal Wiseman, however, appeared more sympathetic to the religious orders and regarded them as important elements in the conversion of England. His successor, Cardinal Manning, not only championed the claims of the secular clergy but distrusted the regular clergy, especially the Jesuits. Labouring 'to raise the status of the secular priesthood, which he considered suffered from the assumption that life as a religious represented a higher calling,' Manning's 'animus against Farm Street had spread to cover the entire Society.'[8] The cardinal fought against the establishment of a Jesuit school in his archdiocese and openly criticised the Society for siphoning off the wealth and influence of English Catholics to the detriment of the secular priesthood.

The real blow to the claims of the religious orders, however, occurred in the Salford diocese. The bishop, Herbert Vaughan, was adamant that no

Jesuit school be established in Manchester, but the Society opened a school against the bishop's expressed wishes while he was in America during 1874-5. On his return to England, Bishop Vaughan was determined to exert his episcopal authority, and he took his case against the Jesuits to Rome. Finally in 1881, Rome issued *Romanos Pontifices,* which effectively gave the English bishops extensive control over the regular clergy: religious orders had to obtain the permission of the local ordinary and the Holy See before the establishment of a residence, church, convent or educational institution. When Vaughan became archbishop of Westminster, however, his rigid attitude to religious orders, especially the Benedictines, began to mellow. Two of the archbishop's brothers, Roger and Joseph, had been Downside monks, and his dream of staffing the new Westminster Cathedral with these Benedictines seemed to place the monks in a favoured position. Friction between the secular and religious clergy seemed inevitable and conflict between priest and archbishop unavoidable.

Richard Joseph O'Halloran was born to Denis O'Halloran and Johanna Roach on 24 December 1856 at Ballyhindon, County Cork. Not much is known about Richard O'Halloran's life in Ireland, his family or any social or clerical connections, except that he had three sisters and three brothers. He received his early education at the French College, Dublin, and St Colman's in Fermoy. On 9 September 1875, O'Halloran entered St Joseph's College, Mill Hill, London, as a candidate for St Joseph's Society for Foreign Missions.[9] One year later, he was admitted into the society on a temporary basis; the records at Mill Hill reveal that the vote for acceptance was unanimous. Minor orders followed quickly, and he was ordained subdeacon and deacon in 1879 and 1880 respectively. But controversy soon coloured his career. While he was master of discipline at a school run by the Mill Hill Fathers in Wales, allegations about his reckless and impulsive behaviour towards some students began to reach his superior in London. O'Halloran tried to justify his actions. He responded to his superior's queries, criticised several members of the staff and pointed out that the complaints from his students were groundless. He argued that a woman addicted to drink, whom he had publicly rebuked and then fired, had fabricated these stories.[10]

In spite of continued complaints from the school, Richard O'Halloran was ordained priest as a member of the Mill Hill Fathers in December 1880 by Bishop John Hedley, auxiliary bishop of Newport and Menevia. But within two weeks the new priest suddenly severed his relations with the society. The log book of the Mill Hill Missionary Society records: 'Jan [uary] 3/81...Left the Society immed[iately] after Priesthood.'[11] The criticism of his work in Wales might have contributed to his dramatic departure, but his reluctance to take an oath required of all members to work in the missions greatly influenced his decision. This bold action and O'Halloran's subsequent refusal to repay Mill Hill for his education ignited a long and fiery conflict between himself and Herbert Vaughan, then bishop of Salford and superior general of the Mill Hill Fathers. And it also marked the start of Richard O'Halloran's long search for a friendly bishop and clerical employment in England.

In 1881, O'Halloran approached Edward G. Bagshawe, bishop of Nottingham, who assigned the young cleric to a small mission in the diocese. Nottingham had become famous as a harbourage for difficult or troublesome priests. Bishop Bagshawe desperately needed clergy to meet the commitments of his expanding diocese. Consequently, 'he increased the number of priests by hasty ordinations and by accepting clergy from other dioceses or religious orders.'[12] Because of this short-sighted policy, Bagshawe 'sacrificed quality to quantity.' Meanwhile, the relationship between O'Halloran and Bishop Vaughan deteriorated drastically and rapidly. After his arrival in Nottingham, Father O'Halloran wrote to Vaughan as his former superior general and requested permission 'to obtain a transfer to some bishop who would think fit to accept my service.'[13] Vaughan refused to act. In the following year, O'Halloran again wrote to Vaughan, complained about the unjust treatment he had received from Mill Hill and then accused him of being 'determined on my ruin.'[14] Bagshawe initially supported O'Halloran. The bishop of Nottingham told the bishop of Salford that Fr O'Halloran was justified in his refusal to take the missionary oath. Moreover, the priest need not reimburse Mill Hill for his education. 'The students in their educational course were,' he lectured Vaughan, 'in a sort of novitiate trying their vocation for the Society, but free (until the time comes for taking its oath) to join it or do missionary work elsewhere.'[15] Soon, however, Bishop Bagshawe's estimation of O'Halloran's character changed. In spring 1882, rumours concerning the impropriety of some of Father O'Halloran's actions reached the episcopal ear. Bagshawe informed O'Halloran of three serious charges against him: that he had verbally abused a parishioner from the pulpit 'to the distress of her family'; that 'you have allowed the Schoolmistress to sleep in your house...in defiance of the public talk which has gone on and is going on about you and her'; and that 'the grossest charges of immorality are brought against you.'[16] Without allowing O'Halloran the opportunity to defend himself, Bishop Bagshawe ordered the disgraced priest to leave Nottingham within a fortnight.

Surprisingly, Father O'Halloran wrote to Bishop Vaughan, pleaded his innocence and asked Vaughan to give him a mission in the Salford diocese. Vaughan refused to welcome this troublesome priest in the Manchester area, but suggested instead that O'Halloran should go to Australia. O'Halloran informed Vaughan that he was 'willing to go to either Sydney or Melbourne,'[17] but he failed to leave Britain. He had secured another temporary haven. In autumn 1882, Bishop Richard Lacy of the diocese of Middlesbrough appointed O'Halloran chaplain to Lady Sykes, who, with her son, had converted to Roman Catholicism, and entrusted him with the care of a small Yorkshire mission. During O'Halloran's stay in the diocese, certain traits and characteristics began to surface. He began to vilify Bishop Vaughan and described their relationship as 'an unchristian transaction and a "scandal."'[18] He also saw himself as a martyr. In one letter, he related how he 'carried on in the greatest poverty and in the face of trying opposition.' Thereafter, his dreams became more grandiose. O'Halloran boasted that he planned to 'erect a school to accommodate 300 children— and to purchase another house and site of land for a convent of nuns.' A final theme also emerged from his letters: a righteous refusal to compromise or negotiate with ecclesiastical authorities. 'I offered *no conditions,*' O'Halloran informed a former Mill Hill superior in London, 'I merely asked your reverence to act as mediator between his Lordship the Bishop of Salford and myself.' None the less, O'Halloran believed that this northern diocese would become the vineyard of his priestly labours. But the eirenic atmosphere soon exploded; Irish Home Rule propelled O'Halloran into controversy. In defiance of the Sykeses, O'Halloran enthusiastically supported Gladstone and Home Rule in the 1886 general election. He offended Bishop Lacy by his involvement in Irish politics. He opposed a candidate backed by the Sykeses. 'As an Irishman I could not withhold my vote from the Home Rule candidate,' he remarked.[19]

O'Halloran later declared that a 'complaint was made to the Bishop of Middlesbrough written by Lady Sykes or another is a matter of no consequence— that this young Irish priest had thrown in his lot with the Irish cause in defiance of his patrons.'[20] According to the priest, 'his lordship did then and there arbitrary [*sic*] abuse his episcopal authority by withdrawing...[my] faculties' to function as a priest in the diocese of Middlesbrough.[21] Bishop Lacy's object 'was to goad me into the commission of some act of folly which might bring about my ruin and serve his ends.'[22] The bishop's tactics were 'infamous,' and he had the personality of an 'irresponsible aristocrat.' All prelates came under O'Halloran's scathing attack: 'as a rule, the bishops light their cigars with the Pope's mandates when not in their own favour, [and] they set themselves up as irresponsible autocrats whilst pretending outwardly to be submissive to the Holy See.' O'Halloran again fancied himself as a martyr sacrificed on the altar of episcopal arrogance and vengeance.

The peripatetic priest next surfaced in the archdiocese of Westminster. According to O'Halloran, Cardinal Manning, 'my good friend, invited me to his diocese of Westminster.'[23] He accepted charge of St Catherine in the Bow and, by this action, claimed that he 'became a priest of Westminster.' However, any hope of tranquillity and stability soon disappeared. His adversary and enemy, Herbert Vaughan, succeeded Cardinal Manning as third archbishop of Westminster in 1892, and the old smouldering conflict immediately flared up. 'Dr. Vaughan had scarcely placed the symbol of jurisdiction around his neck,' O'Halloran later recalled, 'when he sent me a peremptory order to leave the diocese—that he did not want me under him.'[24] The priest complained and argued that he was a legitimate and valid priest of Westminster: consequently, the whim of an archbishop could not force him out of the archdiocese. Cardinal Vaughan, however, contended that Fr O'Halloran belonged to the diocese of Middlesbrough and therefore could be dismissed from Westminster. Both parties took their case to the authorities in Rome, who supported the claims of the cardinal archbishop. The decree from the Congregation of Propaganda Fide stated that O'Halloran was 'not affiliated to the diocese of Westminster and he has no benefice in it, [and] Your Eminence can do with this priest what you think suitable in the Lord.'[25] But, it continued, if O'Halloran desired to remain temporarily in London, he had to sign a document which declared that he did not 'belong to the archdiocese of Westminster and...shall be willing to leave it whenever His Eminence the Cardinal Archbishop shall desire.'[26]

Desiring to remain in the archdiocese, O'Halloran signed the document. Paradoxically, Vaughan gave his fiery cleric a mission in fashionable Ealing, the self-proclaimed 'Queen of the Suburbs.' Vaughan later explained his logic. 'In order that the Rev R. O'Halloran might not be inconvenienced by being suddenly thrown out of work,' Vaughan decided 'to offer him a temporary post so as to give him time to look for employment elsewhere.'[27] O'Halloran also signed another document which stipulated that any debt contracted while at Ealing would be considered a private matter.[28] He eagerly accepted this appointment, and his initial efforts produced noteworthy and successful results. *The Tablet* reported that 'the new mission of SS. Joseph and Peter has made great progress since its commencement.'[29] A leaflet told Ealing Roman Catholics that 'the Mission has made considerable progress...[and] over £5,000 has already been expended upon it.'[30] The same announcement also proclaimed that 'the time has come when school accommodation must be provided for the children.' The congregation grew, and O'Halloran moved services from a private residence 'to a beautiful spot in Mattock Lane off Ealing Green, where services were carried on in the large drawing room of Mattock Lodge.'[31]

Eventually, a new church was built to house O'Halloran's expanding congregation. 'The Church of SS. Joseph and Peter is a modest iron structure,' a London paper noted, 'admirably and even beautifully arranged standing on the freehold land purchased for the permanent structure of Father O'Halloran.'[32] Even a complaint from the Roman Catholics of nearby Hanwell to Archbishop's House testified to O'Halloran's popularity and charisma: the new Ealing priest 'was drawing away the people from their allegiance to the good reverend father of Hanwell.'[33] It appeared that Richard O'Halloran had finally found the stability, success and priestly satisfaction which he had failed to enjoy earlier in his career. In summer 1896, however, a new element convulsed the quiet of Ealing. Cardinal Vaughan wanted Benedictine monks to chant the Divine Office at his new cathedral in central London, and an arrangement was reached with St Gregory's Abbey, Downside, to purchase property in Ealing from which to journey into London to celebrate the liturgy.[34] The arrangement shattered O'Halloran's dreams. Archbishop's House notified Fr O'Halloran that it had been 'arranged, with the approval of the Apostolic See, to place the Mission of Ealing under the charge of the Benedictine Fathers.'[35]

Fr O'Halloran, however, defiantly announced that he would never surrender Ealing peacefully. He immediately appealed to the conscience of the Benedictines and wrote, in 1896, to their superior at Downside, Dom Hugh Edmund Ford,[36] the shrewd-minded prior who was determined to establish a monastic foundation near London. The Ealing priest firmly pointed out that he 'had worked up this new mission in a manner spiritually and financially in every way satisfactory.'[37] 'My work has succeeded and is going on well, and there is no fault whatever to find in it,' he told Ford. 'I have to-day informed the Vicar-General to acquaint the archbishop that I have not the slightest intention of resigning the rectorship of Ealing.' After a threat to carry his battle to Rome, O'Halloran beseeched Ford and begged him to reconsider the Ealing foundation: 'I appeal to you, as an Order of religious men, not to be the cause of bringing on this quarrel between my archbishop and myself.' The arrival of the monks would cause gross injustice and a scandal within the Roman Catholic Church as well. 'Imagine, then, my astonishment that because you want Ealing I MUST GO—after all the labours and money I spent.' 'Why not ask for a new mission—virgin soil—and let me and my work alone.' Ford failed to respond; the monks liked Ealing, and Cardinal Vaughan wanted Fr O'Halloran out of the archdiocese.

In O'Halloran's mind, the Benedictine monks loomed threateningly as interlopers; and it later emerged that he had cultivated a prejudice against religious orders long before his arrival in Ealing. 'Before I came to London, and entered Mill Hill, I knew little about the conflict between the diocesan clergy and the religious orders,' he remarked. It 'was in Mill Hill that I heard of the bitterness between "seculars and religious."'[38] Prelates had encouraged this hatred in his soul: 'The writings of both Manning and the present Cardinal were severely hostile to the claims of monks, and from these writings I imbibed a distrust for all monks.' 'It was Dr Vaughan himself, and no other,' O'Halloran emphasized later in life, 'that led me to look upon monks as the greatest curse on earth to the Church and State.' Accordingly, Cardinal Vaughan—who had just invited the Benedictines into Ealing—was the archenemy of religious communities. 'While I was a student,' O'Halloran claimed, Vaughan had 'led me to regard the religious orders with anything but a friendly eye .'

Unsuccessful with Downside, O'Halloran wrote to Archbishop's House and asked for an explanation or a clarification of the Ealing situation. The vicar general, the Revd Michael Barry, responded by praising his parochial work and claimed that the cardinal's decision to hand over Ealing to the Benedictines was not prompted by their past differences and fights. 'It is simply for the sake of the principle involved,' the letter concluded, 'having in view the order and good government of the diocese.'[39] Cardinal Vaughan even tried to soften the hurt. He later stated that he worked 'to avoid the painful necessity of having recourse to an extreme measure' and claimed that he had obtained a promise from the bishop of Middlesbrough to give O'Halloran a mission in that diocese 'if he would apply for it.'[40] But the Ealing priest snubbed the cardinal's offer. Autumn 1896 was characterized by an uneasy calm, but the omens did not augur well for a peaceful settlement of the Ealing problem.

In December, the archbishop's secretary, Monsignor William Anthony Johnson, warned the Benedictines of 'the opposition of the priest at Ealing.'[41] In January, Archbishop's House informed Prior Ford that Fr O'Halloran 'shows no sign of surrender.'[42] Several weeks later Cardinal Vaughan told Ford that he had 'given O'Halloran notice that on 28th March the Benedictines will take over the Ealing Mission.'[43] But he also informed the Benedictines that they could not expect to take possession of O'Halloran's church or parish property. 'You had better make provision for the people in the large room at Castle Hill [the Georgian mansion purchased by the monks] and not count upon receiving anything whatsoever from Father O'Halloran.' Moreover, ecclesiastical faculties were granted to Dom Bernard Bulbeck, OSB, who arrived in Ealing on 28 March 1897, and to any priest assigned to assist him. O'Halloran's reaction sounded like a declaration of ecclesiastical civil war: 'Death alone removes me from the Rectorship here.'[44] Prior Ford even tried to reason with him. 'It is impossible to go round the church...without a feeling of deep sadness at the thought that a priest of your zeal might be destroyed.'[45]

The authorities in London began to apply pressure. The vicar general informed O'Halloran that Cardinal Vaughan was 'grieved to hear that you have paid no attention to his direction that you should give up the Mission of Ealing into the hands of the Benedictine Fathers.'[46] Barry drew attention to O'Halloran's boast that he would 'not retire and...[would] continue to serve that mission' and reminded him of the promise to leave Ealing 'whenever he [Cardinal Vaughan] should call upon you to do so .' Now, the Ealing Mission 'has been canonically made over to the Benedictine Fathers with the full authority of the Holy See.' Finally, the letter pointed out that the cardinal 'had arranged with your own Bishop to give you a mission in his diocese to which you canonically belong.' Because of his disobedience and arrogance, the vicar general communicated the following decision to Fr O'Halloran:

> The Cardinal is now under the painful obligation of giving you formal notice...that he withdraws the Diocesan faculties which you have hitherto held, and that he forbids you to say a public mass at Ealing on Sunday, unless you publicly announce that you will obey the decision which has been given, and at once hand over the Mission to the Benedictine Fathers.

The drama escalated the following day when Cardinal Vaughan formally entrusted the Roman Catholics of Ealing to the Benedictine monks. The cardinal directed Dom Bernard 'to announce to the Catholics within the Mission of Ealing that the pastoral care of the mission has now been confided to the Benedictine Fathers exclusively.'[47] The faithful were to be informed that 'no other priest within the mission holds faculties or jurisdiction from me' and to be instructed 'to follow and obey their lawful spiritual superiors.' Cardinal Vaughan also announced that the vicar general and dean would meet with Ealing's Roman Catholics on the afternoon of 17 April to answer any questions. This action, however, did not silence or stifle Fr O'Halloran, who still refused to recognise the validity of the Benedictines' claim and continued to say mass for his

Mattock Lane flock. Stronger medicine was needed to bring religious peace to Ealing. Archbishop's House issued a public and formal Decree of Suspension against O'Halloran, 'a refractory cleric,' which stripped him of 'all Ecclesiastical faculties.'[48]

The Benedictines adopted a cautious and conservative approach to the problem they unexpectedly found at Ealing; reserve and diplomacy characterised their response to O'Halloran. Another Downside monk, Benedict Snow, captured the spirit of this policy. During the turbulent month of April 1897, he confessed to Prior Ford at Downside that he did 'not see what we can do about O'Halloran except keep quiet and await events...and do our best not to get mixed up in the quarrel.'[49] 'It will be a scandal and he will probably say and do things that will shock even-minded people.' 'I think our cue should be to say as little as possible and at present do merely the bare requisite of the mission work.' Although the monks had hoped that, if ignored, O'Halloran would strike camp and leave Ealing, it soon became apparent that the neighbouring priest was preparing for a long siege. After the public condemnation by Cardinal Vaughan, Snow again informed Downside that O'Halloran would 'hold out to the bitter end.'[50] Some Roman Catholics began to desert the Mattock Lane church for the orthodoxy of the Ealing Benedictines,[51] but Dom Bernard Bulbeck dashed the hopes of a smooth and peaceful victory. Writing to Prior Ford in October, Dom Bernard stated that 'O'Halloran is flourishing, and [he] told his people his church would be crammed full by another year.'[52] While antagonism between the secular priest and the new monastic enterprise smouldered, Cardinal Vaughan fanned a fire which threatened to consume the Roman Catholic Church in Ealing.

Vaughan took his case against Father O'Halloran to the Congregation of Propaganda Fide. As expected, the cardinal prefect, Miecislas Ledochowski, judged that O'Halloran belonged to the diocese of Middlesbrough and decreed that he 'held [the] office of Rector in the Mission of Ealing...in a temporary way,' pointing out that the suspended priest 'continues to the grave scandal of the faithful, to celebrate mass and to administer the Sacraments.'[53] The Roman document directed Vaughan to convey to Fr O'Halloran the contents of the letter and also urged him to 'give notice to the faithful not to go near the rebellious priest.' The vicar general subsequently visited O'Halloran and informed him of the strongly worded statement from Propaganda. O'Halloran also received a letter from the cardinal prefect which described his refusal to relinquish Ealing to the Benedictines as an act of 'contumacious obstinacy,' deplored the fact that he 'continued to say mass and sacriligiously to administer the Sacraments' and pleaded with the priest to return to Middlesbrough.[54]

Not only did O'Halloran ignore the directive, he threatened to plead his case in Rome and declared that he would not 'resign in favour of the Benedictine monks.'[55] 'If there be a scandal in Ealing, it is produced by the violent and illegal conduct of Cardinal Vaughan and the monks.' Following instructions from Rome, Cardinal Vaughan published a pamphlet which informed Ealing's Catholics about Fr O'Halloran's suspension. *Notification to the Catholics Living in Ealing and the Neighbourhood* chronicled the history of the dispute between Vaughan and the priest and explained the reasons behind the actions taken against O'Halloran: he was not a priest of the archdiocese of Westminster; he had been suspended from his priestly duties because of his refusal to hand over his mission to the monks; and, therefore 'his place of worship is not recognized as a Catholic Church or Chapel, and that no Catholic can frequent it, or receive Sacraments from him, without sin.'[56]

During summer 1897, O'Halloran tried to sow seeds of distrust between the Benedictines and Cardinal Vaughan. He approached the cardinal in July and accused the Ealing monks of saying 'the bleakest things about you.'[57] He informed Vaughan that they were spreading the rumour that 'no lady will allow her maid to come near you—either Catholic or Protestant' and also suggested that 'they hint as much as they dare about me.' Moreover, these monks constantly refer to 'something very black against your past.' The tone of the letter tried to imply some restraint as he darkened the character of the Ealing monks: 'It is for your Eminence to do the rest..[and] it seems to be incredible that the monks (no matter how bitter you and they are against me) could be guilty of such wicked malice and falsehood towards me.' But this transparent tactic failed, and Cardinal Vaughan sent O'Halloran's letter to the Ealing monks with the observation that the woman who made the allegations must have 'been deceived.'[58]

Fr O'Halloran next carried his campaign against the Benedictines into the columns of the press. A local Ealing newspaper, the *Middlesex County Times,* printed a letter by O'Halloran which inveighed against 'the unjust and uncanonical intrusion of the Benedictine monks into Ealing.'[59] When a reader drew attention to the actions of Archbishop Vaughan and Propaganda against O'Halloran, he threatened to raise the standard of schism. 'We believe in the primacy of the Bishop of Rome as the supreme shepherd of the whole Catholic Church,' he told a parishioner, but 'we do not allow that supreme or absolute as attached to the see of Westminster.'[60] Vaughan's actions against him were unchristian and unlawful; Archbishop's House, not Rome, had caused the friction. 'We accept the Bishop of Rome's authority, and in all things lawful and canonical and reasonable we faithfully carry out his will and wishes.' During the following months, the inhabitants of Ealing were treated to a detailed and documented history of the O'Halloran-Vaughan feud. Champions of the rights of the parish priest or the prerogative of the cardinal quickly emerged in the columns of the Ealing press.

Soon the large London papers discovered that the traditional controversy involving the secular and religious clergy had suddenly erupted in one of their suburbs. The *Daily Chronicle* published an article entitled 'Arbitrary episcopal action,' which explained that 'the resistance of the secular priests to the encroachments of the religious orders is the story of a universal conflict that has been measured by centuries.'[61] Within days, the same paper had printed a letter from a secular priest who claimed that 'for a long time an uneasy feeling that the parochial clergy are so many chessmen in the hands of their Bishops' had escalated.[62] The issue was serious: 'The questions raised affect the liberty and happiness of every Roman Catholic in England.'[63] Monks appeared as ecclesiastical villains who represented 'an organized attempt on the part of religious orders to seize the well-established mission of the secular clergy.' And Cardinal Vaughan encouraged this threat to the integrity of English Roman Catholicism. The *Daily Chronicle* told its readers that the archbishop of Westminster 'lent himself to methods which, however familiar they are to the monkish fraternity, seem strongly out of sympathy with his own known geniality of disposition.'

O'Halloran believed that 'the religious orders whilst they keep the secular clergy looking piously up to heaven, take possession of their power and position, both in England and in Rome itself.'[64] He soon became a symbol of liberty and freedom for a number of secular priests who believed that their rights were being usurped by prelates favouring religious orders, and several discontented clerics sought the advice and counsel of the Ealing dissident. 'O'Halloran has a suspended priest, now, as curate, and a third is often with him,' one of the Ealing Benedictines wrote to Downside in 1899.[65] During the following year, the same monk reported that 'a new runaway priest is now *chez* O'Halloran.'[66] Clergy also supported O'Halloran in the press. An unnamed London priest shared some misgivings about the alleged abuse of episcopal power. If O'Halloran could prove that Cardinal Vaughan had wronged him, the Westminster priests would 'back him up,'[67] the writer claimed. But an organized movement led by Fr O'Halloran failed to materialise; he still believed that a compromise could be reached with Archbishop's House.

The Roman Catholic press refused to waste much ink on the antics of Fr Richard O'Halloran. The *Catholic Herald* succinctly expressed the official Roman Catholic position: 'By a Papal decree, the ecclesiastical privileges of the Rev Richard O'Halloran have been withdrawn owing to the refusal on his part to comply with an order of His Eminence Cardinal Vaughan.'[68] In its next edition, the paper pointed out that 'O'Halloran appears...to be doing all that he can to foment trouble in the Archdiocese of Westminster.'[69] *The Universe* made some mention of the Benedictines, but drew attention to O'Halloran's nationality and reported that 'the notoriety created by the Irish priest at Ealing ought to have convinced that foolish ecclesiastic that there is no use in falling out with his superiors in the hierarchy.'[70] The *Catholic Times* printed several of O'Halloran's letters without comment, but then abandoned any hint of neutrality, describing O'Halloran's letters as 'incoherent.'[71] 'His rhetoric is running away with his logic.' The paper addressed the allegation that the freedom of the secular priesthood was under attack and published a letter from a priest of the archdiocese of Westminster which suggested that any 'attempt to represent this as a dispute between the seculars and regulars is hardly honest.'[72] 'The regulars have nothing to do with the dispute which lies entirely between a secular priest and the diocesan and chapter of a secular diocese whose right to rule the diocese and to be obeyed is challenged.'

Fr O'Halloran enjoyed his role as persecuted secular priest and continued to defend his position. He maintained that the monks were 'doing their utmost to attract my people away from this church' and proudly declared that he was 'only doing what other priests should have done when driven pillar to post.'[73] Commenting on the recent defections from his church in Mattock Lane, O'Halloran told the press that the Ealing Benedictines 'have attracted a good many of their bodies but I know I shall have their souls...[and] in time they will come back.' The *Middlesex County Times* reported that a committee had been established to raise funds to assist Father O'Halloran in his struggle. According to a spokesman, 'the fight will be to secure a better status for the Catholic clergy in England...it is hoped this appeal will be responded to by the clergy and the laity of the Catholic Church and other friends of justice.'[74]

In autumn 1897, a faint but clear offer of peace came from Mattock Lane. O'Halloran claimed that 'we interfere with no man...there is room enough in this world for all Christian men to labour for souls.'[75] He also acknowledged that his words and actions had caused some anxiety and grief among the Ealing Catholics. Archbishop's House and the Benedictines, however, did not respond. The prospect of compromise quickly disappeared: the firebrand replaced the olive branch, and the local press again became his platform. 'The Cardinal,' O'Halloran thundered, 'has no more right to send the monks into my mission and attack me...than a highway man has a right by violence to knock down and plunder a respectable citizen, and then abuse him.'[76] He accused Cardinal Vaughan of 'an abuse of his jurisdiction and of gross injustice in bringing monks into Ealing.' In spite of the language, O'Halloran continued to proclaim his loyalty to Rome, and he 'urged his flock...to avoid all those who in Ealing were causing division and bringing scandal on the Roman Church.'[77] Moreover, he tried to soothe Catholic consciences by stressing that 'the Pope removes all sentences of censures or excommunications on whatever course imparted.'

For nearly a year after this outburst, the religious climate of Ealing remained calm. Fr O'Halloran administered the sacraments to his small but loyal flock and continued to explore the possibility of compromise with the Benedictines. Both could work in the vineyard of Ealing. During the final days of 1898, O'Halloran again wrote to Edmund Ford at Downside and proposed that 'you monks have and carry on a separate mission on the Castle Bar Road...there is room enough and to spare for both missions.'[78] 'If you do this, the cause is ended,' he promised the Benedictine superior. But O'Halloran could not veil his anxiety. He threatened that, if no suitable agreement were reached, he would publish a book of documents which would expose the duplicity of Cardinal Vaughan and the Benedictines.[79] 'Rome will no doubt read the book, and all England and the Catholic world will look on to see *if you monks* succeed in your aggression.'[80] The option appeared clear:' Once more I offer you the choice of a separate mission here and let me undisturbed or my public vindication of my position.' Again, O'Halloran did not get the satisfaction of an answer from Downside, and again he retreated temporarily from the field of battle. This cease fire lasted nearly four years.

During this time, O'Halloran began to concentrate his time and energy on his mission, and, in spite of ecclesiastical censure, his small congregation drawn from Ealing's middle-class population, did not die. A census of churches in London conducted in 1904 revealed that approximately sixty-five people attended O'Halloran's Sunday morning mass and forty-three the evening service.[81] In the following year, the *Middlesex County Times* carried a report on O'Halloran's Corpus Christi celebration and noted that 'at the early mass large numbers of parishioners received the bread of life in Holy Communion.'[82]

Fr O'Halloran's rebellious activities became infectious. The rhetoric became more radical, and he began to sound like the leader of an organised party. Some clergy began to listen. In September 1902, O'Halloran announced: 'I take upon myself the responsibility of spokesman for the reforming secular clergy.'[83] Without giving any details or supplying a list of names, he also alleged that he had been 'elected Subsidiary Bishop by "a number of secular priests.'"[84] The *Daily Chronicle* carried the story and reported that the Ealing priest planned 'to lead forth the secular clergy of England in battle array against their ecclesiastical superiors.' O'Halloran's programme sounded similar to that of the priests who had argued for the Restoration of the Hierarchy during the last century. 'We ask for the right of free speech in Synod; we ask for a free Catholic Press; we ask for kindness and fatherly advice from our bishops; [and] we ask for trial by canonical procedure.'[85] But there was 'no intention to deny the rights and claims of the Pope,' he quickly added.[86]

O'Halloran gained an ally in 1902 in his campaign against Cardinal Vaughan. Arthur Galton, an ex-Roman Catholic priest who had converted back to Anglicanism, threw in his lot with O'Halloran, and together they organized the so-called 'Revolt from Rome.' Galton announced that approximately 150 secular priests (who had no intention of breaking with the Roman Catholic Church) were in a state of 'revolt' against their bishops. But when challenged to produce the names of these rebels, he politely refused. O'Halloran's influence in 'Revolt from Rome' soon became apparent. 'The grievances of the secular clergy,' Galton declared, 'are increased by the swelling numbers and the pernicious influence of the religious orders and congregations.'[87]

Another priest soon joined O'Halloran and Galton. In January 1903, the press announced that the first chapel associated with the 'revolt' had opened on 25 January at nearby Gunnersbury. According to the article, it 'is intended as an expression of the dissatisfaction of many priests and laymen with certain details of internal government in the Church' and not separation from Rome. The paper also prophesied that 'other churches in revolt' would soon appear in Acton and Hanwell. But this programme of clerical defiance died quickly. The movement's first convert, Herbert Ignatius Beale, soon parted company. Beale, a convert from Anglicanism and a past disciple of Ignatius of Llanthony, had also been taken in by Bishop Bagshawe of Nottingham. In February 1903, he publicly announced that he was no longer associated with O'Halloran and Galton.[88] The inability to attract numbers and the failure to substantiate its claims of membership and support helped to destroy this clerical grievance committee by summer 1903. The failure of the Roman Catholic authorities and press to take it seriously also contributed to its demise.

O'Halloran could not enlist the secular clergy in his campaign against Cardinal Vaughan, and his attempt to play the Irish card also failed to create sympathy and support for his cause. Because of the troubles caused by his involvement in the 1886 general election and the Home Rule movement, O'Halloran tried to stay clear of Irish politics. His only public remarks on the subject were made in 1910. When asked what party Irish Roman Catholics should support in the next election Fr O'Halloran, not surprisingly, maintained that 'Irish Catholics have nothing whatever to expect from the return of the Conservatives to power.' Drawing attention to ' the declaration of the Liberal Prime Minister that full self-government for Ireland is the Liberal policy makes Home Rule for Ireland a leading issue in the coming election,' he informed readers of the local paper that 'all Irish Catholics will give an unbroken vote for the Liberals in this supremely critical hour.'[89]

O'Halloran did not forsake his Irishness in his feud with Vaughan: the cardinal was portrayed as a bigot and O'Halloran as a poor, persecuted Irish priest. According to O'Halloran's testimony, Cardinal Vaughan had referred to him as a 'beggarly Irish fellow.'[90] When O'Halloran questioned the rationale behind some of the cardinal's actions towards him, Vaughan allegedly replied to an associate that he wanted to 'starve out the beggarly Irishman.'[91] O'Halloran gloried in his background and proudly declared that he 'was born and brought up a pure, simple, Roman Catholic Irish boy.'[92] Moreover, the Irish race had a special devotion to Rome: 'It is characteristic of my race to stick to the Pope, even though we get "stepmotherly" treatment at times.'[93]

No great number of Irish Catholics, however, flocked to O'Halloran's standard; the membership of his mission was not even predominantly Irish. He could find no support on his native soil. The *Irish Catholic* reported that Fr O'Halloran had 'been in Dublin twice within the past year collecting, and now we have a precious trio collecting in his name,'[94] and the public was warned not to contribute any funds until the written permission of the archbishop had been given. In the following year, the *Freeman's Journal* printed a story about a man collecting on behalf of Fr O'Halloran and told its readers not to donate any money unless the individual possessed a letter of introduction from Cardinal Vaughan and the local bishop.[95]

The Benedictines also worked to build up their mission. On 5 January 1899, an energetic and far-sighted monk, Dom Gilbert Dolan, arrived in Ealing to take charge of the monastic foundation. Dom Gilbert purchased land and began the construction of a new church. The congregation had grown considerably, and by 1903 he could report that approximately 500 people attended Sunday mass at St Benedict's Church.[96] Dom Gilbert's strong insistence on a parish school mirrored his optimism, and his arguments also reflected some anxiety about O'Halloran, who showed no signs of surrender. A month after his arrival, Dom Gilbert urged Downside to consider the building of a school:' It won't do to leave the ground open to O'Halloran.'[97] A prosperous school—and not confrontation—would silence their antagonist. Again, in 1902, he argued that 'if it is of importance to "snuff out" O'Halloran it might be said generally that the more St Benedict's becomes a centre of importance and influence the more superfluous and undignified will the position of O'Halloran appear.'[98] He noted that the informed element of the population recognised O'Halloran as a sham, but 'the great majority view the matter very differently.' 'Among the best means to recover our position,' he believed, 'is the establishment of a well-conducted High School.' Consequently, Downside approved his plan for a school, and it opened later in the year.

The apparent success and determination of the Benedictines continued to trouble O'Halloran. Again he embarked upon a course of compromise to save his mission. In 1903, he tried to reason with Aidan Gasquet, the abbot president of the English Benedictine Congregation. O'Halloran did not mince words; he appealed to the 'Christian character of the whole Benedictine Order' in an effort to resolve the impasse.[99] His arguments sounded familiar: the 'title to the Ealing mission...rests on fraud'; and 'I am the valid Rector.' Gasquet was silent. Three weeks later, O'Halloran sent another letter to Downside, but this time the rhetoric sounded more cautious. He asked Gasquet to support him and 'to demand that Rome should grant an independent commission to be convened in London...to investigate our claims— and thus put an end to this dreadful scandal which is detracting the Church in this diocese.'[100] O'Halloran clung to his claim that he was an 'incorporated secular of Westminster' and begged Gasquet to work with him for a peaceful and just settlement. His insensitive choice of words, however, revealed the magnitude of the problem: 'I appeal to you—the Superior General of a numerous, wealthy, and powerful religious order—not to take a mean advantage of the isolated position in which every secular priest is placed to capture my mission and income by brute force and not by the justice and equality of canonical process.'

The directness, simplicity and brevity of Gasquet's response must have infuriated O'Halloran. The Benedictine offered little solace.' I fear that I cannot in any way help you to regularize your position at Ealing, because it is essentially for you to settle with your Bishop.'[101] Throughout September and October 1903, O'Halloran continued to bombard Gasquet with requests to intervene. The letters reflected a growing desperation. 'There is the more peaceful way of compromise,' he suggested.[102] This is a huge district [and] the population here has been increased by thousands since the quarrel began in 1896.' And again: 'There is room enough for two missions and work for many priests.'

Aidan Gasquet simply reiterated that the issue was 'so plainly a question between the Archbishop and yourself.'[103]

In June 1903, O'Halloran's old enemy, Cardinal Vaughan, died; in September, Francis Bourne was translated to Westminster. During the following month, O'Halloran wrote to Bourne and asked 'for an interview to see if we could bring about peace.'[104] The new archbishop declined, but gave his blessing to another meeting between the priest and the vicar general, Patrick Fenton. According to O'Halloran's recollection, Monsignor Fenton made a proposal: the Ealing priest should consider 'a transfer to a diocese in England which is neither Westminster nor Middlesbrough.' O'Halloran balked and told the vicar general that 'the late Cardinal was a most dishonourable man .' His priestly reputation had 'been so damaged by the Benedictine monks and so vilified by Cardinal Vaughan that nothing can induce me to accept any proposal that would lead the public to believe that I was in the wrong.'[105] According to the Ealing cleric, the bishops of England were 'mean, crafty, unreliable, and dishonest'; and he would 'refuse any offer which will not recognize my permanence as Rector of the Ealing Mission.' The Roman Catholic community in Ealing should be divided between the Benedictines and his mission. If this solution presented a difficulty, the case should be settled by an impartial ecclesiastical court.

By autumn 1903, Fr O'Halloran's attempt to negotiate a compromise with the Roman Catholic authorities had floundered. His desire to work through ecclesiastical channels was abruptly destroyed by some remarks made by Archbishop Bourne during a March 1904 visit to Ealing. Bourne castigated O'Halloran and warned the area's Roman Catholics to avoid and shun him. According to Dom Gilbert Dolan, the archbishop told the congregation that 'we cannot shut our eyes to the special difficulty that attaches to the building up the Catholic Church in this district. Unfortunately, there is a schismatical chapel within the limits of this district...[and] the existence of that chapel is an act of open schism.'[106] On the day following this inopportune sermon, O'Halloran protested to Cardinal Rafael Merry Del Val, the English-born secretary of state, condemning Bourne's remarks and requesting an ecclesiastical investigation. 'I ask your Eminence...to bring the sad condition of this Ealing mission, torn by schism, before the personal knowledge of the Holy Father, and let him know our desire for a Canonical Inquiry.'[107] Also, in reaction to Archbishop Bourne's statements, members of O'Halloran's parish published an open letter which charged Bourne with favouritism towards the monks and urged him to cancel any future visits to St Benedict's Church.[108]

The Ealing Benedictines responded quickly to this latest outburst. Dom Gilbert sent copies of the press report to Downside, Archbishop's House, Cardinal Merry Del Val and Aidan Gasquet. Dom Gilbert contemplated legal action against his Mattock Lane rival. He informed Downside that a solicitor friend urged that someone make 'an application to the courts to obtain an injunction to prevent O'Halloran calling himself Roman Catholic Rector of Ealing.'[109] Several Irish bishops and numerous nuns had asked Archbishop Bourne to silence or remove Fr O'Halloran. Bourne, however, cautioned against the law courts and urged Dom Gilbert to proceed slowly. 'Personally I should not like a legal action against Father O'Halloran since I gathered from you that his supporters are few in numbers, and it is better to ignore him as much as possible.'[110] 'Notoriety would be a gain to him.'

In desperation, O'Halloran warmly embraced the columns of the press to regain credibility. During the next several months, he reprinted the old documents, reviewed the well-known history of his struggles with the church authorities and the monks and maintained that he had been robbed of his rightful title to Ealing. In his demand for some judgement from Rome, he displayed anger and frustration that 'no answer has yet come from Rome.'[111] In another attempt to garner support, O'Halloran denounced the monks to a fellow cleric and introduced the question of Catholic education for Ealing. The Benedictine school catered to the wealthy, and consequently 'poor Catholic children have been sent to Protestant schools.'[112] This tactic failed; the unnamed priest quietly forwarded the vengeful letter to Dom Gilbert.

A fragile calm soon shrouded Ealing, and for three years the suburb remained quiet. But in 1907, Rome finally intervened. In April, the Congregation of Propaganda Fide thanked Archbishop Bourne for his patience and expressed relief 'that the troubles excited by him [O'Halloran] are gradually vanishing...due to a lack of supporters and men.'[113] Noting that Fr O'Halloran had frequently addressed petitions to the congregation, the cardinal prefect directed Bourne to advise O'Halloran to abandon 'his rebellion and disobedience and to go away from Ealing.' Propaganda directed Bourne to remind Fr O'Halloran of its earlier decision in 1897, but also offered a compromise: if O'Halloran 'turns to a better attitude, we can see what to decide about his case.' Archbishop Bourne conveyed this information to O'Halloran, who arrogantly interpreted it as a victory for his crusade. He gloated to Gasquet that 'Rome has condemned his [Vaughan's] powers in this Ealing dispute.'[114] 'It is now for you and your monks to decide whether or not you will support Cardinal Vaughan in disobeying Rome and in keeping members of my flock in rebellion against me their lawful pastor.' As the religious temperature remained high, the controversy crept into the chambers of the local educational committee.

O'Halloran believed that a school associated with his mission would give it respectability and a sense of stability, and he opened one in 1904. This operation, however, drained needed funds from his parochial coffers, and he tried to have the school placed on the rates in 1904. No action was taken, and he withdrew his petition.[115] O'Halloran approached the Ealing Educational Committee in 1910 to ask for the needed financial assistance, and contention and strife came to Ealing again. A group loyal to the English Benedictines, the Ealing Catholic Federation, began a movement to sabotage O'Halloran's plan. A delegation approached the Ealing Educational Committee and 'objected to this particular school being regarded as a Catholic school, inasmuch as the application for its establishment did not proceed from the Catholic ecclesiastical authorities.'[116] In short, it was not a Roman Catholic institution. O'Halloran took offense and accused the Benedictines of being the source of this scandalous charge: 'The Ealing Catholic Federation is a political organization presided over by the Benedictine monk, the Abbot Ford, O.S.B.'[117] Even *The Tablet* got involved and printed a letter which warned its readers that O'Halloran was a suspended priest and had 'forfeited all claims to the heritage of Roman Catholicism.[118] Consequently, the history of this dispute, the old arguments and documents again appeared in the secular newspapers. The Roman Catholic press responded. The *Catholic Herald* pointed out that 'a marriage performed by a suspended priest is null and void in the eyes of the Church, just as a marriage performed in a registry office alone is null and void.'[119] In the following month, the same paper alleged that Fr O'Halloran had been consecrated an Old Catholic bishop in 1899.[120]

In spite of this hostile atmosphere, O'Halloran still believed that Rome would reverse its earlier decisions and vindicate his claim to Ealing. A number of his parishioners petitioned Rome on his behalf, but the response was more final and damning than previous ones. The hope for compromise and negotiation had evaporated. A document from the Sacred Congregation of the Council informed Archbishop's House of the petition from O'Halloran's parish and directed Cardinal Bourne to inform the recalcitrant priest of the following decision:

> Since the aforesaid priest actively persists in his contumacy and rebellion against ecclesiastical authority and, despite the warnings and paternal exhortations of the Sacred Congregation of Propaganda Fide, has for a long time remained under the censures thus incurred, no

Catholic may lawfully make common cause with him,
much less acknowledge his spiritual jurisdiction.[121]

Finally, the letter pleaded with Father O'Halloran to abandon his schismatic and rebellious position and to comply with the earlier rulings from Rome.

Cast as a renegade by Roman Catholic authorities, O'Halloran's last chance of legitimacy seemed to depend on the findings of the Ealing Educational Committee. A decision was reached in September 1911: O'Halloran's request was denied. The committee questioned whether he could successfully remedy some of the deficiencies discovered at his school. In reference to O'Halloran's claim that his school was Roman Catholic, the report stated: 'I cannot ignore the fact that, on the evidence before me, he is not in accord with the authorities of the Roman Catholic Church.'[122] Because of the public scandal, parents might refrain from sending their children to this school, and 'for this reason there is some uncertainty as to whether the present numbers can be maintained.' This decision occasioned Fr O'Halloran's last barrage against the hierarchy and the Benedictines of Ealing.

In a long and emotional statement printed in the *Middlesex County Times,* O'Halloran claimed that the inquiry 'was a belated farce' 'brought about by the wire pulling of the monks, who did not produce one ratepayer...at the inquiry.'[123] He was a victim of 'religious persecution at the instigation of the Benedictines.' O'Halloran's wrath against the monks exploded: 'Now at the instigation of the Benedictine Monks, who hold no mandate from the Pope to destroy our schools, whose ecclesiastical claims to enter Ealing rest on deliberate fraud...[to] set aside our rights as citizens and ratepayers...is not just governmental administration.' The Roman Catholic press, on the other hand, simply printed the findings of the educational committee along with O'Halloran's letter of protest.

Fr O'Halloran's outburst in 1911 was the swan song of his controversial career; except for a few lapses his anti-Benedictine language declined. In 1913, a letter from O'Halloran appeared in the local paper which informed his supporters of the monastic conspiracy still directed against him. 'Meanwhile it is my duty to warn you against all misguided persons who seek to lead you astray by their fanaticism or ignorance of Christian teaching and Catholic principles.'[124] In the same year, O'Halloran appealed for justice to the present superior of the Ealing monks, Cuthbert Butler, abbot of Downside. He summed up the history of the long feud: the monks 'have a church here in opposition to me the lawful priest'; numerous fraudulent documents supported their claim; and his title to the

Ealing mission came from 'the *Supreme* authority of the Holy See and General Councils.'[125] Butler chose not to answer.

After nearly two decades of contention and rebellion in Ealing, Rome finally took decisive action against Fr Richard O'Halloran. The Sacred Consistorial Congregation formally excommunicated the Ealing priest in April 1914.[126] The official notification cited the scandalous words and actions which had produced public schism. Surprisingly, the excommunication brought peace and silence to the religious atmosphere of Ealing. Diatribes from his pulpit and attacks in the press ceased, and O'Halloran remained at his Mattock Lane residence in active retirement for nearly ten years. In spite of the Roman prohibition, he continued to say mass 'for himself and his congregation, which steadily dwindled as its members were removed by death,' and 'there was no influx of new life to compensate for the loss.'[127]

Unreconciled to the Roman Catholic Church, Richard O'Halloran died of pneumonia on 13 October 1925 after a week-long bout. A legend developed that the superior of the Ealing Benedictines, Prior Benedict Kuypers, asked the diocesan authorities for permission to visit O'Halloran and to bring him the sacraments, but this was refused. After Fr O'Halloran died, Prior Benedict viewed the body and telephoned Archbishop's House for instructions, especially regarding the Blessed Sacrament.[128] Because of possible legal complications, Cardinal Bourne told the prior that the sacrament could be removed only if the person in charge of the church, the housekeeper, gave her consent. Prior Kuypers decided to wait until after the funeral to approach the woman.

Two days after O'Halloran's death, his housekeeper, Miss Webb, visited Archbishop's House to plead for a priest to conduct a requiem, but this was refused. So laymen conducted a prayer service at the old Mattock Lane church and presided at a graveside ceremony in nearby Hanwell. After the interment, Prior Benedict visited the housekeeper. She expressed her willingness for the prior to take the sacrament, but she also hoped that the cardinal would send a priest to conduct services at O'Halloran's old mission. After some negotiations, Prior Benedict took the Blessed Sacrament. But no priest was sent, and the rebel church was finally closed.

The O'Halloran episode is more than a story about a cantankerous cleric who spent his priestly life in conflict with ecclesiastical authorities and religious orders. The case of Fr Richard O'Halloran sheds some light on Victorian and Edwardian Roman Catholicism. Despite its boast of unity and singleness of purpose, the Catholic community in England did suffer the same internal conflicts that it always attributed to the Established Church. Violent clashes between bishop and priest, the jealousy and suspicion which coloured the relationship of the secular to the religious priesthood and questions involving jurisdiction and the rights of the priests existed beneath the apparently calm surface. The eruption of these tensions during the life of Fr O'Halloran demonstrated that Roman Catholicism faced problems as intense as its Anglican counterpart.

Notes

MHA = Mill Hill Archives; *MCT*= *Middlesex County Times; DC= Daily Chronicle;*
AAW = Archives of the Archdiocese of Westminster; EAA = Ealing Abbey Archives;
CT = *Catholic Times; CH* = *Catholic Herald;* DAA = Downside Abbey Archives

[1] O. Chadwick, *The Victorian Church,* London 1970, i. 278.

[2] Ibid.

[3] J. Bossy, *The English Catholic Community, 1570-1850,* London 1979, 361.

[4] J. Derek Holmes, *More Roman than Rome: English Catholicism in the Nineteenth Century,* London 1970, 59.

[5] Quoted in E. Norman, *The English Catholic Church in the Nineteenth Century,* Oxford 1984, 81.

[6] Ibid. 83.

[7] Bossy, op. cit. 360.

[8] R. Gray, *Cardinal Manning: a Biography,* London 1985, 251.

[9] Founded by Archbishop Herbert Vaughan in 1866, the Mill Hill Fathers opened St Joseph's College in London to train its members for future work in the missions. The archives contain a file on Richard O'Halloran.

[10] O'Halloran to Benoit (the superior of the Mill Hill Fathers), 2 Dec., 1880, O'Halloran File, MHA.

[11] Log Book, MHA.

[12] Holmes, *More Roman than Rome,* 174.

[13] O'Halloran to Vaughan, 19 Feb. 1881, printed in *Cardinal Vaughan and Father O'Halloran: The Rights of the Secular Priests Vindicated,* London 1901. Published by O'Halloran, this pamphlet details the history of the relationship between the two clerics and also contains some of the early correspondence.

[14] O'Halloran to Vaughan, 28 Jan. 1882, MHA.

[15] Bagshawe to Vaughan, 3 Feb. 1882, MHA.

[16] Bagshawe to O'Halloran, 8 May 1882, MHA. O'Halloran later complained to Vaughan that his mission was a 'most immoral place,' and that he had to denounce this public wickedness. He also admitted that he had allowed the school mistress to sleep in his house but claimed he knew of no law forbidding this. Finally, he denied the charges of sexual impropriety. O'Halloran to Vaughan, 11 May 1882, MHA.

[17] O'Halloran to Vaughan, 13 May 1882, MHA.

[18] O'Halloran to Benoit, 21 Feb. 1884, MHA.

[19] *MCT,* 27 July 1897.

[20] *DC,* 20 July 1897.

[21] *MCT,* 7 Aug. 1897.

[22] *Secular Priests Vindicated,* 16.

[23] *MCT,* 15 Aug. 1905.

[24] *Secular Priests Vindicated,* '20.

25 Cardinal Miecislas Ledochowski to Vaughan, 4 May 1894, Vaughan Papers, AAW.

26 O'Halloran Statement, 4 June 1894, O'Halloran File, AAW. O'Halloran later declared that this document was fraudulent, and throughout his life he continued to argue that he belonged to the archdiocese of Westminster.

27 Herbert Cardinal Vaughan, *Notification to the Catholics Living in Ealing and the Neighbourhood*, London 1897, EAA.

28 O'Halloran Statement, 13 July 1894, O'Halloran File, AAW.

29 *The Tablet*, 28 Nov. 1896.

30 Clipping Book, EAA.

31 *Tablet*, 28 Nov. 1896.

32 *DC*, 24 July 1897.

33 *MCT*, 16 Sept. 1899.

34 For an early history of Ealing Abbey and Cardinal Vaughan's plans for the Benedictine monks at his new cathedral see Chapters X & XI of this book and R. Kollar, 'The Arrival of the Benedictines in London,' *Tjurunga*.

35 Vaughan, *Notification*.

36 For a biography of Edmund Ford and his role in the Benedictine foundation in Ealing see B. Hicks, *Hugh Edmund Ford*, London 1947.

37 O'Halloran to Ford, 17 June 1896, printed in *DC*, 28 July 1897.

38 *Secular Priests Vindicated*, 3.

39 Barry to O'Halloran, 16 Sept. 1896, printed in *MCT*, 23 Sept.

40 Vaughan, *Notification*.

41 Johnson to Ford, 7 Dec. 1896, Ford Papers, EAA.

42 Johnson to Ford, 30 Jan. 1897, Ford Papers, EAA.

43 Vaughan to Ford, 11 Mar. 1897, Ford Papers, EAA.

44 O'Halloran to John Brenan, dean of Westminster archdiocese, 22 Mar. 1897, Ford Papers, EAA.

45 Ford to O'Halloran, 2 Apr. 1897, printed in *MCT*, 30 Sept. 1899.

46 Barry to O'Halloran, 8 Apr. 1897, Ford Papers, EAA. This document is a copy of the original sent to O'Halloran.

47 Vaughan to Bulbeck, 9 Apr. 1897, Ford Papers, EAA.

48 Vaughan, *Notification*.

49 Snow to Ford, 20 Apr. 1897, Ford Papers, EAA. Snow was the titular abbot of Glastonbury.

50 Snow to Ford, 2 July 1897, Ford Papers, EAA.

51 Barry to Bulbeck, 26 Aug. 1897, Ford Papers, EAA.

52 Bulbeck to Ford, 1 Oct. 1897, Ford Papers, EAA.

53 Ledochowski to Vaughan, 19 May 1897, Vaughan Papers, AAW.

54 Ledochowski to O'Halloran, 20 May 1897, Vaughan Papers, AAW.

55 O'Halloran to Ledochowski, 31 May 1897, printed in *CT*, 6 Aug. 1897.

56 Vaughan, *Notification*.

57 O'Halloran to Vaughan, 26 July 1897, Ford Papers, EAA.

[58] Brenan to Bulbeck, 24 July 1897, Ford Papers, EAA.

[59] *MCT*, 19 June 1897.

[60] Ibid. 10 July 1897.

[61] *DC*, 22 July 1897.

[62] Ibid. 24 July 1897.

[63] Ibid. 26 July 1897.

[64] *Secular Priests Vindicated*, 7.

[65] Dolan to Ford, 18 July 1899, Dolan Papers, EAA.

[66] Dolan to Ford, 18 Aug. 1900, Dolan Papers, EAA.

[67] *DC*, 24 July 1897.

[68] *CH*, 23 July 1897.

[69] Ibid. 30. July 1897.

[70] *The Universe*, 24 July 1897.

[71] *CT*, 6 Aug., 1 Oct. 1897.

[72] Ibid. 8 Oct. 1897.

[73] *DC*, 22 July 1897.

[74] MCT, 7 Aug. 1897.

[75] Ibid. 3 Sept. 1897.

[76] Ibid. 22 Oct. 1897.

[77] Ibid. 19 Nov. 1897.

[78] O'Halloran to Ford, 20 Dec. 1898, Ford Papers, EAA.

[79] *Secular Priests Vindicated*.

[80] O'Halloran to Ford, 20 Dec. 1898, Ford Papers, EAA.

[81] R. Mudie-Smith, *The Religious Life of London*, London 1904.

[82] *MCT*, 1 July 1905.

[83] *DC*, 2 Sept. 1902.

[84] Ibid. 4 Sept. 1902.

[85] Ibid. 11 Sept. 1902.

[86] Ibid. 20 Sept. 1902.

[87] *St James Gazette*, 30 Aug. 1902.

[88] *DC*, 5 Feb. 1903·

[89] *MCT*, 1 Jan. 1910.

[90] Ibid. 23 Sept. 1899.

[91] *Cardinal Vaughan and Father O'Halloran: The Ealing Case Stated*, London 1901, 6.

[92] Ibid. 3.

[93] *MCT*, 16 Sept. 1899.

[94] *Irish Catholic*, 21 July 1901.

[95] *Freeman's Journal*, 25 Mar. 1902.

[96] *Spiritualia Ministeria*, London 1903, EAA.

97 Dolan to Ford, 27 Feb. 1899, Dolan Papers, EAA. In his invitation to the Benedictines, Cardinal Vaughan had stipulated that the monks could not begin a secondary school without his permission. By 1902 he had reconsidered the situation and gave his permission to establish one at Ealing. The uncertain future of St Charles Bayswater probably influenced the cardinal's change of mind.

98 G. Dolan, 'Report to Downside,' 1902, EAA.

99 O'Halloran to Gasquet, 21 Aug. 1903, Gasquet Papers, DAA.

100 O'Halloran to Gasquet, 14 Sept. 1903, Gasquet Papers, DAA.

101 Gasquet to O'Halloran, Sept. 1903, Gasquet Papers, DAA.

102 O'Halloran to Gasquet, 16 Sept. 1903, Gasquet Papers, DAA.

103 Gasquet to O'Halloran, 29 Oct. 1903, Gasquet Papers, DAA.

104 Quoted in O'Halloran to Gasquet, 18 Oct. 1903, Gasquet Papers, DAA.

105 O'Halloran to Fenton, 17 Oct. 1903, Gasquet Papers, DAA.

106 Dolan to Ford, 22 Mar. 1904, Ford Papers, EAA.

107 O'Halloran to Merry Del Val, 21 Mar. 1904, printed in *MCT,* 26 Mar. 1904.

108 *MCT,* 26 Mar. 1904.

109 Dolan to Ford, 27 Mar. 1904, Dolan Papers, EAA.

110 Bourne to Dolan, 28 Mar. 1904, Dolan Papers, EAA.

111 *MCT,* 2 Apr. 1904.

112 O'Halloran to (?), 10 Apr. 1904, Dolan Papers, EAA. This letter is part of the Dolan Papers, and there is no hint of the identity of the priest who eventually sent it to Dolan.

113 S. Congregazione de Propaganda Fide to Bourne, 2 Apr. 1907, Roman Letters vii, AAW.

114 O'Halloran to Gasquet, 27 May 1905, Gasquet Papers, DAA.

115 *MCT,* 5 Feb. 1910.

116 Ibid. 5 Nov. 1910.

117 Ibid. 12 Nov. 1910. The spokesman later admitted that Ford was the chairman of this organization, but he also maintained 'that Catholic parents cannot in conscience send their children to any school over which the Rev Mr. O'Halloran exercises any sort of control,' ibid. 26 Nov. 1910.

118 *Tablet,* 12 Nov. 1910.

119 *CH,* 28 Jan. 1911.

120 Ibid. 4 Feb. 1911.

121 Sacred Congregation of the Council to Bourne, 5 Dec. 1910, Roman Letters vii, AAW.

122 *MCT,* 30 Sept. 1911.

123 Ibid. 7 Oct. 1911.

124 *Ealing Gazette,* 26 Oct. 1913.

125 O'Halloran to Butler, 29 Dec. 1913, O'Halloran Papers, DAA.

126 *Notificatio,* 16 Apr. 1914, Roman Letters viii, AAW.

127 *MCT,* 17 Oct. 1925.

128 B. Kuypers, 'Memo on Fr O'Halloran,' EAA.

CHAPTER XIII

THE RELUCTANT PRIOR: BISHOP WULSTAN PEARSON OF LANCASTER

Although the Irish accounted for a large proportion of the English Roman Catholic Church during the opening decades of the twentieth century, the Church 'was led by Englishmen too and mostly pretty local ones.'[1] Bourne, McIntyre, Leighton Williams, Henshaw, Thorman, and Singleton represent a few of the native sons who eventually became prelates of their local sees. Likewise, Thomas Wulstan Pearson (1870-1938), born in Preston, was appointed the first bishop of the Diocese of Lancaster in 1925. Dom Wulstan had previously served in the Benedictine parish in Liverpool, an assignment which he cherished. Asked to leave this northern post to become the first prior of Downside Abbey's foundation at Ealing, he unsuccessfully tried to resist. Reluctantly and with serious reservations he followed his abbot's wishes and moved south. His years as the superior of this young priory, however, represent a traumatic break with the sense of personal fulfillment he experienced in Liverpool, but the barren and trying years also served to strengthen his longing and commitment to the pastoral ministry.

Cardinal Herbert Vaughan wanted English Benedictine monks to conduct the liturgy at the new Westminster Cathedral and he invited the monks of Downside Abbey to settle in the capital's western suburb of Ealing in 1896. From there, they could travel daily into London to chant the Divine Office in the precincts of the cathedral. But Vaughan's dream failed to materialize. The refusal of the English Benedictines to support and assist a group of French monks from Solesmes Abbey, whom the Cardinal had also foolishly invited to staff his cathedral, and the bruised feelings of the secular clergy, who felt snubbed at not being offered the honour, forced Vaughan to entrust the liturgy to his cathedral chapter.[2] The English Benedictines, however, did not leave the environs of London.

The Downside mission in Ealing prospered. The parish, founded in 1897, took firm root, and plans for the construction of a church to accommodate the area's Roman Catholic population could not be ignored or postponed. In 1902, Dom Sebastian Cave opened a school to educate young Catholic boys in traditional Benedictine values and ideals. Moreover, a core of Downside monks continued to live the monastic life. And success smiled on these endeavours. Parish officials proudly estimated that the average number of adults who attended Sunday mass during 1913 reached six hundred and fifty. In 1914, the enrolment at the school stood at seventy boys. The physical plant had also been enlarged several times during the early years of the twentieth century to meet the demands of the monks, parishioners, and school boys. But, many began to ask, did the monastic community have a future at Ealing? Should it be trimmed or even abandoned to concentrate resources at Downside? Should Ealing remain exclusively a parish and school? Some Benedictines, however, saw a bright and promising future for the London foundation: it might evolve into a dependent priory; and eventually become an abbey independent of its mother house. The Abbot of Downside, Cuthbert Butler, became the spokesperson for those who wanted the Ealing mission to develop into a canonical priory.

Even before becoming abbot, Cuthbert Butler had taken a keen interest in the unlimited potential of Ealing. Writing from Cambridge to Abbot Edmund Ford in 1902, Butler stated that 'Ealing is at present in an *impasse*.'[3] I have been thinking over it a good deal and I feel moved to give you the outcome of my cogitations.' As a solution, he suggested that Ealing should become a proper Benedictine priory. A suitable superior, for example, could '...run Ealing as a Priory...' But Downside must enthusiastically commit manpower and capital to their London foundation. If it continued to follow a pusillanimous policy, Dom Cuthbert argued that Downside 'better give it up at once' and then try to sell the property to Cardinal Vaughan or to another religious order. Any half-hearted approach should be avoided.

In 1906, Cuthbert Butler succeeded Abbot Ford as Downside's superior, and he resumed his dream of a strong and independent monastic community at Ealing. This new initiative came from Abbot Ford, who had gone to Ealing after his retirement from the abbatial office. In a letter to Abbot Butler, Ford expressed his view that the time had finally arrived to make Ealing a conventual priory. Butler agreed, and appointed a committee to study and plan Ealing's immediate future. He also composed his own report, the 'Ealing Comprehensive Statement,' and distributed it to the committee a week before its meeting, which was scheduled for 5 July 1906.

The title accurately reflected the scope and extent of the abbot's statement. Including his proposals to elevate Ealing to the status of priory, Butler also presented detailed notes on the following topics: property questions, money already expended on the foundation, plans for additional construction, possible sources of income, and the future of the school. In spite of some misgivings, the abbot maintained that Ealing actually represented a monastic gold mine: 'there can be no practical doubt that our Ealing properties...will ultimately become very valuable; so that whatever the outlay on them may be...it may be recovered and more than recovered.'[4] Consequently, the possibility of a proper and vigorous monastic life seemed within reach, and Butler argued that with the addition of a few monks 'Ealing is now in a position that it could become a "Dependent Priory."' He painted a grand and bold picture of Ealing's future: '...there is nothing extravagant in the idea that Ealing Priory should in time become an independent autonomous Benedictine Monastery in London.'

The committee which met at Ealing concurred with Abbot Butler's recommendations:

> The view was strongly held that if Ealing eventually becomes a real, autonomous Benedictine Monastery in London all the expenditure on it will have been worthwhile...This is the time to carry out our original undertaking...to make Ealing a conventual house...and that as soon as it can be done Ealing should receive subjects for itself, and be established as an independent Conventual Priory.[5]

The committee also formulated several resolutions to be submitted to the Downside Council, which would meet later in the month. The Council was reminded of the requirement stipulated by *Diu Quidem* and the Constitutions of the English Benedictine Congregation which governed the establishment of any new priory, namely, a community of at least six monks under a prior appointed by the abbot of the founding monastery, the recitation of the Divine Office in choir, and the observance of the *vita perfecte communis*. Finally, the committee endorsed the following statement: 'Such a Priory would be at first a Dependent Priory, but it is proposed that, as soon as permission can be obtained, subjects should be professed for Ealing, and that every effort should be made to develop as rapidly as possible into a self-standing independent Benedictine Monastery.'

The Downside Council approved these recommendations at its meeting, and consequently its London foundation became Ealing Priory, canonically dependent on Downside. The Council supported the goal of future independence for the Ealing community, and it also suggested that it might be wise to explain this decision at the next conventual chapter, 'so that the community as a whole may be fully aware of the policy which is being pursued, and their sympathy and support secured for it.'[6]

The appointment of the first prior and the names of the monks who would live at this new dependent priory became Abbot Butler's next agenda item. After some correspondence and consultation, Butler quickly reached a decision on the membership. But the office of prior still had to be filled. After a meeting of the Downside Council on 28 July, which discussed the merits of several candidates, Abbot Butler sent each member of the new priory a letter which outlined his dream for the community, and he polled the monks on possible candidates for the job of prior. He also took the opportunity to reveal the mind of the Downside Council: 'the final opinion of the Council was clearly in favour of Fr. Wulstan Pearson but so far he has no knowledge of this, [and] I wish to sound the community before making the appointment.'[7] The Downside abbot also wanted the Ealing monks to consider whether the new prior should be both the monastic superior and headmaster of the priory school.

The name of Dom Wulstan was favourably received at Ealing. One monk, for example, told Abbot Butler that 'Fr. Wulstan would make an excellent superior and I should be very glad to work with him again, as I did so many years at Downside.'[8] Another did not mince words: he argued that Dom Wulstan outdistanced all other candidates 'as head of [the] mission or the whole place.'[9] But Dom Wulstan did not enkindle enthusiasm in the souls of all the Ealing monks. One individual supported him for the job of headmaster, but he did not think that 'Fr. Wulstan would make a good superior for this place, although if he is appointed I personally would not have any difficulty in working under him.'[10] Nonetheless, it became clear that the Downside Council, Abbot Butler, and the majority at Ealing wanted Dom Wulstan Pearson as prior. Moreover, the Ealing monks also voiced general support for combining the duties of the headmaster and the 'head priest,' the so-called 'old system,' in the office of prior.

Abbot Butler next had to convince Dom Wulstan, who was stationed at St. Mary's, Liverpool, to become Ealing's first prior. Born in 1870 in Preston, Dom Wulstan Pearson was educated at Douai and Downside, where he professed solemn vows in 1894. He was ordained a priest three years later. He began his monastic life as a teacher, and 'for nearly twenty years he taught in the school with remarkable success.'[11] Remembered as an accomplished teacher and a stern disciplinarian, he became First Prefect in 1902. After a long tenure at the school, Dom Wulstan was sent to Liverpool in 1912. At this assignment 'he took up his duties as if he had come straight from a seminary—he wanted to learn, not to teach, though it was obvious in a very short time that he was a real master, and an ideal pastor.' Dom Wulstan, moreover, loved his work at St. Mary's, and expected to remain there for many years.

Abbot Butler wrote to him on 7 August 1916, and informed him about the change in Ealing's ecclesiastical status, the membership of the new priory, and raised the question about the office of prior. 'It was I may say the unanimous feeling of the Council, accepted with approval and pleasure by the members of the Ealing community that you are the man to work the place.'[12] Abbot Butler's charge was direct and succinct: 'Accordingly, I hereby appoint you **PRIOR OF EALING**.' Butler then pointed out that the Prior of Ealing would function both as headmaster and head priest: 'the practical experience of the Jesuits is worth learning from in the working of such establishments.' Sensing that there might be some reluctance on the part of his candidate, Abbot Butler told Dom Wulstan that the job represented an 'important and responsible position [and] you will have good will and confidence of all...' He concluded on another positive and affirmative note: 'I have no doubt that you will find it congenial, as you will have...school work, and there is...an element in the mission you will deal with better than anyone there now.'

Shocked and stunned, Dom Wulstan replied in a whimsical but serious manner. 'Fr. Leander used to love dropping bombs,' he told his superior 'but the one you have just exploded is a real high explosive.'[13] He thanked Abbot Butler for the honour, but then confessed that 'the scheme is so vast and the ideas so new that I must have a day or two to pray about them and think over them before replying to you.'

On the following day, therefore, Dom Wulstan composed a long and passionate letter begging Abbot Butler to re-consider this unexpected and undesired change in his life. Expressing his surprise at the abbot's letter and trying to assure him that he had given the matter serious thought, Dom Wulstan stated his position: 'I am quite clear in my own mind that I am not the man for such a work and therefore beg of you to appoint someone else.'[14] Dom Wulstan proceeded to give his reasons. He argued that he was not prepared to deal with any postulants or novices the priory in Ealing might receive. Young people always appreciated him, the letter continued, but 'all I did inspire in them was a sort of fearful respect.' He added: 'If a group of boys was together talking and laughing my joining them was enough to break up the whole thing in a very few moments.' Secondly, he pointed out he did not have the necessary monastic training or experience to guide a fledgling foundation; school duties and work on the missions had snatched him away from the regular observance. 'I should be a fraud and guilty of the greatest rashness,' he pleaded with Abbot Butler 'if I undertook to...guide others in the highest of acts, that of the Monastic life.'

And Dom Wulstan continued to search for other excuses. He told Abbot Butler that 'the Head of a House like Ealing aspires to, should be...known in London and of some position too.' Reminding Butler that Abbot Ford, who had been superior at Ealing after his retirement, had excelled in this important aspect, Dom Wulstan confessed that he knew 'nobody and nobody knows or would know anything of me.' Lack of a financial mind, he also believed, presented another serious impediment. 'I know nothing about the first principles,' he emphasized, adding 'in about six months the whole business would be in such a muddle...' Moreover, Dom Wulstan believed that his brother's drinking problem would jeopardize his effectiveness as a monastic superior, and he explained to Abbot Butler that in the past his brother, while intoxicated, had sought him out several times in Liverpool. This did not create a scandal 'but in a place like Ealing it would be quite different and though the good people there would not consciously take up a different position to me...I should not like it to be the subject of conversation at 5 o'clock tea.' Dom Wulstan concluded his lengthy letter by pleading that 'there are many more reasons' which forced him to decline Abbot Butler's offer, and he told the abbot that his current job in Liverpool represented 'the happiest working years of my life.'

Abbot Butler responded immediately and addressed Dom Wulstan's request, which he described as 'very proper' and one which 'does credit to you [in] all sorts of ways.'[15] The abbot told Dom Wulstan that he would present the case to the Downside Council, but also reminded him that 'if after this I still think it right, I will call on you to submit yourself to my judgment.' Butler again reminded him of the strong support and backing he enjoyed from the Council and from the monks at Ealing and pointed out that 'the quite ideal person is not to be found for any office, abbot downwards—we can only hope for the one who for the whole is best, positively and negatively.' Abbot Butler also assured Dom Wulstan that he was sensitive about his brother's problems with alcohol and the embarrassment it might create in Ealing.

On the following day, Dom Wulstan replied and thanked Abbot Butler for his time and consideration and remarked that 'if the Council would only place themselves in my place they would advise aright.'[16] But the response from Downside smashed all hopes of a compromise. Butler told Dom Wulstan that he had read his letters to the Council and asked for their opinion. 'Their judgment,' the abbot reported, was 'unanimous and unhesitantly that you are clearly the right one for the post; and that being so, that the trouble about your brother being so should not stand in the way of your undertaking the important work to which you are destined.'[17] Abbot Ford, who had extensive personal knowledge of Ealing, attended the meeting at Downside and, according to Butler, stated that the parishioners were fair and gracious and 'even the worse would make no difference in the relations of the congregation to' Dom Wulstan. Abbot Butler's final word contained elements of gentle encouragement. 'And so,' he concluded 'perfectly clear intellectually, but with much emotional distress at putting this strain upon you, I confirm my former letter, with full confidence God will work it...right for you.'

Dom Wulstan accepted his new assignment with resignation and told his abbot that 'in obedience to your order I shall be at Ealing by the end of the week.'[18] But the new prior could still not hide his unhappiness. 'The more I think of it,' he revealed 'the more I am puzzled at the appointment.' 'Four years ago you told me' he continued 'and the Council did also, that my work was evidently on the mission in a big city.' His anxiety at the move became more apparent. 'I am puzzled...because after 20 years of teaching and close connection with boys the idea of renewing this does not appeal to me in the least.' Dom Wulstan realized, however, that even this plea would not change Butler's mind. 'I shall go to Ealing...with the full determination with God's help to make things go. If I do not succeed I promise you it shall not be my fault as far as I can help. And if I do not succeed I only beg of you now not to leave me out there but to move me at once.' Dom Wulstan obediently arrived at his new post in September 1916.

The *Downside Review* informed its readers of Ealing's new status as a Benedictine priory and revealed the name of its new superior. 'Our Mission at Ealing has now been made a properly constituted dependent priory of Downside,' the announcement read, and 'Dom Wulstan Pearson who did so much for Downside during the years he was Prefect, has been appointed prior.'[19] The article announced the membership of the new priory and noted that 'as may be expected, it was necessary for Downside to make some sacrifice for her offspring; and although we do not begrudge what we give, we mourn what we lose.' With his monks finally in place at Ealing, Abbot Butler approached Archbishop's House and notified Cardinal Francis Bourne that Ealing had become a dependent priory of Downside Abbey.

On 17 August, Butler wrote to the cardinal and told him of the appointment of Prior Wulstan as the new superior. Butler then drew attention to the change in ecclesiastical and monastic status. The abbot wrote 'that the church is completed [and] it makes sense to be the time to carry out the original idea of Ealing and make it a "dependent priory"...in which a regular community life will be observed.'[20] Consequently, 'the Superior will have the title of Prior.' Abbot Butler also expressed his hope that Ealing would develop into a centre of religious life and exert a strong influence throughout the London area. Two days later, Cardinal Bourne responded and thanked the abbot for the information about the changes at Ealing. He gave his archiepiscopal blessing: 'I quite approve of the suggested arrangements.'[21]

The shortage of manpower at the London priory confronted the new prior immediately. Earlier requests had fallen on deaf ears at Downside, and the need for Roman Catholic chaplains to serve on the Continent placed additional burdens on Abbot Butler's Somerset monastery. Prior Wulstan emphasized the seriousness of the problem at Ealing by petitioning the Abbot for a temporary dispensation from the recitation of prime in choir. Abbot Butler granted this request. In another letter to the prior, Butler addressed the issue of understaffing. He tried to re-assure Prior Wulstan that he 'would be glad to do what can be done.'[22] But it was the demands of the war effort which strained Downside's resources. 'At the same time I feel the need for Chaplains is the supreme call now,' the Abbot pointed out, and he related how one Downside chaplain 'gave [a] pitiable account of things in France.' Butler told Prior Wulstan that he could probably spare one monk who could say masses and 'help to lighten the burden and could do visiting in the parish.' The prior gladly accepted this offer. He understood the abbot's dilemma and told him that he agreed 'very strongly with you about the chaplain question and I feel that we ought to do everything in our power to help.'[23]

Problems, however, continued to plague Ealing and trouble Prior Wulstan, so much so that he even began to question the wisdom of constituting Ealing as a priory: I have come to the conclusion,' he declared, 'that the starting of the priory during the war was quite a mistake.'[24] We are admittedly short of men,' the prior continued, and 'it would have been far wiser and more discreet to have manned the place as a school and mission than to fill the house with men.' Moreover, he asked the abbot to articulate or clarify Downside's future plans for Ealing. 'If it has to go on as a Priory I do think you ought personally to let it be known what your wishes are...' he begged of Butler. To add to his troubles, the prior also reported a rumour that one of his monks wanted to return to Downside.

Prior Wulstan's continued dissatisfaction with his assignment and his wish for a transfer eclipsed the urgent demand for help at Ealing. Happiness and contentment always eluded Ealing's first prior. Early in 1917, for example, he told Abbot Butler that he still hoped 'that you may see your way to move me...'[25] He could not even hide his anxiety from the monks at Ealing. After the re-assignment of a monk from Ealing, another member of the community found the prior 'quite alarmingly gloomy.'[26] 'As you know his heart is in work like that at Liverpool and he never wanted to come here,' the same monk told Abbot Butler, 'so that if he feels he is not being supported in the way he ought to be by Downside, it is morally certain that the hopes you have of finding in him the solution of the long standing "Ealing difficulty" will be disappointed.' None the less, Abbot Butler still believed that Prior Wulstan possessed the strengths and abilities to become a good monastic leader at Ealing, but the London prior could not remain quiet.

In June 1917, Prior Wulstan again asked to be moved. Responding to this request, Abbot Butler told him that he wanted 'to avoid a mere stop gap arrangement, appointing as Superior someone else "to carry on" who is not the right man...'[27] Butler tried to reason with the prior. A short term or temporary appointment could harm the growth and spirit of the community, or it might mean 'somebody's life would have to be deranged.' The abbot's tactics seemed a bit patronizing. 'My dear Father you worry too much,' Abbot Butler wrote in August, and 'you are doing your best and not failing, in [the] judgment of anyone but yourself.'[28]

Butler's alleged lack of sensitivity finally forced Prior Wulstan to explode. In August, he sent a long and emotional letter to Downside. A homesickness for Merseyside surfaced. 'I can't help but feel...that I was taken away from a place where I was supremely happy,' he began, and 'I am never happy in [the] house' at Ealing.[29] He admitted that he enjoyed the parochial work he did, and urged that the priory should become more involved in parish work. Pastoral activity, and not the monastic routine, should be the primary responsibility or apostolate of the Ealing Benedictines. Prior Wulstan ended this letter to Abbot Butler with a strong and forceful plea: 'Couldn't Fr. Benedict then take charge and free me?' 'I sometimes wonder how much longer I can carry on' he wrote several months later,[30] adding 'I must confess my main interest is to be out of it all.' And again he pleaded with his monastic superior to be assigned to parochial work anywhere, even at Ealing. 'If you would like me to stay here and help on the Parish and [the] general work of the House I am ready to do so,' he admitted but 'honestly I think it would be better not.' Prior Wulstan Pearson's anxiety also had a philosophical or ideological basis, one which had rocked and would continue to threaten the calm of the English Benedictine Congregation. How much emphasis should English

Benedictinism give to the parish work of its monks? The Ealing prior had strong views: 'I don't think Ealing ought to stand in the way of the proper manning of our missions.'[31]

But Butler also had opinions about the role of Benedictine missions and their relation to conventual life. A supporter of the movement which eventually saw the English priories raised to the rank and status of independent abbeys, Abbot Butler always favoured the monastic life over the traditional missionary spirit. The English Benedictine Congregation was not essentially missionary, and this formed the background for his desire to see Ealing grow into a proper Benedictine priory. The need for monks at Downside and the demands from the missions began to stretch Butler's resources, and in 1910 he outlined his policy: 'that it be recognized that the time has come to begin lessening our sphere of missionary activity.'[32] Ealing, therefore, must develop in a new and different direction. The monastic routine and a life of scholarship would supplement work in the parish.

These constant complaints from Ealing succeeded in disturbing Abbot Butler, who responded in strong and harsh terms. 'I cannot but say that the persistence with which you press your wish surprises me' the abbot scolded him, and he told Prior Wulstan that his 'remonstrance before the appointment was perfectly right and so was...[the] appeal in the summer, after 6 months experience.'[33] Then Butler lost his patience: 'But when I definitely...called on you to stick to the post till the end of the War, with virtual promise to release you then, I do think you might have taken it from St. Benedict that so is best, not only for Ealing but for you...' Abbot Butler reminded him of the shortages, demands, and sufferings created by the war. Being prior at Ealing '...is certainly less of a strain than anyone of the millions of men in the trenches are bearing,' he cajoled and 'I must say I don't think it is quite worthy of you.' Prior Wulstan's response seemed apologetic and meek. He agreed that a monk should not be selective about his work; candidates, for example 'should not be received unless they are willing to undertake any of and all of our work.'[34] His final sentence also reflected a spirit of compromise: 'Let us have stability and fixity of policy...that we may go on with our work in peace and confidence.'

Consequently, the relations between the prior of Ealing and the abbot of Downside became less heated and acrimonious. Butler began to hope that Dom Wulstan would remain in charge at Ealing, but by the end of 1918 the prior again asked to be relieved of his monastic duties at Ealing. A tired Abbot Butler told Prior Wulstan that 'it would be an unjustifiable upsetting of another man's life to make him prior in the uncertainties as to whether it would be only for 9 months.'[35] The abbot then praised the work Prior Wulstan was doing among the parishioners: 'I ask myself...what interest at Ealing is the one [that] will suffer if you go out of it,' Butler wrote. 'It is certainly the parish and the pastoral work, the thing you are above all else keen upon.' The abbot tried to convince him that the high and praiseworthy parochial work depended on his willingness to remain as prior. The other monks, in Abbot Butler's opinion, did not possess the necessary 'driving power' to manage successfully a growing urban parish. This letter must have worked some magic. It appeared that Butler finally won the war of words and that Prior Wulstan accepted his fate as superior: the stream of appeals from the prior to the abbot stopped in December 1918.

The prior's discontent and his anxiety over shortages in manpower caused by the war effort, however, could not obscure the success and growth which Ealing Priory enjoyed under his leadership. The economic health of the London foundation improved greatly. Early in 1917, for example, Prior Wulstan started a fund-raising campaign. This wartime drive achieved some success: debts arising from the enlargement of the church were paid off in 1918. The enrolment of Ealing's school reached sixty-five during 1917, but climbed to approximately 100 in 1922. The parish also flourished. A census taken in 1918 estimated the number of parishioners at nearly one thousand six hundred. And some monks began to dream of additional construction to the church to accommodate this growing number.

After eight years as Ealing's first prior, Wulstan Pearson finally realized his dream of returning to pastoral ministry, but in an unexpected manner and style. In December 1924, the Holy See appointed him bishop of the recently created Diocese of Lancaster. The *Downside Review* reported that ecclesiastical gossip had hinted that the first prelate might be a Benedictine 'but his was not among the names that rumour had given us in advance.'[36] The appointment even took the Archbishop of Liverpool, Frederick William Keating, by surprise. Writing to Downside, Bishop-elect Pearson told Abbot Leander Ramsey, who had succeeded Cuthbert Butler in 1922, that the archbishop 'was rather upset, as he had no idea of anything going on till he received the "Bull."'[37] However, Pearson continued, 'he was very kind to me and told me that it would make no difference and that he would do all he could to start me well.' Dom Wulstan also appreciated the problems associated with being named bishop of a new diocese. He wanted to visit Lancaster immediately after his appointment became public 'to break the ice there, and there is a lot of ice about.' The possibility of suspicion and jealousy between the secular clergy and the religious orders haunted him. 'A Benedictine is not wanted,' he confided to Abbot Ramsey. But these misgivings vanished and Dom Wulstan dedicated his life to service in the diocese. On 24 February 1925, Ealing's first prior was consecrated as Bishop of Lancaster, a post he was to hold for nearly thirteen years.

Notes

[1] A. Hastings, *A History of English Christianity 1920-1985* (London: 1986), p. 138. For additional characteristics and similarities of the English bishops during the first century after the restoration of the hierarchy see P. Hughes 'The Bishops of the Century,' in G.A. Beck, ed., *The English Catholics 1850-1950* (London: 1950), pp. 187-222.

[2] See R. Kollar, *Westminster Cathedral: From Dream to Reality* (Edinburgh: 1987).

[3] Butler to Ford, 16 May 1902, Ford Papers, Ealing Abbey Archives, (henceforth EAA), London.

[4] Butler, 'Ealing Comprehensive Statement,' 1916, Ford Papers, EAA.

[5] Report of the Ealing Committee, 1916, Ealing Papers, Downside Abbey Archives, (henceforth DAA), Bath.

[6] Suggestions *Re* Ealing Priory and School, 1916, Ford Papers, EAA.

[7] Butler to the English Benedictines, 28 July 1916, Butler Papers, EAA.

[8] Green to Butler, 29 July 1916, Butler Papers, EAA.

[9] Rylance to Butler, 29 July 1916, Butler Papers, EAA.

[10] Goolden to Butler, July 1916, Butler Papers, EAA.

[11] 'Obituary: Dom Wulstan Pearson,' *Downside Review,* January 1939, p. 1.

[12] Butler to Pearson, 7 August 1916, Butler Papers, EAA.

[13] Pearson to Butler, 8 August 1916, Pearson Papers, EAA.

[14] Pearson to Butler, 9 August 1916, Pearson Papers, EAA.

[15] Butler to Pearson, 11 August, 1916, Butler Papers, EAA.

[16] Pearson to Butler, 12 August 1916, Pearson Papers, EAA.

[17] Butler to Pearson, 13 August 1916, Butler Papers, EAA.

[18] Pearson to Butler, 14 August 1916, Pearson Papers, EAA.

[19] 'Odds and Ends,' *Downside Review,* July 1916, p. 161.

[20] Butler to Bourne, 17 August 1961, Butler Papers, EAA.

[21] Bourne to Butler, 19 August 1916, Butler Papers, EAA.

[22] Butler to Pearson, 3 April 1917, Butler Papers, EAA.

[23] Pearson to Butler, April 1917, Butler Papers, EAA.

[24] Pearson to Butler, June 1917, Pearson Papers, EAA.

[25] Pearson to Butler, 5 January 1917, Butler Papers, EAA.

[26] Hudleston to Butler, 2 March 1917, Butler Papers, EAA.

[27] Butler to Pearson, 24 June 1917, Butler Papers, EAA.

[28] Butler to Pearson, 22 August 1917, Butler Papers, EAA.

[29] Pearson to Butler, August 1917, Pearson Papers, EAA.

[30] Pearson to Butler, 9 December 1917, Pearson Papers, EAA.

[31] Pearson to Butler, 22 January 1918, Butler Papers, EAA.

[32] Quoted in D. Knowles, *The Historian and Character and Other Essays* (Cambridge, 1963), p. 313.

[33] Butler to Pearson, 7 January 1918, Butler Papers, DAA.

[34] Pearson to Butler, 8 January 1918, Butler Papers, EAA.

[35] Butler to Pearson, 11 December 1918, Butler Papers, EAA.

[36] 'The First Bishop of Lancaster,' *Downside Review,* May 1925, p. 85.

[37] Pearson to Ramsey, 26 December 1924, Ramsey Papers, DAA.

CHAPTER XIV

PLANS FOR AN 18TH-CENTURY BENEDICTINE SETTLEMENT IN WESTERN PENNSYLVANIA: BISHOP JOHN CARROLL AND THE ENGLISH BENEDICTINE CONGREGATION

B oniface Wimmer, a monk of St. Michael Abbey in Metten, Bavaria, arrived in Pennsylvania in 1846 with a number of candidates for the monastic life. Wimmer planned to minister to the needs of German immigrants. The Bishop of Pittsburgh, Michael O'Connor, welcomed him into the diocese and donated property at St. Vincent parish in Latrobe. Thus began Benedictine life in the United States.[1]

But during the 1790s others had already thought about introducing Benedictine monasticism into America. Prompted by a letter from an English monk, Bishop John Carroll invited the English Benedictine Congregation to settle in his vast diocese and also suggested a parcel of land which could be purchased for the new foundation. This land, owned by Rev. Theodore Brouwers, was the same site later occupied by Boniface Wimmer and his German monks. But disputes and divisions within English Roman Catholicism, which also touched monasticism in that country, destroyed this early plan to bring Benedictine monks to America.

As the British government began to dismantle the long list of anti-Roman Catholic legislation during the last decades of the eighteenth century, two opposing camps sprang up which claimed to speak for and to represent the interests of English Catholics.[2] The first, the Catholic Committee, founded in 1782, drew its membership from the ranks of the aristocracy and gentry and, when clerical elements did appear, their backgrounds reflected that of the majority. Moreover, John Bossy pointed out, the Catholic Committee represented the interests of the South and Midlands. Another group, predominately clerical, tried to resist this challenge and was determined to lead Roman Catholicism into the promised land of equal political and social rights. The Vicars Apostolic of the North and West provided the moral and spiritual leadership. But this contest to attain first-class citizenship for Catholics nearly devoured the integrity and unity of Roman Catholicism in England. "The last twenty years of the eighteenth century saw the English Catholic community torn asunder by disputes which, to contemporaries seemed certain to end in schism with Rome, and to destroy the heritage of the martyr church."[3]

Radical ideological and theological differences also separated these two Catholic parties, such as the relationship of the Church to society, the infallibility of the Pope and his temporal power, the role of the Vicars Apostolic, and the proper place of English Roman Catholicism in the European intellectual and cultural milieu. The Catholic Committee appealed to Cisalpine principles[4] and labored to bring Catholics into the modern world. Its episcopal and clerical counterpart, the champion of traditional rights and privileges, scoffed at some of the progressive views put forward by the Cisalpines. Eamon Duffy brilliantly captured the intensity of the conflict and the bitterness it generated when he wrote:

> From 1787 onwards English Catholicism was plunged into a series of bitter internal feuds, as Cisalpines and Episcopals struggled for the soul of English popery...their battleground was the history of the English Catholic community, their weapons charges of Popery and Romanism, and countercharges of Republicanism, Jacobinism and Democracy.[5]

This division or tension even divided religious orders and saw two prominent members of the English Benedictine Congregation publicly confront each other, threatened the peace and unity of monasticism in the country, and eventually influenced the development of Benedictinism in North America. Rev. Joseph Cuthbert Wilks, O.S.B., (1748-1829)[6] became a leading spokesman for the Cisalpine Catholics. Professed at St. Edmund's, Paris, in 1764 and ordained in 1772, he was sent on the English Mission in the Southern Providence in 1782. The Congregation soon recognized his talents: Rev. Wilks served as a Definitor of the Regimen, the Abbot President's Council, from 1782-1797. Bernard Ward acknowledged Wilks's theological acumen, his "attractive manners," and unmistakable "signs of true piety and self-denial which are redeeming features in his character...."[7] This Roman Catholic historian, however, had some harsh words for Rev. Wilks, whom he described "as the chief author of the misdeeds of others [the Catholic Committee]." Ward also produced some allegations of unmonastic behavior: "It was said that he was living extravagantly, and that his house was continually open to visitors in a manner unbecoming a monk."

Bishop Charles Walmesley (1722-1797),[8] one of the bright lights of Benedictine intellectual life, emerged as the champion of the Vicars Apostolic and Wilks's chief antagonist. Clothed in the habit at St. Edmund's in 1738 and professed a year later, Walmesley earned a doctorate at the Sorbonne and later became a Fellow of the Royal Society of both London and Berlin. A mathematician, he gained a wide reputation for his numerous works on astronomy, and the British government had consulted him when England adopted the Gregorian calendar. The Benedictines also held him in high esteem: Prior of St. Edmund's (1749-1753), and Procurator in Rome (1754). His abilities did not escape Roman eyes, and Charles Walmesley was consecrated Bishop of Rama and Coadjutor of the Western District in 1756, where he succeeded as Vicar Apostolic in 1764. Roman Catholic writers have been kind to his memory, but also objective. Ward called Walmesley "the most prominent figure among Catholic ecclesiastics of the day..."[9]

> He is described as being of good presence and agreeable
> manners; but his speech, like his writings, was blunt to
> the verge of roughness, a defect which was emphasized
> by a partial deafness with which he became afflicted,
> and which helped to isolate him from those with whom
> he lived.[10]

Another author saw him as a "distinguished bishop," a man of "brilliant talents and solid qualities," and a cleric renowned for "his wisdom and admired [for] his holiness."[11]

During the 1790s, these opposing Roman Catholic groups eventually clashed. "Two mutually antagonistic parties thus confronted one another when Pitt's government finally launched the relief bill in 1791, which was in effect to bring full religious toleration for English Catholics."[12] And the two Benedictines found themselves on opposite sides of the field.

The history of the Catholic Relief Act, which received royal assent on 10 June 1791, shocked and scandalized Roman Catholic England. Laymen made up the membership of the Catholic Committee, which sent a memorial to Pitt asking for legislation in February 1788. In May, however, three clerics joined the group: Bishop James Talbot, Bishop Charles Berington and Rev. Joseph Wilks. The Catholic Committee strongly supported relief measures for the country's Roman Catholics, but their proposed legislation also included a declaration against papal infallibility, an oath which repudiated the "deposing" and temporal power of the Pope, and moreover, any restored political rights would be extended only to those Catholics referred to as "Protesting Catholic Dissenters," who took the questionable oath.[13] Led by Bishop Charles Walmesley, the Vicars Apostolic roundly condemned the oath as heretical.

Consequently, numerous meetings and pamphlets tried to explain the righteousness and correctness of both sides to the bewildered Catholic community. The Cisalpine party attacked the alleged abuse of ecclesiastical power wielded by the Vicars Apostolic and other agents of Ultramontanism. Walmesley's party, on the other hand, accused its opponents of advocating and spreading the evils associated with the Enlightenment, Republicanism, and the French Revolution. Both groups claimed to speak the true voice of English Roman Catholicism, but the episcopal party captured the prize. They lobbied vigorously, and appealed successfully to the Archbishop of Canterbury to use his influence in the Lords to modify the wording of the bill. The title "Protesting Catholic Dissenters," consequently, disappeared, and the less offensive oath from the Irish Relief Act of 1779 replaced the alleged heretical language of the original oath.

Bishop Charles Walmesley's party, therefore, emerged victorious, but divisions damaged and would continue to haunt English Roman Catholicism, and the ranks of English Benedictines were not spared. Before the original measure was introduced in Parliament, Bishop Walmesley had suspended his fellow Benedictine, Rev. Joseph Wilks. The Bishop, along with others, believed that Wilks was responsible for the theological errors put forth by the Catholic Committee. Refusing to comply with Walmesley's order to stop supporting its bill, the committee announced that it planned to appeal to Rome, but the Bishop, however, regarded this action on the part of Wilks as contumacy and in February 1791 suspended him from the exercise of all missionary faculties and all ecclesiastical functions in his district.[14]

Bernard Ward correctly pointed out "that although Bishop Walmesley happened to be a Benedictine, he had no position of authority in the order."[15] Wilks's immediate religious superior was the Southern Provincial, who was subject to the President General of the English Benedictine Congregation. Yet all missionaries held their priestly faculties from the

Bishop in whose district they ministered, and Walmesley merely exercised his prerogative and disciplined Wilks. Ward also suggested that the Southern Provincial approved of Bishop Walmesley's tactics, but the Benedictine Wilks did enjoy some support.

> His own congregation, who were much attached to him, took his side...[and] the embers of the old quarrel between bishops and regulars were re-kindled, for we find some of the latter siding with Mr. Wilkes [*sic*]on the ground that in suspending him without a proper citation or trial, the bishop had infringed upon the rights of the regulars.[16]

In September 1791, Rev. Wilks put his signature to a document which Bishop Walmesley accepted as submission to lawful episcopal authority. But peace did not return to the English Benedictine Congregation. Trying to explain his conduct to the surprised Catholic Committee, Wilks published his side of the story in a pamphlet, but Bishop Walmesley believed that by doing this Wilks had gone back on his word. The Bishop, consequently, again withdrew the priest's missionary faculties. He also appealed to the President General of the English Benedictines and worked to have Wilks sent to the Continent; he eventually left England in May 1792. But Bishop Walmesley did not know when to stop his crusade, and he committed another blunder which helped to blacken his reputation and increased the animosity of some Benedictines against him. Six parishioners of Rev. Wilks's mission at Bath had protested against the removal of their priest, and Walmesley replied to this show of independence and imposed a sentence of excommunication on the parishioners which lasted two years. Shocking events in revolutionary France, however, soon captured the attention and energy of England's Catholics. French refugee priests and members of religious orders fled the persecution and began to make their way into England, and in February 1793, a state of war existed between England and France. Religious houses, including those belonging to the English Benedictines, were suppressed, and some monks were imprisoned for their belief. Some Roman Catholics also cast their gaze across the Atlantic. In May 1794, Rev. Michael Pembridge,[17] an English Benedictine monk and Definitor of the Regimen, wrote to Bishop John Carroll of Baltimore, exploring the possibility of establishing an English Benedictine foundation in North America.

Bishop Carroll enjoyed a special relationship with English Roman Catholicism. Carroll's correspondence with Rev. Charles Plowden kept him informed of ecclesiastical developments in England, and although Bishop Joseph Berington, a Cisalpine sympathizer, influenced his thinking, Carroll also respected Bishop Charles Walmesley, who had consecrated the American churchman a Bishop on 15 August 1790 in Lulworth Castle, England. Moreover, Carroll "never gave up his quest for talented men from England for service in American parishes and schools."[18] Consequently, Bishop Carroll expressed great interest in this suggestion from England. "The proposal was," the Bishop wrote Charles Plowden, his English friend and inveterate crusader against the Catholic Committee and Cisalpine thought, "for the transmigration into the United States of a sufficient number of Eng[lish] Benedictines to form an establishment."[19] Bishop Carroll told Plowden that he "gave it every encouragement in my power...." If the possibility of an English foundation met with Carroll's approval, Pembridge also informed the Bishop that he would present the American plan at the meeting of the English Benedictine General Chapter, scheduled for the summer of 1794.

For some reason, Bishop Carroll did not reply to the English Benedictine's letter for four months. Finally, on 19 September, Carroll wrote to Rev. Michael Pembridge. "I said that your letter was a precious favour," he began, "because nothing can be more pleasing to me than the prospect of having in my diocese a settlement of English Benedictines.'[20] Bishop Carroll then expressed his devotion and attachment to the English Congregation and emphasized the valuable missionary work performed by these monks throughout history. Carroll, naturally, saw his sprawling diocese as a new vineyard for the English Benedictines and expressed this feeling to Pembridge: "If therefore your Venerable Chapter has encouraged your idea, I promise, as long as God grants life, to give to the undertaking every encouragement in my power."

In his letter to Bishop Carroll, the English monk had asked about possible sites for the proposed foundation. Carroll did not fail to address this question, and replied that he had taken into account the "healthiness of situation, cheapness of land, [and] favourable disposition of the laws...." And he offered the following suggestion: "...the neighbourhood of the town, called Pittsburgh, in Pennsylvania...would be the properest place for a settlement and a school." "This situation is as far remote from, and as secure as London, from the Indians," he continued, "and there is a continual communication and regular posts from that settlement to Balte, Philada, and all the trading towns on the Atlantic." Carroll quickly pointed out that the English Benedictines could purchase "three or four acres of good land" for approximately twelve hundred pounds. He ended his letter on a practical note and recommended that "four good laborious lay

Brothers" should be sent "as your great distress there would be for hirelings, and the laws of Pennsylvania admit not slaves."

But Bishop Carroll's letter arrived too late to influence the course of monastic history in the United States. The old animosities that had plagued English Benedictinism destroyed any hope for an American settlement; the General Chapter became a battleground for old feuds. Rev. Charles Plowden sadly informed Carroll of the events of the meeting. According to Plowden, some members of the Chapter eagerly wanted to punish Bishop Walmesley for his past actions against Rev. Joseph Wilks, who had recently returned from the Continent and had been appointed chaplain at Heythrop near Oxford. Walmesley's suspension of Wilks in 1791 had not been forgotten nor forgiven. "Several of the leading capitulars intended to bring forward a string of motions to arraign, condemn, and protest against Bishop Walmesley's conduct toward their confrere Wilks," he told Bishop Carroll, but an act of public censure and the attendant scandal was avoided.[21] Nonetheless, some wanted to express their disagreement with Walmesley's alleged abuse of episcopal power. Plowden noted that "though the vote against the good old Bishop was defeated, the same Chapter elected Wilks to be Vice President of their congregation...."[22]

Bishop Carroll correctly interpreted the mood and actions of the General Chapter in a negative manner. Replying to Plowden's letter, Carroll wrote that "your account of the treatment, which the Ven. Bishop Walmesley met in his own Congregation gave me much pain; and it makes me despair of the success of a proposal" to establish an English Benedictine foundation in this diocese.[23] Consequently, North America had to wait over fifty years before the arrival of Benedictine monks, and this successful enterprise was launched from southern Germany.

Notes

[1] For the early history of St. Vincent and the life of Boniface Wimmer see J. Oetgen, *An American Abbot: Boniface Wimmer, O.S.B.,(Latrobe:* The Archabbey Press, 1976). Felix Fellner, *Phases of Catholicity in Western Pennsylvania During the Eighteenth Century,(Latrobe:* The Archabbey Press, 1942) discusses the religious history of the area and gives some interesting insights into the Brouwers's property and Bishop Carroll's knowledge of it.

[2] J. Bossy, *The English Catholic Community 1570-1850* (New York: Oxford University Press,1976), 330.

[3] Eamon Duffy, "Ecclesiastical Democracy Detected: I (1779-1787)," *Recusant History* 10 (January 1970), 193.

[4] Eamon Duffy, "Ecclesiastical Democracy Detected: I (1779-1787)" traces the origin and development of Cisalpinism.

[5] Ibid., 204.

[6] Henry Norbert Birt, *Obit Book of the English Benedictines from 1606 to 1912* (England: Gregg International Publishers, 1970), 136.

[7] B. Ward, The *Dawn of the Catholic Revival of 1781-1803,* vol. 1 (New York: Longmans, Green and Co., 1909), 125.

[8] Henry Norbert Birt, op. cit., 120-121.

[9] B. Ward, op. cit., 4.

[10] Ibid., 5.

[11] E. Burton, *The Life and Times of Bishop Challoner,* vol. 1 (New York: Longmans, Green and Co., 1909), 369.

[12] J. Bossy, op. cit., 331.

[13] For an excellent discussion on the background to the proposed relief bill and the furor over the oath, see Eamon Duffy, "Ecclesiastical Democracy Detected: II (1787-1796)," *Recusant History* 10 (October 1970), 309-331.

[14] Walmesley to Wilks, 19 February 1791, printed in B. Ward, *The Dawn of the Catholic Revival 1781-1803,* 25.

[15] Ibid.

[16] Ibid., 260.

[17] Henry Norbert Birt, op. cit., 125-126.

[18] T. O'Brien Hanley, ed., "Introduction to Volume Two," in *The John Carroll Papers,* vol. 2 (Notre Dame: University of Notre Dame Press, 1976), iv.

[19] Carroll to Plowden, 15 November 1794, printed in T. O'Brien, ed., *The John Carroll Papers,* vol. 2, 131 - 132.

[20] Carroll to Pembridge, 19 September 1794, Walmesley Papers, Downside Abbey Archives, Downside Abbey, Bath. This letter is also printed in T. O'Brien, ed., *The John Carroll Papers,* vol. 2, 128-129.

[21] Plowden to Carroll, 31 August 1794, Carroll Papers, 6P4, Archives of Archdiocese of Baltimore.

[22] Ibid. Bernard Ward explained the actions of the Benedictine General Chapter in the following manner. "This office carried no duties except in the event of the death of the

President General, in which case he would succeed to that office until the next General Chapter." Ward also did not see the deliberations of the Chapter as representative of the English Benedictines. "It should be borne in mind that the Chapter of 1794 was an incomplete one, several of the most prominent members of St. Gregory's Douai, and St. Edmund's, Paris, being at that time in prison in France." B. Ward, *The Dawn of the Catholic Revival in England 1787-1803,* vol. 2, 66.

[23] Carroll to Plowden, 15 November 1794, printed in T. O'Brien, ed., *The John Carroll Papers,* vol. 2, 131.

CHAPTER XV

BISHOP CHARLES GRAFTON'S DREAM FOR RELIGIOUS LIFE IN THE AMERICAN EPISCOPAL CHURCH: THE INFLUENCE OF THE MONASTIC REVIVAL IN THE CHURCH OF ENGLAND

C harles Chapman Grafton (1830-1912), descendent from a noble Boston family, a Harvard law graduate (1863), and missionary in Baltimore, seemed an unlikely candidate to be attracted to monastic practices usually associated with Roman Catholicism, a religion whose weaknesses and inconsistencies he never failed to trumpet throughout his life. Ordained in 1858 as a priest in the Protestant Episcopal Church in the United States of America, that church in America in communion with Canterbury and since 1970 known as the Episcopal Church, he found himself drawn to the High Church party in England associated with Edward Bouverie Pusey, the Anglican cleric who saw great worth and value in conventual life. It was a sojourn in England, consequently, which inspired young Grafton to introduce the monastic system in America, whose Yankee eyes saw institutions, such as monasteries, nunneries, and brotherhoods as popish.

The religious climate of nineteenth century England had changed since the Reformation and the years of the penal laws. Once feared and ridiculed, monastic practices slowly began to emerge within the Church of England. The courage and example of monks and nuns who fled to England to escape suppression or death during the French Revolution forced many Britons to change their prejudicial attitude. The Romantic Movement, on the other hand, glorified aspects of England's medieval heritage, including the monastic life which the rationalists of the Enlightenment had scorned. But it was the Oxford Movement and its claim to the inheritance of monasticism which helped to give renewed strength to the monastic spirit."[1] The Tractarian theologians "emphasized the importance of the pre-Reformation or Catholic tradition in the Church of England, and consequently, they began to discover the value of many monastic practices."[2] Once condemned or feared, elaborate liturgies, communal recitation of the breviary, and vows now seemed to some Anglicans as a valuable way to strengthen the moral and pastoral fibre of a stagnant Established Church. Moreover, others argued, the spirit and practices of monasticism belonged to all Christians; the monastic life was not the exclusive property of Rome.

Richard Hurrell Froude, for example, sang the praises of unmarried clerics living together in a community and ministering to the spiritual needs of the poor. Frederick William Faber, before his conversion to Roman Catholicism in 1845, also championed the virtues of celibacy and founded a small community at Elton. But Edward Bouverie Pusey supplied both the theological and practical clout. He maintained that the basis or justification for celibacy could be found "in the practice of the primitive Christian communities."[3] Moreover, brotherhoods and sisterhoods engaged in missionary work could spread the Gospel message among the poor and disbelievers who populated England's cities. John Henry Newman also recognized the numerous contributions monasticism had made to western civilization, and he pointed out that a life similar to monasticism had already existed in the early Christian community. Unlike Pusey, however, he believed that modern religious orders must renounce active pastoral work, flee the temptations of the world, and embrace a life of seclusion and prayer. The writings of these Tractarians, especially Pusey, whom Grafton believed represented the moving force and spirit behind the Oxford Movement and its praiseworthy accomplishments, impressed Charles Grafton.

And this Anglo-Catholic revival soon bore fruit in the sudden growth of Anglican sisterhoods, a phenomenon which caught Grafton's eye. First to take vows as an Anglican nun in 1841 was Marian Hughes, who placed herself under the spiritual guidance of Pusey. Others soon followed: the Community of St. Mary the Virgin, Wantage; Priscilla Lydia Sellon's Society of the Most Holy Trinity; the Community of St. John the Baptist, Clewer; and John Mason Neale's Society of St. Margaret. Their laudatory work among the destitute, especially during cholera epidemics, won respect for these sisterhoods and often softened the harsh words of critics. The zeal of the Anglican nuns who journeyed to the Crimea also demonstrated that the religious life did not represent a threatening relic of Roman Catholicism. When Charles Grafton arrived in England during 1864, therefore, he had the chance to experience firsthand the life and work of Anglican religious life.

Charles Grafton's background and training was thoroughly American. Before crossing the Atlantic to England, he ministered in the state of Maryland. Grafton, a supporter of the Unionist cause in the American Civil War, was stationed in Baltimore as a chaplain to a house of deaconesses when the Confederate guns fired on Fort Sumter. As chaplain, he witnessed the powerful work which a religious community could perform. "During the war Fr. Grafton assisted her [Mrs. Tyler, the superior] in the active conduct of the house," the author of the forward to Grafton's autobiography wrote.[4] "Sometimes they had a hundred wounded men come in at night. They were called to witness to Confederate prisoners." Grafton could also look to other examples of community life in America for inspiration and encouragement.

The first attempt to found a religious community of men in the Protestant Episcopal Church in the United States of America took place in 1840. "On 19 June that year Mr. J.W. Miles, of South Carolina, presented a scheme to some of his classmates at the General Theological Seminary, New York, which was approved by Dr. William R. Whittingham, Professor of Ecclesiastical History, who had just been elected Bishop of Maryland."[5] According to Peter Anson, this association of unmarried clerics would undertake missionary work, pledge obedience to the local bishop, and practice communal poverty. Soon after its beginning, a call came from the Bishop of the North-West Territory, and in 1841 three deacons left for an area called Nashotah, 27 miles west of Milwaukee, Wisconsin. Community life started there in August 1842. "Nashotah survived its troubled foundation...[and] evolved first into a moderate High Church seminary, but blossomed out about 1890 as a stronghold of the Catholic party..."[6] The next attempt to graft religious life onto the Protestant Episcopal Church occurred during 1845 in New York, but was short-lived. Another foundation at Valle Crucis, North Carolina, under the direction of the Bishop of North Carolina, Levi Silliman Ives, modeled itself after the Society of Jesus. This community eventually came under attack because of alleged Roman Catholic practices. Bad publicity, departures, and the death of its members signaled the end of this southern brotherhood.[7]

Charles Grafton knew of these American attempts at conventual life, and had personal contact with some of the pioneers. The Rev. Oliver Prescott, one of the founders at Valle Crucis, become his friend and counselor, and also later joined the Cowley Fathers in England with Grafton. Bishop Whittingham, a supporter of Nashotah, later become Grafton's ordaining bishop and encouraged the young cleric in his dream for religious life. By 1865, therefore, Charles Grafton was convinced that his quest for religious life could be realized in England, where Pusey would become his mentor. In May 1865, the Bishop of Maryland, William Rollinson Whittingham, wrote a letter of recommendation to accompany this young cleric: Charles Grafton "as a Presbyter of upright and godly life and conversation, sound learning, and approved fidelity in the holy ministry, is commended while traveling with our permission, on his lawful occasions, to the enjoyment of all Christian offices of love."[8]

Grafton's views on the future of religious life within his American church surfaced during his English sojourn. Writing from London in the summer of 1865, he succinctly outlined his goal: "you know what I have deeply at heart; the revival of Religious Life."[9] A community "of priests bound together by the closest possible ties, would by their love and sympathy support one another and be useful in the saving of souls..." His goal and defense of this brotherhood echoed the beliefs of the Tractarians. "But the Catholic Church has already recognized the religious life as a distinct estate, and that some either because they were weak and could be used in no other way, or for some reason known to the sovereign will, have been called to it."

One of Grafton's first encounters with religious life within the Anglican Church took place when he met Brother Ignatius Lyne,[10] later known as Ignatius of Llanthony, an eccentric and self-styled monk who had established an Anglican Benedictine monastery at Norwich. Ignatius failed to impress Charles Grafton. "Nor is Brother Ignatius the one God has pointed out for men to follow in the way of a religious," a disillusioned Grafton wrote to Oliver Prescott.'[11] "I saw him in London and I heard him at St. Martin's Hall." Unlike some others who heard Ignatius, Grafton thought him "not effective, but tiresome as a preacher."

Grafton, however, did learn a lesson from his encounter with Brother Ignatius: his ideal American brotherhood would not operate as a maverick community, but one which enjoyed the proper relationship with the episcopate. "Either he is under his Bishop or some Anglican Bishop, or as a monk he is under the pope," Grafton argued, and "there must be someone whom he should obey; and the point able and good and thoroughly catholic men make is, what right has he to have public celebrations of the Eucharist in his chapel?" The young American also pointed out the dangers of this unsupervised situation. "The thing is all in a mess. The monks with him are very common persons, and none stay long." Later he strongly expressed his displeasure and disappointment with Ignatius: "I had visited Brother Ignatius at Norwich...but was not drawn to unite with him."[12]

Charles Grafton then began to explore other options and possibilities in his holy quest. Some friends urged him to visit the Roman Catholic Cistercian monastery at Leicester, which was endowed and supported by Ambrose March Phillips de Lisle, a convert to Rome. But the Roman Catholic affiliation was too dangerous for the conservative Grafton. Others told him to approach the Association for the Promotion of the Unity of Christendom, founded by George Frederick Lee in 1857. Dedicated to promote the reunion of Canterbury and Rome, the A.P.U.C. also scared Grafton who immediately saw this connection with Roman Catholicism as a source of trouble. He told Prescott that he "would not make the A.P.U.C. a prominent part of our work."[13] "It will be enough for us to be religious, without giving anyone a cry against us." Fear of popery, therefore, prompted Grafton to avoid this early ecumenical organization: "...I don't want Brotherhoods to be damaged by that cry, or have anything to hear except straightforward attacks."

E.B. Pusey, however, became his mentor and gave Grafton the inspiration and encouragement he needed. "In Pusey," Grafton later wrote, "God raised up for the Anglican Church a great saint, wonderful in his colossal learning, more wonderful in his deep humility and burning zeal for God."[14] Grafton had always worshipped Pusey and his influence on the High Church revival, "of which Dr. Pusey was the centre..."[15] Later in life, Grafton pointed out another significant influence of Pusey's life and thought on the development of Anglican religious communities: "It called upon the clergy to live higher and more self-sacrificing lives. Parish houses, workingmen's clubs, schools of all kinds...Church homes, penitentiaries, refuges, guilds, religious orders, deaconesses, sisterhoods, all the machinery of the modern parish came into existence."[16]

A sympathetic Pusey eventually directed Grafton to other like-minded churchmen who wanted to establish religious life in the Anglican Church. In February 1865, Bishop Alexander Penrose Forbes of Brechin, the Rev. R.M. Benson, Mr. Charles Wood, Mr. George Lane-Fox, and Charles Grafton met at St. Mary's, Soho. Wood, later known as Lord Halifax, soon noticed Grafton's enthusiasm. He "had come over from America influenced by the same ideas in regard to a revival of the Religious Life as those animating Father Benson and others in England, and was then staying at the Clergy House at All Saints, Margaret Street."[17] Lord Halifax later wrote that at the meeting many "...possibilities were discussed with much consideration as to what might be God's Will as to the hopes and wishes in regard to the formation of a Community of clergy and laity living together under Rule for spiritual purposes, and in reference to what might be the individual duty of those concerned in the undertaking."[18] According to Halifax, Benson and Grafton "definitely expressed the desire to give themselves to such a life."[19] This idea, not surprisingly, sounded similar to Pusey's plan, and consequently within a few days another meeting took place in the presence of E.B. Pusey. When asked for his advice, Pusey urged the group to organize first, and then seek the necessary ecclesiastical approval and blessing.

Charles Grafton was ecstatic. Writing during the summer of 1865 to his friend Oliver Prescott, he could not control his emotions. "By a series of wonderful providences, men are being drawn to a religious life, and are being drawn together," and moreover, he continued, "it is the most aweful and solemn of anything I ever knew."[20] Grafton then pointed out that "Some of England's saintliest men will direct by their counsel the work, and some of them will be in it." "God is educating and raising up saints here," he proudly declared. Agreeing with Pusey's suggestion, Grafton thought it better to approach the bishops with a *fait accompli* and then ask for episcopal approbation.

And concrete plans for the brotherhood did develop quickly. "As soon we can," Grafton wrote, "we...will meet at a place near Oxford, Mr. Benson's parish, and commence living by Rule and receiving instructions in the spiritual life and rules of a community."[21] He also revealed that some Anglicans interested in the conventual life had already visited some Roman Catholic religious communities, including Monte Cassino, and others planned to go to the Continent to experience personally the life of established monastic brotherhoods. Grafton wanted "to see Religious orders...and learn," but he also revealed that "I don't think it is very important now, as these persons know more than I do..."

During the summer of 1865, the theological principles of the future Society of St. John the Evangelist, the Cowley Fathers, began to take shape. Members of the brotherhood would be bound by vows of poverty, obedience, and celibacy, and "the general line will be rather like that say of the modern orders, the Redemptorist or Jesuit, than the ancient Monastic ones." Vows, always an emotional and contentious issue with some Anglicans who still feared popery and Roman influences on the Church of England, had to be defended. And Grafton did not miss this opportunity. "Religious life," he argued, meant "the life based on the three vows."[22] Vows, he believed, liberate and do not imprison. "Putting before one then the conditions of Poverty, Obedience and Celibacy in their rigor, ask we of God guidance that we may know His will in our regard and grace to promptly follow it." Now the taking of vows is part of the Christian religion," he later wrote, "it is the teaching of our Book of Common Prayer."[23] He pointed out that Jesus Christ approved of vows and sanctioned them: "He called men to take as celibates a permanent estate, and there could be no way of entering into such a state spiritually save by a vow."

After receiving the sanction of the Bishop of Oxford, William Wilberforce, this new Anglican brotherhood took root. In August 1865, Charles Grafton and R.M. Benson set up house in Oxford and began to live the conventual life. And on 27 December 1866, Grafton, Benson, and S.W. O'Neill "made their religious professions; promising to live in celibacy, poverty, and obedience as Mission Priests of St. John the Evangelist until life's end."[24] Grafton always hoped to transplant this seed of religious life on American soil, and consequently in 1871 he accepted the position of rector at the Advent Parish, Boston, where he began work to establish the Cowley Fathers in North America. But this plan did not succeed. Both Grafton and Fr. Prescott left the Society of St. John the Evangelist because of a dispute with Benson, who refused to grant independence to any American affiliation. Yet Charles Grafton continued to pursue the dream of an American religious community.

"In 1882," he later admitted, "I was led by certain provinces to found a sisterhood in America."[25] And he acknowledged his indebtedness to the Anglican religious communities he had experienced. "My connection with the communities in England as a special director and confessor had given me a knowledge of their constitution and rule such as, I suppose, no other one clergyman then possessed." During that year, therefore, Grafton devoted all his energies to the foundation of the Sisterhood of the Holy Nativity. Again drawing on knowledge of English sisterhoods, Grafton noted that these early communities "began to take up a large number of different kinds of works."[26] This American sisterhood would thus encourage "...large room for the cultivation of the spiritual life, and which would especially be given to aid the parochial clergy, and have as a chief object the winning of souls." The Sisterhood of the Holy Navitity would not administer or staff large institutions, such as hospitals and orphanages. These American sisters, on the other hand, would "give themselves especially to the cultivation of the interior life..."

With the help and guidance of Sister Ruth Margaret, this sisterhood became quickly involved in the parochial work of the Church of the Advent. And when Grafton was later appointed Bishop of Fond du Lac in 1889, "he moved its mother house to his cathedral city, so that the Sisters should be under his personal guidance."[27] This sisterhood, according to Peter Anson, naturally benefited form Grafton's English experiences. "Having been trained by Fr. Benson at Cowley in the principles of the Religious Life, the bishop imparted the same austere ideals to his Sisterhood."[28] Anson identified these traits as personal sanctification and the love of God, pastoral work, and a life based on the Rule of St. Augustine.

While still living in Boston, Charles Grafton also developed ideas for communities of American men. Again, one cannot miss his Cowley background. Writing at the request of a friend on the possibilities of an American foundation, Grafton put forth his principles in August 1885. "It is noticeable," he began, "that, in any portion of Christendom blest with a priesthood and Sacraments, and thus fully organized for its work, great religious movements are usually accompanied by the formation of persons associated together under various rules of Christian living."[29] Grafton drew attention to the successes associated with the revival of community life in the Anglican Church, and argued that religious life was another sign of the catholicity of his American church. Clergy possessing various talents and educated laymen, who would enjoy the same privileges as the cleric, would form its ranks.

Like his sisterhoods, moreover, his ideal brotherhood would also be involved in active apostolic work. Grafton's association of religious men "could do a great work for God by its life of study and prayer and by aiding the bishops and clergy in their missionary and parochial labors."[30] These men "would help to dissipate the spirit of worldliness and self-satisfied respectability which hangs over the Church like a miasma poisoning her life." Grafton believed that such a brotherhood could exert a tremendous influence on the church. Members could staff retreat centers or supply temporary help for parishes. And, Grafton argued, the need was so great. Moreover, he maintained that his proposed brotherhood would testify "...against worldliness, witnessing of the unseen glories of man's coming union with God."[31]

This community of clergy and laymen must be American in character and spirit, and Grafton based his dream upon several principles. First, "such a society *must not be an imitation or attempted reproduction of anything in the past.*"[32] "It will not be an imitation but an original work."[33] Secondly, "the society *must be an American one.*" By this Grafton meant that the superior must be American and the central organization located there. Charles Grafton's next point also flowed from his insistence on the American character of the brotherhood, namely, it must develop out of and meet the needs and demands of the contemporary North American church. This vineyard, he believed, was large. Work among the former slaves in the South, among the impoverished in the rural areas, and also among the destitute in the urban slums would occupy the brotherhood.

This new American brotherhood, moreover, would not develop or exist independently of official church supervision. Again drawing on his experience abroad, Grafton maintained that a proper religious society must receive episcopal approval and sanction. He strongly believed that the society *in its teaching should be loyal to the Church.*"[34] The principles and formularies of the Book of Common Prayer provided the necessary guidelines. Commenting on this necessary relationship to proper church authority, Grafton again argued against any easy imitation of past or existing orders: "if they are to be men of such a character, it is obvious that the society *should have its own definite spirit.*"[35]

Charles Grafton's keen interest in religious communities did not cease after he became Bishop of Fond du Lac in 1889. He never failed to write and promote brotherhoods and sisterhoods within the American Episcopal Church. The Sisterhood of the Holy Nativity, which moved from Boston in 1905, continued to exist throughout the twentieth century. But fortune did not smile on the growth of brotherhoods within Grafton's Wisconsin diocese. Bishop Grafton supported and encouraged the development of St. Dunstan's Abbey, a self-styled Benedictine community, but this group did not survive Bishop Grafton's death in 1912.[36] Grafton also hoped to cooperate with the Anglican Abbot of Caldey Island in South Wales, Aelred Carlyle. The Bishop of Fond du Lac had ordained Carlyle an Anglican priest during his visit to America in 1904, and plans soon began to develop which might have led to an affiliation between the Fond du Lac and Caldey communities. But Grafton's death also destroyed this plan.

Although not successful in all his efforts to introduce religious life into the American Episcopal Church, Charles Grafton worked persistently to educate the faithful to the benefits which could be derived from brotherhoods and sisterhoods. If a common theme can be discovered in his efforts, Grafton's firsthand experiences of conventual life which he observed in England, especially his association with the Cowley Fathers and E.B. Pusey, emerge as the significant factor in his dreams for religious life in the American Episcopal Church.

Notes

[1] R. Kollar. "The Oxford Movement and the Heritage of Benedictine Monasticism," *Downside Review*, October 1983. p. 281.

[2] O. Chadwick, *The Mind of the Oxford Movement* (Stanford: Stanford University Press, 1960), p. 12.

[3] R. Kollar, "The Oxford Movement and the Heritage of Benedictine Monasticism," p. 281.

[4] E. Wenslow, "A Forward," in C. Grafton, *A Journey Godward* (Milwaukee: The Young Churchman Co., 1910), p.10

[5] P. Anson, *The Call of the Cloister. Religious Communities and Kindred Bodies in the Anglican Communion* (London: SPCK, 1964), p. 533

[6] P. Anson, *The Call of the Cloister*, p. 535

[7] P. Anson, *The Call of the Cloister*, p. 539.

[8] E. Wenslow, "A Forward," p. 10.

[9] Grafton to Fay, 18 July 1865, printed in C. Grafton, *Letters and Addresses* (New York: Longmans, Green and Co., 1914), p. 47

[10] For biographies of Ignatius of Llanthony see: D. Attwater, *Fr. Ignatius of Llanthony* (London: Cassell and Co., 1928); A. Calder-Marshall, *The Enthusiast* (London: Faber and Faber, 1962); The Baroness DeBertouch, *The Life of Father Ignatius, O.S.B.* (London: Methuen and Co., 1905).

[11] Grafton to Prescott, 17 July 1865, printed in C. Grafton, *Letters and Addresses*, p. 32.

[12] C. Grafton, *A Journey Godward*, p. 40.

[13] Ibid.

[14] Ibid., p. 42.

[15] C. Grafton, *Pusey and the Church Revival* (Milwaukee: The Young Churchman Co., 1908), p. 70.

[16] Ibid.

[17] C. Wood, *The Cowley Evangelist*, February 1915, quoted in J. G. Lockhart, *Charles Lindley Viscount Halifax*, Part I (London: Geoffrey Bles, 1935), p. 117.

[18] Ibid., pp. 117-118.

[19] Ibid., p. 118.

[20] Grafton to Prescott, July 1865, printed in C. Grafton, *Letters and Addresses*, p. 37.

[21] Ibid.

[22] Grafton to Fay, 18 July 1865, printed in C. Grafton, *Letters and Addresses*, p. 47.

[23] C. Grafton, *A Journey Godward*, p. 101.

[24] P. Anson, *The Call of the Cloister*, p. 78.

[25] C. Grafton, *A Journey Godward*, p. 103.

[26] Ibid.

[27] P. Anson, *The Call of the Cloister*, p. 561.

[28] Ibid., p. 562

[29] "An American Religious Community," 15 August 1885, printed in C. Grafton, *Letters and*

Adresses, p. 90.

[30] Ibid., p. 92.

[31] Ibid., p. 94.

[32] Ibid., p. 96.

[33] Ibid., p. 97.

[34] Ibid., p. 101.

[35] Ibid., p. 102.

[36] In 1912, Grafton even published a guideline, *A Commentary on the Rule of the Benedictine Abbey of St. Dunstan.* For a brief outline of Grafton's plans and the eventual failure of this community see P. Anson, *Call of the Cloister*, pp. 192-193.

✌

INDEX

Titles of religious are included in the index. Numbers in italics reference a footnote: n., or
several footnotes on the same page nn.

❧

ALSO BY RENE KOLLAR

Westminster Cathedral: From Dream to Reality.

The Return of the Benedictines to London.
A History of Ealing Abbey: 1896 to Independence.

Abbot Aelred Carlyle, Caldey Island,
and the Anglo-Catholic Revival in England.

GENERAL THEOLOGICAL SEMINARY
NEW YORK